Nineteenth-Century British Premiers

GW00385545

Also by Dick Leonard

A CENTURY OF PREMIERS: SALISBURY TO BLAIR
THE BACKBENCHER AND PARLIAMENT (edited with Val Herman)
CROSLAND AND NEW LABOUR (edited)
THE ECONOMIST GUIDE TO THE EUROPEAN UNION
ELECTIONS IN BRITAIN: A VOTER'S GUIDE (with Roger Mortimore)
GUIDE TO THE GENERAL ELECTION
PAYING FOR PARTY POLITICS
THE PRO-EUROPEAN READER (edited with Mark Leonard)
THE SOCIALIST AGENDA: CROSLAND'S LEGACY (edited with David Lipsey)
WORLD ATLAS OF ELECTIONS (with Richard Natkiel)

Nineteenth-Century British Premiers

Pitt to Rosebery

Dick Leonard

© Dick Leonard 2008

All rights reserved. No reproduction, copy or transmission of this publication may be made without written permission.

No portion of this publication may be reproduced, copied or transmitted save with written permission or in accordance with the provisions of the Copyright, Designs and Patents Act 1988, or under the terms of any licence permitting limited copying issued by the Copyright Licensing Agency, Saffron House, 6-10 Kirby Street, London EC1N 8TS.

Any person who does any unauthorized act in relation to this publication may be liable to criminal prosecution and civil claims for damages.

The author has asserted his right to be identified as the author of this work in accordance with the Copyright, Designs and Patents Act 1988.

First published 2008 by
PALGRAVE MACMILLAN

Palgrave Macmillan in the UK is an imprint of Macmillan Publishers Limited, registered in England, company number 785998, of Houndmills, Basingstoke, Hampshire RG21 6XS.

Palgrave Macmillan in the US is a division of St Martin's Press LLC, 175 Fifth Avenue, New York, NY 10010.

Palgrave Macmillan is the global academic imprint of the above companies and has companies and representatives throughout the world.

Palgrave® and Macmillan® are registered trademarks in the United States, the United Kingdom, Europe and other countries.

ISBN-13: 978–1–4039–3909–8 hardback
ISBN-10: 1–4039–3909–8 hardback
ISBN-13: 978–0–230–20985–5 paperback
ISBN-10: 0–230–20985–8 paperback

This book is printed on paper suitable for recycling and made from fully managed and sustained forest sources. Logging, pulping and manufacturing processes are expected to conform to the environmental regulations of the country of origin.

A catalogue record for this book is available from the British Library.

A catalog record for this book is available from the Library of Congress.

10 9 8 7 6 5 4 3 2 1
17 16 15 14 13 12 11 10 09 08

Printed and bound in Great Britain by
CPI Antony Rowe, Chippenham and Eastbourne

To Mark and Gabrielle
Miriam and Phiroze

Contents

All illustrations by kind permission of the Government Art Collection (GAC)

Introduction

This is the second volume to appear of a trilogy of books describing and re-assessing the careers of each of the 51 British Prime Ministers, from Robert Walpole to Tony Blair. The first volume, *A Century of Premiers: Salisbury to Blair*, was published in 2005; the third, *Eighteenth Century British Premiers: Walpole to the Younger Pitt* will follow in 2009. The present volume deals with the 20 Premiers who held office during the nineteenth century.

This was a period during which Britain's international standing was at its peak. It could fairly claim to be the first world power, its economy was the strongest in the world and its naval power dwarfed that of any other nation, though its military strength was less than that of several continental European countries. The British Empire grew almost inexorably throughout the century, even under Prime Ministers as strongly anti-imperialist as Gladstone, and by the end of the century nearly a quarter of the world's land area was coloured red on the maps which decorated every classroom in the nation's schools.

Three-quarters of the Prime Ministers came from the landed aristocracy, while five were from middle class backgrounds – Addington being the son of a doctor, Peel and Gladstone the sons of wealthy manufacturers or traders, while Canning was fathered by a failed barrister and Disraeli by a scholarly author. Eighteen out of the 20 received a university education, 10 from Oxford and eight from Cambridge, though Russell and Palmerston both also attended Edinburgh University, and Melbourne, Glasgow. Only Wellington and Disraeli were not university-educated. Disraeli was the only nineteenth-century Premier not to be educated at a leading 'public' school, apart from William Pitt who was taught by private tutors. Nine Prime Ministers attended Eton, five Harrow, two Westminster and one each, Winchester and Charterhouse. Few of the Prime Ministers followed occupations, other than managing their own estates, before embarking on a political career. Pitt, Addington and Perceval were lawyers, as was Melbourne (though he only appeared in one case), Wellington a soldier, Aberdeen a diplomat, and Disraeli an author. The majority of them became

Prime Ministers, for the first time, in their forties or fifties; the youngest during the nineteenth century being Lord Liverpool, at 42 years and one day, though the Younger Pitt had started his first premiership, back in 1783, at the age of 24 years and 205 days. The oldest Prime Minister to take office, for the first time, was Lord Palmerston, at 71 years and 109 days, though Gladstone was 82 years and 230 days old when he began his fourth premiership, retiring only at the age of 84, the oldest Premier in British history. The longest serving Prime Minister during the century was Lord Liverpool, who served continuously for 14 years and 305 days; the shortest was his immediate successor, George Canning, who died in office after only 119 days.

Of the 20 Prime Ministers, 12 were Tories or Conservatives and eight Whigs, Peelites or Liberals. Altogether, the Tories were in office for just over 60 years during the century and their opponents for just under 40. Eleven of the Premiers were members of the House of Lords throughout their premierships, and seven were in the Commons. Two – Russell and Disraeli – served as Prime Minister both in the Commons and in the Lords. All the peers, except Aberdeen and Rosebery, began their political careers in the Commons before being transferred to the Upper House.

Throughout the period, Prime Ministers owed their initial appointment to the Monarch, and subsequently attempted to maintain a majority in the House of Commons. During the course of the century, however there was a profound change in the balance of power between these two forces, a change which was primarily due to the extension of the franchise in parliamentary elections. Before the 1832 Reform Act, the King felt able to ride rough-shod over the wishes of Parliament, dismissing governments which enjoyed a good majority in the Commons. Most notoriously in 1783, when George III ejected the predominantly Whig government, led by the Duke of Portland, to make way for William Pitt, and again in 1807 when he ousted Lord Grenville's government of' 'All the Talents', and reinstated Portland, who was now a Tory (see Chapters 1 and 3). When William IV attempted a similar manoeuvre in 1834, replacing the Whig, Lord Melbourne, with the Tory, Sir Robert Peel, he came a cropper. Peel dissolved Parliament, but failed to win a majority at the subsequent general election, and William was forced to reinstate Melbourne (see Chapter 11). This was the last occasion when a monarch tried to dismiss a sitting government.

The 1832 Act had in fact spelled the end of a long era in which monarchs were able, through the widespread use of patronage and outright bribery, to determine the result of elections. Although the Act provided for only a modest extension of the franchise, enlarging it from approximately 5 to 7 per cent of the adult population, the accompanying abolition of 'rotten' and 'pocket' boroughs greatly increased the legitimacy of the electoral process, which was opened up to the rapidly expanding middle class. Further Reform Acts, in 1867 and 1884, extended the franchise to all male heads of households and opened the way to the formation of mass political parties. Thus during the course of the century, the choice of government was effectively transferred from the Monarch to the House of Commons, and eventually to the wider electorate. It was a great achievement of the British political class to achieve, without bloodshed, and by incremental measures, this transformation from rule by an oligarchy to the threshold of democracy, though it was to take another 18 years in the new century before full manhood suffrage was achieved, and 29 before women were entitled to vote on the same terms as men.

The nineteenth-century Prime Ministers who presided over these great changes varied greatly in their ability, and in the extent to which their governments were successful. In my book on twentieth-century Premiers, I published a rank-order of Prime Ministers, based on a survey by the BBC of historians, commentators and politicians. As far as I am aware, no comparable exercise has been attempted with regard to the nineteenth century, and it is with some diffidence that I offer my own rather arbitrary assessment, based not only on their achievements as Prime Minister, but on the overall impact of their political careers. On this basis, George Canning, who served less than four months, appears much higher in the list than many of his fellows whose incumbency was far longer. For what it is worth, here is my list:

1 = Peel
1 = Gladstone
3 Grey
4 Canning
5 Pitt
6 Disraeli
7 Salisbury
8 Russell
9 Palmerston
10 Liverpool
11 Grenville
12 Perceval
13 Melbourne
14 Derby
15 Wellington
16 Addington
17 Aberdeen
18 Goderich
19 Portland
20 Rosebery

Note on titles and the House of Lords

Readers unfamiliar with the niceties of British peerages and other hereditary titles may be confused by references to titled persons who have been Prime Ministers or held other government posts, while serving in the House of Commons. Two categories are principally concerned – those who hold courtesy titles as the sons of peers, and those who have Scottish or Irish peerages which did not make them automatically entitled to membership of the House of Lords. In the first category was Lord North, Prime Minister between 1770–82, whose title derived from his being the son and heir of the Earl of Guildford. In the nineteenth century, Lord John Russell owed his title to being a younger son of the Duke of Bedford. He later was created an Earl in his own right, and transferred to the House of Lords before his second premiership. Lord Palmerston was an Irish peer, and spent the whole of his long political career in the House of Commons. One leading politician who spanned both categories was Lord Castlereagh, Foreign Secretary and Leader of the House of Commons between 1812 and 1822. He owed this title to being the eldest son of the Marquess of Londonderry. This happened to be an Irish peerage, and in the last year of his life he succeeded his father as the second Marquess, but remained in the House of Commons.

Bibliographical note

Short bibliographies are included at the end of each chapter. In addition, a work of reference should be mentioned which has been of use to the author throughout the book – Dermot Englefield, Janet Seaton & Isobel White, eds., *Facts about the British Prime Ministers*, 1995, New York, H.W. Wilson Company.

1
William Pitt, the Younger – Reformer Turned Reactionary?

THE RIGHT HON.ᴮᴸᴱ WILLIAM PITT;

CHANCELLOR OF THE EXCHEQUER, &c. &c.

When the nineteenth century opened, the British government was led by a mature 40-year-old politician, who had already been Prime Minister for 16 years – longer than anybody else, before or since, except for Robert Walpole, whose nearly 21 continuous years in the office may never be equalled. Pitt the Younger owed his preferment, at the age of 24, to two other men. The awesome reputation of his recently deceased father – William Pitt the Elder – known as 'The Great Commoner' (though he finished up as the Earl of Chatham) gave a head start to his own political career. Equally helpful was the favour of King George III, who cynically chose him as the means to drive out of office his own *bête noir*, Charles James Fox. That he was subsequently able to maintain himself in power for so long was almost entirely due to his own considerable abilities.

If ever anybody was pre-programmed to be Prime Minister, it was William Pitt the younger. He was born, in Kent, on 28 May 1759 – the very year in which his father gained lasting renown as a war leader in the Seven Years' War. The elder Pitt was not, then, actually Prime Minister, but he planned and directed Britain's military and naval operations, which saw France driven out of its possessions in both Canada and India, and worsted in conflicts in West Africa and the West Indies. Although his subsequent term as Prime Minister, in 1766–68, was a disappointment, his achievements in 1759, combined with his passionate patriotism, rare incorruptibility and soaring oratory established him as Britain's outstanding eighteenth-century political leader.

The elder Pitt came from a well-established landed family, with a tradition of public service, whose fortune derived from his grandfather, Thomas Pitt, a trader in India, who became Governor of Madras. William the Elder married Hester Grenville, whose brother, George Grenville, was also to be Prime Minister (in 1763–65), so the young William grew up in a family which was deeply political on both sides. William was the second son, and fourth child (out of five) in the family, but from the outset his father had marked him out as the one to carry forward the flame of his own burning ambition.

Partly because of his delicate health, but also because of the elder Pitt's unpleasant memories of Eton, which he described as 'a stultifying and brutal place' (Turner, p. 6), William was educated at home by a private tutor, but his father took a very active role in his instruction. He coached him in oratory, getting him to translate, verbally and at sight, passages from Greek and Latin authors, and hearing him recite. By the age of seven, William was already looking forward to following in his father's footsteps. Very quick to learn, he was judged at 14 to be the equal or superior of most 18-year-olds, and started to study at Pembroke Hall, Cambridge, with the Rev. George Pretyman (whom he was much later to nominate as Archbishop of Canterbury, only to be over-ruled by George III) as his tutor. His health soon broke down, and he spent much of the next three years at home, suffering, among other ailments, from gout. His doctor, Anthony Addington (father of his successor as Prime Minister, Henry

Addington), prescribed a bottle of port every day as a cure. It seemed to work, but it left William with a heavy dependence on alcohol, which was to do him no good in the long run.

As an undergraduate, he lived a solitary life, meeting few people other than his tutor, Pretyman. He proved a diligent student of Latin and Greek, showed a taste for mathematics and learned French, but no other modern languages and showed little interest in contemporary culture. In 1776, still aged only 17, he graduated as a Master of Arts, without taking an examination. He stayed on in Cambridge, and his social life at last took off, bringing him into contact with a group of well-bred young men, several of whom were later to become his political associates. One of these was William Wilberforce, the famous campaigner for the abolition of the slave trade, who left a record of Pitt's life at Cambridge, describing him as being always 'remarkably cheerful and pleasant, full of wit and playfulness' (Ehrman, I, pp. 17–18). This view was corroborated by others, including Pretyman, and he was undoubtedly very popular with his fellows, but at the same time he was remarked as being gawky and awkward, and painfully shy with strangers. He was in no doubt that politics was his vocation, and he travelled frequently to London to listen to parliamentary debates, on one occasion being introduced to Charles James Fox, the leading Whig orator, who commented favourably on his lively intelligence. He attended the House of Lords on 7 April 1778, to hear his father's last speech, a passionate appeal to make peace with the American rebels, and when the Earl collapsed before reaching his peroration, helped to carry him out of the Chamber. Chatham died a month later, and – in the absence of his elder brother, John, who was on military service overseas – Pitt was left to make the funeral arrangements and attempt to sort out his father's tangled financial affairs. He was deeply in debt, having – unlike most of his contemporaries – refused to enrich himself from his ministerial duties, and though Parliament voted to pay off the debts and to establish an annuity of £4,000 attached to the Earldom (which went to his brother), Pitt received no legacy, and himself went into debt, which – with ups and downs – continued for the rest of his life.

It was necessary to earn a living, and Pitt now started eating dinners at Lincoln's Inn, with the intention of working at the bar. He qualified in June 1780, and in August went to work on the Western circuit. In September, however, a general election was called, and he hastily returned to Cambridge, where he was nominated as a candidate for one of the University seats. He was just over 21 years old, and wrote enthusiastically to his mother that it was 'a seat of all others the most desirable, as being free from expense, perfectly independent, and I think in every respect extremely honourable' (Turner, p. 13). The only disadvantage was that Pitt, despite his long residence in Cambridge, had very little support. He came bottom of the poll, in fifth place with less than 14 per cent of the votes. In order to secure election at such an early stage, it would be necessary, he concluded, to surrender some of the independence he (like his father) so craved. When he was approached by a notorious 'boroughmonger', Sir James Lowther, to take over, with all expenses paid, the representation of Appleby (in Westmorland) – one of his string of 'rotten boroughs', which had become immediately vacant – he accepted with little hesitation. Lowther was an admirer of his father, and, as Pitt explained to his mother, 'No Kind of Condition was mentioned, but that if ever Our Lines of Conduct should become opposite, I should give Him an Opportunity of chusing another Person. On such Liberal Terms, I should certainly not hesitate to accept the Proposal, than which Nothing could be in any respect more agreeable' (Ehrman, I, p. 26). Accordingly, on 8 January 1781, Pitt was returned unopposed at a by-election, without setting foot in the constituency.

The Parliament to which Pitt was elected was divided as much by faction as by party. The historical division between Whigs and Tories had become somewhat blurred during the 20 years that George III had occupied the throne. The long domination of the Whigs throughout the reigns of the first two Georges, which had seen the Tories steadily decline in both numbers and influence, was a thing of the past. The Whigs still saw themselves as the guarantors of the Glorious Revolution of 1688–89, believing in a limited monarchy, the supremacy of Parliament, a vigorous and basically anti-French foreign policy, free trade and relative religious tolerance. Led by an oligarchy of enlightened aristocrats, they tended to be arrogant, self-satisfied and behaved as though they were born to rule. The main Whig factions were led by three peers – the Marquess of Rockingham, the Earl of Shelburne and the Duke of Portland, with Charles James Fox the dominant figure in the House of Commons.

The Tories, representing primarily the gentry, were strong supporters of the royal prerogative and the Church of England, tending to believe in the divine right of monarchs, and were long tainted by suspicions of Jacobitism, though this was less of a factor after the failure of the 1745 uprising of Bonnie Prince Charlie. They were also protectionist, and more isolationist in international affairs, putting their trust in the British Navy to keep the nation out of danger. Their long eviction from power was ended by the accession of George III, who distrusted the Whig oligarchs and was determined to assert his own personal role. In 1762, he installed a Tory, the Earl of Bute, a personal favourite, as Prime Minister, but his ministry lasted for less than a year. There followed four short-lived Whig governments, one of them led by the elder Pitt as Earl of Chatham, but in 1770, George succeeded in imposing a second Tory administration. This was led by Lord North MP, a much more substantial politician than Bute, who was to continue in office for 12 years. When Pitt was elected, his long rule was nearing its end, and he was largely discredited by the disasters of the American War of Independence.

Pitt's entry into Parliament aroused great interest, almost entirely because of his father, to whom he bore much physical resemblance, with his long, thin face and tall body, though at six feet his was longer and more ungainly than his father's. He also made much of his adherence to his father's principles, of putting patriotism before party advantage, and of refusing to enrich himself at the public expense. He did not disappoint the high expectations: after hearing his maiden speech, which made a deep impression on the Commons, Edmund Burke declared 'he is not a chip of the old block, he is the old block himself' (Duffy, p. 4).

Like the Elder Pitt, William described himself as an 'independent Whig', and loosely attached himself to the faction led by the Earl of Shelburne, who had been one of the two Secretaries of State in his father's administration. He proved himself an incisive critic of the North government, making a powerful speech, on 12 June 1781, in favour of Fox's motion for peace with the American colonies. A year later, with his reputation as an up-and-coming force already well established, and the government clearly on its last legs, he rashly declared that he would 'never accept a subordinate situation' in any successor administration. North resigned a few days later, and the Marquess of Rockingham was summoned to form a new Whig government, in which Shelburne became Home, and Fox, Foreign Secretary. Pitt was offered the post of Vice-Treasurer of Ireland, which his father had briefly held in 1746. It carried a salary of £5,000, which Pitt could well have done with, but he felt trapped by his earlier words and declined, choosing instead to support the new government from outside. Pitt now moved swiftly to assert himself as an advocate of electoral reform, moving a resolution to appoint a select committee to consider the state of representation, supporting one to shorten the duration of parliaments and a bill to check bribery. Pitt's efforts failed, but he resolved to return to the charge on a more auspicious occasion. Meanwhile, the Rockingham government lasted a mere four months, the Prime Minister dying suddenly of influenza in July 1782. The King chose Shelburne as his successor, and Fox, who had quarrelled with him over the peace negotiations with America and France, declined to serve under him and resigned his post, as did Burke, who had been paymaster-general. Shelburne, the bulk of his Cabinet being peers, was desperate to recruit debating strength in the Commons to counter these two formidable adversaries, and offered Pitt the post of Chancellor of the Exchequer. This was not then as senior a post as it subsequently became, as the First Lord of the Treasury (i.e., the Prime Minister) was primarily responsible for financial and fiscal affairs, nevertheless it was a stunning promotion for a man of 23 with no previous ministerial experience.

Pitt's period as Chancellor lasted a mere eight months, during which he made his mark by reorganizing customs duties, cutting out wasteful expenditure and reducing the extent of jobbery in public offices. Meanwhile, Shelburne, a highly intelligent man but lacking in political skills, was having great difficulty in seeking approval for the peace terms which had finally been negotiated with the Americans. An unholy alliance was formed between the followers of Fox, the leader of the 'advanced' Whigs and the main critic of the American War, and the Tory Lord North, who had been responsible for its conduct. Shelburne realized that he would have to break up this alliance if his policy and his ministry were to survive. He made overtures to some of North's supporters who, however, insisted that North should be included in the government, which Pitt was not prepared to countenance. Shelburne then sent Pitt to see Fox to invite him to rejoin the government. Fox refused, saying that for a new coalition to be formed, Shelburne would have to resign. Pitt stormed out, saying, 'I did not come here to betray Lord Shelburne', and the two men, who previously had been mutual admirers, were never to meet in private again (Turner, p. 43). The Commons passed a censure motion against the peace terms, by 207 to 190 votes, on 22 February 1783, and Shelburne resigned two days later, much to the King's chagrin. In the final Commons debate, Pitt had made an extraordinarily eloquent appeal on Shelburne's behalf, and castigated the opportunism of the two previously sworn enemies, Fox and North, who were clearly putting themselves forward as joint heads of a new government. 'If this ill-omened marriage is not already solemnised', he said, 'I know a just and lawful impediment, and, in the name of public safety, I here forbid the banns' (Duffy, p. 10).

George III made a last desperate effort to avoid giving office to the pair, one of whom was his most inveterate critic, and the other whom he felt had abandoned him by insisting on resigning after the collapse of the British position in North America. He offered the premiership to the 23-year-old Pitt, on Shelburne's recommendation, and renewed the offer twice more over the succeeding six months. In Duffy's words, Pitt's 'refusals show a great degree of political maturity and judgment in being able to control his ambition'. Pitt was clear in his own mind that he could not hope to form a viable government without being able to command a majority in the House of Commons, and this he could only do with the co-operation, or at least the acquiescence, of Lord North, a man he held 'responsible for the misuse of Crown influence to corrupt Parliament, and for the confrontation with the colonies which had hastened the death of his father, who had exhausted himself in battling against it, and resulted in the loss of America' (Duffy, pp. 12–13).

Eventually, the King had to agree to the Fox–North coalition, which was nominally led by a Whig grandee, the Duke of Portland, with Fox resuming his tenure of the Foreign Office and North becoming Home Secretary. It took office on 2 April 1783, but from the beginning George III was determined to overthrow it at the earliest opportunity, and refused point-blank to sustain the government with the powers of royal patronage normally put at the disposal of his ministers. The King, however, had to act with some circumspection, as the new government enjoyed a comfortable majority in the House of Commons. He seized his opportunity towards the end of the year, when the government introduced legislation to bring the East India Company, which governed territories whose population greatly exceeded that of Britain itself, under closer control. It proposed that the management and patronage of the company should be transferred to parliamentary commissioners appointed for a four-year term. The King, and Pitt, thought that Fox would use the extensive patronage of the Company to the government's advantage, to compensate for the royal patronage which it lacked. They also recalled that Fox's father, Henry, the first Lord Holland, had used the patronage at his disposal, when he had been Paymaster-General in 1757–65, to build himself a large fortune, and were determined to block the Bill.

Fox appeared to have little difficulty in getting it through the Commons, and though George was insistent on his right to veto legislation, this power had not been used since the reign of Queen Anne, and it was widely thought to have fallen into desuetude. In a plan cooked up with Lord Thurlow, a former and future Lord Chancellor, in which Pitt was complicit, it was resolved to use the House of Lords to defeat the measure. The King authorized Lord Temple, a cousin of Pitt's, to tell peers that anybody who voted for the India Bill 'was not only not his friend, but would be considered by him as an enemy' (Duffy, p. 18). The Lords duly obliged, defeating the Bill, on 17 December 1783, by 95 votes to 76. Both Pitt and George III had expected the government to resign immediately, but it decided to cling to office, not least because it secured 2–1 majorities in votes in the House of Commons attacking the use of the King's name and those who advised its use in the Lords. The King waited a further day, and then sent messengers at midnight to Portland, Fox and North requiring them to surrender their seals of office. Pitt was appointed First Lord of the Treasury on 19 December, with Lord Thurlow as Lord Chancellor, but few other men of any standing were prepared to associate themselves with a government which had been brought to power in such an underhand way, and Pitt was attacked for forming a government of mediocrities. Few people expected it to survive for long, and it was quickly dubbed the 'mince pie government', on the assumption that it would not last beyond Christmas. In such inauspicious circumstances began a premiership which was to last for over 17 years (and almost 19 years, in all, including Pitt's second ministry in 1804–1806). Pitt was aged 24 years, 205 days – almost nine years younger than any other British Prime Minister – his closest rival, the 3rd Duke of Grafton, being just over 33 on his appointment in 1768.

Pitt endured a scary few months, being repeatedly defeated in votes in the House of Commons, but – to Fox's exasperation – refused to resign, secure in the knowledge that he retained the King's confidence. During this period, however, his personal stock rose sharply, due to the skill with which he defended himself in parliamentary debates. The burden on him was considerable, as his entire cabinet was made up of peers, and he had to act as the government's spokesman on every conceivable issue. Pitt's reputation also grew outside Parliament, partly because of his forbearance in declining to appoint himself to a sinecure office, the Clerkship of the Pells, worth £3,000 a year, which was in the Prime Minister's gift. He also gained from public revulsion at an attack on his carriage by a Foxite mob on his return from receiving the Freedom of the City of London. Salvation came with the dissolution of Parliament in March 1784 – three-and-a-half years before the end of its term. Pitt knew that the odds were overwhelming that he would emerge with a comfortable majority from the election. He had already made deals with 'borough mongers', and the full weight of royal patronage (and Treasury money) was at his disposal. Indeed, throughout the eighteenth century, no sitting government was ever to lose an election. It was the King who gave ministers their marching orders, not the electors, who were few in number and largely influenced by a relatively small number of aristocratic landowners. The general election of 1784 was no exception: no detailed breakdown of the results has survived, but it was generally estimated that the government secured a majority of around 120 in a House of 558. The opposition was divided between about 130 MPs committed to Fox, and 70 to North, who had been the main loser in the election, and whose support subsequently fell away (Derry, p. 52). For Pitt, the election brought another cause for satisfaction: he was able to exchange his 'pocket' borough of Appleby for his first love – Cambridge University – where this time he came top of the poll, and was easily elected, retaining the seat for the rest of his life.

With his solid parliamentary majority, and the renewed support of the King, Pitt no longer seemed vulnerable, and he settled in for a long innings in Downing Street, though nobody foresaw that it would prove quite as long as it did. His cabinet was still devoid of parliamentary talent, and he himself chose to retain the office of Chancellor of the Exchequer throughout his premiership, but he was able to bring along two close associates of high ability, who were eventually to fill the most senior posts. These were his cousin, William Grenville, son of a former Prime Minister, who was to rise successively to Home and Foreign Secretary, and Henry Dundas, a formidable political 'fixer' from Scotland, who became his chief 'trouble shooter', and was also to be Home Secretary, and later Secretary for War and the Colonies. His main handicap was that the King insisted on choosing the ministers himself, and ruled that Lord Thurlow, a man whom Pitt found highly uncongenial and disloyal, should continue as Lord Chancellor. Thurlow's relationship to George III was much closer and warmer than his own, which Pitt resented but was unable to do anything about.

Across the floor of the House of Commons, he had regularly to face Fox, now the undisputed leader of the Whigs, and his only rival, and perhaps superior, as a parliamentary orator. Always credited by history with both his forenames, he was invariably known as Charles or Charley during his lifetime. Ten years older than Pitt, and himself the second son of a distinguished political father, Fox was also known for his precocity, having first been elected to Parliament at the age of 19. This was two years below the legal limit, but in the less rule-bound ways of the eighteenth century, nobody objected when he took his seat. His own political career was to be blighted by Pitt's rise to power, and by George III's unrelenting hostility. He was effectively to be the leader of the opposition (though the title did not then exist) for 23 years, and his sole periods in Cabinet office were three stints as Foreign Secretary, each lasting only a few months, in 1782, 1783 and 1806. On more than one occasion, Pitt sought to include Fox in his government, but Fox demanded that they should both serve under a nominal superior, such as Portland, while Pitt invariably insisted on retaining the premiership. The two leaders' long rivalry prefigured that of Gladstone and Disraeli nearly a century later, and they were an equally contrasting pair, both in appearance and character. Pitt was tall, stiff and withdrawn; Fox fat, warm and gregarious. Pitt was cautious, calculating and conservative; Fox radical, impulsive and untidy. Pitt's political judgement was excellent, and he never (except on Ireland much later in his career) attempted to push hard for policies that had little chance of being acceptable to Parliament or – more importantly in his eyes – the King. Fox's judgement was poor, and though he was capable of wild opportunism, consistently pursued policies calculated to alienate the King. Fox was dissolute – a gambler and womaniser, who eventually contracted a happy marriage with a former courtesan, Elizabeth Armistead. Pitt was highly disciplined, had little apparent interest in women, and has – on the basis of rather slender evidence – become something of a gay icon (see page 23, below). Nearly everybody loved 'Charley', whose charm was a by-word. Except for a few bosom friends, with whom he was able to unbend in moments of alcoholic revelry, Pitt was respected but not greatly liked. They had some causes in common – electoral reform and the abolition of the slave trade – and in other circumstances their complementary talents could have drawn them together and made a formidable team. But raw ambition drove them apart in 1782–84, and they were never to be reconciled. Indeed, Pitt revealed a vindictive streak in his character, following his sweeping victory in the 1784 election, when he persisted for several months in an attempt to get Fox unseated from his Westminster constituency on – by eighteenth century standards – very minor evidence of irregularities. He was only finally dissuaded from this course when he was defeated on the issue by a House of Commons vote. (It was by no means unusual for the government to lose parliamentary votes, at a time of weak or non-existent party discipline, and when those in general support of the government, or even cabinet ministers, felt no particular obligation to deliver their votes except on major issues.)

Pitt's over-riding objective during his first years in office was to restore national confidence, and the declining economy, after the setbacks and disasters of the American War. His purpose was to stimulate trade – particularly with Europe to offset the loss of North American markets (which was to prove only temporary) – to improve the public finances and to usher in a period of political stability. On any reckoning, he was largely successful in his endeavours, and within a relatively short time, not only King George but a large proportion of the 'political' class, came to view him as the indispensable head of government. One of Pitt's principal tools was his annual budgets, but he did not make a name for himself, at least in his earlier years, as a tax pioneer. He relied on traditional forms of taxation and did not noticeably expand the tax base, concentrating as Ehrman convincingly argues (Ehrman, I, pp. 250–6), primarily on increasing the yield from existing taxes, by improving methods of collection and by cracking down more effectively on smuggling. His most important innovation, in 1786, was to establish a sinking fund, with the objective of eventually paying off the national debt, which had doubled to around £213 million as a consequence of the American War. Pitt's proposal was well received, and steady progress was to be made in reducing the debt over the first half dozen years, but the outbreak of war with France in 1793 meant that it rapidly resumed its upward trend. Pitt was also active in cutting out wasteful expenditure, and, wherever possible, reducing or terminating the award of pensions and sinecures, though he was not above using such means for *political* purposes, including to strengthen the government's position in the House of Lords.

Pitt was also successful in his efforts to promote trade, though he suffered a setback in 1785, when he was forced to withdraw proposals for free trade between England and Ireland. He had more success with a commercial treaty, negotiated with France, in 1786, which led to a sharp increase in trade between the two traditional enemies. Pitt was to return to his earlier campaign for electoral reform, introducing a bill, in April 1785, which provided for a very modest extension of the franchise in county constituencies, while granting one million pounds to compensate the electors of 36 rotten boroughs which were to be disfranchised, while the 72 seats thus made available were to be transferred to London, Westminster and the more populous counties. Neither the King nor several of his ministerial colleagues approved of the measure, and nor did Lord North and his followers, though Fox supported the Bill. The King did not try to prevent its introduction, but insisted that it should be introduced in Pitt's personal capacity rather than as a government measure. Pitt made a powerful speech seeking leave to introduce the Bill, but it was defeated by 248 to 174 votes. A disappointed Pitt decided to cut his losses, and never again raised the issue, indeed opposing reform bills introduced by private members on three occasions in the 1790s and 1800s. So parliamentary reform had to wait nearly another half century until the 'great' Reform Bill of 1832. Nor did Pitt's enthusiasm for reform extend to support for the repeal of the Test and Corporation Acts. These two measures, dating from the mid-seventeenth century, had the effect of excluding Protestant dissenters (later known as Nonconformists) from membership of municipal corporations or from holding a wide range of public offices or commissions in the army and navy. Although these acts were only enforced in a spasmodic manner, they remained a standing grievance, particularly to the business community, in which many dissenters had gained prominence. Pitt appeared to have no strong views on the subject, and he consulted the Archbishop of Canterbury, who informed him that only 2 out of 16 bishops favoured reform (Hague, p. 239). Unwilling to alienate the Church of England, Pitt threw his weight against the proposed repeal, which was duly defeated, in March 1787, by 176 votes to 98. Pitt was a strong supporter of the abolition of the slave trade, and he encouraged his friend Wilberforce to bring motions before the House of Commons to secure this objective. On one occasion, in April 1792, he made what was regarded as one of the greatest speeches of his career in support of Wilberforce's demand for 'immediate' abolition, but the House preferred to adopt an amendment tabled by Dundas, substituting the word 'gradual', which stripped the motion of any practical effect. William Hague describes Pitt's inability to secure the final abolition of the trade as his 'greatest failure'. He writes:

> The sincerity of his opposition to this dreadful trade was all too plain, but so is the fact that he lost the energy, focus and will to pursue the matter to a successful conclusion … The fact that abolition was so speedily secured by Grenville and Fox soon after Pitt's death suggests that he too could have secured it if he had marshalled his forces to do so. (Hague, p. 589)

By the late 1780s, an increasingly frustrated Fox followed the course pursued by earlier opposition leaders in the reigns of George I and George II, by transferring his allegiance to the court of the Prince of Wales, who was at daggers' drawn with his father. More intelligent and much more cultured than the philistine King, the future George IV was far from being an admirable character. Dissolute, vain, extravagantly self-indulgent, lacking in judgement and profoundly untrustworthy, Fox and his fellow Whigs would have been well advised to keep him at arms-length. Instead, Fox and he became bosom companions, and few doubted that the first act of young George if he were to succeed his father would be to dismiss Pitt from power and restore Fox and Portland to their former posts. In 1788 George III was 50 years old, and had already reigned for 28 years. Given the average expectation of life, it was not fanciful to suppose that before long the Prince of Wales would ascend the throne. His – and Fox's – opportunity seemed to have arrived in November 1788, with the

Regency crisis, brought on by the onset of George III's first serious attack of porphyria, a little understood hereditary illness, whose symptoms included temporary insanity. The King's principal doctor, Warren, declared that he was incurable and unlikely to live for long. The Whigs, in Fox's absence on holiday in Italy, were persuaded by Richard Sheridan, the Irish playwright and leading Foxite MP, to demand the immediate installation of the Prince as regent. Pitt, sensing the great danger he was in, played for time, insisting that all the relevant precedents should be studied and that an Act of Parliament should be passed setting out the terms of the regency. He also consulted his own former doctor, Anthony Addington, who gave a much more favourable prognosis, saying that he had seen worse cases than the King make a full recovery. Pitt's regency bill sharply curtailed the powers of the regent, in particular, preventing him from granting peerages and making official appointments (except on a temporary basis), and placing the King's person and property wholly in the Queen's hands. Fox, who had hastened back to London, in a poor physical state, stricken with dysentery, then made a crucial blunder. The self-proclaimed 'tribune of the people' declared in the House of Commons that the Prince had an hereditary right to the regency, implying that Parliament had no business in seeking to define the limits. Pitt immediately seized his chance, whispering to his neighbour 'I'll unwhig the gentleman for the rest of his life', and proceeded to point out that this went directly against the long-standing Whig principle of parliamentary sovereignty. Despite, the disloyalty of his Lord Chancellor, Thurlow, who was negotiating behind his back with the Foxites and the Prince, to ensure that he kept his own post in the event of a change of government, Pitt was able to rally his Cabinet and a majority of the House of Commons, who adopted the Bill on 5 February 1789. It then went to the Lords, but further progress was made unnecessary by the King's sudden recovery.

The outcome of the Regency crisis was as great a triumph for Pitt and a disaster for Fox, as the overthrow of the Fox–North coalition in 1783. The King's inveterate hostility to Fox became even greater, and his gratitude to Pitt knew few bounds. He sought to make him a Knight of the Garter, which Pitt declined, suggesting instead that the honour went to his elder brother, the 2nd Earl of Chatham, who was currently First Lord of the Admiralty. A couple of years later, he finally overcame Pitt's reluctance to accept a sinecure office, appointing him as Warden of the Cinque ports, worth £3,000 a year, and with a fine residence, Walmer Castle, to go with it. Pitt's stout defence of the King's position, against the intrigues of his eldest son, also increased his own standing with the public. Unlike his two Hanoverian predecessors, who were disliked as foreigners who made little effort to endear themselves to their new countrymen, George III was widely popular, despite his authoritarian tendencies. He looked and behaved like an English country squire and fully shared the tastes and prejudices of a majority of his subjects.

Pitt's advantage over Fox was consolidated by the general election of 1790, where his supporters improved even further on their major success in 1784, with 340 seats going to the government, 183 to the opposition and 35 to 'others' (Turner, p. 118). Meanwhile, Pitt had begun to make his mark on the international stage, reducing his ineffectual Foreign Secretary, the Marquess of Carmarthen (later, Duke of Leeds) to little more than a cipher. He chanced his arm by ordering mobilization in 1787, when France threatened to intervene in the Netherlands on the side of the Republicans in their struggle for power with the *Stadhouder*, the Prince of Orange. Together with the King of Prussia, who was the Prince's brother-in-law, he threatened a military riposte, and Prussian troops actually crossed the Dutch border, whereupon the Republicans' resistance collapsed. The French then hastily backed down, and Pitt was able to claim a triumph without firing a shot. Three years later, he was able to repeat the trick with Britain's other traditional enemy – Spain – over the Nootka Sound dispute. This concerned the establishment of a British trading post on Vancouver Island, in territory long claimed by Spain. The Spanish reacted by stopping a British ship and arresting the traders, while demanding that the British should recognize Spanish sovereignty over the entire west coasts of the American continents. The British cabinet prepared for war, and called on Spain to compensate the arrested traders. Spain proved obdurate until it transpired that its long-time ally, and fellow Bourbon kingdom, France, distracted by the early phases of the Revolution, was in no mood to go to war on its behalf. It then smartly climbed down, agreed to compensate the traders and conceded that British subjects could enter areas not actually settled by the Spanish and fish in the Pacific.

Pitt had followed up his Dutch success by concluding a 'Triple Alliance' between Britain, Holland and Prussia, and now aspired to expand this into a general 'Concert of Europe', whose purpose would be the peaceful settlement of disputes and the confirmation of European boundaries as they had existed in 1787. In particular, he aimed to associate Austria and Russia with the project, which would leave France isolated if it declined to participate. This grand design, which prefigured the system imposed after the Congress of Vienna in 1815, collapsed at its first test, in 1791, when Catherine the Great of Russia proclaimed the annexation of the fortress of Ochakov (Odessa), which had been captured during a war with Turkey. Britain and Prussia sent an ultimatum to Catherine that she should return it to the Turks, and Pitt prepared to send British fleets to the Black and Baltic seas to add to the pressure. But the Austrians declined to join in, and Catherine showed herself to be unexpectedly obdurate. Pitt also faced strong parliamentary and cabinet opposition, and – deeply humiliated – sent a message to the Prussians to withdraw the ultimatum, telling Joseph Ewart, the British Ambassador to Berlin, 'with tears in his eyes, that it was the greatest mortification he had ever experienced'

(Ehrman, II, p. 24). His projected 'Concert' was dead, and two years later he looked on helplessly as Russia, Prussia and Austria proceeded to the second of their three partitions of Poland. The Duke of Leeds resigned as Foreign Secretary, in protest against his handling of the Ochakov affair, which caused Pitt no anguish, as it enabled him to promote his cousin, and close associate, William Grenville, in his place.

The storming of the Bastille on 14 July 1789 marked a watershed in Pitt's long premiership. Before then he had been a highly successful peacetime Prime Minister, and a moderate reformer. Later he was to be a markedly less success-ful war leader, and what might be most accurately described as a moderate reactionary (if that is not a contradiction in terms), though it was to be nearly another four years before Britain was actually at war with France. Initially, Pitt welcomed the early stages of the French Revolution, as did the great majority of Britain's political class. It came in the midst of the hundredth anniversary cel-ebrations of the 'Glorious Revolution' of 1688–89, and the general feeling was that France was at last catching up with Britain and would develop into a con-stitutional monarchy with enhanced liberties for its citizens. Even as disorders spread, Pitt remained sanguine, as he believed that this would weaken France as a great power, which would be to the British advantage. His attitude hard-ened after the September massacres of 1792, and the execution of Louis XVI the following January, yet he still resisted pressure to join Austria and Prussia in their war against France. Eventually, it was France which declared war, in April 1793, after Britain had objected to its invasion of Holland.

Meanwhile, serious splits developed within the opposition. Fox had wel-comed the Revolution unequivocally, exclaiming after the fall of the Bastille, 'How much the greatest event it is that ever happened in the world!, and how much the best!'. Many of his younger supporters, including a future reform-ist Prime Minister, Charles Grey, were inspired to seek to revive the movement for parliamentary reform, which was largely dormant since the failure of Pitt's Bill in 1785. They founded a body called Friends of the People, and argued for much more thoroughgoing changes, including Household suffrage. This, however, fell well behind the demands of more rank-and-file bodies, such as the London Correspondence Society, led by a shoemaker, Thomas Hardy. These included universal male suffrage, the abolition of the property qualification for MPs, equal electoral districts, the payment of MPs, annual parliaments and the secret ballot. These demands horrified the more conservative Whigs, including Portland, who regarded their advocates as no better than 'Jacobins', and feared for the defence of their own property. They were even more appalled by the pub-lication, in 1791, of Thomas Paine's *Rights of Man*. The earliest and most painful defector from Fox was Edmund Burke, formerly his closest friend and collabora-tor. Showing extraordinary prescience, Burke, at an early date, foresaw all the more nefarious consequences of the Revolution – the growth of fanaticism, the descent into chaos and civil war, the destruction of liberty and the military adventurism, which would plunge Europe into a generation of war. He spelled out his fears in his pamphlet, *Reflections on the Revolution in France*, published in November 1790, and advocated immediate action to forestall them. Pitt himself was by no means convinced, and for more than another two years maintained a policy of strict neutrality towards the events in France.

Once war was joined, however, in 1793, he became fully committed to conducting it to a successful conclusion. This did not, in his view, necessarily involve the restoration of the monarchy, which most of his allies wished to proclaim as a war aim, but it did mean that France should cease to be a constant threat to the security of its neighbours. Pitt was emphatic that only he should lead the government, but was anxious to strengthen its position by recruiting heavyweight figures from the opposition who were prepared to sever their connections with Fox. An opportunity had already arisen, in January 1793, when Thurlow had finally exhausted Pitt's – and the King's patience – by attacking the government's fiscal policies in the House of Lords. Pitt successfully demanded his resignation, and was able to replace him as Lord Chancellor by the Whigs' leading lawyer, Lord Loughborough. Detailed negotiations then followed with Portland and other leading Whigs, but they were not yet ready to abandon Fox. Eighteen months later, however, in July 1794, Pitt pulled off a considerable coup, when Portland, who became Home Secretary, and four of his leading colleagues, joined the cabinet, bringing a large parliamentary following with them. The Portlandites drove a hard bargain: 'The alliance could not have been arranged without Pitt's generous offer of five places in the cabinet, five peerages and one promotion in the peerage, a pension for Burke, two offices in the royal household, the lord lieutenancy of Middlesex, and the promise of the lord lieutenancy of Ireland' (Turner, p. 118). Some of Pitt's supporters criticized him for ceding too much, fearing that he would lose control over his own cabinet, six of whose 13 members were now his former political opponents. But Pitt was careful to keep the main portfolios connected to the war effort in the hands of his own loyalists, and the effect of the whole exercise was to hamstring the opposition. Portland was able to bring 62 MPs over to the government's side, 'leaving the Foxites in the Commons as a small and isolated party of about fifty-five members' (Turner, p. 132). In any event, the cabinet, as a whole, seldom played a significant role in determining war policy. Pitt was in the habit of settling decisions with his two closest collaborators – Grenville, the Foreign Secretary, and Dundas, War Secretary, and provided these three were of one mind there was little chance of their being successfully challenged. The only other person of great influence was the King, who liked to be consulted and was not bashful about making his own suggestions. On some occasions he was to over-rule Pitt, but most of the time the Prime Minister got his own way.

Pitt's reputation as a reformer did not long survive the onset of war. Backed by his new Home Secretary, Portland, he introduced a series of repressive measures which, while ostensibly aimed at would-be violent supporters of the French Revolution, were, in practice, employed against the essentially peaceful advocates of electoral reform, such as the leaders of the London Correspondence Society, who were actually arraigned in a treason trial which carried the threat of the death sentence. Fortunately, a London jury had the good sense to acquit them, though in Edinburgh one man was hanged on similar charges, and others imprisoned or sent to Botany Bay. Pitt himself took part in the cross-examination of several of those arrested, but was highly embarrassed when he was subpoenaed to appear as a witness in the trial of the noted radical, John Horne Tooke. Here he was forced to admit the similarity between the views attributed to Tooke and his own advocacy ten years earlier. Pitt's measures, which included the suspension of *habeus corpus* for several periods, were bitterly opposed in the Commons by Fox and his depleted band of supporters, but were carried by large majorities. Fox denounced them as a concerted attack on liberty, but the historian John Derry attempted to put them in perspective when he wrote:

> But Pitt and Portland did not preside over anything like a reign of terror. Something like a total of 200 prosecutions over a period of ten years hardly merits such a description. Many of the cases ended in acquittal or the charges being dropped and the proceedings discontinued. The pressure of convention and the weight of public opinion achieved more in damping down radicalism than either the Seditious Meetings Act or the Treasonable Practices Act. With the ascendancy of loyalism and the popular identification of radicalism with Jacobinism, radicals suffered more from the prejudices of the community than from the force of law. (Derry, p. 97)

Pitt's war strategy closely paralleled that of his father during the Seven Year's War, utilising Britain's naval supremacy to facilitate attacks on France's overseas possessions, while subsidizing European allies to bear the brunt of military operations on the continent. Consistently, however, he failed to match the achievements of the elder Pitt. While most of the French possessions in the Caribbean were over-run, British troops had great difficulty in consolidating their conquests, and were decimated by tropical diseases. They had more success in their operations against France's allies, Spain and Holland, conquering Trinidad from the former, and the Cape Colony and Ceylon (Sri Lanka) from the latter. On the continent, however, direct British military operations – against Toulon, the Vendée (in support of French royalists) and Flanders – all ended in disaster. Nor did Britain's allies – either in the First coalition (1792–97), or the Second (1798–1801), fare any better.

Whereas his father had had the good fortune to ally himself with a military genius – Frederick the Great – none of the Younger Pitt's more numerous allies revealed conspicuous fighting qualities, their armies being regularly rolled over by French generals, from Carnot to Bonaparte. They then hastened to make peace, often on humiliating terms, leaving the British to fight on alone. The British troops, also, were poorly led, notably by Frederick, Duke of York, the favourite son of George III, whose ineffectiveness as commander during the Flanders campaign has been immortalized in the famous song, *The Grand Old Duke of York*. Virtually the only successes Pitt had to celebrate were periodic victories by the Navy, a deserved recompense for the assiduity he had shown in modernizing and expanding the fleet throughout the 1780s.

Pitt was to prove persistently optimistic in his conduct of the war, but failed – despite his Herculean labours – to pursue a consistent path, while his organization of public business was chaotic. Nor did his close personal alliance with Grenville and Dundas remain untroubled. The former was critical of his readiness to strike at France at any time and at any place, whenever an opportunity arose, believing that the available forces should be concentrated and only used in carefully planned and well-resourced campaigns which offered a good prospect of success. He also became exasperated at Pitt's continuance in paying subsidies to Prussia at a time when it was proving to be an inactive and unreliable ally, much more interested in carving up Poland, in successive partitions, with Austria and Russia, than in fighting against the French. Dundas proved an efficient organizer, but was inclined to defeatism and favoured an essentially defensive policy, giving priority to forestalling the probably exaggerated fears of a French invasion. Pitt had never anticipated a prolonged war, believing that the French economy would quickly collapse under the strain, and was distressed to find that it was the British economy which appeared to suffer most, with recurrent food shortages, labour unrest and the national debt reaching unprecedented heights. Periodically he was tempted to seek a negotiated peace, but George III was reluctant to agree. On two occasions, however, in 1796 and 1797, serious talks began, with Pitt essentially offering a deal on the basis of the return of the conquered French colonies in exchange for a withdrawal from the Low Countries. This was not sufficient bait to attract even the more moderate members of the *Directoire*, which replaced the terror regime in 1795. Pitt's wisdom in sticking to these conditions may be questioned. Certainly, Fox, and Pitt's friend Wilberforce, firmly believed that a continuation of the war was not in Britain's interest, and that a perfectly reasonable settlement could have been reached if the British negotiators had been more flexible. It could also be argued that the continuation of the war led to what Britain most feared – a permanently aggressive and expansionist France, which was assured by the rise to power of Napoleon, a direct result of his victories in the War of the Second Coalition, which Pitt organized after 1798.

Pitt wore himself out, and largely destroyed his health through his wartime exertions, becoming more and more dependent on alcohol. While attempting to supervise every detail of the war effort, he was also single-handedly running the Treasury, having retained his post as Chancellor of the Exchequer throughout his premiership. He found it increasingly difficult to finance the war, balancing tax increases with very extensive borrowing, but he continued to show tenacity and ingenuity in introducing his annual budgets. One of these, in 1798, was to introduce Income Tax for the first time. Intended only as a temporary measure, and initially raising far less than he had envisaged, it was eventually to become the principal resource on which subsequent Chancellors of the Exchequer have depended to fill the coffers of the state. He continued to carry a heavy load as Leader of the House of Commons, all his senior ministers, with the exception of Henry Dundas, being in the Lords, which meant that he had continually to speak for the government on a very wide range of subjects.

He was an increasingly isolated figure. Both his sisters, to whom he was devoted, had died in childbirth, his younger brother, James, a naval captain, had perished at sea, and his brother-in-law, Edward Eliot, who became his closest companion, died in 1791. Devoted associates of his youth, such as William Wilberforce, gradually drifted away, and he found it difficult to cultivate new friends. Although he remained throughout his career a masterly presence in the House of Commons, he did not use it as a means to build up a circle of close personal supporters. He was the object of immense respect, but little warmth, among his fellow MPs. A much-quoted account by the great parliamentary diarist, Sir Nathaniel Wraxall, describing his first appearance in the House as Prime Minister, is revelatory of the general disdain with which he treated them:

> From the instant that Pitt entered the doorway, he advanced up the floor with a quick and firm step, his head erect and thrown back, looking neither to the right nor the left, not favouring with a nod or a glance any of the individuals seated on either side, among whom many who possessed £5,000 a year would have been gratified even by so slight a mark of attention. It was not thus that Lord North or Fox treated Parliament.

With a few of his ministers he enjoyed greater intimacy, particularly Henry Dundas, who became his main drinking companion and whose home, close to his own house at Holwood in Kent, he often visited. Also nearby lived Lord Auckland, the former William Eden, a distinguished former ambassador, who had negotiated Pitt's commercial treaty with France. Pitt spent much time at his home in the autumn of 1796, relaxing with Auckland and his extensive family, not least his eldest daughter, the attractive 19-year-old Lady Eleanor Eden. Pitt made no declaration, but apparently Eleanor and both her parents assumed he was working up to a proposal of marriage, a prospect which gave them enormous pleasure. Rumours began to spread, and even reached the newspapers, and in January 1797 Pitt felt constrained to send an embarrassed letter to Auckland, disclaiming any such intention, and saying that, however, desirable such a union would be, there were 'decisive and insurmountable' obstacles. Auckland apparently concluded that these were of a temporary and financial nature, and wrote back suggesting that Pitt should come round 'and talk about the whole at leisure and again and again' (Hague, p. 391). Pitt was therefore forced to write a further and less circumspect letter, making it brutally clear that his mind was 'unalterably' fixed.

This episode, which caused a considerable stir, is discussed in detail by Pitt's most exhaustive biographer, John Ehrman, and more recently by former Tory leader William Hague. Both are disinclined to believe that Pitt's main motivation in backing off was the chaotic state of his financial situation (over which he exercised none of the conscientious care which he lavished on the nation's finances as First Lord of the Treasury), though this could have been a subordinate factor. Both conclude that, when it came down to it, Pitt simply could not face the prospect of marriage, either with Eleanor or any other woman, given his apparent lack of carnal interest in the opposite sex. Ehrman does not believe that he was actively homosexual. 'If he had any homosexual "potential" it would seem to have been very mild', he writes, 'and it is much more likely that he had no strong sexual inclinations at all' (Ehrman, I, p. 109). Ehrman does, however, add that 'If there was a homosexual relationship in Pitt's life, Canning might appear the most obvious candidate' (Ehrman, III, p. 94). The future Foreign Secretary, and briefly Prime Minister, was one of a number of young junior ministers – among them Castlereagh, Huskisson. Perceval and the future Lord Liverpool – with whom Pitt enjoyed friendly and relaxed relations, but Canning was clearly his favourite, and he was reported to be in a 'trance' when he attended his young protégé's wedding. That there was mutual affection is clear, but there is only the slightest evidence that it took a physical form. Ehrman quotes Pitt as having told his niece, Lady Hester Stanhope, many years later, that he must stay 'a single man for my King and country's sake'. 'He stood apart', he concludes, 'untouched as a priest stands untouched at the centre of his avocations; a priest in this instance of politics and government!' (Ehrman, III, p. 97).

Lonely, in failing health, depressed by the continued lack of success in the war, as the eighteenth century drew to its end, Pitt began to show occasional signs of losing his grip. In May 1798, he provoked a duel with an opposition MP, George Tierney, after carelessly impugning his patriotism in a parliamentary exchange. It took place on Putney Heath, both men fired twice, but neither was injured, Pitt firing his second shot into the air. More seriously for his survival as Prime Minister, he failed to keep George III regularly informed of the government's intentions. This had fatal consequences in 1801, when Pitt proposed to his Cabinet colleagues that legislation should be brought in to enable Catholics to vote in parliamentary elections, and to be appointed to public office. Intended as a *quid pro quo* for the Union of the British and Irish Parliaments, which had been approved the previous year (though only after extensive bribery of Irish MPs to vote their own chamber out of existence), the proposal fell foul of several of Pitt's colleagues, notably the Lord Chancellor, Lord Loughborough. He hastened to inform the King of what was proposed, and George angrily declared that he could not approve the measure which was a breach of his Coronation oath to defend the Protestant religion. Pitt feeling himself morally bound to proceed with the legislation, in the light of informal assurances which had been given to Irish Catholics, promptly offered his resignation to the King. Perhaps he hoped that George would not accept it, and would acquiesce in Catholic emancipation in order to keep the services of the man who had loyally served him for 17 years. But George had grown tired of Pitt's growing independence, and – crucially – now had an acceptable candidate for the premiership in view and was no longer fearful of opening the way to Fox, whose influence in Parliament had sharply declined since the defection from him of the Portland Whigs. He turned to Henry Addington, the popular Speaker of the House of Commons, and a friend of Pitt's, many of whose ministers (but not Grenville or Dundas) were willing to serve under him. Pitt himself was happy to lend his support to Addington, whom he probably thought was in a better position than himself to seek a peace treaty with France, which he now believed to be necessary.

Addington duly succeeded in negotiating the Peace of Amiens, within a year of assuming the premiership. Described by Canning as 'the peace everybody was glad of and nobody was proud of' (Derry, p. 121), it broke down after 14 months, after both sides had breached its terms, Napoleon by invading Switzerland and the British by refusing to evacuate their troops from Malta. War resumed in May 1803, and Addington quickly revealed himself as a less than inspiring war leader. Agitation soon arose for the return of Pitt, celebrated in a song composed by Canning as 'The Pilot that weathered the Storm', and Addington twice attempted to recruit him to his government. Pitt made it clear, however, that he would come back only as Prime Minister, and in May 1804, Addington, bowing to the inevitable, tended his resignation. George welcomed Pitt back with a clear conscience, his new Prime Minister having promised him that he would not raise the subject of Catholic emancipation again during the King's lifetime.

The government which Pitt formed, in May 1804, was not the one he intended. He had wanted to form a 'grand coalition', uniting all the significant parliamentary factions in a patriotic government pledged to resist the threat of a French invasion which, with Napoleon massing his forces outside

Boulogne, seemed a much more serious threat than at any time since 1793. In particular, he wished to include Fox and his supporters, as well as those of his cousin, Grenville, from whom he had become estranged, partly because of the pledge he had given the King over Catholic emancipation, and who, together with Fox, had led the opposition to the Addington ministry. The King was perfectly prepared to accept Grenville in the government, but drew the line at Fox, whereupon Grenville himself refused to participate. The result was that Pitt's government was largely composed of Addington's ministers, plus a few of his own strong supporters, notably George Canning. Dundas, who had been ennobled as Viscount Melville, returned as First Lord of the Admiralty, but was soon forced to resign when he, by the casting vote of the Speaker, was impeached for alleged malversation of funds during his earlier service as Treasurer of the Navy. Tears were reported to have rolled down Pitt's cheeks 'in one of the rare occasions on which he lost control of his feelings in public... at the destruction of his old and loyal colleague' (Derry, p. 131). Melville was ultimately acquitted, but his removal was a heavy blow to Pitt, an exhausted, seriously ill and depressed man, who showed little of the resilience of 20 years earlier, when he had formed his first administration.

With infinite difficulty, Pitt now managed to construct the Third Coalition, luring Austria and Russia to put large armies into the field, with Prussia also limbering up. In October 1805, Nelson's great victory at Trafalgar, destroying the cream of the French and Spanish fleets, and removing the threat of invasion, restored Pitt's spirits and his customary over-optimism, only for these to be smashed by Napoleon's comprehensive defeats of the Austrians and Russians at Ulm and Austerlitz. When news of Austerlitz reached Pitt, in December 1805, he pointed to a map of Europe and said: 'Roll up that map; it will not be needed these ten years', a prescient estimate of how long it would take before Napoleon's final defeat at Waterloo. A month later, on 23 January 1806, Pitt was dead. The cause was long suspected to be cancer, but, according to Hague, who consulted expert medical opinion, the most probable cause was a peptic ulcer. 'Two hundred years later he would have been cured in a few days by therapy with antibiotic and acid-reducing drugs. In 1806, there was nothing that could be done for him' (Hague, p. 577).

The Younger Pitt was a new kind of Prime Minister, compared to whom the great majority of his predecessors were amateur dilettantes. No premier before, and few since, has dedicated his life so completely to his calling, working exceptionally long hours, suppressing most of his other interests and possible sources of pleasure, and establishing such a command over the political scene. He was able to expand the informal, if not the formal powers of the premiership, establishing his authority, at least to a limited extent, over other departments than the Treasury, which was the only one where the writ of previous premiers had actually run, though most of them had had considerable influence over foreign policy and defence issues. Partly because he had to deal with an exceptionally opinionated and stubborn monarch, whom he was reluctant to challenge directly, Pitt was never able to establish his own right to appoint, shift or dismiss ministers, nor to be accepted as the only minister to have direct access to the King and the sole right to advise him. Nevertheless, the fact that he was known to seek these objectives made it easier for his successors to pursue them from more pliable monarchs, though it was not until the end of the reign of Queen Victoria that these were unequivocally conceded.

Though not particularly efficient in his own working methods, being notoriously unwilling to reply to letters, and tending to postpone decisions on routine matters until they reached crisis point, he was concerned to improve the overall performance of the administration and was always on the lookout for improvements, if not fundamental reforms, to be introduced. He was always exceptionally cautious, if not conservative, in constitutional matters, and became more so as he grew older, tending to conform to George III's own view that the British constitution, as defined by the legacy of the Glorious Revolution, was a perfect instrument and should not be tampered with. Pitt was singularly concerned about his own reputation, wishing to be seen as a selfless public servant, always putting the national interest above any narrow party or factional interest, and utterly incorrupt in all his dealings. These principles he claimed to have inherited from his father, and he could certainly be said to have followed them exceptionally closely, even to the extent of leaving behind him massive debts – largely caused through his being systematically swindled by servants and tradesmen – which had, like his father's, to be posthumously redeemed by a vote of the House of Commons. He was a far more successful politician than his father, and much better at handling his relations with George III than the Elder Pitt had been with George II. Pitt was not a party man, and never called himself a Tory, though history has so assigned him and the modern Conservative Party has recognized him as one of its founding fathers. He could fairly lay claim, nearly 200 years before Harold Wilson, to the title of the Great Pragmatist, and was the first Prime Minister who actively sought to mould public opinion to reinforce his position in Parliament and with the Court.

He was undoubtedly a less great man than his father, and infinitely less capable as a war leader. Indeed, one modern historian, A.J.P. Taylor, has argued that it was wrongheaded of Pitt to get involved in war in the first place. 'What was the war about?', Taylor asked. 'Pitt claimed to be fighting for the liberties of Europe. What he was fighting for was the liberties of princes and for the aristocracy. The decision to go to war with revolutionary France in 1793 was a catastrophe for free principles' (Taylor, p. 22). This was, of course, the view that Fox took at the time, and it is one of history's great might-have-beens to ponder what would have happened if he, rather than Pitt, had been George III's choice as his Prime Minister.

Works consulted

Stanley Ayling, 1991, *Fox*, London, John Murray.

John W. Derry, 1990, *Politics in the Age of Fox, Pitt and Liverpool*, Basingstoke, Macmillan.

Michael Duffy, 2000, *The Younger Pitt*, London, Longman.

John Ehrman, 1969, *The Younger Pitt: I The Years of Acclaim*, London, Constable.

John Ehrman, 1983, *The Younger Pitt: II The Reluctant Transition*, London, Constable.

John Ehrman, 1996, *The Younger Pitt: III The Consuming Struggle*, London, Constable.

William Hague, 2004, *William Pitt the Younger*, London, HarperCollins.

Frank O' Gorman, 1997, *The Long Eighteenth Century*, London, Arnold.

Oxford Dictionary of National Biography, 2004, Oxford, Oxford University Press.

A.J.P. Taylor, 2000, *British Prime Ministers and Other Essays*, London, Penguin.

Michael J. Turner, 2003, *The Younger Pitt: A Life*, London, Hambledon.

2

Henry Addington, 1st Viscount Sidmouth – Better than His Reputation?

Whoever succeeded the Younger Pitt was likely to be regarded as something of an anti-climax, and this was certainly the fate of Henry Addington, whose premiership lasted from March 1801 to May 1804, bridging the period between Pitt's two administrations. The butt of a spiteful jibe by George Canning that 'Pitt is to Addington as London is to Paddington', he was long dismissed as ineffectual, though his reputation was, very belatedly, partially restored by a perceptive biography by Philip Ziegler, appearing only in 1965. This argued that he led his government with some ability, and that his major – and fatal – shortcoming was one of communication.

Addington was the first middle-class Prime Minister. He was descended from a long line of yeoman farmers, whose fortunes had been transformed by his grandfather, who, thanks to two advantageous marriages, was able to educate his son, Anthony, at Winchester and Trinity College, Oxford. Anthony became a physician, specializing in mental illness, and ran a private lunatic asylum next door to his house in Reading. After some years, he took the risky step of transferring his practice to London, becoming a Fellow of the Royal College of Physicians, and eventually acquiring a string of fashionable patrons, of whom the most distinguished was the first Earl of Chatham, the Elder Pitt, to whom he became a family friend as well as physician. Dr Addington was to have six children, of whom the fourth, and the elder son, was Henry, born 30 May 1757. This was two years before the birth of the Younger Pitt, whom he got to know as a child, and to whom, at the age of 17, Dr Addington prescribed a bottle of port a day in an apparently successful attempt to cure him of gout (see Chapter 1).

Henry, a placid, congenial and moderately intelligent child, was sent to a top-drawer 'prep school' at Cheam, and subsequently followed his father to Winchester and Oxford, where he was enrolled in one of the more scholarly colleges – Brasenose. At Cheam and Winchester, he was regarded as a model pupil, but – according to Ziegler – had the misfortune to fall at Winchester under the influence of a fanatically narrow-minded and reactionary tutor, the Reverend George Huntingford, whom he was to reward with the Bishopric of Gloucester when he became Prime Minister. Huntingford quite possibly had homo-erotic feelings for the young Henry, but if so was apparently able to suppress them: it was Henry's mind rather than his body which was corrupted by the association. Friendly by nature, Henry's main ambition in life was to be liked by his fellows, and in this he was largely successful. He made close friends at both his schools, and was later to include several of them in his government, while at Oxford much of his time was taken up by what would now be called networking. In particular, he was able to win the friendship of two of the grandest young men in the University – William Grenville, himself the son of a Prime Minister and first cousin to William Pitt, and Lord Mornington, later Marquess Wellesley, whose younger brother, Arthur, was to become the Duke of Wellington.

Addington graduated in February 1778, but stayed on at Oxford for another year, largely for social reasons, only establishing himself in London, to read for the bar, in the autumn of 1780. In the meantime, he had spent much of the summer at Devizes, with his wealthy brother-in-law, James Seaton, who was one of the two local MPs. Seaton may already at this time have indicated to Addington that he intended to promote him as his successor for the seat. This duly occurred in 1784, when Addington, a Tory, was returned unopposed for the constituency, which he continued to represent until 1805, when he took a peerage as Viscount Sidmouth. In the meantime, Addington had acquired a wife, Ursula Mary Hammond, the daughter and joint heir of a local Cheam businessman of gentle birth. They married in September 1781, when Henry was 24 and Ursula 21. It was a genuine love match, which had the added attraction that the bride brought an income of £1,000 a year. It proved a happy marriage, which lasted until Ursula's death, in 1811 at the age of 51, and produced four daughters and four sons, one of whom was to die in infancy.

Addington's parliamentary career began very quietly; he made no attempt to speak during his first two sessions, but continued his practice of networking, making a wide circle of friends, mostly among the country gentry. Then, in January 1786, he was asked by Pitt to second the address at the beginning of the parliamentary session, an honour usually reserved for bright, up-and-coming young backbenchers, a description which hardly fitted the rather stodgy, if still youthful, MP for Devizes. He performed the task adequately but without distinction, and the few subsequent speeches he made during his first Parliament did little to suggest that he was destined for higher things. Normally a consistent and uncritical follower of Pitt, he was however – due to the now deeply ingrained conservatism he had first imbibed from the Rev. Hungerford – unable to bring himself to support the very moderate bill for parliamentary reform, which his childhood friend unsuccessfully introduced in April 1785. If Pitt was disappointed by his abstention, he did not hold it against him for long, as four years later he plucked him from obscurity, and proposed him as Speaker of the House of Commons. Pitt was motivated not just by friendship: he wanted a docile supporter of his government in the Chair, and one who was prepared if necessary to use his casting vote on the government's side; no nonsense about choosing an impartial arbiter.

Pitt's choice was widely criticized by MPs who thought a more senior and more distinguished candidate should have been chosen, but Addington was duly elected thanks to the large Pittite majority in the House. Those who opposed his election were in for a pleasant surprise. Addington turned out to be an excellent Speaker, with a good grasp of parliamentary procedure, the patience to endure long hours of tedious debate without losing his good humour and notably fair in his treatment of the Foxite opposition. He soon became popular in all quarters of the House and gained the trust of the great majority of

MPs. This did not prevent him being treated with condescension by the more aristocratic Members, who looked down on his humble origins and referred to him, disparagingly, as 'the Doctor'. As Speaker he was expected to do a lot of entertaining, which, as a man of modest means, he was ill equipped to do. The House responded by voting him a salary of £6,000 a year and the provision of an official residence within the parliamentary precincts. Addington became ever closer to Pitt, who got into the habit of dining with him at the Speaker's House, together with his closest ministerial colleagues, William Grenville, Henry Dundas and the Lord Chancellor, Lord Loughborough. Here they discussed the government's problems in a frank and informal manner, and Addington offered sage and commonsense advice, which Pitt clearly appreciated. Such a close association with ministers would be regarded as highly improper for a modern Speaker, but – though it was generally known – it did not appear to affect adversely Addington's growing reputation for fair-mindedness. Nor did his highly conservative views on most political (and religious) issues mean that his mind was closed to the need to make parliamentary procedures more flexible. When the Clerk of the House tried to prevent evidence on the slave trade being presented to a special committee on the grounds that it would break with precedents, he over-ruled him, saying 'It does not follow that because a mode is new it must therefore be improper' (Ziegler, p. 73). Addington further endeared himself with MPs by turning down an offer, in 1793, by Pitt to make him Home Secretary, preferring to continue as Speaker. This was favourably compared to the action of his predecessor, William Grenville, who had abandoned the Speakership after a mere few months in order to accept the same Cabinet post.

Two events, in 1797 and 1798, underline his increasingly warm personal relationship with Pitt. It was to Addington that the Prime Minister chose to confide his difficulties in backtracking from his wooing of Lady Eleanor Eden. A year later, Addington rode out to Putney Heath to observe, from a discreet distance, Pitt's duel with the Foxite MP George Tierney. This was an act of friendship and moral support, but it may also be a sign of a bad conscience that he had not intervened more decisively from the Chair to get Pitt to withdraw the aspersions he had cast on Tierney's patriotism during a parliamentary debate. Then, in 1800, when Pitt's health temporarily broke down, it was to Woodley, Addington's small estate near Reading, that he retired to recuperate (Cookson, p. 304).

It was Addington, too, who, in 1798, when Pitt was at a loss to find additional sources of finance to sustain the war effort, suggested that taxpayers should be invited to make voluntary contributions, in excess of the sums for which they had been assessed. The project was remarkably successful, at least in its first year of operation, when it yielded over £2.8 million, including £20,000 from the King, and £2,000 each from Pitt, Dundas and Loughborough. Addington also subscribed £2,000, just over one-fifth of his total income, saying that 'the strict fifth would have given too much the appearance of minute *calculation*' (Ziegler, p. 79). Altogether, Addington was to serve as Speaker for over 11 years, the longest term since the legendary Arthur Onslow, who served for over 33 years, until 1761, and he succeeded in restoring the dignity and authority to the Chair, which it had lost under Onslow's successors. On Addington's own career, however, it had one malign effect. According to Ziegler,

> Addington's years as Speaker destroyed whatever chance there might have been that he would become a competent parliamentary debater. The free- dom from interruption, the invitation to pomposity and prolixity, the need for objectivity which went far to rule out any form of dramatic expression or emotional appeal: all these ensured that his delivery remained pedestrian and his matter so displayed as to appeal neither to the imagination nor the intellect. (Ziegler, pp. 74–5)

This was to prove a severe deficiency when Addington succeeded to the Premiership, and proved incapable of defending his policies effectively in the House of Commons, in marked contrast to his predecessor.

It was in 1797 that the first suggestion was made that Addington should take over the premiership. Pitt, depressed after the failure of peace negotia- tions, thought of retiring for a while, and installing Addington as a temporary successor, who would keep the seat warm until he was ready to return. He dis- cussed the possibility with George III, who was ready to go along with it, but Pitt's spirits suddenly returned and he decided to labour on. Four years later, when he somewhat impetuously offered his resignation to the King, after he had vetoed Pitt's proposals for Catholic emancipation (see Chapter I), neither he nor George III considered any other possible person for the premiership. There was, however, a difference in their attitudes. Pitt still saw Addington as only a stand-in; the King, who had tired of Pitt's growing independence and his increasing tendency not to confide in him, now saw Addington (an opponent of Catholic emancipation) as a contender for office in his own right. What is clear, however, is that Pitt genuinely encouraged Addington to accept the King's commission, and called on his friends and supporters to rally to the new government, and that Addington was still in awe of Pitt and was far from wishing to supplant him. He showed a marked reluctance to become Prime Minister, but responded when the King said to him 'Lay your hand upon your heart, and ask yourself where I am to turn for support if *you* do not stand by me'. When Addington finally agreed, the King embraced him, saying 'My dear Addington, you have saved your country' (Zeigler, pp. 93–4).

Despite Pitt's goodwill, several of his closest associates refused to join Addington's government. The most prominent was Grenville, a convinced supporter of Catholic emancipation, who subsequently had a fierce row with Pitt when the latter promised George never to raise the issue again during the King's lifetime. Other devoted Pittites, such as George Canning, were so distressed at their master's fate that they could not bring themselves to serve under Addington, whom they regarded as a usurper. George Rose, who had been Pitt's Secretary to the Treasury for 17 years, was even heard to remark that he would 'as soon assent to the prostitution of his daughter as remain in office' (Ziegler, p. 98). Addington peremptorily dispensed with Loughborough, the Lord Chancellor, whom he rightly regarded as an unscrupulous intriguer, but was distressed when other central figures of Pitt's administration, such as Henry Dundas, Earl Spencer and William Windham, declined to continue in office. Their replacements were, for the most part, a mediocre lot, including several old school friends of Addington's, his brother Hiley, and brother-in-law, Charles Bragge. Among the more able were the new Foreign Secretary, Lord Hawkesbury (later Lord Liverpool) and the Solicitor-General, Spencer Perceval, both future Prime Ministers. The biggest shortcoming of Addington's new government was its dearth of parliamentary orators, which – given the Prime Minister's own deficiency in this department – was to prove a grievous handicap.

Addington's first, and over-riding priority – with which Pitt was in full agreement – was to negotiate a peace treaty with France. The war had reached a total stalemate, with France, now led by Napoleon Bonaparte as First Consul, seemingly unbeatable on the European continent, and Britain, with its naval supremacy, dominant elsewhere, having captured a string of French and Dutch colonies, as well as the Spanish island of Trinidad. The nation was suffering from war weariness and the new Prime Minister could conceive of no possible advantage in continuing hostilities. Yet he had few illusions that a lasting peace was obtainable, given his well-founded suspicions that Napoleon's imperial ambitions were by no means fully satisfied. The country, however, needed a breathing space, in which to recuperate its economy, and which would leave it in a stronger position if, unfortunately, it proved necessary to resume the war at a later date.

After Addington had been in office for almost exactly a year, on 25 March 1802, the Treaty of Amiens was signed, ending war with France, Spain and Holland. The terms which Addington's negotiators had been able to obtain were, perhaps, marginally inferior to those which Pitt had rejected during the earlier abortive negotiations in 1796 and 1797, but in the meantime Britain's continental allies had been decisively defeated in the War of the Second Coalition. In these circumstances, Addington drove as hard a bargain as could realistically be expected. Under the terms agreed, all the conquered French and Dutch colonies were returned, with the exception of Ceylon, while the island of Malta was to be handed back to the Knights of St. John. Britain was to keep Trinidad, while the French were to withdraw from Naples, and relinquish their claim to the Ionian islands. Nobody in London thought the peace terms glorious, but they were grudgingly accepted, while Pitt (who privately regretted the return of the Cape Colony to the Dutch) enthusiastically endorsed them, and they were carried with large majorities in both Houses of Parliament. In the country, as a whole, the response was more positive, and Addington gained greatly in popularity as the man who had finally brought peace after ten dis-piriting years of conflict.

Within a month of the signing of the treaty, Addington produced his first peacetime budget, abolishing Pitt's income tax, which had proved highly unpopular and inefficient, and which he believed was no longer justified as the war had come to an end. His proposals also contributed markedly to tidying up the government's finances. Despite the gross nepotism which Addington, untypically, then displayed, in appointing his 16-year-old son, Henry, to the lucrative sinecure of Clerk of the Pells, he retained his popularity, and in July 1802, had no difficulty in maintaining his majority in a general election, with-out resorting, his biographer reported, 'to the morass of bribery and abuse, blackmail and threats which made up the traditional pattern of a British general election' (Ziegler, p. 160). Addington was also able to strengthen his ministerial team, by bringing back Castlereagh, who had been Irish Secretary under Pitt, while the Whig, George Tierney, who had fought a duel with Pitt four years earlier, was a welcome addition to the government's feeble debating strength in the Commons. Tierney had hoped to bring over other leading Whigs with him, but in the end they decided to remain loyal to their party leader, Charles James Fox, who was now working closely with Grenville in opposition.

Addington's relations with the King could hardly have been better. George much preferred his cordiality to Pitt's icy correctness, and gave many signs of his personal favour, notably assigning his Prime Minister the use of a prestig-ious residence, White Lodge, in Richmond Park. If peace could only have been maintained, there was every prospect that his 'stop-gap' government could have settled in to a lengthy and moderately successful term of office. Yet rela-tions with France soon began to deteriorate, exacerbated by Napoleon's inva-sion of Switzerland and Britain's refusal to evacuate Malta under the terms of the Amiens Treaty. In the end, it was a British decision to resume the conflict, in May 1803, and the very unmartial-looking Addington made a complete fool of himself by dressing up in the uniform of the Berkshire militia and going down to the House of Commons to announce the declaration of war in a bombastic statement. From that moment, it became clear, possibly even to Addington, that it was only a matter of when, rather than whether, Pitt would replace him as the wartime leader. Pitt was only too willing to assume the bur-den, but a certain fastidiousness held him back from plunging the knife into the back of his former protégé. It is a fascinating exercise to trace the gradual development of his relations with Addington and his government, as he slipped almost imperceptibly from warm encouragement to benevolent neutrality to disdainful indifference and, in the final weeks, to active hostility. Right from the beginning, he was urged by his closest followers, notably George Canning, who conducted a poisonous campaign of calumniation against Addington, to deliver the *coup de grace*, but Pitt held back and did his best to restrain the ardour of his supporters. Addington was not lacking in his own loyalists, who were strongly represented on the government backbenches, and included many distinguished men in public life, notably Admiral Lord Nelson. He also possessed his own 'spin-doctor', in his younger brother, Hiley Addington, who was highly successful in manipulating the press, including, in particular, *The Times*, which was always ready to accept articles written anonymously by him, defending his brother and attacking Pitt and his followers.

As Prime Minister, Addington grew in self-confidence, and lost much of his awe for Pitt, though he recognized that his government would be immensely strengthened if he could entice him to join. Even before the war was resumed, he made overtures to Pitt in a series of three meetings in January 1803. Pitt made it clear that he would not be willing to serve under Addington, and a few weeks later Addington proposed that he and Pitt should effectively share power by serving under a figurehead premier, whom, he suggested, might be Pitt's elder brother, the 2nd Earl of Chatham. Pitt again refused, using the occasion to give his own definition of the requisites of the premiership:

> There should be an avowed and real minister possessing the chief weight in council and the principal place in the confidence of the King. In that respect there can be no rivality or division of power. That power must rest in the person generally called the First Minister; and that minister ought, he thinks, to be the person at the head of the finances. (Quoted in Hague, p. 505)

Addington then made the extraordinary offer of standing down in favour of Pitt, and accepting a subsidiary position himself in the government, provided his cabinet colleagues agreed. Even this was not good enough for Pitt, who insisted on forming an entirely new government, ejecting most of Addington's supporters and including Grenville and other figures from the opposition. Addington, he suggested, should leave the government altogether, and take on an honorific role, such as Speaker of the House of Lords, a post which, he said, had once existed and could be reconstituted. This was too much for the Addington cabinet to stomach, whereupon Pitt broke off negotiations, saying that he would only return to power at the express request of the King. His personal relations with Addington then sharply deteriorated.

Canning convinced himself, and the bulk of Pitt's supporters, that, as soon as war was declared, an overwhelming public demand would ensure his early return to power. In the event, the force of the demand was limited, while George III felt no necessity to rid himself of a Prime Minister whom he valued highly, and who was conducting his government with reasonable competence. Addington remained in office for a full year after the resumption of hostilities, introducing a wartime budget, restoring income tax, but putting it on a much sounder footing than Pitt had done. Pitt had relied on voluntary compliance, and his tax had brought in a great deal less than had been estimated. Addington insisted that the tax should be deducted at source, the basis of direct taxation both in Britain and all other modern countries until the present day, and the yield dramatically increased. Pitt and his friends were not amused that Addington was proving himself a more successful Chancellor of the Exchequer than his predecessor.

Addington's war aims were distinctly unheroic and commonsensical, but were probably better suited to the situation in 1803–1804 than the more active strategy adopted by Pitt both before and after. In Addington's view, there was a stalemate between Britain and France, with the former supreme at sea and the latter on the land. The only way in which this could be broken, given the failure of successive coalitions against France, would be to tempt Napoleon to try to invade Britain, and hope to destroy his army either at sea or on the beaches. He therefore determined to build up a massive force of militias and regular forces to ensure the defeat of any invasion, and to rely upon the assurances of his friend, Nelson, that the bulk of Napoleon's forces would not make it across the Channel. In the meantime, the British proceeded, once again, to mop up the bulk of the French and Dutch colonies, facing very little resistance. Addington's government can be absolved of making any really fundamental mistakes, but there were inevitably organizational muddles in recruiting a large militia force in a relatively short period, and this caused a great deal of discontent. His real failure was in rousing the spirit of the nation – the series of fumbling and pedestrian speeches which he made in Parliament during the first year of war were inevitably compared unfavourably with the orations of Pitt. Gradually, Addington's parliamentary support began to crumble, particularly after Pitt moved into open opposition in the spring of 2004. In successive divisions in the Commons, his majority fell from 58 to 52 to 37. The personal pressure on Addington, a sensitive man, became unbearable. 'By 1804', wrote his biographer, 'the affable and complacent figure who had presided so urbanely in the Speaker's chair had been reduced to a haggard neurotic, sleeping badly, short-tempered, scenting insults and hostility even when there were none, doubting his own capacities and pathetically uncertain even of his closest friends...the last few months in office had come close to destroying his spirit' (Ziegler, p. 219). On 29 April 1804, he told George III that his position was 'hopeless', and on 10 May he resigned, the King immediately sending for Pitt. 'On the whole his government's record on finance, foreign policy and national defence was a good one', according to the latest authoritative assessment (Cookson, p. 310). Yet many of his contemporaries, and much later opinion, regarded him as a failure. According to Ziegler, there were three reasons for this 'He was not an aristocrat, he was not an orator and he was not William Pitt' (Ziegler, p. 110). There was another, perhaps more fundamental reason – his long post-Prime Ministerial career. Addington was just under 47 when he resigned, becoming Viscount Sidmouth soon after. He was to live nearly another 40 years, for 14 of which he served as a Cabinet Minister, under four Prime Ministers – Pitt, Grenville, Perceval and Liverpool. During this period, he deservedly acquired the reputation of an arch reactionary, particularly during his ten years as Home Secretary in the Liverpool government, when he was blamed for the 'Peterloo massacre', and much repressive legislation (see Chapter 6). His long period in office ended in 1824, when he resigned in protest against the diplomatic recognition of the revolting Spanish colonies in South America. He continued to oppose reform in the House of Lords, voting both against Catholic emancipation in 1828 and the Great Reform Bill in 1832. He thus became something of a bogy figure to 'progressive opinion', which refused to accept that he could have been anything but a disaster as Prime Minister. This unjust verdict has been largely qualified by modern scholarship, which has also concluded that, despite his unfortunate political record, he had many admirable human qualities. Ziegler's conclusion has substantially been borne out by later scholars:

> He was not a great man, let alone a great Prime Minister. He was almost as convinced a reactionary as he has been depicted. His talents were in no way extraordinary … Yet I am left in no doubt that he has been monstrously misused by history. As a Minister he was responsible, conscientious and far from ineffectual. As a man he was kindly, courteous and sincere. His honour and his integrity would be remarkable in any age and any profession. Less can be said for many men whose reputation stands immeasurably higher. (Ziegler, p. 11)

Works consulted

J.E. Cookson, 2004, Article in *The Oxford Dictionary of National Biography*, Oxford, Oxford University Press.

John W. Derry, 1990, *Politics in the Age of Fox, Pitt and Liverpool*, Basingstoke, Macmillan.

William Hague, 2004, *William Pitt the Younger*, London, HarperCollins.

W.H., 1885, Article in *The Dictionary of National Biography*, London, George Smith.

Philip Ziegler, 1965, *Addington*, London, Collins.

3
William Grenville, 1st Baron Grenville – Not Quite 'All the Talents'

Only two men in British history have had the distinction of following their own fathers in the top office. One was William Pitt; the other, his first cousin, William Grenville. Like Henry Addington's, William Grenville's career was largely shaped by his relationship with Pitt, his almost exact contemporary. Yet Grenville was a more independent character, and was never so much in awe of Pitt, even though he became his closest associate and a leading ministerial colleague throughout most of Pitt's long first premiership. Thereafter, the two men drifted apart, and Grenville largely transferred his loyalty to Pitt's great rival, Charles James Fox.

William Wyndham Grenville was born on 24 October 1759, the third son and sixth child of George Grenville and Elizabeth Wyndham, two of whose nine children were to die in infancy. The Grenvilles were descended from a Norman family, who had been landowners in Buckinghamshire since the twelfth century, living at Wotton, near Aylesbury. Their fortunes had taken a distinct change for the better at the beginning of the eighteenth century, through inter-marriage with the neighbouring and more powerful Temple family, with their magnificent residence at Stowe. The Temples amassed considerable wealth and political influence, controlling a number of parliamentary seats, which enabled members of both branches of the family to embark on political careers. This 'cousinhood' was extended in 1754 into the Pitt family, when George Grenville's sister Hester married the elder Pitt. George preceded Pitt (later the Earl of Chatham) into the premiership, in 1763. He proved to be an able administrator and reformer of the public finances, but was an indifferent manager of men and soon became unpopular, not least because of the alacrity with which he, like other members of the Temple clan, availed himself of valuable sinecures. His premiership lasted a little over two years, after which 'the King [George III] took the opportunity of ridding himself in 1765 of a prime minister he came to regard as a self-opinionated bore' (Jupp, 1985, p. 8).

Whatever his failings as a public man, George Grenville was a fond father to William and his siblings, and established a happy home environment at Wotton, together with his wife Elizabeth. She also came from a political family, her father having been the leader of the Hanoverian Tories in the House of Commons under George I and George II (The Temples and the Grenvilles were Whigs). Little is known, in detail, about William's childhood, which effectively came to an end at the age of 11 when, shortly after his arrival at Eton, both his parents died within a year of each other. He was later to describe this as 'a misfortune which every subsequent period of my life has given me fresh occasion to lament'. His eldest brother, George, who was soon to inherit the title Earl Temple from his uncle, assumed the role of head of the family at the age of 17, and became a sort of surrogate father to William. He continued to be the largest, if not the controlling, influence in his life until William was at least in his late twenties and was already a senior politician in his own right.

By then, it was already clear to most observers, if not to themselves, that the younger brother was far superior to his elder, both in intelligence and judgement. There was an intermediate brother, Tom, who was less dependent on, and less influenced by, Earl Temple.

William, who of the three was the most similar to his father in character and outlook, had also inherited his probing intelligence and addiction to hard work. After Eton, he proceeded to Christ Church, Oxford, where he proved to be an outstanding student, excelling in the classics, English and mathematics, winning the Chancellor's Prize for Latin Verse and achieving a very good grasp of modern languages, particularly French. He went on to read for the bar at Lincoln's Inn, but never practised, his brother, Earl Temple, drafting him in as MP for one of the family boroughs – Buckingham – in place of his brother-in-law, Richard Aldworth Neville. He was 22 years old, and was returned unopposed in a by-election in February 1782. It was in the dying days of Lord North's government, and Grenville immediately allied himself with the Whig opposition, led by the Marquess of Rockingham, as had his two elder brothers and the entire Temple-Grenville clan. When North resigned, one month later, Rockingham formed his second administration, in which Temple was disappointed not to make the cabinet. Instead, he was fobbed off with the Lord Lieutenancy of Buckinghamshire, while Tom Grenville joined the new Foreign Secretary, Charles James Fox, who sent him to Paris as plenipotentiary in the peace negotiations with France and the United States.

The new government was not a happy team, Fox soon falling out with the Home Secretary, the Earl of Shelburne, who insisted on butting in on the peace negotiations on the pretext that the colonies came under his department. On 29 June, an exasperated Fox precipitately offered his resignation, a maladroit move whose effects were exacerbated by the totally unexpected death, from influenza, of Rockingham, on 1 July. The King called on Shelburne to take over the premiership, and Fox insisted on resigning, being supported by the great mass of Rockingham's supporters, including Tom Grenville. Temple, however, who now aspired to being appointed to one of the great two Secretaryships of State, now vacated by Fox and Shelburne, rallied to the support of the latter, as did William Grenville. Shelburne was hard pressed to form a viable government, in the absence of the Foxites, but declined to include Temple in his cabinet, offering him instead the Lord Lieutenancy (or 'viceroy') of Ireland. Temple accepted, and set off for Dublin, taking William Grenville with him as Chief Secretary. Grenville thus achieved significant office at the age of 22 years and nine months, and after only five months in Parliament. His cousin, William Pitt, only five months older, did even better: he was appointed Chancellor of the Exchequer.

As soon as Grenville had found his bearings in Dublin, he was despatched to London by his brother to act as his eyes and ears, and general fixer, in the imperial capital. He was Temple's main means of communication, albeit unofficially, with the government. Temple was actually subordinate to the Lord President of the Council, Earl Camden, a veteran minister who was not particularly energetic or interested in Irish affairs. Grenville soon proved himself highly effective, and his role became even more important when a decision in a court case put in doubt the sovereignty of the Irish Parliament, subject only to its allegiance to the King. This caused an uproar in Dublin, and – at Temple's prompting – Grenville began to lobby hard for the passage of a 'Renunciation Bill' disclaiming the right of the House of Commons to over-rule decisions of the Irish Parliament. He personally drew up a bill, and managed to overcome strong opposition within the cabinet to its introduction. The motion to approve the bill was moved in the Commons by the Home Secretary, Thomas Townshend, but Grenville was allowed to second it, and made a powerful impression with his speech, which was only the second time he had addressed the House. The whole affair redounded greatly to his credit, fostering the belief that he was 'a coming man'.

Shelburne's government, however, lasted only for eight months, being defeated in a Commons vote, as recounted in Chapter 1, in March 1783, when the supporters of Fox and Lord North united to reject the peace terms agreed with the American colonists. George III was furious, but felt himself impotent to prevent the formation of a Fox–North coalition, under the nominal leadership of the Duke of Portland. He resolved, however, to take the first opportunity that presented itself to unhorse the new government. In this resolution, he was supported by William Pitt, and by two of the three Grenville brothers, who declared themselves 'king's men'. Tom, once again, went his own way, continuing to support Fox. The fact that Temple and William Grenville decided to throw in their lot with the King was remarkable, in view of their undoubted resentment at his action 18 years earlier in peremptorily dismissing their father, George Grenville, from the premiership. One reason for their decision may have been the loyalty they felt to the Earl of Shelburne, but Temple, in particular, whose appetite for office, honours and fat sinecures was known to be insatiable, may have calculated that his long-term prospects would be better served by sucking up to the King. Grenville's appetite, while far from negligible, was more moderate, and he may well have followed Temple out of fraternal regard and a desire to promote the broader family interest.

George III did not have to wait long before seizing the opportunity to dispense with the Portland government, and Temple, together with William Pitt, was the chief actor in the *dénouement*. The occasion, as recounted in Chapter 1, was the introduction of the India Bill, in the autumn of 1783, fiercely opposed by the East India Company and other city interests. The bill easily passed the Commons, but the King then authorized Temple to tell his fellow peers that anybody who voted for the bill 'was not only not his friend, but would be considered by him as an enemy'. Sufficient peers took the hint for it to be defeated by 95 votes to 76, and the King promptly dismissed the Portland–Fox–North ministry, after only 260 days in office, even though it still commanded a large majority in the Commons. Pitt, who had earlier twice refused the premiership, this time accepted eagerly, but had difficulty in forming a cabinet as few senior statesmen were prepared to associate themselves with what they held to be unconstitutional conduct by the King. As a result, Pitt took the extraordinary step of appointing Temple to both Secretaryships of State, Home and Foreign Affairs. This caused such an outcry in the Commons that Temple was forced to resign within a few days, and Pitt scraped around to fill his cabinet, which few expected to last for long, with essentially 'second eleven' figures, all from the House of Lords.

Temple's reputation was severely damaged by the episode, and he was never again to be seriously considered for cabinet office, though he did serve a second term as Lord Lieutenant for Ireland in 1787–89. He also, like his father before him, had demanded and received the extremely valuable sinecure office of Teller of the Exchequer, worth £14,500 a year (Jupp, 1985, p. 428). Temple felt that the King owed him more recompense than this for the service he had rendered, and lobbied hard for a dukedom. George III, however, considered that new ducal creations should be restricted to royal princes, and was not prepared to go beyond a marquessate, which Temple, nursing a strong sense of grievance, reluctantly accepted, becoming the 1st Marquess of Buckingham. There was nothing unusual in politicians of the eighteenth and early nineteenth centuries seeking sinecures or honours for themselves, or patronage for their relatives and friends, nor was the practice generally regarded as reprehensible. The two William Pitts, father and son, were, in fact, seen as being rather eccentric in failing to enrich themselves or their families in this way. The Grenvilles, by contrast, were regarded as being altogether too greedy, and as pushing the system beyond its acceptable limits.

William Grenville had played no significant role in the plot to replace Portland by Pitt, but he was to become one of the main beneficiaries. Henceforth, he was progressively to replace his brother as the most influential figure in the 'Grenville connection', which counted up to 30 adherents, by no means all family members, in the two Houses of Parliament. Crucial to his advance was his relationship with Pitt. They had hardly known each other as children, and were only distant acquaintances when Grenville reached the House of Commons in February 1782, one year after his cousin. They then became close friends, and Pitt formed the highest opinion of Grenville's capacity and readiness to involve himself in complex and difficult issues. Grenville was to benefit also from the mediocre quality of Pitt's cabinet, which led the Prime Minister more and more to seek help from, and devolve responsibilities to, more junior figures who held only subordinate government posts. Together with Henry Dundas, a Scottish lawyer, he became Pitt's closest associate, and general workhorse, during the early years of his ministry, becoming joint Paymaster-General, and a member of the Board of Control and the Board of Trade.

In 1784, Pitt proposed to make him Governor-General of India, a sure route to fame and riches, and a remarkable temptation to the 24-year old younger son of a landed family who was determined to make his own way in the world and relieve himself of his dependence on his brother, who had provided his parliamentary seat, and in whose London house he felt obliged to live. Although their personal relations were good, Grenville obviously felt uncomfortable about his situation, having described 'dependence', in a letter to a friend, as ' the greatest curse in nature' (Jupp, 1985, p. 15). However, one of Grenville's most marked characteristics, along with his sharp intelligence, was an ingrained caution, and he regarded the internal situation in India as so unpredictable that he was not prepared to take the risk of failure.

Though not lacking in self-confidence, Grenville did not set his personal ambitions at the highest level. He defined them, in a letter to Buckingham, in 1786, 'as a cabinet post which would not involve topics of great parliamentary interest and, in addition, a sinecure for life'. Earlier he had written to a friend of the difficulty 'of carrying off an heiress', which suggests that he was not looking exclusively to public service as a way of securing his fortune. He was to tell the same friend, 'I have treasured up in my mind a saying... which was repeated to me frequently by my uncle... that there is nothing within the compass of a reasonable man's wish he may not be sure of attaining provided he will use the proper means' (Jupp, 1985, p. 15).

Grenville had a number of close friends, with whom he was able to unbend, and who described him as a warm and charming companion. But his public persona was more forbidding. He was regarded as stiff and haughty and completely lacking in small talk. Nor did his personal appearance do him any favours. He had bulging eyes, an over-sized head and a more than ample posterior, was untidily dressed and short-sighted, which meant that he wore spectacles, or an eye-glass, from an early age. He soon became the butt of cartoonists, such as James Gillray, and acquired the nickname of Bogy, or Bogey, on account of his goblin-like appearance. In his biography, Peter Jupp cites a much quoted piece of verse, which first appeared in a scandal sheet when Grenville was in his mid-twenties:

> Lord Bogy boasts no common share of head;
>   what plenteous stores of knowledge may contain
> The spacious tenement of Bogy's brain.
> Nature in all her dispensations wise,
>   who formed his head-piece of so vast a size,

> Hath not, 'tis true, neglected to bestow
> Its due proportions on the part below;
> and hence the reason, that to secure the State
> His top and bottom may have equal weight.

Grenville also suffered from a certain diffidence which inhibited him from putting himself forward. Thus, when Pitt invited him, in 1783, to move the acceptance of the peace terms with America in the House of Commons, he declined, saying: 'I do not like to stand forth so conspicuous in public questions, which I had always rather follow than lead...'. It was this quality which made Grenville, for all his abilities, a natural number two rather than a leader, and Pitt never seems to have felt any danger that his talented supporter would turn into a rival. In most respects, he was in fact Pitt's equal if not superior, though he fell far short of him as an orator, despite developing into a very competent parliamentary debater.

It was to Grenville that Pitt turned in 1787, when a difficult situation arose in the Netherlands, with Dutch Republicans, supported by the French government, vying for power with the hereditary *stadhouder*, the Prince of Orange, whose brother-in-law, the King of Prussia was threatening to intervene on his behalf. Pitt was anxious to prevent the growth of French influence in the Low Countries, but did not want lightly to run the risk of renewed war, and wanted an assessment of first the level of support for the Prince in the Netherlands and second of how likely the French would be to take to arms in the event of Britain and/or Prussia providing him with military help. Grenville travelled first to the Hague, and then to Paris, having detailed discussions in both capitals and was able to report back that the Prince's position was retrievable, while the French had little appetite to involve themselves in armed hostilities. This encouraged Pitt to take a robust attitude, and when the Prussians sent an army across the Dutch border they met little resistence, and the French stood idly by while the Republicans were routed.

Pitt was delighted with Grenville's conduct of a difficult diplomatic mission, and resolved to bring him into his cabinet at the earliest opportunity. He offered to make him First Lord of the Admiralty in 1788, but Grenville declined, partly on the grounds that he was poorly informed and poorly qualified for this post, and preferred to wait until something more attuned to his talents became available, evidently having the Home Office, currently occupied by Lord Sydney (the former Thomas Townshend), in mind. It seems to have been agreed between him and Pitt that he should have the reversion of this post, as soon as an appropriate occasion arose for moving Sydney. Before this happened, however, Pitt once again called on his services to meet a short-term contingency. This arose during the Regency crisis, beginning in November 1788 (see Chapter 1), when Pitt was desperately anxious to prevent the House of Commons voting to grant the Prince of Wales unlimited powers as Regent. The sudden death of the Speaker came as a severe embarrassment to him, and he resolved to appoint one of his most faithful supporters in an attempt to keep the House in line and to steer the conduct of their debates. His choice fell on Grenville, who at the age of 29 became the youngest Speaker since Medieval times. There was strong resistance to his election from the Foxite opposition, but he was chosen by 215 votes to 144 on 5 January 1789. Eleven days later, he made a lengthy and highly persuasive speech, from the Chair, in favour of the government's proposals for sharply circumscribing the powers of the proposed Prince Regent, and Pitt was more than satisfied with his performance. The recovery of George III from his illness, in early March, removed the necessity for him to preside over the Commons, and on 5 June, he duly resigned the Speakership and was immediately appointed Home Secretary – a move bitterly resented by many MPs, who thought their House had been made a mere convenience of the government. Grenville, however, who some months earlier had been appointed to the sinecure post of Chief Remembrancer of the Exchequer (worth £2,400 a year), was able to congratulate himself on achieving the two main ambitions he had previously confided to his brother, Buckingham, and that while he was still on the right side of 30.

Grenville regarded the Home Office as the ideal post for his interests and talents, and looked forward to a lengthy tenancy, which, however, was not to be. His main impact on the Office, which was responsible for control of the colonies, as well as a wide range of domestic responsibilities now shared by up to half a dozen different ministries, was drastically to overhaul its antiquated practices. He instituted, his biographer recalls, 'the practice of having précis made of all incoming and outgoing correspondence... [and] established a register for letters that were circulated amongst cabinet ministers for information' (Jupp, 1985, pp. 89–90). The chief piece of legislation for which he was responsible was the 1791 Canada Act. This divided the territory into two provinces, Upper and Lower Canada (the modern provinces of Ontario and Quebec), providing each of them with bicameral representative assemblies, the upper house hereditary and the lower subject to popular election, with a wider franchise than existed in Britain at the time. These constitutional arrangements remained in force for some 40 years, and were a clear improvement on what went before, but, according to Jupp, it worked only 'moderately well'. Yet Grenville's role in government was by no means confined to his responsibilities as Home Secretary. He had by now clearly emerged as the number two man in the government, a fact underlined by his promotion to the cabinet ahead of Pitt's two other close advisors – Henry Dundas and Lord Hawkesbury (later the Earl of Liverpool). Most of the cabinet were still in the House of Lords, and Grenville became, after Pitt, the government's main spokesman in the Commons, speaking on a wide range of subjects, including foreign affairs, for which he had no ministerial responsibility He was dubbed as 'Pitt's Vice-Chancellor' by Richard Sheridan, the Irish playwright and leading Whig MP.

Grenville's tenure of the Home Office came to an end after two years – in June 1791 – when he reluctantly accepted Pitt's request that he should take over the Foreign Office. The vacancy had occurred through the resignation of the Duke of Leeds, over the Ochakov affair (see Chapter 1), when Britain had threatened war with Russia, and then rather ignominiously backed down. Grenville had accepted a peerage some months earlier, due to Pitt's desire to strengthen his position in the upper house, of which Grenville became the leader. Although Grenville's long-term ambitions had included a peerage, he was far from certain that his removal from the Commons at this stage would not hinder his subsequent political career. Nor did he share the vainglorious aspirations of his brother, Buckingham, settling without argument for a barony, the lowest rank in the peerage, and not seeking a territorial title, styling himself simply Lord Grenville. He was 31 years old, and became one of the longest-serving Foreign Secretaries, continuing for nearly ten years in the office, combining it for the whole period with the leadership of the House of Lords, in which capacity he was universally recognized as being outstandingly successful. It was an extremely arduous period in his life, dominated from start to finish by the conflict with revolutionary France. As noted in an earlier chapter, he became, with Pitt, and Henry Dundas (who succeeded him as Home Secretary) part of a triumvirate which was jointly responsible for framing war policy, subject to spasmodic interference by George III. For the first year and a half of his Foreign Secretaryship, Britain was neutral in the war against France conducted by Austria and Prussia, a policy which he strongly supported, secure in the conviction that the two Germanic powers would prove victorious, and unwilling to commit Britain to making the restoration of the Bourbons an objective of its policy. However, the French occupation of the Austrian Netherlands and threat to invade Holland convinced him that French expansionism must be resisted, and the stiffening of the British attitude provoked a French declaration of war in February 1793. From then onwards, it became his firm conviction that no peace with France would be acceptable until she disgorged her conquests in the Low Countries.

By this time, a major change had occurred in Grenville's personal life. On 18 July 1792, he had married a cousin, Anne Pitt, the 19-year-old daughter of the first Lord Camelford, a wealthy nephew of the Elder Pitt. He had first proposed to her two years earlier, in what would effectively have been an arranged marriage, both Camelford and the Marquess of Buckingham being strongly in favour of the match. But the feisty 17-year-old had turned him down, largely on the grounds that she hardly knew him. Grenville had persisted in his wooing, and she became more and more attracted to him as she got to know him better, and after a long wait Grenville's patience was rewarded. Jupp comments that he had been 'completely smitten by a teenager who, although not a beauty, possessed considerable intelligence and, like his mother and himself, was a devout Anglican. It is possible that this was his first physical relationship with a woman and it was certainly his last' (Jupp, 2004). Part of her original attraction to him was undoubtedly her father's wealth, and she brought him a dowry of £20,000. The long-term benefit of the union was to be even greater, putting Grenville's finances permanently on a solid footing. Anne's brother, the dissolute second Lord Camelford, was killed in a duel in 1804, and the family's spacious Cornish estate, Boconnoc, reverted to her as well as the equally grand Camelford House, which Grenville was to make his London home. The dowry had partly been used to help Grenville buy a small estate in Buckinghamshire, Dropmore Park, which became their principal home. Grenville's marriage delighted his friends, who thought it had had a very beneficial effect on his persona. Lord Mornington, the future Marquess Wellesley, who had been his fellow student at Oxford, wrote to him, in October 1792,

> I cannot tell you with how much pleasure I saw your ménage. I told Pitt that matrimony had made three very important changes in you which could not but affect your old friends, 1). a brown lapelled coat instead of the eternal blue single breasted, 2). strings in your shoes, 3). very good perfume in your hair powder.

The marriage appears to have brought lasting happiness to both partners, though it was not to be blessed with children.

At the Foreign Office, Grenville lost little time in imposing a marked improvement in practices and administration, as he had earlier at the Home Office. In this, he was following in the footsteps of his father, George Grenville, who had implemented comparable improvements at the Treasury 30 years earlier. The two Grenvilles may justly claim to have been among the most *efficient* ministers until modern times. With one notable exception, Grenville did not engage in much personal diplomacy, preferring to operate through a voluminous correspondence and the use of ambassadors and special envoys, including his brother, Tom. The exception was the negotiation of the so-called Jay Treaty, signed in London in November 1794. Britain had been on the verge of renewed war with the United States, owing to disputes concerning the American-Canadian border, frontier posts, debts, trade with the West Indies and the British demand to be able to seize and search neutral ships trading with France. President George Washington sent Chief Justice John Jay to London in an attempt to negotiate a settlement of all these disputes, and after overcoming their initial distrust, the two men, both distinguished intellectuals, hit it off in a big way, and were able to reach compromises on all the questions at issue. By and large, the Americans came out best on the territorial issues, while the British view prevailed on the right of search. Historically, the main importance of the Jay Treaty was the precedent it set for the use of arbitration in the settlement of territorial disputes. Otherwise, the almost exclusive focus of Grenville's activities as Foreign Secretary was the continuous search for allies in the war against France, and the offering of inducements to keep their armies in the field. The principal objects of Grenville's attention were the trio of Austria, Prussia and Russia, but he also paid close attention to Spain and the Netherlands, as well as smaller powers, such as Denmark, Portugal, the kingdoms of Sardinia (Piedmont) and the Two Sicilies, many of the smaller German states, and even Turkey. As noted in chapter 1, although the three ministers responsible for directing the war effort worked together in general harmony, they did have their differences of approach. Grenville was critical of Pitt's impulse to attack France on any and every occasion, believing that it was preferable to strike only when numerical superiority was assured. He did not, however, share Dundas's preference for a wholly defensive war, with British efforts reserved for overseas expeditions, where its naval dominance should ensure success. On the question of internal security, Grenville fully supported the repressive efforts of Pitt and of Lord Portland, who succeeded Dundas (who became War Secretary) as Home Secretary in 1794. It was he who moved the Habeus Corpus Suspension Bill in the Lords, in 1794, and the Treasonable Practices and Seditious Meetings bills two years later.

As the 1790s proceeded, with the successive defeats of the First and Second Coalitions against France, Grenville's disagreements with Pitt over war policy became stronger. He objected to Pitt's insistence on continuing to pay subsidies to Prussia long after it had ceased to be an effective ally against France, and put his faith instead in a closer alliance with Austria and Russia, where the unpredictable Tsar Paul, had succeeded his mother, Catherine the Great, in 1796. Normally exceedingly cautious, Grenville took the lead, in 1799, in organizing a pincer movement to overwhelm the French occupiers of the Low Countries, by an Austrian attack from the east and an Anglo-Russian invasion of Holland, which, he wrongly predicted, would be supported by a mass uprising. In the end, the Austrian thrust proved ineffective, the Russians sent fewer troops than promised and the uprising failed to materialize. The invasion turned out to be a fiasco, the only compensation being the capture of the Dutch fleet, and the Russian forces had to be ignominiously evacuated to the Channel Islands, where they sat out until the following year, when the Tsar withdrew from the war, and recalled his troops. A chastened Grenville concluded that he was no strategist, and concentrated instead on trying to ensure that Britain was not forced into peace negotiations with France at a time of military weakness. He was not able to prevent preliminary talks taking place with the French, in 1796, 1797 and 1800, but was able to insist on a stiffening of the British terms sufficient to make them unacceptable to the French negotiators. It seems likely that without his energetic intervention, Pitt would have been prepared to settle for rather less, and a peace agreement comparable to that reached at Amiens, in 1802, would have been possible. By then, of course, Grenville, as well as Pitt himself were out of office.

They had resigned, as recounted in chapter 1, in February 1801, when George III had vetoed cabinet proposals for Catholic emancipation. Grenville had been one of the strongest advocates of this measure, partly because of his belief in religious toleration, but more importantly because his experience of dealing with Irish affairs had convinced him that it was a necessary means to assure solid Irish backing for the war effort. He then fell out with Pitt, when the latter – possibly in the hope of an early recall to office – gave the King an assurance that he would not raise the issue again in his lifetime. Grenville refused to serve in Henry Addington's government, which took office in March 1801, and watched with growing dismay as he negotiated a peace treaty with France, which left it in control of the Low countries and provided for the return of most of Britain's colonial conquests. He was the most senior politician to denounce the treaty, which was accepted as an unfortunate necessity by the great majority, including Pitt, and brought short-term popularity to Addington from a war-weary nation. Grenville became the leader of a 'new opposition' to Addington, which included most of the Portland Whigs (but not the Duke himself), in contrast to the 'old opposition', a more numerous body still headed by Charles James Fox. Gradually, the two oppositions began to co-ordinate their activities in Parliament, despite their strong differences over war and peace. To a large extent, Grenville fell under the potent charm of Fox and the two men became close associates and friends. There was a third opposition grouping, the Pittites – led by George Canning – who were unable to accept the fact that their hero had been supplanted by Addington. After the war with France resumed, in May 1803, Grenville became convinced that it could only successfully be pursued under a government of national unity – a 'Ministry of All the Talents' – led by Pitt, but including the Addingtonians and all three elements of the opposition. This was also now Pitt's preference, and when he resumed the premiership, in May 1804, he asked to include both Grenville and Fox in his team. George III had no objection to Grenville, but firmly vetoed Fox, at which Grenville said that he himself would not serve, despite Fox saying that he would not stand in his way. This offer of self-abnegation by Fox greatly touched Grenville, and bound them even more closely together, the 'new' and 'old' oppositions virtually combining their forces. This new constellation was greatly helped by a visit which Fox had made to France, during the 14 months' peace, when he had had an interview with Napoleon. He was offended by his imperious attitude, and the growing evidence of his dictatorial excesses, and returned much less of an advocate of 'peace at any price' than he had previously been.

The death of Pitt, at the age of 46, in January 1806, came at a particularly bleak moment in the resumed war against France. If the battle of Trafalgar, the previous October, had made Britain safe from invasion, the more recent victories of Napoleon at Ulm and Austerlitz had shattered the Austrian and Russian armies and destroyed the Third Coalition. George III was presented with an unwelcome choice. His strong preference was that Pitt's government should continue, with the members of the cabinet proposing a new Prime Minister from amongst their number. They were, however, unwilling to do this, and firmly recommended to the King that he should instead appoint Grenville, as much the most experienced and respected figure who had been in government over the previous 20 years. George realized he had no choice in the circumstances, and invited Grenville to propose a government 'with no exclusions', an acknowledgment that he was no longer in a position to block Fox's return to office. Grenville was in no hurry to accept, proposing instead that Earl Spencer, a leading Whig peer, should be Prime Minister. It was not only diffidence, and a sense of weariness which made him hesitate, but also a concern for his own income, despite the fact that the death of his brother-in-law two years earlier had left him a very wealthy man. Writing to his brother, Buckingham, he complained that he would have to give up his sinecure post of Auditor of the Exchequer, and that 'I should in fact receive no addition to my present income and must incur a very great additional expense'. Fox removed this difficulty for him by agreeing to introduce a bill placing the auditorship temporarily in the hands of a trustee, and Grenville went ahead and drew up a list of ministers to present to the King. Although his government became known as The Ministry of All the Talents, only three of the four main party formations were, in fact, included – hostility between the Whigs (who had been in the wilderness for a generation) and the Pittites (now generally regarded as Tories) preventing them from working together. So the government was made up of the Grenvillites, the Whigs, led by Fox and the young Charles Grey, and the Addingtonians, whose leader had become Viscount Sidmouth. Grenville would have liked to find posts for the abler Pittites, notably Canning, Castlereagh, Perceval and Hawkesbury (later Lord Liverpool), and hoped it would be possible for some of them to join the government at a later stage, but this did not happen,

The result was that he was to lead a largely inexperienced team, which was particularly weak in debating power in the Commons, apart from Fox, who was to die within seven months. Grenville's being in the Lords was to prove a major disadvantage, particularly after Fox's death. Unlike Pitt and Addington, Grenville did not choose to combine the Premiership with the Chancellorship of the Exchequer, to which post he appointed the 26-year-old Lord Henry Petty (later the Marquess of Lansdowne). Sidmouth became Lord Privy Seal; Earl Spencer, Home Secretary; Fox, Foreign Secretary; Grey, First Lord of the Admiralty and William Windham, War Secretary. Predictions that the government would soon split due to foreign policy differences between Grenville and Fox proved groundless, and though Fox attempted to negotiate peace with the French, he agreed to seek a joint negotiating position with the Russians, Britain's only remaining ally. This precluded any agreement being reached with the French. Ill-advised and badly conducted military operations were then undertaken against France and her allies, in such diverse locations as Buenos Aires, the Dardanelles, Sicily and Alexandria. None was successful, and Britain was henceforth to adopt Grenville's own 'defensive and husband-ing system', which effectively meant a policy of armed vigilance, while wait-ing for Napoleon to commit the mistakes which would ultimately lead to his downfall. It was to be a long wait, but Grenville would live to see it as a still semi-active politician, but one who had been out of power for eight years.

Grenville had clear ideas about his government's objectives, but was less cer-tain about the means to be employed, and was largely deficient (as he himself was to admit) in the skills required to galvanize his fellow ministers into effec-tive action. According to Jupp, the 'central features' of Grenville's plan for a 'systematic government' included:

> First, a reorganization of the armed services which Grenville, in the company of others, had been urging since the renewal of the war with France. Second, a reform of national finances so as to deal with the recurring problem of raising enough money to pay for the war. Third, a policy of 'conciliation' towards Ireland in terms of both political management and measures. (Jupp, 1974, p. 260)

For Grenville, an essential element in this 'conciliation' was progress towards Catholic emancipation, a conviction which was inevitably to set him on a course of conflict with his monarch. The clash, when it came, was made worse by Grenville's less than tactful handling of his relations with the King. This particularly concerned his demand to hold a general election in October 1806, ostensibly to legitimize the reconstruction of the government, following Fox's death. Grenville's purpose was to boost his own authority, and to demonstrate to the Pittites, who now formed the opposition, the strength of his support in the country. George III considered the election unnecessary, as the government already enjoyed a large majority in Parliament, and very reluctantly agreed, while refraining from making the customary royal financial contribution to the government's electoral expenses. Grenville's initiative was successful, in so far as he succeeded in increasing his majority by between 20 and 30 seats, but the cost to him of alienating the King was disproportional. Thereafter the King was wary of his Prime Minister, and this was exacerbated by Grenville's lack of the ready charm which had, for example, made Addington so adept at handling his prickly sovereign. In this – as in many other respects – Grenville's government was irreparably weakened by Fox's death. Against all expectations, Fox had got on famously with the King once he had admitted him into government, and George was heard to confess after his death that he had never thought 'he would miss him so much' (Derry, p. 133).

From Dublin, the demand for progress towards Catholic emancipation grew ever stronger, and Grenville and his leading colleagues (with only Sidmouth dissenting) felt that the minimum concession to the agitation should be the introduction of a Bill throwing senior posts, in both the Army and Navy, open to Catholics. This was similar to, but went rather further than, a Bill to which the King had given his consent in 1793, which applied only to service within Ireland, and excluded the Navy. Grenville and his colleagues unwisely concealed from the King the extent to which the new Bill differed from its predecessor. When the King was informed of this by Sidmouth, he reacted angrily, and demanded that the Bill be withdrawn. To this the government reluctantly agreed, but then the King went further and demanded an assurance from all his ministers that they would never again raise the question of Catholic relief in his lifetime – the same demand to which Pitt had acceded in 1801. Grenville and Grey, who had succeeded Fox as Foreign Secretary and leader of the Whigs, refused, and the government was effectively dismissed. Grenville had been Prime Minister for one year and 42 days, almost exactly half as long as his father, also dismissed by George III some 42 years earlier, after 2 years and 85 days.

Grenville's government was largely a failure – with one shining exception. Almost entirely due to the personal efforts of Grenville and Fox, it had pushed ahead with measures to abolish the slave trade, which despite all the efforts of William Wilberforce, and the encouragement of Pitt, who had however lacked the final commitment to force it through, had languished as a political issue for a generation. The abolition bill obtained the royal assent on the very day that Grenville and his ministers handed in their seals of office. Grenville was not sorry to retire from office, having found the experience of leading a government dispiriting, and doubting his own competence to do it. Shortly before, he had written to Buckingham that he longed 'daily and hourly ... for the moment that my friends will allow me to think that I have fully discharged (by a life of hitherto incessant labour) every claim they, or the country can have upon me'. He added: 'I want one great and essential quality for my station and every hour increases the difficulty ... I am not competent to the management of men. I never was so naturally, and toil and anxiety more and more unfit me for it' (Jupp, 1985, p. 409).

Grenville was still only 47, but his thoughts now lay in a quiet retirement at Dropmore, where he could relax with his wife, carry on with his classical and literary studies and indulge his passion for landscape gardening. His reaction to a request from Charles Grey to attend a meeting to discuss co-ordinating opposition to the incoming government, led by the Duke of Portland, was most discouraging. 'I feel very repugnant to any course of very active opposition', he wrote, 'having been most unaffectedly disinclined to take upon myself the task in which I have been engaged, and feeling no small pleasure in an honourable release, I could not bring myself to struggle much to get my chains on again'. However, Grey, who shortly afterwards inherited an Earldom from his father, joining Grenville in the Lords, was adamant: Grenville must lead the opposition, even though his parliamentary faction was much smaller than his own, and Grenville became the acknowledged leader of the Whig Party until 1817. For Grenville, this was very much a part-time activity, from which he probably derived far less satisfaction than from the Chancellorship of Oxford University. He succeeded to this post after Portland's death in 1809, but only after a fierce election campaign in which he engaged with a great deal more energy than he had ever shown in fighting parliamentary elections. His narrow victory was all the sweeter because his principal opponent was no other than Lord Eldon, Lord Chancellor in Perceval's government and a noted anti-Catholic, who was widely suspected of having influenced George III in his dismissal of Grenville's government.

Although Grenville's political activity was now spasmodic, his influence over his followers was considerable, for example, converting them to the importance of free trade, leading them to oppose the Corn laws in 1815, and he was expected to negotiate on their behalf whenever an opportunity arose for returning to office, either in coalition with the Pittites or replacing them, should arrive. There were no fewer than five occasions, between September 1809 and June 1812, when this seemed possible, but on four of these the terms proposed were unacceptable to the Whigs. The exception was in February 1811, when the renewed madness of the King led to the Prince of Wales taking over the regency, which he retained until George III's death in 1820, when he succeeded him as George IV. The Regent was keen to turn out the Perceval government, and restore his Whig friends to power, but Grenville botched his exploratory meetings with him and exasperated his colleagues by once again making an issue about retaining his sinecure office should he become premier. The Prince Regent lost heart and allowed the Perceval government to continue, confirming it in office, under the Earl of Liverpool, when Perceval was assassinated in 1812. Grenville continued to lead the Whigs until 1817, when he bowed out of active politics, leaving Earl Grey as the undisputed leader. It was not quite the end: he continued to attend the House of Lords occasionally, and in November 1820, was approached by the new King with an offer to form a government to replace Liverpool's administration, with which he was at loggerheads over the treatment of Queen Caroline, whom he wished to divorce. Much to the chagrin of the Grenvillites, and particularly his nephew, the second Marquess of Buckingham, who saw in this approach the restoration of their own political fortunes, Grenville turned the King down on the spot, and advised him to compose his differences with his ministers. Grenville's last speech in the House of Lords – generally reckoned to be one of his greatest – was in favour of yet another unsuccessful Catholic Emancipation Bill. He suffered a debilitating stroke, the first of several, in 1823, but was delighted to be able to vote by proxy in 1829 for the Bill finally carried by the Duke of Wellington's administration. 'I may now say', he said to his nephew, Buckingham, 'that I have not lived in vain'. He died five years later, at Dropmore, aged 74.

Although his premiership was to be short and lacking in achievement, Grenville was a leading political actor over a spread of some 40 years, during which his influence was arguably exceeded only by Pitt and Fox. An essentially conservative figure, he had a high intelligence and an exceptionally clear mind, and was noted for his strong sense of personal loyalty, which he exhibited successively to his eldest brother, to Pitt, and to Fox. Despite sharing the venal instincts of other members of the Grenville clan, he was essentially a man of integrity who showed remarkable consistency in his views and commitments, whether it was the abolition of slavery, Catholic emancipation or the obstinate refusal to condone a peace with France which did not guarantee Britain's essential interests, as he saw them. Highly effective as a departmental minister, and as Leader of the House of Lords, he was to lack some of the qualities, not all of them admirable in themselves, which might have made him equally successful as a Prime Minister.

Works consulted

John W. Derry, 1990, *Politics in the Age of Fox, Pitt and Liverpool*, Basingstoke, Macmillan.

John Ehrman, 1969, *The Younger Pitt:I The Years of Acclaim*, London, Constable.

John Ehrman, 1983, *The Younger Pitt: II The Reluctant Transition*, London, Constable.

John Ehrman, 1996, *The Younger Pitt: III The Consuming Struggle*, London, Constable.
    Peter Jupp, 1985, *Lord Grenville 1759 –1834*, Oxford, Oxford University Press.

Peter Jupp, 1974, 'Lord Grenville' in Herbert Van Thal, (ed.), *The Prime Ministers:* Vol. One, London, Allen & Unwin.

Peter Jupp, 2004, Article in *Oxford Dictionary of National Biography*, London, Oxford University Press.

4
William Henry Cavendish-Bentinck, 3rd Duke of Portland – Whig into Tory

His Grace the Duke of Portland

The Duke of Portland had the singular distinction of leading both a predominantly Whig and a Tory administration. Twenty-five years separated his two governments, and in each case he was a mere figurehead, the government being dominated by more powerful nominal subordinates. In between his two brief premierships, however, Portland played a prominent political role.

William Henry Cavendish-Bentinck was born on 14 April 1738, the eldest son and third child of the 2nd Duke of Portland and of Margaret Cavendish-Holles-Harley, granddaughter of Robert Harley, Earl of Oxford, a prominent minister under Queen Anne. William's great-grandfather, Hans William Bentinck, had come over from the Netherlands with William III, in 1689, and was his closest friend and most influential adviser, being created Earl of Portland, and awarded extensive estates in several English counties. The title was upped to a dukedom by George I in 1716, and the family holdings were further enlarged, when the second Duchess inherited Welbeck Abbey and an income of £12,000 a year from her mother and her cousin, the third Earl of Oxford. The second Duke is described by the historian, A.S. Turberville, as 'retiring, unambitious, inconspicuous, a much less remarkable personality than his wife...but wise, gentle, and kindly' The Duchess was a much stronger personality, who outlived her husband by 23 years, and – through her control of the family purse-strings – was something of a restraining influence on her elder son up till and even after his first premiership.

William was educated at Westminster School and Christ Church, Oxford, qualifying Master of Arts in 1757. He seems to have been an adequate but not outstanding student, and at the age of 19 set out for the Grand Tour, spending three years, mostly in Italy, but also visiting Hamburg, Prussia and Warsaw. Judging from his portraits, an exceptionally handsome young man, known by his courtesy title as the Marquess of Titchfield, he soon acquired a reputation as a philanderer and rapidly got into debt. His parents gave him an allowance of £2,500 a year, which they regarded as more than adequate for his needs, but he wrote plaintively to his father asking for this to be increased to £5,000. When this was refused, he addressed himself to his two elder sisters, one of whom, Elizabeth, was married to Viscount Weymouth, with no greater success. William aspired to a diplomatic career, hoping for a cushy post in a European capital, but his family doubted if he had sufficient experience, and his sister Elizabeth wrote to him suggesting that a political career might be more appropriate. Her husband controlled the Herefordshire constituency of Weobley, and, in March 1761, shortly before his twenty-third birthday, and even before his return from the continent, he was elected unopposed as one of its two MPs.

He sat in the Commons for exactly one year, and there is no record of any activity on his part. But in March 1762, his father, who had played no part in politics, died. The young Lord Titchfield became the third Duke, immediately taking his seat in the House of Lords, and attaching himself to the largest of the Whig factions, led by the ageing former Prime Minister, the Duke of Newcastle. Newcastle's protégé, the Marquess of Rockingham, was poised to take over, and Portland, in turn, became his protégé and close associate.

A poor and infrequent speaker, Portland may appear to have been an indifferent recruit to Newcastle's ranks, but his high social standing made him a prize catch. Dukes (other than royal dukes) were thin on the ground, and to find one who was young, personally agreeable, keen and prepared to give generously of his time and money in organizational activities, including the financing of elections, was an unlooked for opportunity. In a very short space of time, Portland was accepted as one of the leading Whig peers.

On his return from the continent, he was also seen as a highly eligible bachelor, but before settling down he embarked on love affairs with two ladies who would have been unlikely to commend themselves to the Dowager Lady Portland as suitable marriage mates for her son. One was a beautiful young widow, Maria Walpole, the illegitimate daughter of Sir Edward Walpole, and niece of the writer, Horace Walpole. Married to the Earl of Waldegrave, who was twice her age, she was left with three young children while still in her early twenties. Portland wooed her passionately, but she set her cap at even higher prey. As Horace Walpole put it, in his Memoirs, 'the young Duke of Gloucester, who had gazed at her with desire during her husband's life, now openly shewing himself her admirer, she slighted the subject, and aspired to the brother of the crown'. She became his mistress, and later his wife, much to the fury of George III, who introduced the Royal Marriage Act into Parliament, shortly afterwards, one of his other brothers, the Duke of Cumberland, also having contracted an unsuitable match (Turberville, p. 44).

Disappointed by Maria, Portland now directed his attention to Anne Liddell, the estranged wife of the Duke of Grafton, who was himself to be Prime Minister in 1768–70. He lavished presents on her, including two horses, and her surviving letters to him reveal that she more than reciprocated his feelings. Suddenly, however, Portland's side of the correspondence grew more distant, and, in March 1766 he wrote announcing his engagement to Lady Dorothy Cavendish, daughter of the fourth Duke of Devonshire. Judging from her portrait, the future Duchess of Portland was a great deal less attractive than either of her rivals, and she was certainly less vivacious. She was, however, universally seen as a suitable match, and their marriage, which took place the following November, seems to have been a happy one. The advantage to Portland was obvious, He was marrying into one of the greatest aristocratic and political families of the realm, and his new brother-in-law, the 5th Duke of Devonshire, obligingly lent him Burlington House, in Piccadilly, as his London residence, an ideal venue for political entertaining (Turberville, pp. 44–51). As for the Duchess of Grafton, she did not remain broken hearted for long. She soon took up with the Earl of Ossory, bearing him a son in 1768, and marrying him as soon as her marriage to Grafton had been dissolved by Act of Parliament in 1769. (It is intriguing that another future Prime Minister, Harold Macmillan, was to marry a Lady Dorothy Cavendish, daughter of the 9th Duke of Devonshire, over 150 years later, in 1920).

What sort of man was the Third Duke of Portland, and what beliefs and principles underlay his political career? First and foremost, he was an almost perfect exemplar of the creed of *noblesse oblige*, as was illustrated by a letter he addressed to his wastrel younger brother, Lord Edward Bentinck, urging on him his duty to accept nomination as a Member of Parliament:

> Since I have been able to exercise my reason, I never could persuade myself that men were born only for themselves. I have always been bred to think that Society has its claims on them, & that those claims were in general proportioned to the degrees of their fortunes, their situation, and their abilities.... (Turberville, p. 68)

Secondly, Portland was a strong party man, and the party he had chosen was the Whig party, which he saw as the natural protector of the Bill of Rights of 1689. This prescribed a limited monarchy, and parliamentary government, and it was the duty of the Whig aristocracy, in Portland's view, to ensure that this doctrine prevailed. Throughout the reigns of the first two Georges, they had successfully carried out this mission, but the young George III, who ascended the throne in 1760, had lost little time in challenging it, turning out of office Whig governments led successively by the Dukes of Newcastle and Devonshire, and substituting one led by a royal favourite, the Earl of Bute.

Portland, a mild-mannered man, was nevertheless capable of strong emotions, and conceived a deep aversion to Bute, and a keen distrust of the King. For his part, George refused to accept that he was acting against either the letter or the spirit of the Bill of Rights. He believed that his right to appoint or dismiss ministers at his will was underwritten by this Act, and that it was only the laziness of his great grandfather, George I, and his grandfather, George II, which had allowed this power to be usurped by a Whig oligarchy. He was doing no more, he believed, than reclaiming the powers awarded to William III by the 1689 Act.

Despite, his Whig principles, Portland was no democrat, and in general held highly conservative views. He was opposed to parliamentary reform, to Catholic emancipation and the abolition of slavery. This might have brought him into conflict with Charles James Fox, the undisputed leader of the Whigs in the House of Commons, but in fact the two men acted in almost complete harmony for many years, and were only driven apart by the impact of the French Revolution, in the years after 1789. The basis of Portland's influence was his position as a great territorial magnate, with estates in Buckinghamshire, Cumberland, Hampshire and Soho. Yet he was constrained by two factors – his relationship with his mother, and his own spendthrift ways. The Dowager Duchess of Portland loved her elder son dearly, but was fiercely protective of her own rights. The Cavendish interest, including large estates in Nottinghamshire and Derbyshire and a grand London residence, which she had inherited from her mother, remained hers until her death in 1785, while Portland only controlled the Bentinck inheritance until then. The Dowager chose, however, to make her home at Bulstrode, in Buckinghamshire, the main Bentinck residence, allowing her son, in exchange, to live in Welbeck Abbey, the Nottinghamshire base of her branch of the Cavendish family, conveniently close to Portland's new Cavendish in-laws, the Devonshires, at Chatsworth. There were periodic conflicts between mother and son over the control and management of the different estates, and in addition sharp political differences, as the Dowager was an intimate friend of Lady Bute and had many close contacts with courtiers of the King. In addition, Portland's brother-in-law, Lord Weymouth, who had provided him with his parliamentary seat, was a Tory, who served for many years, without distinction, in Lord North's government.

Portland was a benevolent landlord, and was regarded as an 'easy touch' by many of his large circle of friends and dependents. He was continually bailing out Lord Edward Bentinck, described by Horace Walpole as his 'idle and worthless younger brother', and lent as much as £56,000 to his rakish friend George Byng (Lord Torrington), which he never got back. In addition, he recklessly spent large sums of money in the general election of 1768 in a determined attempt to win parliamentary seats in Cumberland, where he was a large landowner, from the control of the notorious 'boroughmonger', Sir James Lowther. In the short-term, he was notably successful, doubling the number of seats he directly controlled in the House of Commons, from four to eight, but in the long-term it was ruinous to his finances. Lowther retaliated by launching a lawsuit against Portland, challenging the legality of his Cumberland holdings which had been granted to his great grandfather by William III. Lowther was immensely wealthy and boasted 'I would at any time spend £20,000 to make the Duke of Portland spend fifteen, for I know I can hold out longer than he can, and my meaning is to ruin the Duke of Portland'. The case dragged on for ten years, at enormous expense, and though Portland eventually prevailed, 'it proved a joyless victory, which resulted in the sale of most of his Cumberland estates' (Wilkinson, 2003, p. 24). Wilkinson points out that, though Portland was by most measures a very wealthy man, his assets palled in comparison with those of other territorial magnates. Prior to his mother's death, in 1785, his net income was some £9,000 a year, which then rose to £17,000. 'These figures should be compared with fellow grandees, such as the Duke of Devonshire and the Marquess of Rockingham, whose net incomes were in the region of £40,000 p.a.' (Ibid., p. 61).

Portland did not have long to wait to win ministerial office. In July 1765, three years after he succeeded to the dukedom, the King ejected George Grenville, Bute's successor, from office, and turned once again to the Whigs to form a government. The Marquess of Rockingham became Prime Minister at the age of 35, and invited Portland, then 27, to become Lord Chamberlain, outside the Cabinet. The duties were not very arduous, and were largely routine, such as the organization of 'state ceremonies, the preparation of apartments for royal visits, the redecoration of ballrooms, the purchase of new furniture and similar topics' (Turberville, p. 88). Portland found it all rather boring, but proved efficient at his post, and when the King dismissed the Rockingham government, after just over a year, he was one of a number of ministers asked to stay on in the new government led by the Earl of Chatham (the elder Pitt). Portland was not an admirer of Chatham, whom he referred to as 'Lord Cheat'em', and had no qualms in resigning after a few months, when Rockingham called on his supporters to quit the government. In opposition, he stayed close to Rockingham, and remained so for the ensuing 16 years until Rockingham was again asked to form a government, in March 1782. This was in succession to Lord North, whose 12 years in office came to an end with the collapse of the British position in the American War of Independence. Rockingham nominated him as Lord Lieutenant, or 'viceroy' of Ireland, but less than three months after his arrival in Dublin the sudden death of the Prime Minister brought the government to an abrupt end.

The Rockinghamites met to appoint a successor, whom they optimistically assumed would be asked by George III to form a new government. Much the most able of the Whig peers was the Duke of Richmond, an illegitimate descendant of Charles II, who had served with distinction in both the Rockingham governments, and would dearly have loved to be chosen. Yet, in Horace Walpole's words, quoted by Turberville, 'with a thousand virtues, he was nevertheless exceedingly unpopular'. One reason was his ardent advocacy of Parliamentary reform, which did not go down well with many of the Whig magnates, who feared the loss of their 'pocket' boroughs. 'What', asked Turberville,

> of the party's most active and brilliant representative in the Lower House – Fox? It is exceedingly doubtful whether this most intensely aristocratic of all political connexions would ever have selected a commoner as its head: but there was a fatal objection apart from that – Fox was anathema to the King. It was Fox himself who proposed the solution which found general favour – the election of the Duke of Portland. (Turberville, 1939, p. 180)

So it was that one of the least qualified people ever to lead a British political party was chosen. As his grandson, the nineteenth century diarist, Charles Greville, also quoted by Turberville, put it:

> My grandfather was a very honourable, high-minded but ordinary man; his abilites were very second- rate, and he had no power of speaking, and his election to the post of leader of the great Whig party only shows how aristocratic that party was...they would never have endured to be led by a Peel or a Canning. (Ibid., pp. 180–1).

George III never seriously considered asking Portland to become Prime Minister, and hastened to appoint the Earl of Shelburne, formerly a close associate of the Elder Pitt, who asked Portland to stay on as Lord Lieutenant of Ireland. Soon afterwards, however, he resigned, joining the bulk of the Rockinghamites in opposition, and beginning a long and harmonious partnership with Fox, who was the undisputed Whig leader in the Commons. As recounted in Chapter 1, Shelburne's ministry did not last long, being defeated in February 1783, in a House of Commons vote on the American peace terms, due to the coming together of the forces of Fox and of Lord North MP, the former Tory Prime Minister. The King, with great reluctance, agreed that they should form the next government, but insisted that someone else should be Prime Minister. His preference was the young William Pitt, then only 23, but he was unwilling, and in any case was unacceptable to both Fox and North, who both insisted that Portland should be chosen. He agreed to take office, but the new government, installed on 2 April 1783, was totally dominated by Fox, as Foreign Secretary, and North as Home Secretary, both being in the House of Commons. In effect, Portland's role was principally to act merely as Leader of the House of Lords, but he enjoyed excellent relations with both of his nominal subordinates, and seemed quite comfortable to be seen as a figurehead.

From the outset, George was determined that the government, to whom he refused all patronage, should be of brief duration, and his resolve was only strengthened when it proposed to him a generous formula for clearing the debts of the spendthrift Prince of Wales and substantially increasing his official allowance. The King expressed his 'utter indignation and astonishment' at so large a sum being proposed (far larger than *he* had enjoyed as heir apparent), and charged the Duke with 'neglecting the interests of the Sovereign and of the public to gratify the passions of an ill-advised Young Man'. Portland replied with an emollient letter proposing a compromise, which the King accepted, and – untypically – apologized to Portland for his earlier ill temper. Despite this apparent reconciliation, George was still determined to remove the Portland government at the earliest opportunity, which – as described in Chapter 1 – occurred when Fox enthusiastically pushed through the Commons a Bill, drafted by Edmund Burke, sharply curtailing the independence of the East India Company and transferring its powers of patronage to parliamentary commissioners. In a plot carefully contrived with the former (and future) Lord Chancellor, Lord Thurlow, and with the Younger Pitt, the latter's cousin, Earl Temple, was authorized to tell members of the House of Lords that the King would regard any of them who voted for the Bill as his 'personal enemy'. Rumours of what was afoot reached the government, and Portland referred obliquely to them in his speech proposing the Second Reading of the Bill in the Lords. Perhaps there was nothing to be done about it, but Portland badly mishandled the situation, making no serious attempt to persuade peers of the merits of the Bill, and then bungling the parliamentary procedure for its approval. The Bill was defeated by 19 votes, but the government, which still enjoyed a large majority in the Commons, refused to resign. It was then unceremoniously dismissed by the King, who sent personal messengers at midnight to the homes of Portland, Fox and North to demand the return of their seals of office. Portland's premiership, which came to an end on 18 December 1783, had lasted a mere 260 days. The King's intervention was described, by the leading historian of this period, as 'indefensible according to both the constitutional theory and practice of his own day' (Cannon, p. xiii). Portland received no blame from his colleagues for his maladroit performance. He was regarded by them as a martyr for the Whig cause, and 'it became impossible to conceive of the return of the whigs without his reinstatement [as Prime Minister]' (Wilkinson, 2004).

Such a return seemed probable late in 1788, when the first bout of madness of George III appeared to open the way to the appointment of his son (later George IV), a bosom friend of Fox and other leading Whigs, as Prince Regent. The King's recovery, the following March, before a regency bill had been passed, forestalled this possibility, and the main body of the Whigs were to remain in the wilderness for many years to come. Portland, however, was restored to office, though not to the premiership, some five years later.

The French Revolution, in 1789, had opened up deep divisions within the Whig Party, with Fox enthusiastically welcoming it, and Edmund Burke reacting sharply against. Portland's initial reaction was mildly favourable, but as the excesses mounted up, he, together with many other Whig aristocrats, began to fear for his property if French revolutionary ideas were to cross the Channel. When war broke out with France, in 1792, he became even more concerned, and succumbed to the patriotic fervour whipped up by Pitt's supporters. He was, however, deeply reluctant to break with Fox, who was opposed to the war, and for long refused to respond to feelers from Pitt to join his government, as Lord Loughborough, the leading Whig lawyer, had done, in becoming Lord Chancellor in January 1793. It was another 18 months before he was prepared to take the plunge, finally, as recounted in Chapter 1, becoming Home

Secretary in July 1794. He was accompanied by four other conservative Whig defectors, who joined the cabinet at the same time, and he succeeded in bringing over to the government side more than half of the Whig representation in the Commons. This greatly bolstered Pitt's majority, and left Fox in charge of a diminishing rump of largely demoralized supporters.

The Portlandites also obtained numerous peerages and other honours, as well as appointments to non-cabinet posts, of which the most important was the Lord Lieutenancy of Ireland. This went to Earl Fitzwilliam, Rockingham's nephew and a close friend of Portland's. On his arrival in Dublin, Fitzwilliam embarked on a purge of government officials, replacing supporters of Pitt with Irish Whigs and, without obtaining Cabinet approval, expressed his sympathy for Catholic emancipation. Portland was horrified, and immediately recalled Fitzwilliam, offering, however, as a token of friendship, to resign as Home Secretary, and telling Fitzwilliam that the King had agreed to appoint him to a Cabinet post as compensation for his dismissal, provided he affirmed his –support for the ministry. With all the pride of a leading Whig magnate, Fitzwilliam rejected this offer out of hand, and his friendship with Portland was at an end. As Home Secretary, Portland continued to be responsible for Irish affairs and, following the unsuccessful United Irish uprising, led by Wolfe Tone, in 1798, took a leading role in the moves to incorporate the Irish Parliament into the British Parliament at Westminster. This was only achieved by the massive employment of patronage, and outright bribes to Irish MPs to induce them to vote their own Parliament out of existence. This policy was carried through by the men on the spot in Dublin, the Marquess of Cornwallis, as Lord Lieutenant, and Viscount Castlereagh MP, as Chief Secretary. When Portland left office, in 1801, there were substantial funds missing from the Home Office accounts, which was promptly covered up. For nearly 200 years, Portland, who was known to be in financial difficulties at the time, was suspected of having diverted the money (more than £30,000) for his own purposes. It was only with the release of the Home Office secret service papers, in the 1990s, and sharp detective work by the historian, David Wilkinson, that it was revealed that the missing money had, in fact, been illegally transmitted to Dublin to grease the palms of Irish Protestant legislators (Wilkinson, 2003, pp. 148–58).

Portland's Whiggish instincts did not long survive his recruitment to the Pitt government, and his previous animus against Pitt, who had usurped his premiership a dozen years earlier, and against George III, soon evaporated. Indeed, he became a fervent admirer of Pitt, whom he found a considerate colleague, and of the King, with whom he developed good relations and whom he came to see as a model patriotic monarch. For all intents and purposes, Portland became a Tory, though he never described himself as such, and his record as Home Secretary showed him to be one of the most hard-line of Pitt's ministers. He was largely responsible for introducing and implementing the oppressive legislation directed against alleged supporters of the French Revolution and of parliamentary reform, and he did not scruple to use secret service informers and *agents provateurs* to harry their activities. Nor did he show himself sympathetic to those suffering from serious food shortages, following a series of bad harvests, setting his face against proposals to fix food prices or make government purchases of imported grain. Only on two occasions, in 1795 and 1800, did he relent, in the face of strong pressure from other ministers.

When Pitt resigned, along with other leading cabinet ministers, in February 1801, in protest against George III's vetoing of Catholic emancipation, Portland did not join them. He carried on as Home Secretary in Henry Addington's government, later switching to become Lord President of the Council, a position he retained in Pitt's second ministry, formed in May 1804. The following year, he relinquished the post to make room for Addington (now Lord Sidmouth), but remained in the Cabinet as Minister without Portfolio. He went into opposition when Lord Grenville formed his 'Ministry of All the Talents', on Pitt's death in February 1806, becoming the nominal leader of the Pittites, who were excluded, or excluded themselves, from the government because of their incompatibility with the Whigs, who formed the largest element in Grenville's team. The Pittite group included such strong characters as George Canning, Spencer Perceval, Lord Hawkesbury (the future Lord Liverpool) and Viscount Castlereagh, whose mutual rivalry was assuaged by their common agreement to unite under the emollient Duke.

Portland was now an elderly man, and his health was far from good, and it looked as though his ministerial days were at an end. Yet when, in early 1807, George III once again came into conflict with his ministers on the issue of Catholic emancipation (see Chapter 3), Portland wrote an ill-advised letter to the King urging him to stand his ground. Grenville and his leading colleagues agreed to withdraw their Bill granting the rights of Catholics to hold senior positions in the Army and Navy, but refused to promise the King never to raise the issue again. Thereupon, he peremptorily dismissed them, and appealed to Portland to take Grenville's place. With evident misgivings, Portland complied, forming what was effectively a Tory government, with the leading positions all filled by Pittites. On paper, at least, it was a strong team, with Spencer Perceval as Chancellor of the Exchequer, George Canning as Foreign Secretary, Lord Hawkesbury (shortly to succeed to the Earldom of Liverpoool) as Home Secretary and Viscount Castlereagh MP as Secretary for War and the Colonies. In practice, it proved a great deal weaker than the sum of its parts. This was because of the lack of direction which it received from Portland, who attended cabinet meetings only spasmodically, and hardly ever the House of Lords, where he remained silent throughout his premiership. Wilkinson did not put it too bluntly, when he wrote: 'Portland was worse than useless as prime minister. Not only did he fail to direct policy, he also bungled the lesser role of conciliator' (Wilkinson, 2003, pp. 164–5). Contemporary comment, especially from Whig supporters, who felt betrayed by him, was even more unkind. Wilkinson quotes, at length, a poem published in the *Morning Chronicle*, and beginning:

> He totters on a crutch;
> his brain by sickness long depressed,
> has lost the sense it once possessed,
> though that's not losing much. (Ibid., p. 137)

The government faced serious problems, not least in promoting the war against Napoleon, where the campaign in Spain and Portugal was going badly, and the expedition to the Dutch island of Walcheren, with the aim of seizing Antwerp, planned by Castlereagh, went disastrously wrong. They were compounded by a scandal involving the King's second son, the Duke of York, who was Commander-in-Chief, and whose mistress was accused of selling army commissions. The worst feature of Portland's government, however, was the intrigues conducted by individual ministers against their colleagues. The main culprit was George Canning, who – sensing that the Portland ministry would not last long – endeavoured to manoeuvre himself into a position where he would be well placed to succeed him. His main rival was likely to be Perceval, but the man he had in his sights was Castlereagh, and he approached Portland, threatening to resign if Castlereagh was not removed from the War Office and replaced by Lord Wellesley, the elder brother of General Sir Arthur Wellesley, later the Duke of Wellington. Portland agreed, in principle, and squared the matter with the King, but insisted that the change could not be made until after the outcome of the Walcheren expedition was known, and that until then the decision should be kept from Castlereagh so as not to undermine him. He also suggested that the bad news should ultimately be conveyed to Castlereagh by Earl Camden, the Lord President of the Council, who was his uncle, and who nobly offered to give up his own post in his nephew's favour, in order to soften the blow. Yet when the time came, after the failure of the Walcheren expedition, his nerve failed him, and shortly afterwards Portland had an apoplectic seizure while on his journey from London to Bulstrode, and was taken out of his carriage 'speechless and insensible. He made a partial recovery of both mind and speech, but no hopes were entertained of his ultimate restoration to health' (Turberville, p. 301). His family wanted Portland to retire immediately, and when Perceval also recommended him to do so, he decided to call it a day, a decision which alarmed Canning, as he thought it had come too early for his own chances of the succession. When Castlereagh learned of Canning's conduct, he was outraged, and immediately demanded satisfaction. The two men met on Putney Heath for a duel, in which Canning was slightly wounded (see Chapter 7), and the scandal added to the ignominy of the collapse of Portland's government.

Portland resigned on 4 October 1809, after a premiership of two years and 187 days. This was more than three times as long as his first premiership, but whereas he had played a useful role as a mediator the first time round, he was almost a complete passenger in his second administration. Perceval went on to form a government from which both Canning and Castlereagh were excluded, and the former had to wait another 13 years before he was restored to office. Portland agreed to continue in Perceval's cabinet as Minister without Portfolio, but died three weeks later, after a second apoplectic attack, on 30 October 1809, aged 71. He left debts of £500,000, and it was only by effecting painful economies, including the sale of the main Bentinck estate at Bulstrode, that his son, the 4th Duke, who eschewed any political participation, was able to mend the family fortunes.

Portland's long political career had seldom risen above the level of mediocrity. As opposition leader in the 1780s, he lent respectability to the otherwise somewhat raffish Whigs, and his patience and affability helped to hold the party together in a difficult period. A conscientious, if reactionary, Home Secretary between 1794 and 1801, he would probably have been wiser to bow out of politics at that stage, and devote his evidently waning powers to the management of his still extensive estates. Yet a misguided sense of duty, and a desire to please the King, to whom he was now devoted, forced him to carry on. His historical importance lies chiefly in his action in 1794 of bringing the more conservative Whigs over to Pitt. He thereby paved the way for a reconstituted Tory party, which was to become the dominant political force in the first three decades of the nineteenth century.

Works consulted

John Cannon, 1969, *The Fox–North Coalition*, Cambridge, Cambridge University Press.
John W. Derry, 1990, *Politics in the Age of Fox, Pitt and Liverpool*, Basingstoke, Macmillan.
E. Anthony Smith, 1973, 'The Duke of Portland', in Herbert Van Thal (ed.), *The Prime Ministers*, Vol. I, London, Allen & Unwin.
H.M. Stephens (H.M.S), 1885, Article in *Oxford Dictionary of National Biography* London, Smith Elder & Co.
A.S. Turberville, 1939, *A History of Welbeck Abbey and its Owners*, Vol. II, London, Faber and Faber.
David Wilkinson, 2003, *The Duke of Portland: Politics and Party in the Age of George III*, Basingstoke, Palgrave Macmillan.
David Wilkinson, 2004, Article in *Oxford Dictionary of National Biography*, Oxford, Oxford University Press.

5
Spencer Perceval – Struck Down in His Prime

Spencer Perceval has gone down in history as one of the least known of nineteenth century Prime Ministers, being remembered – if at all – as the only one to have been assassinated. Otherwise, he has been noted for his fervent evangelical Christianity and for being one of very few practising lawyers to have made it to 10 Downing Street. Yet, he had an unusual political career, and – after a tentative beginning – was at the height of his powers when he was killed in 1812. Had he lived, he might well have served for a lengthy term, perhaps for much of the 15 years that his successor, the 2nd Earl of Liverpool, was to occupy the post.

Although he came from an aristocratic and highly political background, Perceval had largely to make his own way in the world. Born on 1 November 1762, he was the second son, of the second marriage of his father, the second Earl of Egmont, who was First Lord of the Admiralty under George Grenville and in the first administration of the Marquess of Rockingham, in 1763–6. He was to die, when the young Spencer was only eight years old, leaving seven children from his first marriage, and nine from the second, of whom Spencer was the fifth born. Spencer's mother, Catherine Compton, was related to the Earls of Northampton, and was the great-niece of Spencer Compton, the Earl of Wilmington, who had been the second British Prime Minister, in 1742–3, and after whom Perceval was named. She became a Baroness in her own right (in the Irish peerage, as Baroness Arden), in 1770, the title being inherited by Spencer's elder brother Charles, together with a considerable fortune, while his much older half-brother John, became the third Earl of Egmont. Spencer himself was to inherit an income of only £200 a year, and his whole career was to be dominated by his need to earn enough money to maintain his own large family of six sons and six daughters.

Spencer was under-sized, and sallow if not sepulchral in appearance, an effect that was exacerbated by his always being dressed in black. He was known at school, and frequently in later life, as 'Little P'. At Harrow School, his headmaster, Joseph Drury, was to recall many years later, 'hard work and singleness of purpose were his cardinal virtues', while he succeeded in avoiding the temptations of 'desultory reading which could only vitiate his taste and confuse his ideas' (Gray, p. 4). Already at Harrow, Perceval was noted, together with his close friend Dudley Ryder (later Lord Harrowby) for his strong commitment to evangelical Anglicanism, which was to dominate his life. He won many prizes at school, and in 1780, proceeded to Trinity College, Cambridge, where he graduated MA two years later. The University was then known as a centre for hard drinking and general riotousness, but Perceval held aloof, devoting himself to his studies and associating mainly with a small group of fellow Evangelicals. 'Perceval', wrote his biographer, 'was undoubtedly studious; perhaps, for most tastes, he was a little too serious-minded [and] may sound too good to be true'. Yet, he added, 'there was a lighter side', referring to his 'guileless, guiltless jokes', and his fondness for hoaxes (Gray, p. 6). It was probably this which saved him from acquiring a reputation for priggishness, though he was famously described by Sydney Smith as 'an odious evangelical'.

When he left Cambridge, Gray records, 'there was no money for the usual grand tour of Europe', and he enrolled at Lincoln's Inn to read for the bar, also joining a debating society, meeting at the *Crown and Rolls* public house in Chancery Lane, where he honed his public speaking skills which were to prove invaluable at the bar, and much later in the House of Commons. He qualified as a barrister in 1786, and attached himself to the Midland circuit, where, however, money and clients were hard to come by. An anonymous contemporary memoir, quoted by Gray, refers to him hiring a horse to travel from town to town rather than buying his own, and how he would keep a careful note 'of the shilling spent on his dinner at a wayside inn, or of the florin which covered both dinner and breakfast, of the sixpenny tip to the chambermaid and the hostler, and of the cost of oats for his horse'. Somewhat lacking in self-confidence, and with an 'excess of modesty, which, at that period, almost amounted to timidity', he eventually became the leader of the circuit, and proved a popular figure. The eminent barrister, Sir Samuel Romilly, recalled in his *Memoirs* how 'With very little reading, of a conversation barren of instruction and with strong invincible prejudices on many subjects, yet by his excellent temper, his engaging manners and his sprightly conversation he was the delight of all who knew him'.

In 1787, the still penniless barrister was to fall in love. Revisiting, with his brother, Charles, the old family home in Charlton, Kent, which had been sold to Sir Thomas Wilson, an old soldier who had fought at the battle of Minden, they were immediately attracted by two of his daughters. Charles, now Lord Arden, an MP and a Lord of the Admiralty, with a large income, was warmly welcomed by Sir Thomas as a suitor, and was soon to marry the elder sister, Margaretta, in the private chapel of Charlton House. Spencer had less luck in courting the younger daughter, Jane, who was 18 years old, and her father refused point-blank to consent to her marriage to a young man of such poor prospects. The couple decided to bide their time for three years until she came of age.

Perceval's precarious finances received some modest relief by his appointment as Deputy Recorder of Northampton, in 1790, obtained through the influence of his maternal grandfather, the Earl of Northampton, and a year later he obtained two small sinecures at the Royal Mint, worth a little over £100 a year. By then, he and Jane were married, possibly having eloped, she arriving for the ceremony in her riding habit. Sir Thomas's anger was soon appeased, and he accepted his new son-in-law with good grace, assuring him that his daughter's eventual dowry would be no less than if she had wed with his consent.

Yet the young couple were certainly a great deal poorer than most of their social equals, setting up home in lodgings over a carpet shop in London's Bedford Row. Perceval was now 27, and the couple lost little time in establishing a family, six children being born in the first six years of their marriage, and another six over the subsequent decade. It was a happy marriage and Spencer doted over his wife and children. To bring them up in comfortable circumstances, he needed to maximize his income, and he made steady progress at the bar, becoming a King's Counsel in 1796, and a Bencher at Lincoln's Inn, his legal fees rising to about £1,000 a year. Through his brother, Lord Arden's influence, he also became counsel to the Board of Admiralty, and he was also appointed a commissioner in bankruptcy. In 1791 and 1792, he took the first tentative steps towards a political career by publishing, albeit anonymously, two pamphlets, one on the impeachment of Warren Hastings, the former governor-general of India, the other arguing for more repressive action to be taken against sympathizers of the French Revolution. The latter pamphlet attracted the favourable attention of the Prime Minister, William Pitt, and Perceval was appointed as junior counsel for the prosecution in the trials of two leading radicals, Thomas Paine and John Horne Tooke, in 1792 and 1794.

Despite his urgent need of money to sustain his family, Perceval throughout his life made generous charitable gifts, usually anonymously. He regarded this as his simple Christian duty, which also made him a fierce critic of hunting, gambling, drunkenness and adultery, and a fairly strict sabbatarian. Wilberforce said of him that 'Perceval had the sweetest of all possible tempers, and was one of the most conscientious men I ever knew; the most instinctively obedient to the dictates of conscience, the least disposed to give pain to others; the most charitable and truly kind and generous creature I ever knew', while a fellow Evangelical, William Roberts, is quoted by Gray as describing him as 'Christianity personified'. 'Perceval's spotless private life', Gray comments, 'was one of the greatest assets in his later political career... he set a new standard in fair-dealing and candour in politics, even at times to the detriment of his own interests'. Perceval's instincts, however, were deeply conservative, which led to an exaggerated deference to existing practices and a horror of innovation. He was, nevertheless, a fervent supporter of the abolition of slavery, and a believer in reform within the Church of England, where he campaigned for the restriction or abolition of absentee appointments to clerical livings, the payment of decent salaries to curates and the building of new churches in industrialized areas. His strong Anglicanism, however, made him an implacable opponent of Catholic emancipation, while his close study of the more prophetical books of the Bible laid him open to some of the more absurd millenarian superstitions which took hold in the late 1790s. In 1800, he was to publish a pamphlet entitled *Observations intended to point out the application of a prophecy in the eleventh chapter of the Book of Daniel to the French Power*. It is perhaps going too far to describe Perceval as a religious bigot, but he was not far off.

In January 1796, Perceval was surprised to receive a letter from the Prime Minister, William Pitt, offering him the vacant post of Chief Secretary to the Irish government. The new Lord Lieutenant, the Earl of Camden, had proposed his nephew, Viscount Castlereagh MP, but Pitt and the Home Secretary, the Duke of Portland, both felt that his Northern Irish connections would prove prejudicial to his acceptance in Dublin. Taking account of Perceval's financial worries, the offer included a promise of 'some provision of a permanent nature' and implored Perceval not to refuse because of 'misplaced diffidence'. Immensely flattered by the offer, which he described as 'so vastly beyond anything I could have imagined would ever have been submitted to my choice', Perceval nevertheless immediately wrote back declining, because of his family responsibilities. He ruled out the prospect of accepting the implied offer of a lucrative sinecure, saying that such terms 'would be so much too great for any service I could offer to the public, that you could not grant them with any degree of credit to yourself, or indeed without the imputation of inexcusable profusion of the public money' (Gray, pp. 13–14). Thus did the high-minded Evangelical exclude himself from an arrangement which would have been regarded as absolutely normal by the vast majority of contemporary politicians without large private means. Pitt made no further effort to persuade him, and Castlereagh duly embarked upon his own long and distinguished ministerial career.

Perceval's own entry into politics was not, however, long delayed. As the Deputy Recorder of Northampton, he had given some useful advice to the local corporation in a dispute over the town's charter in the spring of 1796, and when shortly afterwards one of the town's two MPs, his cousin Charles Compton, inherited his father's seat in the House of Lords, Perceval, aged 33, was returned unopposed in the ensuing by-election. Within less than a month, however, he was compelled to fight a vigorous campaign to hold the seat in a general election. Northampton had a reputation for fiercely fought election campaigns, having a relatively wide franchise with 1,000 voters on the electoral roll, and three rival interests usually competing for the two seats. The three groups were, respectively, the Compton family interest, the local corporation and the Whigs. Perceval received the support of the first of these, the new Earl of Northampton paying his election expenses, and easily topped the poll in a three-cornered contest, the second seat going to a Whig. Perceval, who proclaimed himself a supporter of Pitt, was returned unopposed in six further contests, and represented the borough for the rest of his life.

Perceval made an immediate impact upon the House of Commons, largely by a rollicking speech roundly attacking Charles James Fox, which left the opposition squirming. It was described by Pitt as 'in all respects one of the best I ever heard'. A year or so later, when Pitt fought his duel with Tierney (see Chapter 1), his second, Dudley Ryder, posed the delicate question of who should succeed if he were killed. He was astonished at Pitt's reply that 'he thought that Mr Perceval was the most competent person, and that he appeared the most equal to Mr Fox' (Gray, p. 41). Certainly, Perceval soon established himself as the most effective parliamentary debater on the government side, apart from Pitt. He was not asked to join the government, but in 1798 was appointed Solicitor-General to the Queen and solicitor to the Board of Ordnance. When Pitt resigned, in January 1801, the new Prime Minister, Henry Addington has-tened to add Perceval to his team, largely to boost its debating strength in the Commons. Perceval became Solicitor-General, and a year later was promoted to Attorney-General. In this capacity, he successfully conducted two impor-tant prosecutions – one against Colonel Edward Despard, who was executed for high treason, the other against Jean Peltier, a French exile, who was found guilty of a criminal libel against Napoleon Bonaparte, during the Peace of Amiens. Perceval was able to continue with private legal work, transferring his practice from the King's Bench to Chancery. Within a year his fees had dou-bled, reaching almost £10,000 by 1804. 'For the first (and only) time in his life he felt free from private financial worries' (Gray, p. 47). Perceval continued as Attorney-General in Pitt's second ministry, in 1804–1806, and showed himself unexpectedly liberal in several of his decisions. He refused to interpret the anti-trade union Combination Acts in the interests of the employers, and tried to extend the scope of the elder Peel's Cotton Manufacturing Apprentices Bill, which sought to protect young workers. When Pitt died, he declined to join the 'Ministry of All the Talents', formed by Lord Grenville, in February 1806.

He went into opposition, along with the great majority of those who regarded themselves as 'the friends of the late Mr Pitt', but who were seen by their oppo-nents as Tories. They included a number of men of great ability, but mutual jealousies were so strong that they were unable to agree among themselves on who should be chosen as party leader. They fell back on the unsatisfactory solu-tion of acknowledging the ageing Duke of Portland, who a generation earlier had led a predominantly Whig government, as their titular chief, but nobody was designated to lead them in the House of Commons. Neither Canning nor Castlereagh, the most able of them, were prepared to serve under the other, while the third of the trio of former senior ministers, Robert Jenkinson, who was to succeed to the title of Earl of Liverpool in 1808, was already in the House of Lords, having been created Baron Hawkesbury in 1803. Perceval slowly emerged as the *de facto* leader in the Commons, and proved by far the most effective spokesman. The most dramatic incident involving Perceval during his period in opposition was the appointment by the King of a Commission to consider the alleged misconduct of Princess Caroline, the separated wife of the Prince of Wales, who was rumoured to have become pregnant by a commoner.

This enquiry, known as the 'Delicate Investigation' failed to substantiate the most serious charges against the Princess, and the Cabinet accordingly recommended to the King that she should again be received at Court, though a Cabinet minute warned her that she 'must be more circumspect in her future behaviour'. The Princess's principal legal adviser throughout the process was Perceval, and the 156-page letter he drafted in her defence was widely hailed as a masterful effort, described by Gray as 'the last and greatest production of Perceval's legal career' (Gray, p. 83). The episode undoubtedly enhanced his reputation, though he risked permanently alienating the Prince of Wales (the future Prince Regent), who had hoped to use the enquiry as a basis for a divorce action. By now, the Grenville government, fatally weakened by the death of Fox, in September 1806, was coming to its end, and Perceval helped it on its way by strongly opposing its Bill to make concessions to Irish Catholics. Perceval's stand, which was supported by the bulk of opposition MPs, probably emboldened George III to insist on the dropping of the Bill and then to present his ministers with an ultimatum to renounce any future initiatives along similar lines or face instant dismissal. Grenville and Grey and their leading colleagues then refused to give such an undertaking, and the King invited Portland to form a government, which was to consist exclusively of the 'friends of Mr Pitt'. The most important offices went to Canning, as Foreign Secretary, Castlereagh as Minister for War and the Colonies, Hawkesbury as Home Secretary and Perceval, as Chancellor of the Exchequer and Leader of the House of Commons. Perceval was highly reluctant to take on this double portfolio, preferring to resume his previous role as Attorney-General, or alternatively to take the Home Office. He pleaded his ignorance of financial matters, but his real objection was that he could not afford to take on the Chancellorship of the Exchequer, with its relatively small salary of less than £3,700 a year, compared to £6,000 for the Home Secretary and the assurance of large legal fees to supplement the Attorney-General's salary. He finally agreed under pressure from his colleagues to accept the additional post of Chancellor of the Duchy of Lancaster, during the King's pleasure, which would considerably augment his salary.

In accepting these posts, Perceval was taking on an enormous double burden. In facing the 'Talents' across the floor of the House, he was encountering one of the strongest opposition teams – both in numbers and debating power – for many years, with relatively little supporting strength at his own disposal. As Chancellor, he was not only handicapped by his lack of experience, but by the effective absence of a First Lord of the Treasury, who normally took the major responsibility for Treasury policy and administration, with the Chancellor playing only a subsidiary role (comparable, perhaps, to the modern post of Chief Secretary to the Treasury). The Duke of Portland, who was a mere figurehead as Prime Minister, took no part in the Treasury of which he was the nominal head, leaving Perceval to run the most important department of the government virtually single-handed.

Perceval's main challenge as Chancellor of the Exchequer was to raise enough money to continue the war against Napoleonic France, which threatened to become a crippling burden. In 1807, the retiring Prime Minister, Lord Grenville, had told his closest associates that Britain was capable only of waging a defensive war. Any major continental campaign was, he said, beyond our means. Yet, wrote Perceval's biographer: 'Over the succeeding five years, the Portland and Perceval administrations maintained British garrisons in all parts of the world, subsidised Austria, Portugal, Sicily and Sweden, launched the Walcheren expedition, and supported Wellington's lengthy and expensive campaigns in the Peninsula' (Gray, p. 323).

The Peninsular War was sparked off by Napoleon's ill-considered action, in March 1808, of deposing the Portuguese and Spanish dynasties and installing his brother, Joseph, as King of Spain. This provoked national uprisings in both countries, providing Britain for the first time with an opportunity of military intervention with significant support from the local population. Despite initial success, it proved a far longer and more hazardous commitment than was originally conceived, but it was to play an important part in Napoleon's eventual downfall. The Walcheren expedition (see Chapter 4), by contrast, was to prove a humiliating failure. Perceval played no direct part in the planning of either operation, which was primarily the role of Castlereagh, yet it was his efforts which made them possible. Perceval's budgets were not particularly innovative, but he managed to raise unprecedented sums to finance the war effort, without raising taxes. This he achieved by careful administration, cutting out unnecessary expenditure, and by raising large sums through long-term loans at very favourable rates of interest. The confidence he created by his own evident integrity undoubtedly influenced bankers to advance larger sums than they would otherwise have been inclined to do.

In Parliament, Perceval faced constant harassment from the Whig opposition, confident that the government's hold on power was increasingly precarious. The three issues on which they concentrated were Catholic emancipation, the conduct of the war and the linked questions of government patronage, corruption and parliamentary reform. On the Catholic issue, Perceval, to the delight of George III, gave no quarter. In the by-election, in the event unopposed, which he fought in April 1807, caused by his appointment as Chancellor of the Exchequer, he adopted the slogan 'No Popery', a stance he maintained on all the subsequent occasions on which the issue was raised in Parliament. On other issues, he showed a more subtle approach, seeking by amendment to weaken the impact of bills, such as that introduced by the leading Whig, J.C. Curwen, in 1809 to abolish the practice of selling parliamentary seats. The most difficult issue with which Perceval had to deal was the concerted effort to secure the dismissal of the Commander-in Chief of the Army, the Duke of York, following the scandal over the alleged sale of commissions by his former mistress, Mary Anne Clarke (see Chapter 4). The Duke had been hopeless as a field commander in the Flanders campaign a decade earlier, but was an effective administrator and was very popular with the troops because of his evident concern for their welfare. Moreover, there was no serious evidence that he had been involved in corruption. Perceval made a brilliant speech in the House defending the Duke, managing – against all expectation – to secure the defeat of the principal motion against him. Yet the Duke's enemies were not prepared to relent, and a further motion, backed by William Wilberforce and his group of high-minded Christians known as 'the Saints', and with whom Perceval was himself often associated, was tabled calling for his removal on account of his 'immoral conduct'. Combined with the Whig and Grenvillite opposition, this was almost certain to be carried, and Perceval succeeded in convincing an unwilling Duke, and his father, George III, that the only way to salve the situation would be for the Duke to resign, leaving open the possibility that he might be re-appointed when the excitement died down. (This is what in fact happened two years later, when Perceval as Prime Minister, recommended the Prince Regent to restore his younger brother, on the retirement of his elderly replacement, General Sir David Dundas).

The final months of the Portland government were darkened by the intrigues of the Foreign Secretary, George Canning to evict the War Secretary, Lord Castlereagh from office, and to prepare the way for his own succession or that of another figurehead Prime Minister, in the form of the Earl of Chatham (the Younger Pitt's elder brother), whom he would hope to manipulate (see Chapter 4). Perceval held himself aloof from the intrigue, and Canning overplayed his hand, repelling his colleagues by his conduct, while Chatham's prospects of the leadership evaporated with his inept conduct of the Walcheren campaign, of which he was the military commander. The consequence was that the bulk of the cabinet concluded that Perceval was the most suitable candidate for the Premiership, a view with which George III heartily concurred. The King was attracted by Perceval's anti-Catholic views, and expressed the opinion that he was 'perhaps the most straightforward man he had ever known'. The Cabinet doubted, however, that with the resignations of Canning and Castlereagh, it would be strong enough to carry on without reinforcement from the other side of the House. With the King's consent, Perceval and Liverpool therefore approached Lord Grenville and Grey to discuss the possibility of their co-operating in the formation of a new government. Perceval, who had no driving ambition to be Prime Minister, contemplated that this post would probably fall to Grenville, and hoped to take over the Home Office himself. Grenville and Grey, however, deeply distrustful, did not realize that a wide coalition, in which they would play a very considerable role, was intended. They assumed that the object was to split the opposition by offering only a few token places in what would continue to be a Pittite government, and declined to respond. They no doubt believed that, without their support, the new government would collapse, and that they would soon be called back to office. In fact, they missed their best opportunity, and condemned the Whigs to another 21 years in opposition.

In fact, it was only with the greatest difficulty that Perceval, aged just under 47, was able to construct his government. Conscious of his weak position in the House of Commons, he made an attempt to attract the support of Lord Sidmouth (formerly Henry Addington) and of Lord Melville (the former Henry Dundas), each of whom commanded the support of a significant *bloc* of MPs. Aware, however, that each of them was personally unpopular, and that their inclusion in the government might alienate other potential allies, he did not want to offer either of them cabinet posts. Instead, he sought their consent, or at least acquiescence, to an approach being made to their own leading supporters, such as Melville's son, Robert Dundas, whom he wished to appoint as Secretary for War and the Colonies. Most people in Perceval's position would have attempted to camouflage their motives, but he wrote candidly to both men setting out exactly the difficulty he was in. Neither of them reacted positively, so Perceval had to proceed initially without their support, though Robert Dundas later joined the government in a more junior capacity, while Sidmouth became Lord President of the Council over two years later. Perceval also found it impossible to find a suitable successor to himself as Chancellor of the Exchequer, a post he was most anxious to relinquish. Altogether, he approached no fewer than five possible candidates, including the young Lord Palmerston, but none of them was willing to serve. Eventually, he agreed to continue in the post, though he insisted on giving up the salary, which he was entitled to receive in addition to that of the First Lordship of the Treasury. It had taken him six weeks to form his cabinet of nine members, seven of whom were in the House of Lords.

The principal offices were filled by Richard Ryder, younger brother of his friend Dudley Ryder, as Home Secretary; the Earl of Liverpool as Secretary for War and the Colonies, Lord Eldon as Lord Chancellor and Marquess Wellesley (elder brother of the future Duke of Wellington) as Foreign Minister. Apart from Liverpool, it was not a strong team, and Perceval found that he had to carry an even heavier burden than he had under Portland. During his first year of office, he was under particular stress: his government was defeated six times in major parliamentary divisions, and it was only the stubborn support of George III, which enabled it to survive.

Several of the government defeats arose over the parliamentary enquiry into the failure of the Walcheren expedition, which had been forced by the Opposition. The government was gravely embarrassed by the attitude towards the enquiry of the Earl of Chatham, the expedition's military commander, who served in the cabinet as Master-General of the Ordnance. It was only his very belated resignation which saved the government from losing the crucial vote condemning the whole conduct of the expedition, which would certainly have led to the resignation of the government as a whole. Perceval won praise for his handling of an extremely tricky situation, but he was himself mainly to blame for the next crisis to hit the government – the arrest of the radical MP, Sir Francis Burdett.

Burdett, one of the Members for the City of London, had addressed an open letter to his constituents criticizing the House of Commons for its 'arbitrary and tyrannical use of privilege'. This followed a vote, from which Burdett had been absent through illness, committing to prison the secretary of a radical debating society, which had described the decision to exclude the public from the debates on the Walcheren enquiry as 'an insidious and ill-timed attack upon the liberty of the press, as tending to aggravate the discontents of the people, and to render their representatives objects of jealous suspicion'. Despite the view of many of his colleagues that a reprimand at the bar of the House would be a sufficient punishment for Burdett, Perceval insisted that he should be committed to the Tower of London, and forced through a motion to this effect, by 189 votes to 152. The attempt to arrest Burdett provoked the most serious street riots in London since the Gordon riots of 1780. Burdett was eventually arrested in his own home, where he was calmly teaching his son to translate the *Magna Carta*, and was transported to the Tower, where he was held from April to June 1810, when he was quietly released after Parliament had gone into recess. This episode reflected no credit at all on Perceval, but was consistent with the strong support he had given in the 1790s to the repressive actions taken against radical organizations by the Pitt government.

In October 1810, Perceval faced perhaps his greatest challenge, when the King finally plunged into insanity. The Prince of Wales, supported by all his younger brothers, exerted strong pressure to be appointed without delay as Prince Regent, with no strings attached. But Perceval refused to be hurried, and insisted on introducing a parliamentary bill, which was a replica of Pitt's measure of 1788–9, in particular severely limiting the Regent's powers of patronage during the first 12 months of his regency. Fully aware that the Prince was most likely to turn him out of office in favour of the Whigs as soon as he was appointed, Perceval refused all opportunities to appease him, and succeeded in carrying his Bill though both Houses of Parliament. It came into effect in February 1811. Then, to general surprise, after a great deal of coming and going with the main opposition leaders, Lords Grenville and Grey, the Prince Regent changed his mind about a change of government, and confirmed Perceval in office. It seems clear that Grey and Grenville, the latter in particular, mishandled their relations with the Regent, who found them less willing to defer to his wishes than he had expected. More likely, though, he had been influenced by reports from his mother that the King was well on the way to recovery, and feared what his father would do if he resumed his powers after a short interval and found that his son had dismissed his ministers for no good reason. In the event, there was no recovery; the King lived for another nine years, during which the regency continued. After 12 months, the restrictions on the Regent expired, but – an essentially indolent man – he was loath to face the disruption which a change in administration would bring. He was disappointed by his old Whig friends, and found he had more in common than he had expected, with Perceval, whose anti-Catholic views now chimed in well with his own, which more and more resembled his father's, as he grew older.

The vexed question remained of the Prince Regent's Privy Purse and what financial provision should be made for the Queen and for the now much-restricted circle of courtiers of the King. The Regent petulantly dismissed the government's proposals, demanding separate establishments for the Queen and for each of the royal princes and princesses and that Parliament should be invited to discharge his own accumulated debts, which he estimated at £522,000. Perceval would have none of this, and, after consulting the cabinet, wrote to one of the Prince's advisers to the effect that

> it was, in his opinion, best for the real dignity of the Prince Regent and 'for the maintenance of his popularity and high estimation in the country' that he should accept a scheme by which his debts 'should be discharged by means of his own privations and not by means of fresh burdens on the people'. (Gray, p. 438)

The cabinet's united front was, however, broken by Wellesley, the Foreign Secretary, who had already proved himself a most unsatisfactory colleague. Putting on the grandest airs, while grievously neglecting his routine duties, and justly suspected of intriguing behind their backs with Canning, he now saw an opportunity of ingratiating himself with the Prince Regent, in the hope of himself supplanting Perceval as Prime Minister. He therefore let it be known to the Regent that he was in favour of a more generous settlement, and when he was brought to book by an otherwise united cabinet announced his intention to resign. After much toing and froing, the Prince Regent finally acceded to the bulk of the government's proposals, and Wellesley departed from the government, to the general relief. Perceval seized the opportunity to strengthen his team by bringing in Castlereagh to succeed him, while Lord Sidmouth (Addington) finally joined the government as Lord President of the Council. The embittered Canning was left out, and sourly commented that, like measles, every one had to have Sidmouth once. (The former Prime Minister, in fact, succeeded in joining the governments of no fewer than five of his successors – Pitt, Grenville, Portland, Perceval and Liverpool). Finally, the death of the first Lord Melville left the way open for his son and heir, Robert Dundas, to take the senior post of First Lord of the Admiralty. It looked as though Perceval's government had at last reached calmer waters, and that he could look forward to a long and secure tenure of his office. Then, without warning, on the afternoon of 11 May 1812, he was shot dead in the lobby of the House of Commons. He was 49 years old, and had been Prime Minister for two years and 221 days.

His assassin, John Bellingham, was unknown to him. A merchant's clerk, working in Archangel for a Liverpool firm, he had fallen into debt, and had spent five years in a Russian prison. Convinced that the British Ambassador in St. Petersburg, Lord Granville Leveson-Gower, had done nothing to facilitate his release, he repeatedly petitioned the British government on his return to Britain for financial compensation, and worked himself up into a mania, when none of his attempts proved successful. He was determined on revenge for what he believed was a gross injustice, and thought first of killing Leveson-Gower, now a leading politician, but at the last moment decided to target the Prime Minister. As Perceval entered the lobby, he rushed up to him, held a pistol against his breast and discharged a single shot. Perceval staggered forward, cried out 'I am murdered, murdered', and fell down dead. Bellingham quietly sat down, beside his smoking pistol, and waited to be arrested. A shocked House of Commons met the next day, and voted an annuity of £2,000 for Perceval's widow and a grant of £50,000 for her children. Bellingham was tried three days later at the Old Bailey. A plea of insanity was made on his behalf, but he addressed the jury for two hours with such lucidity, saying amongst other things that he wished in retrospect that he had killed Leveson-Gower instead, that it was not seriously entertained. The jury took only ten minutes to convict him of murder. He was hanged on 18 May, a week after the assassination.

Perceval was not a great Prime Minister, but – with all his limitations – was remarkably successful in achieving what he set out to do. Assuming the premiership, which he had not consciously sought, in extremely difficult circumstances, he succeeded in rallying all the disparate factions which had supported the Younger Pitt, with the exception of the Canningites. He achieved a mastery of the House of Commons, pursued the war against France more fruitfully than any of his predecessors, handled the nation's finances with dexterity and, without appeasing the self-indulgence of the Prince Regent, managed to establish a reasonable *modus vivendi* with that difficult and unpredictable character. At the time of his death, his government had achieved more authority, and seemed more stable, than any of its predecessors since the first administration of the Younger Pitt. A highly conservative figure, he nevertheless showed surprising flexibility in handling controversial issues, with the exception of Catholic emancipation, to which his rocklike opposition was second only to that of George III. The main criticism that historians have made of Perceval is that he was too rooted in the past, and to the ideas of the Younger Pitt, to set Britain on a fresh path, and enable it to grasp the new opportunities presented by the opening years of the nineteenth century. Nor was that task adequately fulfilled by his immediate successors over the following two decades. It was, essentially, left to later leaders, both Whig and Tory, who came to power only in the 1830s, such as Grey, Melbourne and Robert Peel.

Works consulted

John W. Derry, 1990, *Politics in the Age of Fox, Pitt and Liverpool*, London, Macmillan.
Norman Gash, 1984, *Lord Liverpool*, London, Weidenfeld and Nicolson.
Mollie Gillen, 1972, *Assassination of the Prime Minister*, London, Sidgwick & Jackson.
Denis Gray, 1963, *Spencer Perceval: The Evangelical Prime Minister 1762–1812*, Manchester, Manchester University Press.
J.A. Hamilton, 1895, Article in *Dictionary of National Biography*, London, Murray.
Lucille Iremonger, 1970, *The Fiery Chariot*, London, Secker & Warburg.
Peter Jupp, 2004, Article in *Oxford Dictionary of National Biography*, Oxford, Oxford University Press.

6

Robert Banks Jenkinson, 2nd Earl of Liverpool – Keeping the Show on the Road

The R.t Hon.ble Robert Banks
EARL of LIVERPOOL.

The third longest-serving British Prime Minister was the second Earl of Liverpool, who took over the leadership of Spencer Perceval's government, following his assassination in 1812, and remained in office until April 1827. He was, effectively, the product of a one-parent family, his mother dying one month after his birth and his father not remarrying until he was 12 years old. Robert Banks Jenkinson was born in London on 7 June 1770. His father, Charles Jenkinson, was descended from a long line of baronets going back to the reign of Charles II, but whose fortune dated back to Anthony Jenkinson, a sea captain and merchant venturer in the reign of Queen Elizabeth, who had finished up as her ambassador to the Tsar of Russia and the Shah of Persia. Charles Jenkinson was a successful politician, who had become the leader of 'the King's friends' in the House of Commons, and a minister under both Lord North and the Younger Pitt. In 1769, at the age of 41, he made a financially beneficial marriage to the 18-year-old Amelia Watts, the partly Indian daughter of William Watts, a former governor of Fort William in Bengal, who had made a considerable fortune as one of the more rapacious associates of Robert Clive. She was to die, from the delayed effects of childbirth, at the age of 19, on 7 July 1770. Robert was brought up in his father's household, but spent his holidays near Winchester, either in the house of his grandmother Amarantha Cornwall, or his Aunt Elizabeth, whose husband, Charles Wolfram Cornwall, was Speaker of the House of Commons in 1780–9. Charles Jenkinson, who was to become one of the closest associates of Pitt, was created Baron Hawkesbury in 1786, and Earl of Liverpool, in 1796. He also inherited the family baronetcy in 1789, becoming the 7th Baronet. He was to marry, for a second time, in 1782, to Catherine, the wealthy widow of Sir Charles Cope. Two children were born to this marriage, Charlotte, in 1783, and Charles Cecil, in 1784.

The older Jenkinson was an able administrator, and a learned, if rather pedantic man, who wrote several scholarly works. Immensely ambitious for his son, he carefully supervized his education, which began at Albion House, a private boys' school at Parsons Green, Fulham, and continued, as a boarder, at Charterhouse, a 'public' school then located in the heart of London, near Smithfield and the Old Bailey. His father plied him with advice, both on his studies, and his manners and his personal appearance, writing on one occasion that he and the rest of the family 'look forward with anxiety to the figure you will hereafter make in the world'. He added that the chief happiness he expected to enjoy in his declining years would be derived from his son's 'prosperity and eminence' (Gash, 1984, p. 12). At 16 he left school, to enrol at Christ Church, Oxford. Though somewhat emotionally under-developed, he was better educated and much better informed than the vast majority of his fellow undergraduates, having met and conversed with such famous figures as Pitt, Edmund Burke and Lord Chancellor Thurlow at his father's dinner table. Jenkinson, who applied himself with great diligence to his studies, was admired and looked up to by many of his fellow students. These included the young George Canning, who came up to Christ Church seven months after Jenkinson, and wrote to his uncle that he was 'very clever and very remarkably good natured'. Canning and Jenkinson became very close friends, being known among their fellows as 'the inseparables', and were leading members of a small debating society, in which Jenkinson argued from a Tory, and Canning from a Whig point of view. They were, indeed, very different characters: Jenkinson, sober and industrious, distinguished himself by actually spending less than his annual allowance of £200 in his first year at Oxford. Canning, wild, witty, malicious, had a much quicker mind than his friend and rival, but was nevertheless greatly influenced by him, soon shedding his own Whig views. Jenkinson was regarded by many as being stiff and pompous, but was generally well liked; Canning soon acquired an incorrigible reputation for levity, and his mercurial temperament won him adoring friends and bitter enemies in almost equal numbers. Both of them were highly ambitious, but Jenkinson was much the more skilful at concealing this.

Jenkinson interrupted his undergraduate career after only 26 months to embark on the first stage of the Grand Tour, which was a common feature of the lives of young aristocrats in the late eighteenth and early nineteenth centuries. This took him to Paris in July 1789, where his father had arranged for him to meet a range of dignitaries, and where he planned to perfect his already good knowledge of French. A week after his arrival, on 14 July, he happened to be, his biographer recalls, among 'the great crowd of Parisians who watched the storming of the Bastille and saw the rioters, including numbers of women, at their horrid work of destruction and slaughter. It was a spectacle which gave him a distaste for revolutions' (Gash, 1984, p. 16). He returned to Oxford in October, and the following May, being excused, as the son of a peer, from taking the BA examination, was proclaimed as a Master of Arts. Within a month, he had been elected a Member of Parliament, in the June 1790 general election, won easily by the Pitt government. His father arranged for him to stand in two constituencies, Appleby in Cumberland, controlled by the famous borough-monger, Lord Lonsdale (formerly Sir James Lowther) and Rye, in Kent, a pocket borough controlled by the Treasury. In both constituencies he was elected unopposed, but chose to represent Rye, which continued to elect him unopposed until 1803, when he was elevated to the peerage. Jenkinson was just 20 years old, and did not attempt to take his seat until a year later, when he attained the legal minimum of 21. Instead, he embarked on the second stage of his Grand Tour, which took in Rome, Naples and Florence.

Jenkinson's maiden speech was given in February 1792. A confident performance, lasting over an hour, it was devoted to foreign affairs, discussing the European balance of power, the value of the Prussian alliance and the apparent military weakness of France. By contrast, he was highly critical of the growing strength of Russia, which he foresaw would represent a serious threat to the European balance. The speech was favourably received, being praised by Pitt in his reply to the debate, and also in his written report to the King. Thereafter, Jenkinson spoke only sparingly in the House, on one occasion opposing Wilberforce's motion to abolish the slave trade. It was an unconvincing speech, probably made to please his father, now Lord Hawkesbury, who was a leading opponent of abolition in the House of Lords.

When the House rose for the summer recess, in June, Jenkinson resumed his continental travels, leaving for Holland, Germany and France. He visited the Austrian and Prussian forces now massing to cross into France in the confident hope of squashing the French revolution, and sent back letters to his father shrewdly assessing their relative competence, being much more impressed by the Prussians. News of the visit by this well-connected young MP soon spread, and in French circles it was widely believed that Jenkinson had been personally sent by Pitt in order to make contact with their enemies. This seems improbable, but Jenkinson certainly returned from his travels in a much more hostile mood towards France. Relations between the two countries were fast deteriorating, and the opposition, led by Charles James Fox and Charles Grey, tabled a resolution urging the dispatch of a mission to Paris to negotiate a settlement of all outstanding difficulties so as to prevent the slide to war. Jenkinson fiercely attacked the motion, saying that it would be 'infamous' to send an ambassador to 'bow his neck to a band of sanguinary ruffians'. Jenkinson's attitude was shared by the bulk of the House of Commons, and Fox's motion was negatived without a division. Hostilities with France began in February 1793, and when Fox moved a set of resolutions condemning the outbreak of war, Jenkinson was put up by the government to move the previous question, bringing the debate to a premature end. Pitt was, again, mightily impressed, and wrote to George III described his speech as one of 'uncommon ability and effect' (Gash, 1984, p. 24). Two months later, he created a less favourable impression in a debate on the unsuccessful operations at Toulon and Dunkirk, suggesting that the 'soundest military strategy would be to strike at the heart of the enemy and march on Paris itself'. This seemed a far-fetched notion to a generation brought up on eighteenth century principles of warfare and he was widely ridiculed for his supposed naivety. Gash points out, however, that this was to be precisely the strategy soon to be followed against his enemies by Napoleon, with devastating effect, and that it might well have been the best course for Britain to take in 1793 (Gash, 1984, p. 24).

Jenkinson resumed his friendship with Canning, and almost certainly was instrumental in drawing him to the attention of Pitt. This may well have helped Canning's own search for a parliamentary seat, and in June 1793 he was returned unopposed at a by-election in Newtown, Isle of Wight (the first of no fewer than seven constituencies which he was to represent in a tumultuous parliamentary career). They then again became almost as inseparable as they had been at Oxford, dining frequently together at Jenkinson's house in Conduit Street, before proceeding together to the House of Commons. While the friendship was wholehearted on Jenkinson's side, Gash suggests that

> Canning's feelings towards Jenkinson still had an element of contempt of a kind not uncommon in a clever, witty young man towards a duller, loyal companion. It was an example followed by many of Canning's friends and admirers ... His moral seriousness, his slightly odd physical appearance, made him something of a butt among the bright, amusing, somewhat malicious young men who gathered round Canning. (Gash, 1984, pp. 25–6)

Although tall, Jenkinson did not present an impressive figure. He had a melancholy air, a conspicuously long neck, and an awkward, shambling gait, much parodied by cartoonists. To the young Canningites, Gash adds, 'it was vexing that such an unmodish figure should be ahead of them in the parliamentary race'. Jenkinson did not have to wait long before Pitt offered him preferment. In June 1793, shortly after his twenty-third birthday, he was appointed to the Board of Control set up to supervise the affairs of the East India Company. The other members were all senior figures, including Pitt himself, Henry Dundas, Lord Grenville and Lord Mornington (the future Marquess Wellesley). At Pitt's urging, too, Jenkinson, who had already enrolled in the militia organized in the face of the threat of a possible French invasion, assumed a colonelcy in the Cinque Ports Regiment of Fencible Cavalry, organized by the Prime Minister himself. He took his duties extremely seriously, and much of his time was now absorbed by military activity, despite the mockery of Canning, who once reduced Jenkinson to tears by mercilessly lampooning him in the company of their friends. The ever-forgiving Jenkinson soon made it up with him, after an estrangement lasting several weeks. It was at about this time that Jenkinson fell in love. The object of his affections was Lady Louisa Hervey, the youngest daughter of the eccentric 4th Marquess of Bristol, an inveterate traveller after whom the numerous Bristol hotels in European cities were named. A former Bishop of Derry, who had unexpectedly inherited the marquessate after the death of his two elder brothers, he promptly separated from his wife of 30 years' duration, leaving her to bring up Louisa in a very strait-laced household in the country. His two, much older, elder daughters both made disastrous marriages, and then attained notoriety by their promiscuousness, so the whole family was living under something of a cloud. Louisa, who was three years older than Jenkinson, shared neither the eccentricities of her father nor the vices of her sisters, but was nevertheless regarded by the elder Jenkinson (now Lord Hawkesbury) as an unsuitable wife for his son. He did not want his family to be associated with that of Lord Bristol, who, apart from his other shortcomings, was a Whig. It was only after Pitt, and even George III, had personally remonstrated with him that he gave his consent to the marriage, which took place on 25 March 1795. He then soon forgot his earlier opposition and warmly welcomed Louisa into the family fold. Jenkinson was then 24; he and Louisa became a devoted couple, though they were to remain childless.

In 1796, his father was created the 1st Earl of Liverpool, and Jenkinson assumed the courtesy title of Lord Hawkesbury, by which he was known until he inherited the earldom in 1808. Three years later, he was appointed Master of the Mint, previously a sinecure, but now involving a number of duties, for which he was offered the salary of £2,500 a year, which, at his father's prompting, he negotiated up to £3,000. With this appointment came membership of the Privy Council, and it seemed only a matter of time before Pitt would bring him into his government. Instead, Pitt resigned in 1801, when the King vetoed his proposals for Catholic emancipation. Pitt urged his friends to carry on and support the new Prime Minister, Henry Addington, but many refused to do so, including Lord Grenville, the Foreign Secretary, Henry Dundas, Lord Spencer and William Windham, from the cabinet, and Castlereagh, Canning and Granville Leveson-Gower from more junior posts. When Addington offered the 30-year-old Lord Hawkesbury the Foreign Office, his father, who was also in the cabinet, was delighted; Hawkesbury, over-awed by his lack of experience, rather less so. He would probably have preferred a less dazzling promotion at this stage, but having assured himself of Pitt's goodwill, nevertheless accepted. His immediate brief was to negotiate peace terms with France, but Addington, himself a poor parliamentary performer, was also desperately in need of his debating power in the House of Commons, his other cabinet ministers all being in the House of Lords.

It was not easy for the young Hawkesbury to take control of the Foreign Office. Many of the senior diplomats, loyal to Lord Grenville throughout his long tenure as Foreign Secretary, found it difficult to adjust to a younger and inexperienced chief. Grenville himself, though initially giving Hawkesbury friendly encouragement, became more and more critical as the peace negotiations (with which he fundamentally disagreed) proceeded. Hawkesbury was also, understandably, the object of jealousy from contemporaries (including Canning and his circle) who felt he had been promoted beyond his merits. Nevertheless, he created a favourable impression by his parliamentary speeches, and the negotiations continued until, in March 1802, the Treaty of Amiens was signed (see Chapter 2). It proved widely popular in a war-weary nation, and was welcomed by virtually all political leaders with the exception of Grenville. Some of them, however, privately felt that too much had been conceded to the French negotiators, who were led by the wily Talleyrand.

The peace gradually unravelled over the following 14 months, largely because of Napoleon's continued intervention in the affairs of neighbouring states, including Switzerland, and Holland, and the British reluctance to withdraw from Malta under the terms of the Treaty. The British ambassador to Paris reported that the payment of a large bribe to the Bonaparte family might secure agreement to the British annexation of the island, suggesting £2 million, as an appropriate sum. Hawkesbury responded with an offer of a mere £100,000, and nothing came of the proposal. A last minute offer from the Tsar of Russia to mediate between the two countries was rejected, causing anger to the Tsar, a possible ally in the renewed war which Britain declared in May 1803. In retrospect, Hawkesbury and his colleagues have been criticized both for their handling of the peace negotiations and for precipitating the renewed outbreak of war. As Gash put it, 'having been too conciliatory in 1801–2, they were too inflexible in 1802–3' (Gash, 1984, p. 48). The consequence was that when the Addington government finally resigned, in May 1804, to make way for Pitt's second administration, Hawkesbury's tenure of the Foreign Office was not seen as an unmitigated success. He had shown himself a good administrator, and his parliamentary performances had been impressive, but his political judgement and general 'feel' for the situation left something to be desired. Nevertheless, having spent three years holding very senior office, he emerged from the government with a greatly enhanced status. He had also ceased to be a member of the House of Commons, being created Baron Hawkesbury, in his own right, in November 1803, to become Leader of the House of Lords. It was not a move he welcomed, but he loyally agreed when Addington told him it was essential to counter the growing opposition from Lord Grenville, who was a dominant figure in the upper house. In any event, he was destined for the Lords on the death of his father, who was still President of the Board of Trade, but seldom attended cabinet meetings because of ill health. In fact, he was to live for another five years.

When Pitt formed his second government, he was determined to retain the services of Hawkesbury, but not as Foreign Secretary. This he gave to Lord Harrowby, the former Dudley Ryder, and Hawkesbury reluctantly accepted the less senior and, in his eyes, less interesting post of Home Secretary. This was, nevertheless one of the most important posts in the government, and Hawkesbury retained his position as Leader of the Lords. He was undoubtedly one of the pivotal members of the cabinet, which was made up in almost equal parts by survivors from the Addington administration and by Pitt's personal followers. These, to his chagrin, did not include the impatient George Canning, who, with ill grace, had to content himself with the non-cabinet post of Treasurer of the Navy. When Harrowby was forced to relinquish his office through ill health, Canning brashly volunteered himself as a successor, only to be rebuffed by Pitt, who excused himself by saying he did not want to hurt Hawkesbury's feelings. He nevertheless did not restore him to his former post, but instead appointed the relatively uncontroversial Lord Mulgrave. The resentful

Canning then proceeded to intrigue against Hawkesbury, which strained their friendship to the limit. Hawkesbury's tenure of the Home Office was uneventful, but he showed his qualities as a thoroughly reliable team player, while the post brought him into close contact with George III, who formed the highest opinion of his abilities.

When Pitt died, in January 1806, Hawkesbury was the King's first choice as his successor. Believing that he would not be able to form a viable government, Hawkesbury declined, but the King then pressed on him the valuable sinecure of Warden of the Cinque Ports, which had been held by Pitt. This was worth £5,000 a year, which, together with an increased allowance from his father, enabled him fully to maintain his income when the King next turned to Lord Grenville and invited him to form his 'Government of All the Talents'. This, as recounted in Chapter 3, did not include the Pittites, and Hawkesbury went into opposition for the first time since his election to Parliament. He then formed part of a quartet of experienced former ministers, along with Castlereagh, Perceval and Canning who, under the nominal leadership of the Duke of Portland, were responsible for organizing the parliamentary opposition in both Houses. They did not have to wait long to return to office. Just over a year after being sworn in, the Grenville government was sent packing by George III for refusing to give an undertaking not to revive the issue of Catholic emancipation during the King's lifetime. The Duke of Portland was asked to form a new government, in which Hawkesbury returned to the Home Office, Perceval became Chancellor of the Exchequer and Leader of the House of Commons, Canning Foreign Secretary and Castlereagh Secretary for War and the Colonies. Hawkesbury, who retained the leadership of the House of Lords, was a pivotal member of the Cabinet, and – together with Perceval – was responsible for whatever degree of co-ordination there was between ministries in what, under the feeble leadership of Portland was essentially a 'government of departments' rather than a centralized team. When he learnt of Canning's intrigues against Castlereagh (see Chapter 3), he was appalled, and he threw his weight decisively in favour of Perceval when he and Canning appeared to be the most likely candidates to succeed Portland as Prime Minister. The scandal of the duel between Canning and Castlereagh in the dying days of the Portland government, in any event, put both of them out of the running for inclusion in the new government, which Perceval formed in October 1809. By then, Hawkesbury had succeeded to the Earldom of Liverpool, on the death of his father the previous year, and in Perceval's government he succeeded Castlereagh as Secretary for War and the Colonies. The new Home Secretary was Richard Ryder (Lord Harrowby's younger brother), and the Foreign Secretary was Marquess Wellesley.

Liverpool continued to act as Leader of the House of Lords, and was now generally regarded as the number two man in the government. His over-riding concern as War Minister was to sustain the up-and-down campaign of the British forces in the Iberian Peninsula. The commander, now known as Viscount Wellington, was much the ablest of the British generals, but was notoriously grumpy and difficult to deal with. He had a low opinion of politicians, with the exception of Castlereagh, whom he regarded as the only minister who had ever given him solid support. He therefore did not initially welcome Liverpool's appointment, but gradually warmed to him, as he discovered that the new minister was determined to fight his political battles for him, and would do all he could to maximize the flow of reinforcements, supplies and financial support, while leaving him a maximum of flexibility in military strategy. Liverpool did not, of course, have an entirely free hand; not only the Treasury, but also the Commander-in-Chief and the Master-General of the Ordnance were intimately involved in many of the decisions which needed to be taken. His biographer probably understated Liverpool's problems in writing: 'With the Treasury, controlled by politicians like himself, Liverpool's relations were close; with the two successive commanders in chief, first Sir David Dundas and then, from May 1811, the Duke of York, they were correct; with the Ordnance, distant and sometimes difficult' (Gash, 1984, p. 82).

Liverpool, however, whose diplomatic skills were formidable, usually managed to get his way, and by the time he left the War Office, in June 1812, the ultimate success of the Peninsular campaign seemed no longer in doubt. A month later, Wellington's great victory at Salamanca sealed all his efforts. By then, Liverpool was ensconced in 10 Downing Street, a transition which had been far from smooth. The assassination of Perceval, on 11 May 1812 left the cabinet devastated, but they rapidly came to two conclusions. One was that the only possible successor, among their midst, was Liverpool. The second was that it would be difficult, if not impossible, for the government to remain in office unless it was reinforced by at least one of the opposing groups in Parliament. Their preference was to approach Canning and Wellesley rather than Grenville and Grey, the leaders of the Whigs. These conclusions were reported to the Prince Regent, who authorized an approach to Canning and Wellesley, both of whom rejected the offer to serve under Liverpool, Canning on the ostensible grounds of the government's refusal to consider Catholic emancipation, while Wellesley, who still hoped to secure the premiership for himself, advanced a number of objections. Soundings with Grenville and Grey were no more encouraging, and the Regent then invited Wellesley to form an administration, but the existing cabinet was unanimous in refusing to serve under him, as were Grenville and Grey. Wellesley then threw in the towel, and the exasperated Regent then passed the commission on to Lord Moira, a professional soldier and long-time favourite of the Prince. The best he could come up with was a sort of 'second eleven' of Pittites, with himself as a figurehead Prime Minister and Canning as First Lord of the Treasury and Leader of the House of Commons. The Regent was sensible enough to see that this would not do, and told Moira to 'settle it all with Eldon [the Lord Chancellor] and Liverpool', leaving them a free hand as to ministerial appointments. This was not the way his father, George III, had conducted his cabinet-making.

Liverpool became Prime Minister on 8 June 1812, the day after his forty-second birthday. Two months earlier, he had personally persuaded Lord Sidmouth to join Perceval's cabinet as Lord President of the Council, and he now decided that the best way to strengthen the government was to give him a more central role, thus cementing the support of the sizeable Addingtonian group in the Commons. Sidmouth thus became Home Secretary, his brother-in-law, Charles Bragge, Chancellor of the Duchy of Lancaster, and his leading supporter, Nicholas Vansittart, Chancellor of the Exchequer. Castlereagh remained Foreign Secretary and Leader of the House of Commons, and Lord Eldon continued as Lord Chancellor. A year later, in June 1813, he made another attempt to persuade Canning to join his government, offering him the post of Foreign Secretary, which Castlereagh was prepared to relinquish. Yet Canning, as so often, overplayed his hand, demanding that he should also become Leader of the House of Commons – something which Liverpool was not prepared to concede.

Liverpool's first three years in office were dominated by the concluding stages of the Napoleonic Wars, victory in which was his over-riding priority. Napoleon's retreat from Moscow had fatally weakened him, and Liverpool responded by enabling Wellington to step up the pressure in Spain, leading to the victory at Vitoria, in June 1813, and the crossing of the Pyrenees into France on 1 August. The final battle in the campaign was won at Toulouse, in April 1814. Meanwhile, Liverpool's resourceful Foreign Secretary, Viscount Castlereagh MP, was equally active on the diplomatic front, successfully offering subsidies to Prussia, Sweden and Austria to join Russia, and re-enter the war against Napoleon's depleted forces. Their decisive victory at Leipzig, in the so-called Battle of the Nations, in November 1813, foreshadowed Napoleon's final defeat, though it was only in the following April that he abdicated and surrendered to the allied forces.

The victory, after so many years, was celebrated with great enthusiasm and pageantry in London, which welcomed the visits of the Tsar Alexander, the King of Prussia, and Marshal Blücher, in June 1814, while Wellington received a dukedom, and both Liverpool and Castlereagh were invested as Knights of the Garter. Liverpool then despatched Castlereagh to Vienna, where the rulers of the victorious powers were to be engaged for many months in redrawing the map of Europe. As with Wellington, in the Peninsular War, Liverpool gave Castlereagh maximum flexibility, having agreed with him, and the cabinet, in advance on Britain's principal aims. These included the re-establishment as independent powers of Portugal, Spain and the Netherlands (now to include Belgium), and the restriction of France to its borders of 1790, without, however, stripping her of any of her ancient territories. Liverpool feared that if this were to happen it would so weaken the authority of the restored Bourbon monarchy that it would be vulnerable to a further Revolution, probably led by Jacobins. All these objectives Castlereagh was able to achieve, but the restoration of Poland, another British aim, was beyond even his powers of negotiation. In fact, the main business of the Congress was an uninhibited struggle to grab territory between the three main eastern allies, with the future of Poland and Saxony being the main bones of contention. On Poland, the issue was essentially whether Russia should be permitted to swallow up the whole country, with Austria and Prussia being compensated by gains further to the west, including Alsace and part of Lorraine from France. The alternative was that the three countries should each retain the parts of Poland, which they had annexed in three successive partitions between 1772 and 1795. Castlereagh considered that this was the lesser of two evils and threw his influence behind this arrangement, which was eventually agreed, though the Russian share of the spoils was substantially increased. The Kingdom of Saxony had been an ally of Napoleon, and both Austria and Prussia sought to annex it outright. At one point, the two Germanic powers were on the brink of going to war over the issue, but cooler heads eventually prevailed and, though truncated, it was awarded to neither power, preserving a precarious independence, which lasted until 1871, though formally until 1918.

No sooner was Castlereagh back in Britain than Napoleon escaped from Elba, and Liverpool and his government were adamant that he should be prevented, at all costs, from re-establishing himself. A Commons motion moved by the radical MP, Sir Francis Burdett, that Britain should follow a policy of non-intervention, attracted a mere 37 votes. It was clear that the government's determination was supported by an overwhelming majority of the public. Wellington, who happened to be in the Netherlands on a visit, was instructed to remain, and prepare a new British army around the small garrison already stationed there, which was immediately reinforced by the dispatch of several regiments from Ireland. Between April and June, the force was increased from 4,000 to over 32,000 men. Castlereagh sent instructions to the British delegation in Vienna to offer yet further subsidies to the allied powers to accelerate their own military preparations. That Napoleon's comeback was definitively halted at Waterloo, on 18 June, was as much due to Liverpool's urgent reaction as it was to the soldiers of Wellington and Blücher. When Napoleon surrendered to a British ship a month later, Liverpool insisted that there should be no question of negotiating with him, and that he should this time be exiled to an island under British control, much more remote and better guarded than Elba. He was duly dispatched to St. Helena in the warship *Northumberland* less than two months after the battle. At the resumed Congress of Vienna, Castlereagh revived an old vision of the Younger Pitt's, by successfully seeking agreement that the great European powers should establish a 'concert of Europe', consulting on a regular basis on how to maintain peace and resolve international conflicts. Four other congresses were held between the four powers, until 1822, when the British walked out of the Congress of Verona, in protest against a decision by the other three powers to authorize a French intervention in Spain to quell a revolt against the restored Bourbon monarchy. Nor did Britain formally adhere to the Holy Alliance, advocated by the Tsar Alexander and enthusiastically endorsed by Austria and Prussia, which soon degenerated into an instrument to maintain the *status quo* by intervening in the affairs of sovereign states to prevent political change. A final congress was held in St. Petersburg, in 1825, not attended by Britain, and the congress system was then abandoned.

Liverpool and his government emerged from the war with greatly enhanced prestige, though this soon evaporated, as post-war problems built up, and an economic recession set in. Unemployment, boosted by a precipitate demobilization of the armed forces, soared, and civil disorders abounded. A prominent element was the Luddite movement of hand-workers displaced by new machinery. They banded together to smash up the machines, but were met by savage repression from the government, including numerous hangings and transportations. By 1818 the Luddite movement was effectively destroyed, but its place had been taken by an upsurge in political radicalism, with the formation of numerous political clubs and societies. They presented renewed demands for electoral reform, going far beyond the relatively modest demands supported by the Whig opposition. The government, thoroughly alarmed, feared that revolutionary violence would soon break out, and responded by reactivating some of Pitt's repressive legislation of the 1790's, including the suspension of *habeas corpus*. The so-called Peterloo massacre, in August 1819, when local magistrates sent cavalry in to break up a mass open-air meeting in St. Peter's Fields, Manchester, address by the radical orator, Henry Hunt, causing 11 deaths and 400 hundred injuries, was the worst act of repression, and prompted the Whigs to organize mass protest meetings throughout the country. One of these, in Yorkshire, was sponsored by the great Whig magnate, Earl Fitzwilliam, the Lord Lieutenant of the county, who was promptly dismissed by the government from his post. The government then brought in even harsher legislation, known as the 'Six Acts', which Liverpool admitted in the House Lords was 'odious' to him, but which he regarded as a temporary necessity. In practice, the Acts were applied very sparingly, but this did not prevent his government from being labelled as one of the most reactionary in British history. Much of the blame was attributed to Castlereagh, who carried the legislation through the House of Commons, and was famously stigmatised in a poem by Shelley:

> I met Murder on the way
> He had a mask like Castlereagh

The real authors of the Six Acts, however, were Lords Sidmouth and Eldon, who had to be restrained by their Cabinet colleagues from introducing even more draconian measures. It is easy to categorize Liverpool's government as paranoid, seeing non-violent advocates of reform as bloodthirsty Jacobins. Not all the revolutionary plots dreamed up by informers and *agents provocateurs*, however, were imaginary. The Cato Street conspiracy, of 1820, was a plan to murder the entire Cabinet, while it dined at the house of Lord Harrowby, the Lord President of the Council, and subsequently to seize control of London. The conspirators, led by the extreme radical, Arthur Thistlewood, were arrested just in time; five were hanged and five transported for life.

At no time during his premiership was Liverpool (whose position was made more difficult by his membership of the House of Lords) in command of a solid majority in the House of Commons. The membership was fragmented, and though the Pittites (most of whom now recognized themselves as Tories) and the Whigs were the two largest factions, there was a large number of uncommitted MPs, mostly country gentry, who though they usually voted with the government could never be taken for granted. The great majority of MPs were landed aristocrats, or their nominees, and in the post-war period they had two overwhelming objectives. The first was to reduce taxation, in particular the hated income tax, and the other was to secure the landed interest in a time of recession. Also the support of the monarch was not anything like as potent a force as in earlier times. George III may have had strong prejudices and little patience with ministers who were unwilling to follow his will, but he was, on the whole, a popular figure in the country and the object of deep respect and deference from almost the entire political class. If he wished to sustain even an unpopular ministry he had many ways, including the generous use of patronage, to keep it in power. With the Prince Regent (later George IV), it was a different matter. Regarded as a lazy voluptuary, he enjoyed neither popularity in the country, nor respect from his ministers. His available powers of patronage had, moreover, been greatly reduced by reform legislation under Pitt, Grenville and Perceval which had led to the abolition of many sinecure posts, including even that held by Liverpool himself, the Wardenship of the Cinque Ports, or at least the salary attached to it.

The consequence was that, in order to placate MPs, Liverpool had to take two painful decisions, which went very much against his own convictions. Alarmed at the high level of the national debt, after more than 20 years of conflict, he wished to continue with the temporary wartime expedient of income tax for at least a few years, in order to help reduce the size of the debt. The House of Commons would have none of this, and, in March 1816, roundly defeated the government's proposal by 238 votes to 201. In consequence the government was forced to abolish the tax, borrow an additional £5–6 million from the Bank of England, and embark on successive rounds of expenditure cuts, gravely weakening the armed force in the process. Even before this, in order to protect the prosperity of the agricultural interest, the government felt compelled to introduce the notorious 'Corn law', under which foreign grain could not be imported unless the price of wheat climbed to over 80s. a quarter. Liverpool, a close student of the works of Adam Smith, was a convinced free trader, and tried to water down the government's bill, proposing a sliding scale, rather than an inflexible cut-off point at 80s. He was not able to convince his colleagues. The original proposal went through, guaranteeing protectionism for agriculture for over 30 years, and laying up trouble for his protégé, Sir Robert Peel, when he became Prime Minister in the 1840s (see Chapter 12).

By 1820 economic recovery had set in, and the government's position seemed a great deal more secure. But the death of the old, blind, mad King, after 60 years on the throne, presaged a major political crisis. Now that he was on the throne in his own right, George IV determined to secure a divorce from his Queen, the former Princess Caroline, who had lived abroad since 1814. Having appointed his own three-man commission to investigate the apparently ample evidence of her sexual misdemeanours, George pressed the cabinet to introduce a 'Bill of pains and penalties' to strip the new Queen of her title and to end her marriage by act of Parliament. The government, rightly fearing that the proceedings would be infinitely damaging to George himself, as it would inevitably throw the spotlight on his own multiple infidelities throughout the 25 years of their marriage, was highly reluctant to take this step. George thereupon promptly invited Lord Grenville to form a new government, an offer which the former Prime Minister of 'the government of the all the talents' abruptly declined (see Chapter 3). Liverpool and his colleagues then agreed, in August 1820, to introduce the Bill in the House of Lords. Known popularly, if inaccurately, as the Trial of the Queen, who sat in the public gallery throughout its proceedings, it was one of the most dramatic and sensational events in parliamentary history. Huge numbers of people tried to attend the debates, which were reported by a press overwhelmingly sympathetic to the Queen and hostile to the King, as was virtually the whole of the opposition. The proceedings went extremely badly for the King, and the Bill only scraped through the House with a majority of nine votes. Realizing that there was no possibility of it passing the House of Commons, given the state of public opinion, Liverpool announced on 10 November that he was withdrawing the Bill. The Queen became something of a national hero, but her popularity did not last long. At George's coronation, to which she was not invited, in July 1821, she tried to force her way into Westminster Abbey, but her way was barred, and she was heartily booed by the crowd. A current epigram reflected the fickleness of public favour:

> Most Gracious Queen, we thee implore
> To go away and sin no more

> But, if that effort be too great
> To go away at any rate. (Smith, p. 147)

Within less than a month, Caroline was dead, struck down by an intestinal complaint.

Liverpool was constantly on the alert for possibilities of strengthening his Cabinet, and in 1816 at last succeeded in recruiting Canning, who – by now desperate to regain office – accepted the relatively junior post of President of the Board of Control, effectively the minister for Indian affairs. He represented a considerable reinforcement of the government's debating power in the Commons. Two years later, he carried off an even greater coup by persuading the Duke of Wellington to join the cabinet as Master-General of the Ordnance. His prowess as a parliamentary debater was less obvious, but his enormous prestige added greatly to the general standing of the government. Of all Liverpool's colleagues, the key figure during his first 10 years in office, was Castlereagh. He carried the double burden of Foreign Secretary and Leader of the House of Commons. In both tasks, he was a conspicuous success. Not an outstanding orator, by unfailing courtesy and quiet diligence, he commended himself to his fellow MPs, and the government consistently did far better than expected in the division lobbies. Castlereagh was highly valued by Liverpool, who undoubtedly saw him as his favoured successor. Yet he was probably a manic-depressive, and the accumulated strain of performing two such demanding jobs for so long eventually got the better of him. In August 1822, a year after he had succeeded his father as the 2nd Marquess of Londonderry, he cut his throat with a penknife, after receiving a blackmail threat over his alleged, but far from substantiated, homosexuality. Liverpool was devastated, but soon concluded that the only possible successor would be Canning, who was about to leave for India to take up the appointment of Governor-General. The problem was that Canning had become *persona non grata* to George IV, who regarded him with as much hostility as George III had shown to Charles James Fox. But the younger George lacked his father's iron will, and when Liverpool firmly insisted on the choice of Canning, he reluctantly gave way. Canning took over both of Castlereagh's posts, carrying on the general lines of his foreign policy, but with rather more *panache*. In the Commons, he was markedly less conciliatory, but proved a more effective expositor of government policy. Also, in 1822, a significant promotion brought the 30-year-old Sir Robert Peel to the Home Office, replacing Sidmouth, who remained in the cabinet, though without portfolio. At this time, Liverpool brought off another notable feat, by cementing an alliance with the Grenvillites, who had broken off their alliance with the main opposition Whigs some years earlier. Lord Grenville himself was no longer interested in office, but Charles Wynn joined the cabinet as President of the Board of Control, and a dukedom was offered to Grenville's nephew, Lord Buckingham, an honour that his father had vainly sought on several occasions from George III. With the adherence of the Grenvillites, Liverpool had finally succeeded in reuniting all the factions which had supported the Younger Pitt. In January 1823, there was a further reconstruction of the government, when Frederick Robinson replaced Vansittart as Chancellor of the Exchequer and William Huskisson became President of the Board of Trade. Both these men were supporters of Canning, and their appointment reflected his growing influence in the government. These changes set the pattern for the final years of Liverpool's ministry.

In June 1821, Liverpool's wife, Louisa, who had been in bad health for some time, died at the age of 54. He was severely affected, but sought to bury himself even more deeply in his work than before. Eighteen months later, at the age of 52, he was to marry a second time. His 46-year old bride was Mary Chester, a long-time close friend of his first wife. There were no children from either marriage. Liverpool's health, also, began to decline at this time; he suffered from a painful form of thrombophlebitis in his left leg, and often had to take the waters at Bath. Though basically a calm man, he became more irritable, and was described by one of his ministers as 'a great fidgett'. Despite his failing health, the beginning of the 1820s marked the most successful period of his premiership. The post-war difficulties were effectively over, with the economy now booming and the upsurge of radicalism on the wane. In 1819, Liverpool had geared himself up to make a stand against the incessant demands of the Commons for tax cuts, and presented a budget involving some £3 million in new taxes, with the aim of producing an annual surplus of £5 million. He made it clear that this was a matter of confidence, telling his fearful Lord Chancellor that 'If we cannot carry what has been proposed, it is far, far better for the country that we should cease to be the Government' (Gash, 2004). Despite a fierce onslaught by George Tierney, the leader of the Whigs in the Commons, a large majority of MPs swallowed their dislike of the new tax proposals and backed the government in what proved a turning point in their economic policies. From then onwards, there was a steady surplus in the national accounts, and the national debt began to fall. By the middle of the decade, when tax cuts became a realistic possibility, Liverpool insisted that these should be directed at the reduction of tariffs, encouraging home consumption and lowering the cost of raw materials. 'The budgets of 1824 and 1825 constituted the first free trade budgets of the century', according to Gash (2004). He thus established a claim to be considered as a forerunner of Cobden and Gladstone, as a pioneer of free trade. The fortunate presenter of these two budgets, the Chancellor of the Exchequer, Frederick Robinson, collected most of the credit for their immediate beneficial effects, and was accorded the sobriquet 'Prosperity' Robinson.

Yet apart from its later budgetary and free trade policies, Liverpool's government could in no sense be categorized as a reforming ministry. It was essentially a conservative administration, and it largely chose to ignore the two most pressing *political* issues with which it was faced: the twin demands for electoral reform and Catholic emancipation. Liverpool was opposed to both, though in a less stubborn way than, for instance, Perceval or Sidmouth (Addington). In each case, he was prepared to countenance minor concessions in order to stave off more far-reaching changes. Thus, while firmly opposing all the general reform bills presented by opposition MPs, he acquiesced in the demand to disfranchise one of the most notorious 'rotten boroughs'. In 1821 Lord John Russell had carried a bill in the House of Commons to take away the two seats from Grampound, after a case of gross corruption, and award them to the fast-growing city of Leeds, which had no separate representation. When the Bill reached the House of Lords, Liverpool rejected the award of the seats to Leeds, and successfully amended the proposal to grant them to the County of Yorkshire, then the most populous constituency in the country, with 20,000 electors. Henceforth it was to have, uniquely, four members.

Similarly, on Catholic emancipation, Liverpool was prepared to accept Catholics on the electoral roll but not as Members of Parliament. The Catholic issue was evenly more divisive and explosive than political reform. George IV was not such a hard-line opponent as George III had been, but largely shared his father's views and would not lightly have consented to legislation. The political world, including Liverpool's own government, was deeply split, and the only way that Liverpool could hold his team together was by declaring government neutrality on the issue, leaving individual members free to express their own views. Initially, the division of opinion within the Cabinet was fairly even, but with the passage of time, and especially after Canning joined the cabinet, the proportion of pro-Catholics grew steadily, until eventually only Liverpool and his Home Secretary, Robert Peel, were opposed. Meanwhile, during the 1820s – partly under the stimulus of Daniel O'Connell's campaigning Catholic Association in Ireland – pressure for change reached boiling point. In 1821, for the first time, a bill was passed in the House of Commons for the enfranchisement of Roman Catholics. Prompted by a hostile speech by the Duke of York, heir presumptive to the throne, it was defeated by the House of Lords.

The following year, the Commons backed a bill, proposed by Canning (temporarily out of the government), to admit Catholics to the House of Lords, by a majority of 12. Again it was reversed by the Lords, and Liverpool thought that the writing was on the wall. He now concluded that emancipation was inevitable, but that his would not be the administration to bring it in. When a third Bill, proposed by Sir Francis Burdett, passed the Commons in 1825, he and Peel both decided to resign unless, which they did not expect, it was rejected in the Lords by a wide margin. This would have opened the way to a new government pledged to carry the measure. The cabinet, alarmed by this prospect, rallied round, and despite the objections of Canning, helped to ensure its defeat, by the substantial majority of 48 votes. Both Peel and Liverpool then agreed to carry on, but Liverpool's health was now fast declining, and few expected him to wait much longer before quietly bowing out. In fact, the end of his premiership came abruptly, when, on 17 February 1827, he had a massive cerebral haemorrhage, and was temporarily paralysed. The King waited for a decent interval, and then sent for Canning to form a new government. Liverpool had served for 14 years and 305 days, a term only exceeded by Robert Walpole and the Younger Pitt. He recovered partially, and was to outlive his immediate successor, who died the following August. He lingered on, a mere shadow of his former self, until 4 December 1828, when he died aged 58.

Liverpool has hardly received his due from posterity. Too facilely dismissed by Disraeli as an 'arch mediocrity', he has been strangely neglected by historians. The only full-length biography appeared as long ago as 1868, though Norman Gash's much shorter life, which appeared in 1984, is highly informative and perceptive. What emerges from his picture is a man who was not highly gifted, but possessed a multitude of small talents, which together made him an extremely effective politician. Pre-eminent among these was his ability to win the confidence of his colleagues. At all times, his cabinet contained powerful and controversial figures, along with the normal complement of nonentities, yet he managed to harness their energies in such a way that it worked together as a cohesive team, perhaps more so than any of its predecessors. He effectively established the principle of collective cabinet responsibility, to which the Younger Pitt had unsuccessfully aspired. This greatly strengthened him in his dealings with the Prince Regent, who soon discovered that there was no point in trying to intrigue with individual ministers in order to undermine the Prime Minister. If, as was often the case, he was tempted to dispense with Liverpool's services, he was aware that the whole cabinet would resign with him, and that he would have to look to the Whigs to form an alternative administration, a prospect which became increasingly unattractive to him as he became older and more set in his ways.

Technically, Liverpool was undoubtedly one of the most proficient of British Prime Ministers. Vastly experienced before he took office, having occupied each of the three Secretaryships of state, he kept a firm overall control over decision-making, while allowing his colleagues a very free hand in running their departments. Immensely patient, pragmatic, a good listener, and regarded even by his opponents as being exceptionally fair-minded in debate, never attempting to misrepresent their arguments, it is not difficult to understand how he was able to win the fierce loyalty of his colleagues. Not expected at the outset, either by himself or by others, to serve a lengthy term, he managed to keep the show on the road for almost 15 years. The strength of this achievement can be measured by what came afterwards – the rapid disintegration of the Pittite coalition, which he had so painfully reconstructed. Half his cabinet refused to serve under Canning, who was forced to include the Whigs in his government, while 'Prosperity' Robinson, now ennobled as Viscount Goderich, who was to succeed Canning after his death four months later, was himself able to survive in office only for a further four months before his own exceptionally argumentative government collapsed around him.

Works consulted

John W. Derry, 1990, *Politics in the Age of Fox, Pitt and Liverpool*, London, Macmillan.

John Ehrman, 1983, *The Younger Pitt: III The Consuming Struggle*, London, Constable.

Norman Gash, 1984, *Lord Liverpool*, London, Weidenfeld & Nicolson.

Norman Gash, 2004, Article in *Oxford Dictionary of National Biography*, Oxford, Oxford University Press.

Denis Gray, 1963, *Spencer Perceval: The Evangelical Prime Minister 1762–1812*, Manchester, Manchester University Press.

Lucille Iremonger, 1970, *The Fiery Chariot*, London, Secker & Warburg.

E.A. Smith, 2005, *A Queen on Trial; the Affair of Queen Caroline*, London, Sutton Publishing.

7
George Canning – in the Footsteps of Pitt

The shortest-serving Prime Minister in British history was George Canning, whose premiership lasted a mere 119 days, before he died in office. The irony is that he could well have been one of the longest-serving – if it was not for his unbridled ambition and apparent passion for intrigue, which alienated both the King and his Cabinet colleagues, he might have been appointed 18 years earlier. On the other hand, the wonder was that somebody from his own unconventional background reached high office at all. Born in London, on 11 April 1770, of Protestant Irish descent, his father's family were minor gentry who had been established in co. Londonderry since 1618. His father – also George – was a raffish figure, who had been a barrister, radical pamphleteer and a failed wine merchant in London, before being disinherited by his own father. He had married Mary Ann Costello, a ravishing beauty, also from Ireland, in 1768, and rapidly had three children, of whom only George survived, before dying in 1771, on George's first birthday, leaving his still only 24-year old wife destitute, with an allowance from his grandfather of only £40 a year to bring up the young George. A resourceful woman, she decided to seek her fortune on the stage, but after an unsuccessful debut at the Drury Lane Theatre, tried her luck in the provinces, where she did rather better. She became the mistress of a dissolute actor, Samuel Reddish, by whom she had five illegitimate children (including two pairs of twins), of whom only three survived infancy. She then married again, to Richard Hunn, a draper, and went on to have five more children. George spent his infancy travelling round with his mother, and her increasing ménage, staying in cheap theatrical lodgings, until – at the age of eight – he was plucked out of poverty and obscurity by his uncle, Stratford Canning, a merchant banker, who became his guardian, and took him into his own home. Soon after, he sent George to a prep school in Hampshire, and four years later to Eton. Part of the bargain was that he would not see his mother, except with his guardian's consent, though he kept in touch by letter, and was devoted to her. It was, in fact, eight years before he was to see her again.

At Eton, George proved a precocious scholar and at the age of 16 distinguished himself by producing, with three friends, *The Microcosm*, a superior kind of school magazine, published weekly in Windsor, and of which both King George III and Queen Charlotte became devoted readers. Much the most brilliant of the contributions, signed merely 'B' or 'Gregory Griffin', were written by Canning himself. Non-political in content, they were highly satirical in tone, and included a number of poems of good quality. Canning's uncle was well in with the Whigs, and at his house he met such luminaries as Charles James Fox, Edmund Burke and Richard Sheridan. When he went up to Christ Church, Oxford, in 1787, he was a convinced Whig. By this time, his guardian had died, and the role had been taken over by his business partner, William Borrowes, though the Rev. William Leigh, a wealthy clergyman married to George's Aunt Elizabeth, also took a close interest in his welfare. George, who wrote to his mother that he 'loved them very much' (Hinde, p. 16), spent his holidays with them, and looked to them for his main source of guidance and advice. His paternal grandmother had also died, bequeathing him a small estate in Ireland, which gave him an uncertain income of £400 a year, £50 of which he directed should be paid to his mother. In his first term in Oxford, Canning took the lead in setting up a small private debating society, consisting of only six members, the most prominent of whom, Robert Banks Jenkinson, was the son of the President of the Board of Trade in Pitt's government. They had a fine conceit of themselves, wearing a distinctive uniform, with buttons labelled D, C, P and F – after Demosthenes, Cicero, Pitt and Fox, whom they regarded as the greatest orators of all time. Word of their activities soon spread – and in particular of Canning's enthusiastic advocacy of Whig causes, and the Dean of Christ Church, Dr Cyril Jackson, who had become a warm admirer and supporter of Canning's, thought it was time to have a quiet word in his ear. He seems to have put it to him diplomatically that it was all very well for wealthy aristocrats, like his fellow members, to play at politics and even to aspire to a parliamentary career, but that Canning had his own way to make in the world, and that it would be better to look to the law, or some other profession to make his fortune. In the meantime, too open an association with politics might do his prospects harm. Canning took the hint, and promptly resigned from the club, much to the chagrin of his fellow members. He remained friendly with Jenkinson, who, however, soon left the University to embark on his Grand tour, and Canning made new friends.

One of these, Lord Granville Leveson Gower, was the son of the Marquess of Stafford, the Lord Privy Seal, and he soon invited Canning to visit the family seat at Trentham. Here he met many leading Tory politicians and their wives, nearly all of whom were charmed by this lively, witty, intelligent and handsome (he had inherited his mother's dark good looks) friend of the youngest son of their host. Meanwhile, Canning was becoming a figure of note within the University, winning the Chancellor's Medal for Latin Verse, and being pointed out by the former Prime Minister, the Earl of Shelburne (now the Marquess of Lansdowne), as a likely future premier. In 1789, at Dr Jackson's instigation, he was elected to a fellowship at his college, which, while the stipend was low, gave him an excellent position and free lodgings. He now decided to concentrate on reading for the bar, being in no position to accompany his wealthy friends, such as Leveson Gower, on a year-long Grand tour. The most he could manage was a short tour of the Netherlands, just after going down from Oxford in 1791. He then enrolled at Lincoln's Inn, and took chambers in Paper Buildings, but the lure of politics was too great, and he set his heart on getting quickly into Parliament, without waiting to get established as a lawyer. Yet before he could seek election, he had to decide under whose colours he would stand. Torn between his Whiggish background and his new Tory friends, he took some time to decide, before throwing in his lot with the latter. His motives were almost certainly mixed. On the one hand, personal advantage probably lay with shifting his allegiance. The Whigs were overwhelmingly an aristocratic group, and without family interest or a large private income it was unlikely that he would prosper in their ranks. Moreover, they were in opposition, and had no access to patronage. The Tories, by contrast, were less uniformly aristocratic, and could offer the prospect of ministerial or other official appointments.

On the other hand, Canning found himself less and less in sympathy with the Whigs, and in particular his friends, Sheridan and Fox, as a result of their response to the French Revolution. Canning had shared their initial enthusiasm, but as the excesses of the revolutionaries grew found himself more and more alienated. When Burke, one of his heroes, broke with Fox over the issue, he had much sympathy for him. Canning's attitude to the French republic was that it was 'an interesting experiment', and republicanism might well be a preferable system for some other countries, but not his own. Writing to a friend in 1792, he said:

> As to this country, though I am not so enthusiastically attached to the beauties of its constitution, and still less so determinedly blind to its defects, as to believe it unimprovable – yet I *do* think it much the best practical Government that the world has ever seen…I do think it almost impossible to begin improving now. (Hinde, 1973, p. 24)

He therefore concluded that he was, broadly, in favour of the *status quo*, and reacted unfavourably when Fox's young lieutenant, Charles Grey, formed the Association of the Friends of the People, to campaign for a radical scheme of parliamentary reform. It was this which finally prompted him, he later recalled, to sit down on 26 July 1792 and write a letter to the Prime Minister, William Pitt, whom he had never met. Pitt, however, was well aware of Canning's existence, and may well have been forewarned by Jenkinson, who had been a Pittite MP since 1790, and was himself highly regarded by the Prime Minister. The letter from the 22-year-old Canning could hardly have been more brash. He wrote asking permission to call on the Prime Minister, saying that 'although he was on terms of familiar friendship with some of the more eminent members of the opposition, he was not in any way committed to them politically. He also made it clear that although he wanted to enter Parliament, he lacked the financial resources to bring himself in' (Hinde, p. 25). Pitt immediately replied in the most courteous terms, and a meeting was arranged for 15 August. Here, Pitt, obviously charmed by his young visitor and on the look-out to poach a promising recruit from the opposition,

> explained that the amount of patronage directly at his disposal was tiny, but that sometimes owners of seats were prepared to dispose of them simply at his recommendation. Canning replied that this would be acceptable so long as it was clear that he owed the seat to Pitt's recommendation and not to the owner's choice. He also expressed the hope that he would be allowed to make up his own mind on issues that were not of major importance to the government, like the Test Act on which he knew he and the prime minister disagreed. Pitt accommodatingly replied that thinking men could not always be expected to agree, especially on 'speculative subjects' and that what he hoped for from Canning was a 'general good disposition towards Government'. (Hinde, p. 27)

Canning did not have to wait long before his *chutzpah* was rewarded. The following June, the MP for Newtown, Isle of Wight, Sir Richard Worsley, indicated to the government that he was willing to give up his seat in exchange for a government post. Pitt immediately informed Canning that, at no expense to himself, he could have the constituency 'exactly in the manner which will be agreeable to your wishes as you explained them in your letter and when I had the pleasure of seeing you' (Hinde, p. 28). A week later, he was returned unopposed, without visiting the constituency, and his political career was launched. Most of his Whig friends concluded that he had turned his coat for dishonourable reasons, but several of them, notably Sheridan, maintained amicable relations. Canning's arrival in the House of Commons was not widely seen as an extraordinary event. His maiden speech was well received, but it took a little time before he became – as he undoubtedly did – one of the most effective debaters in the House, perhaps excelled only by Fox and Pitt. On the other hand, he was immensely gratified by the reception he received from Pitt. On his very first night in the House, he was invited to dinner with the Prime Minister and with other senior cabinet ministers, including the Foreign Secretary, Lord Grenville and Henry Dundas, the Secretary for War. Thereafter, Pitt frequently had him over for dinner or supper, often à *deux*, and could not have been more friendly or encouraging. Meanwhile, he continued fitfully with his law studies, but by the summer of 1795 had to take a serious decision on whether to commit himself to the bar. He decided against, but needed to earn some money, and was most disinclined to seek a sinecure post. It would be discreditable, he wrote in his journal, to give up the law for 'an office of mere income and idleness'. He consulted Pitt, who immediately responded by saying that ministerial office would solve his problem, but that, unfortunately, no vacancy existed at the moment (Hinde, p. 41). Within a few months, however, he contrived to find a post for Canning as one of two Under-Secretaries at the Foreign Office, to serve under Grenville. He took up the post in January 1796, at the age of 25.

His fellow Under-Secretary was frequently away on diplomatic missions, while Grenville preferred to work much of the time at his country residence at Dropmore, so Canning was often effectively in control of the Office, and handled the bulk of the routine work. A workaholic, he revelled in his new responsibilities, even though they made heavy inroads into his busy social life. His greatest difficulty arose during the two unsuccessful bouts of peace negotiations, in 1796 and 1797, when he was responsible for liaising with Lord Malmesbury, the chief British negotiator at meetings in Lille and Paris. Canning's – and Malmesbury's – problem was that, whereas Pitt genuinely wished the talks to succeed, Grenville (and George III) did not, and his loyalties were often stretched. He solved the problem by ensuring that Grenville did not see some of the more sensitive dispatches, but in spite of this both sets of negotiations failed, mainly due to intransigence on the French side.

Canning's ministerial and parliamentary duties did not exhaust all his energies. At the beginning of the 1797–8 parliamentary session, he agreed with Pitt to launch a pro-government newspaper, which would combat the 'lies' told by the opposition press and counter radical views by proclaiming a vigorous patriotic message. It was supposed to be anonymous, but it soon got around that Canning himself was the principal contributor, with Pitt chipping in with the odd article. Entitled *The Anti-Jacobin*, it ran for 35 weekly issues, and obtained a healthy circulation of some 2,500 copies, which its proprietors implausibly boasted represented a readership of 50,000. A high-class propaganda sheet, it pulled few punches, and its final issue was devoted to a long epic poem, largely composed by Canning, ridiculing the lack of patriotism of the radicals. This included the couplet 'A steady patriot of the world alone/ The friend of every country – but his own'. It is, however, mostly memorable for containing the most famous words Canning ever wrote, which have since appeared in numerous anthologies:

> But of all plagues, good Heav'n, thy wrath can send,
> Save, save, oh! Save me from the *Candid Friend*.

The *Anti-Jacobin* was discontinued at the end of the parliamentary session, in June 1798, most of its contributors, including Canning, moving on to the Tory *Quarterly Review*. Canning's period as Under-Secretary came to an end in March 1799, when he was appointed a member of the Board of Control for India, which effectively supervised the activities of the East India Company. The Board was presided over by Dundas, who regarded it as almost a full-time job added to his responsibilities as War Secretary (it was soon to be made a cabinet post in its own right). Canning seemed to consider the post as something of a resting place, to broaden his experience, before Pitt was ready to bring him into his cabinet. This impression was strengthened by his appointment as a Privy Councillor and Joint Paymaster-General of the Forces in March 1800. Canning was not Pitt's only young protégé, but there is no doubt Canning was his favourite. Their relationship became exceptionally close, and Canning wrote to a friend, in 1796, saying 'I could not love or admire him more, even if I had no obligations to him'. Pitt's feelings for Canning are unrecorded, but his actions spoke louder than words – and – at least up to Canning's marriage, in July 1800, he showed him exceptional favour. The question inevitably arises whether part of Canning's attraction to him was sexual. The author of the most thorough, indeed monumental, biography of Pitt – extending to three long volumes – John Ehrman, thinks it is improbable that there was a homo-sexual relationship, but expressed the view that if Pitt did have a male lover Canning was the most obvious candidate. In fact, the only evidence pointing to this was a single occasion when Canning was seen to put his hand familiarly on Pitt's shoulder (Ehrman, p. 94).

Whatever Pitt's sexual predilections, there is little doubt that Canning's were heterosexual. The first person with whom he was believed to be involved was Princess Caroline, the estranged wife of the Prince of Wales. A notorious sexual predator, like her husband, she made a dead set at Canning, when he met her at Lord Palmerston's house. He was obviously strongly attracted to her, as he revealed in a letter to his aunt, Mrs Leigh, four days later, without, however, revealing her identity, but he was also fearful of the consequences of getting involved with her. It was, after all, a capital offence to have carnal relations with the wife of the heir to the throne. The probability is that they never became lovers, though the future George IV believed that they did, and this accounts for his prolonged hostility to Canning, and his great reluctance to accept him as a member of Lord Liverpool's cabinet many years later. What is clear is that they became close friends, and she later became godmother to Canning's eldest son. Canning was, perhaps, saved from succumbing to her charms by falling deeply in love with a wealthy heiress he met soon after. This was Joan Scott, the youngest of three daughters of General John Scott, who had made a fortune through gambling, and when he died left £100,000 to each of them.

He set out to woo her, though very circumspectly, as he was only too aware that, given his lower social status and lack of means, he would be suspected of trying to marry her for her money. An added difficulty was that her eldest sister was married to the Marquess of Titchfield, the son and heir of the Home Secretary, the Duke of Portland, and that she regarded him as acting *in loco parentis*. Titchfield was not in favour of the match, but Canning was not with-out powerful allies. These included Pitt, whom he took into his confidence, and who helped plan his marital strategy with him, and Lady Jane Dundas, the wife of the War Secretary, whose husband was related to Joan Scott, and who was more than happy to put a word in on his behalf. Eventually Joan made it clear that she wanted to marry Canning, and he then tackled Titchfield directly and succeeded in winning him over. They were married in London, on 8 July 1800, and Pitt, whose emotions were almost certainly mixed, was reported as being in a 'daze' throughout the ceremony. The marriage turned out to be totally satisfactory from Canning's point of view. He may not have acted from pecuniary motives, but from now on his income was assured, and provided a firm base for his political career. Moreover, Joan proved to be a perfect partner for him, acting as his secretary, following his career with great interest, offering unending support and usually good advice, while herself avoiding the limelight. It was a very happy union, which produced three sons and a daughter, though unfortunately the eldest son, George Charles, was afflicted with ill health, and was to die before his nineteenth birthday.

On the morrow of his marriage, at the age of 30, Canning's prospects could hardly have appeared brighter. Utterly confident in Pitt's continuing goodwill, and believing that promotion to the cabinet was only a matter of time, he had already built up his own following among the younger Pittite MPs, and was widely acknowledged to be the most able of Pitt's lieutenants. He had good grounds for believing that, if all went well, he would emerge as his political heir and eventual successor. There were, however, some clouds on the horizon. One was represented by his mother. Although a keen theatre-goer, Canning was only too aware that acting was not regarded as a respectable profession, and was always badgering his mother to give it up. If not, he was determined that she should remain in the provinces, rather than coming to live in London, as she threatened to do once her marriage to Mr. Hunn broke up. Canning was generous to her, sending as much money as he could, even when he himself was still hard up, and putting himself out to help his numerous half-siblings. In practice, she was only a minor embarrassment to him, but Canning's love for her was blended with an extreme wariness. Much more damaging to him was his unwillingness to suffer fools gladly, and his propensity to include a large proportion of mankind in that category. He was apt to make witty and malicious remarks at their expense, which not unusually got back to them, creating unnecessary enmities. His friends were very aware of this, and some of them remonstrated with him to be more careful in future. He resolved to do so, but was all too often unable to live up to his resolution. This, coupled with envy and resentment at the excessive favours he received from Pitt, meant that his numerous admirers were balanced by a perhaps equal number of critics.

Then, in March 1801, the bottom fell out of Canning's world, with the sudden resignation of Pitt as Prime Minister. This followed the refusal of George III to agree to his policy of Catholic emancipation. Canning insisted on also resigning, despite Pitt's plea to him to carry on in support of the new premier, Henry Addington. In doing so, and in becoming Addington's unremitting scourge throughout the three years of his ministry, Canning proved himself more royalist than the King, more Catholic than the Pope, or more precisely, more Pittite than Pitt. Although Pitt eventually joined in the criticism of Addington, and was happy to return to office in May 1804, he was immensely embarrassed by Canning's activities, genuinely believing that Addington should be given a fair chance to succeed. When he formed his second administration, he included two of Canning's contemporaries, in senior posts – Jenkinson as Home Secretary and Castlereagh as Secretary for War and the Colonies – much to his disgust, Canning had to put up with the non-cabinet position of Treasurer of the Navy. Even this post, he threatened to resign, in protest against the inclusion of Addington (now Viscount Sidmouth) in the cabinet. Pitt persuaded him to stay, but Canning made an enduring enemy of Sidmouth, who was to remain an influential political figure for another two decades. Subsequently, he was rebuffed by Pitt when the Foreign Secretary, Lord Harrowby, was forced to stand down temporarily because of ill-health. Canning, believing that his previous experience as Under-Secretary made him well qualified for the post, volunteered to stand in for him, without, he told Pitt, insisting on either the title or the salary. Pitt appeared to receive the suggestion well, without committing himself, but when, shortly afterwards, Harrowby insisted on resigning for good, he overlooked Canning, and appointed Lord Mulgrave, the Chancellor of the Duchy of Lancaster, in his place.

Canning was mortified, and bitterly resented having to be, after Pitt, one of the main spokesmen in the House of Commons for policies approved by the cabinet, of which he was not a member. It was only ten months later, in October 1805, when Pitt suddenly invited him to dinner, that he had an opportunity to pour out to the Prime Minister the full extent of his frustrations. Pitt immediately responded, by promising Canning that he would join the cabinet the following January, either keeping his present post of Treasurer of the Navy, or – if he preferred – becoming President of the Board of Control. Canning was delighted, and felt that all his old intimacy with Pitt would now be restored, as it indeed was over the following weeks. These, however, were a period of immense strain and disappointment for Pitt, with the unravelling of the Third coalition against France, which he had laboriously put together, with Napoleon's rout of the Austrian and Russian armies at Ulm and Austerlitz. The triumph at Trafalgar, which guaranteed Britain against invasion, was a welcome relief, despite the death of Lord Nelson, but it only fleetingly lifted the transcendental gloom into which Pitt was descending in the final months of 1805. He was to die in office, in January 1806, before carrying out his promised cabinet reshuffle.

Canning was devastated by Pitt's death, and was unprepared for politics without him, though he had taken a small step towards asserting his independence at the 1802 general election, when he relinquished the seat he held at Pitt's behest, and purchased an Irish rotten borough, at Tralee, for the rumoured price of 4,000 guineas. 'The friends of the late Mr Pitt', as they styled themselves, were excluded from the new government formed by Lord Grenville, who had foreseen an administration of 'All the Talents', but had no room left for them after he had provided places for his own followers, the Whigs led by Charles James Fox, and the supporters of Lord Sidmouth. The Pittites could not agree on who should be their leader, but settled on the elderly Duke of Portland as their nominal head. In practice, Jenkinson, now Lord Hawkesbury and soon to become the Earl of Liverpool, led them in the Lords, while Canning, together with Perceval and Castlereagh, formed an uncomfortable triumvirate in the Commons. It was not long before Grenville began to regret the omission of the Pittites, and particularly of Canning, whose abilities he greatly admired. He made two separate approaches to him, in July and August 1806, with pressing invitations to join the cabinet, which Canning would have loved to accept, but he felt constrained to consult his colleagues, and then replied that he would only be willing to accept if the entire cabinet was reconstructed to bring in all the leading associates of Pitt. This Grenville was unwilling to do, as it would almost certainly provoke the resignation of Sidmouth and his associates, whom he regarded as an essential element in his coalition. Then, in September, came the death of Charles James Fox, his Foreign Secretary and Leader of the House of Commons, which left a gaping hole in his government. Charles Grey was appointed to fill his posts, but his father, the 1st Earl Grey, was believed to be a dying man, which meant that he would soon be wafted into the House of Lords and no longer able to lead the Commons. This was an absolutely crucial post when the Prime Minister was in the Lords, and Grenville made a tentative approach to Canning to enquire whether he would be willing to accept it – if as expected – Grey went up to the Lords. This offer was so tempting that Canning might well have done so, despite the obligation which he felt towards his fellow Pittites. Before the issue arose, however, Grenville was out of office, sacked by George III, in March 1807, because his government refused to give a pledge not to revive the issue of Catholic emancipation (see Chapter 3).

George III was tempted to appoint the Earl of Chatham, the Younger Pitt's elder brother, as Prime Minister, but was strongly advised by the leading Pittites to choose the Duke of Portland. This elderly, ineffective grandee, who a generation earlier had led a predominantly Whig government, was incapable of giving any direction to his ministers, who, in Perceval's words, became 'a government of departments'. The chief posts went to Liverpool, as Home Secretary and Leader of the House of Lords, Perceval as Chancellor of the Exchequer and Leader of the Commons, Castlereagh as Secretary for War and the Colonies, and Canning as Foreign Secretary. In this post, he was – initially at least – supremely happy, despite, the difficult international situation, as the war against Napoleon continued to go badly.

Within three months of his appointment came the disaster of the Battle of Friedland, which knocked Russia and Prussia out of the war, and was followed by the meeting at Tilsit between Napoleon and Tsar Alexander I, at which the latter effectively became an ally of Napoleon. He agreed to join his Continental System, aimed at blockading Britain by closing all continental ports to British shipping and commerce. Canning, probably the keenest 'hawk' in the cabinet, in his determination to carry on the war as vigorously as possible, was especially concerned about rumoured secret clauses to the Tilsit treaty which he suspected included plans to bring the neutral state of Denmark into the war on the French side. He sent a large fleet to Copenhagen, with a threat to bombard the City if the Danes did not hand over their fleet to Britain for the duration of the war. The Danish Regent refused and a three-day bombardment commenced, resulting in 2,000 deaths and the destruction or damage of a third of the buildings in the city, before the Danes yielded. The British then seized the Danish fleet and sailed it back to Britain. The action was strongly criticized by the Whig opposition, but was popularly received within the country, and added to Canning's fast-growing reputation, despite the fact that it had the inevitable consequence of bringing Denmark into the war on the opposing side. Canning thereupon decided on an equivalent response on the southern extremity of Europe, where, following a French invasion, there was a severe risk of the powerful Portuguese fleet falling into enemy hands. An ultimatum was sent to Prince John, the Portuguese Regent, to go into exile in Brazil, and take his fleet with him, or face an attack from British ships blockading Lisbon's harbour. A few hours before Marshal Junot's forces reached Lisbon, a reluctant Prince John sailed off to Portugal's largest colony, escorted on his way by the British ships.

The French invasion of Portugal, followed by Napoleon's action the following year, in deposing the Spanish king and imposing his brother Joseph in his place, marked the beginning of the Peninsular War. The spontaneous Spanish insurgency against their French occupiers provoked an excited response in London, and a determination by Canning and his colleagues to do everything they could to assist their new Spanish allies. A British army, with General Sir Arthur Wellesley (later the Duke of Wellington) in temporary command, was sent to Portugal, and routed the French forces, under Junot, at the battle of Vimeiro. On the morrow of the battle, two more senior generals, Sir Hew Dalrymple and Sir Henry Burrard arrived from Britain and took over command from Wellington. They then proceeded to negotiate an armistice with the French – the Convention of Cintra – which provided extraordinarily generous terms for their defeated enemy. Under its provisions, the British agreed to repatriate the French troops to France in their own ships; there was no restriction on these troops re-entering the war; the French were guaranteed their 'property' (most of which had been plundered from the Portuguese), and any reprisals against the pro-French party in Portugal were forbidden. Canning was furious and raged against all the generals, including Wellesley, and demanded their recall. Under the influence of Castlereagh, a great admirer of Wellesley, the cabinet, however, more wisely decided only to sanction Dalrymple, who was later to be rebuked by a Court of Inquiry. Neither he nor Burrard were ever to be employed again. The frustrations of Portugal were soon to be amplified by the outcome of the British intervention in Spain. An army under the command of General Sir John Moore, found it impossible to liaise effectively with the scattered and divided forces of the Spanish insurgency, and after manoeuvring indecisively for several months concluded that its position had become untenable, and set out for the long march, through wild and inhospitable country, from central Spain to the northern port of Corunna to be evacuated back to Britain. Pursued by Napoleon's forces, it repelled a French attack on the outskirts of Corunna, in which Moore was killed, an action celebrated in a famous poem by Charles Wolfe. Moore's somewhat bedraggled army then sailed away.

Canning added to his growing reputation as an orator by his forceful speeches defending these events in the Commons, but he was deeply dissatisfied with their outcome. It was, perhaps, because of this that, in March 1809, he sat down and wrote a letter which was to have the most injurious effect on his own subsequent career. It was addressed to the Prime Minister, and listed a series of complaints about the conduct of the war. He subsequently met Portland at his country seat at Bulstrode for several days of discussions, during which he made the blunt demand that Castlereagh should be removed from the direction of the war. If not, Canning insisted, he himself would resign. A deeply embarrassed Portland discussed this with other cabinet ministers, and then with George III, all of whom agreed that it was essential to prevent Canning's resignation. It was also agreed that the best plan would be to offer Castlereagh an alternative post, perhaps in the House of Lords, but that no change should be made until after the outcome of the Walcheren expedition (see Chapter 3), which had been planned by Castlereagh, was known. The Lord President of the Council, the Earl of Camden, who was Castlereagh's uncle, agreed to break the news gently to him, and even offered to relinquish his own post to make way for his nephew. When it came to the point, however, he could not face telling Castlereagh, and already regretted his impetuous offer to make way. So weeks, and months went by, without Castlereagh having the merest suspicion that his days were numbered, while virtually all the other cabinet ministers became aware of what was afoot. Then, on 15 August, Portland had an apoplectic fit, and the whole question of Castlereagh's replacement got caught up in the manoeuvring for the prime ministerial succession. In this, Canning clearly overplayed his hand, and his position was severely weakened by his apparent plotting against Castlereagh, though it had not been his idea to keep Castlereagh in ignorance and he was not to blame for the long delay in putting his plan into effect. He had a frank discussion with Perceval, saying that in his view the new Prime Minister must come from the House of Commons, and that he and Perceval were the only feasible candidates. While he had the deepest personal respect for Perceval, he hoped he would understand that it would be impossible for him to serve under him, and suggested that Perceval should go to the House of Lords, possibly as Lord Chancellor. Perceval replied that he, too, would be unwilling to serve under Canning, and proposed that both of them should keep their present posts, and that another Prime Minister should be appointed from the Lords, whom they would both find acceptable. Canning retorted that it was essential for the premier to be in the Commons. The following day he had an audience with George III, which went disastrously badly, as recounted by one of his biographers. Canning told the King that:

> There is no substitute for Portland, for 'he is not one of a species, he is an individual, the last of his species – there is nothing like him to be found'. As to alternative prime ministers in the Lords, Chatham, who had once seemed obvious, was ruled out by his apparent mishandling of the Walcheren expedition. He renewed his threat to retire if Perceval was chosen, but told the King that if the Government failed to stand he would have an alternative in Canning and his friends. The King told Perceval later that this was 'the most extraordinary' conversation he had ever heard. Edward Cook, Castlereagh's Under-Secretary, called it 'the most insolent proposition that was ever obtruded upon a Monarch by a presumptuous Subject'. (Dixon, 1976, p. 136)

It was not surprising that the only effect of this conversation was to convince the King that his already existing preference for Perceval was fully justified. Soon after this, Castlereagh finally heard from his uncle the details of Canning's proposal to supplant him, and after brooding on it for 12 days, sent an angry letter to Canning demanding satisfaction:

> You continued to sit in the same Cabinet with me, and to leave me not only in the persuasion that I possessed your confidence and support as a colleague, but you allowed me, tho' virtually superseded, in breach of every principle both public and private to originate and proceed in the Execution of a new Enterprise of the most arduous and important nature [Walcheren], with your apparent concurrence and ostensible approbation. (Dixon, p. 136)

The following day, Canning, who had never fired a pistol in his life, met Castlereagh on Putney Heath at 6 a.m., and each man fired two shots. Castlereagh was uninjured, but Canning was lightly wounded in his left thigh.

The damage to his reputation was much worse. Castlereagh was also criticized for his pride and apparent desire for revenge, but Canning was almost universally condemned for provoking the quarrel. Both men were left out of the government formed by Perceval a few weeks later, though Castlereagh was welcomed back, as Foreign Secretary in 1812, and continued in this office, which he doubled up with the leadership of the House of Commons, for another ten years under Lord Liverpool. Canning was twice invited to join Liverpool's government – in 1812 – and was even offered the Foreign Secretaryship, but again grossly overplayed his hand, demanding the leadership of the Commons as well. He consequently remained in the wilderness until 1816, when, swallowing his pride, he accepted the much more junior post of President of the Board of Control (of India).

The general election of October 1812 provided a new experience for Canning. It was his tenth parliamentary contest, but on each previous occasion he had been returned unopposed for a pocket or rotten borough. This time, he was one of two Tory candidates facing opposition from Whigs in Liverpool, a borough with a large parliamentary franchise, and a long history of fiercely fought partisan contests. He had been invited to fight the seat, at no expense to himself, by the local Tories, led by John Gladstone, father of the future Liberal Prime Minister. It was a genuinely uncertain contest, with two strong rivals, in Henry Brougham, the leading Whig orator and future Lord Chancellor, and Thomas Creevey, the famous diarist. In the end, Canning headed the poll, with his fellow Tory in second place. He had finally tasted the rough-and-tumble of a pre-Reform Bill election and had found it exhilarating, and was by no means better disposed to reform than he had previously been. During the course of the campaign, he made a remarkable declaration of his continuing loyalty to Pitt, and of his independence from all other politicians: 'To one man, while he lived, I was devoted with all my heart and all my soul. Since the death of Mr. Pitt I acknowledge no leader...I have adhered and shall adhere to [his] opinions as the guides of my public conduct' (Dixon, p. 164).

From now on, his relationship with his constituency was to be transformed, with large numbers of constituents expecting favours, and no question of his getting away with never setting foot in the borough he represented in Parliament. During the next couple of years, he pursued an uncertain political course. Together with his small band of rather over a dozen supporters, he alternated between supporting the government and backing initiatives by Whig MPs. He was a deeply frustrated man – watching his great rival, Castlereagh, emerge as an international statesman and the star of the Congress of Vienna, with the knowledge that he himself could have played the same role, and that it was his own fault that it had been denied him. He had conceded this in a letter to his old friend Granville Leveson-Gower, in which he wrote: 'I am afraid no possible combination of circumstances can place me again where

I stood...and it is no use to reflect where I might have been now had that time been taken at the flood' (Rolo, p. 93).

For at least 10 years, Canning, and his wife, had been desperately anxious about the health of their dearly loved eldest child, George Charles. who was lame in one leg and almost perpetually ill. In 1807, they had moved house to the distinctly unfashionable town of Hinckley, in Leicestershire, 100 miles from London, purely because of the presence there of a Mr Chesher, who was known to have effected some remarkable cures of other lame children. Joan and the other children went to live there, which meant that they were separated for long periods from Canning, who, of course, spent most of his time in London. By 1814, little George had got a lot worse, and his parents became convinced that he needed to live in a warmer climate. The Prime Minister, his old friend, Lord Liverpool, came to their aid, suggesting that Canning might like to take up the post of Ambassador to Lisbon. It was expected that the Regent, Prince John, later King John VI, who had withdrawn to Brazil at Canning's instigation in 1807, was about to return, and it was thought fitting that Canning should be in Lisbon to welcome him back. So, in November 1814, Canning duly took up the post, and established his family in the grand ambassadorial residence. Yet John showed himself in no hurry to return, and Canning had a frustrating time dealing with the Portuguese government, who constantly had to wait weeks or months before committing themselves while instructions were awaited from Rio de Janeiro. His son's health did not improve, and Canning needed no persuasion when, in June 1816, on the death of the Earl of Buckinghamshire, Liverpool offered him the vacant cabinet post of President of the Board of Control. This time, Canning made no awkward conditions, and returned to the cabinet a much chastened man, in a post far junior to that he had previously held.

He had to fight a by-election, which was vigorously contested by a radical candidate, before he could take up his position. The opposition made much of supposed corruption involved in Canning's appointment to Lisbon, circulating the ditty:

> Fourteen thousand a year is a very fine thing
> For a trip to a Court without any King. (Dixon, p. 182)

Canning was elected with a good majority, and took up his new post, which consisted of overseeing the East India Company. Within the cabinet, he managed to work with Castlereagh, and even Sidmouth, in tolerable accord. In the Commons, Canning provided heavy reinforcement to the government's debating strength, while in his own department, he worked with quiet efficiency and unwonted tact. His relations with the governor-general, the Marquess of Hastings (formerly Lord Moira), however, never got beyond the stage of formal correctness. An appalling snob, Hastings resented being responsible to man he regarded as a parvenu. Canning remained at his post for four years, until 1820, when the government reluctantly agreed, at the behest of the new King, George IV, to introduce a bill enabling him to divorce Queen Caroline (see Chapter 6). As a personal friend of the Queen, Canning felt that he could not be associated with a move against her, and proffered his resignation. Liverpool, thinking that this was, in reality, a bid by Canning to secure a more senior post, offered him the Home Secretaryship, in succession to the ageing Lord Sidmouth. Canning, however, declined, writing to Liverpool that 'Lord Sidmouth's office is just the one upon the daily details of which this unhappy question must operate with the most sensible and constant effect' (Rolo, p. 102. So Canning retired, with the unspoken understanding that he would return to office once the divorce issue was out of the way. Yet when, a year later, with the withdrawal of the Bill and the subsequent death of the Queen, Liverpool proposed to bring him back, George IV vehemently objected. When it was suggested that Canning should instead go to India as governor-general, in succession to Lord Hastings, there was a barrage of dissent, led by Hastings himself, who argued that the Indian princes would never accept someone of such low birth. The King, however, anxious to get Canning as far away from his court as possible, enthusiastically accepted the nomination, and Canning prepared to pack his bags to depart for Calcutta, reflecting that the ample emoluments would at least permit his wife to replenish her somewhat depleted fortune. Both of them had been devastated by the death of young George Charles, in March 1820, which had knocked the raw edge off Canning's political ambitions, and perhaps predisposed them to the prospect of starting a new life together in the Far East. But, shortly before they were due to sail, the hand of God struck: in August 1822, Castlereagh committed suicide (see Chapter 6).

Liverpool was now adamant that Canning must return to the cabinet as Castlereagh's successor, both as Foreign Secretary and Leader of the Commons. The King, still hostile, made indirect inquiries to see whether the Prime Minister would regard his refusal as a resigning matter, and – not being prepared to take the risk – very reluctantly agreed. He told the Lord Chancellor, Lord Eldon (a firm opponent of Canning) that he had been called upon to make 'the greatest personal sacrifice that a sovereign ever made to a subject, or indeed, taking all *the circumstances*, that man ever made to man' (Rolo, p. 113). At the age of 52, Canning finally regained the position he was in 1809, the intervening 13 years being largely wasted in terms of his political advance. Yet he was an older and a wiser man – more patient, less arrogant and much less inclined to intrigue. In fact, during the five years of his second Foreign Secretaryship, he was much more intrigued against than intriguing. The main intriguers were the King himself, and the ultra-Tory element in the Cabinet, which comprised virtually all the ministers in the House of Lords with the exception of Liverpool himself, who was his firm and constant ally. Although temperamentally very different from his predecessor, and fellow Irishman, Castlereagh, their views were rather similar. Both of them, though Protestants themselves, were strongly in favour of Catholic emancipation, and both of them believed in following what might be described as a 'liberal' foreign policy. This principally meant dissociating themselves from the Holy Alliance powers of Austria, Prussia and Russia, who were bent on intervening in smaller states to suppress liberal or nationalist movements. Canning effectively carried on with Castlereagh's policies, though he enunciated them far more clearly and defended them with great oratorical effect in speeches both in the House of Commons and on public platforms. The effect of these speeches was to greatly increase his popularity in the country, while mitigating the hostility of the Whigs, who broadly approved, while upsetting many of his fellow Tories.

His most effective opponent within the cabinet was the Duke of Wellington, who became the chief spokesmen of the 'ultras', and whose standing was boosted by his close relations with the King. George IV, who sympathized with the Holy Alliance, actively plotted with the 'ultras' to undermine Canning, egged on by their ambassadors, who were frequent visitors to his Court. A notable intriguer was the Princess Lieven, whose husband was the Russian Ambassador, but who, more significantly, was the mistress of the Austrian Chancellor, Metternich. She was to leave a vivid picture of the machinations around the court and government in her letters to Metternich and other personalities, published long after her death. With Liverpool's backing, Canning was able to see off all the plots against him, but meanwhile worked hard to overcome the King's hostility. In this, he was to be helped by the current, and last, of the long line of royal mistresses, Lady Conyngham, with whom the King was completely besotted. Canning offered a vacant Under-Secretaryship in his department to her son, Lord Francis Conyngham, which pleased the King mightily. He was even more delighted when Canning recommended the appointment, as Ambassador to the newly established republic of Buenos Aires (later Argentina), of Lord Ponsonby, a previous lover of Lady Conyngham, whom George IV wished to be sent as far away as possible. As both Foreign Secretary and Leader of the Commons, Canning was necessarily in frequent contact with the King, who, easily bored with public affairs, was surprised to find him a much more congenial interlocutor than the great majority of his colleagues. He was charmed by Canning's wit and candour, and began to develop some of the affection for him that he had felt for Fox, when he was a young man, 40 years earlier. From being a ferocious opponent, he became a strong supporter of Canning, and lent no further countenance to those plotting against him.

The first crisis that Canning had to deal with, which he inherited from Castlereagh, was the determination of the Holy Alliance to use French troops to intervene in Spain, to suppress a liberal constitution and enforce the dictatorial rule of the new Bourbon monarch, Ferdinand VII. Canning used every means he could to discourage this venture, but when the French invasion began, in April 1823, it was clear that the only recourse left to him was to go to war with France, with Britain's recent allies firmly lined up on the other side. Canning might conceivably have stayed the French hand by the mere threat of war, but – though sorely tempted – he refrained from doing so, partly at least because it was far from clear that he would have been supported by the King and his cabinet colleagues if he had attempted this. Acutely conscious that he had suffered a setback, he determined that, if France had regained control over Spain, she should not also be allowed to extend her influence to the New World by helping to restore Spanish control over her revolted colonies in Latin America. He made it clear that the British Navy, which he also employed (with only very partial success) to help suppress the international slave trade, would prevent this from happening. This – together with the proclamation of the Monroe doctrine by the US President in January 1823 – effectively guaranteed the independence of the newly established states. Independence was one thing, diplomatic recognition quite another, and Canning had a long and difficult struggle before he was able to persuade the King and his cabinet colleagues to extend it. It was only in 1825 that the first Latin American ambassador, from Colombia, was able to present his credentials. Canning's prime motivation was undoubtedly to further British interests by opening up the whole of Latin America to British trade and investment, but he successfully dressed up his policies in liberal and internationalist rhetoric, famously declaring, in a parliamentary speech in December 1826: 'I resolved that if France had Spain, it should not be Spain with the Indies. I called the New World into existence to redress the balance of the Old.'

Canning became a popular hero throughout Latin America, and to this day his statue dominates many city squares, and there is hardly a major town which does not have a street named after him. In Greece, he is less celebrated, unlike Byron, whose death at Missolonghi in 1824, during the Greek national uprising against the Ottoman Turks, brought him lasting renown. Arguably, however, Greek independence, recognized by the great powers in 1829, owed much more to Canning's subtle diplomacy. This aimed equally at stopping the Turks from brutally suppressing the uprising and at forestalling Austrian and Russian military intervention. It did not prevent an eventual war between Russia and Turkey after Canning's death, but it gave vital breathing space to the Greeks and set at least a temporary limit to Russian expansion into the Balkans. Canning's final foreign policy success was in Portugal, following the death of John VI in 1826. His legitimate successor was his eldest son Dom Pedro, who preferred to remain in Brazil, where he had been proclaimed Emperor four years earlier. He abdicated in favour of his eight-year-old daughter, Maria, appointing his sister Isabella as Regent, and granting the country a liberal constitution. Yet Dom Pedro's younger brother Miguel, claimed the throne for himself, and amassed an army of right-wing sympathizers on the Spanish side of the frontier, ready to invade his country with the backing of the Spanish government, egged on by the French ambassador. Miguel's forces crossed into Portugal in November 1826, but Canning reacted with commendable dispatch, and immediately mobilized 5,000 troops to send to Lisbon, whose arrival galvanized the Portuguese resistance, and Miguel's troops were driven out by the following January. Canning achieved one of his great debating successes, when he defended his action in Parliament, on 12 December, saying: 'We go to Portugal, not to rule, not to dictate, not to prescribe constitutions, but to defend and preserve the independence of an ally. We go to plant the standard of England upon the well-known heights of Lisbon. Where that standard is planted, foreign domination shall not come' (Dixon, p. 250).

This intervention, and this speech, foreshadowed many made two or three decades later by Lord Palmerston, who was already a junior member of Liverpool's government, and who counted Canning as his mentor. Doubling up his Foreign Secretaryship with the leadership of the House of Commons put enormous strain on Canning, as it had on his predecessor, Castlereagh. He had to spend long hours listening to virtually every debate in the House, and was the government's principal spokesman on a wide range of issues, which had little or no connection with foreign policy. He once admitted that the two jobs ought not to be combined, but said that 'he would rather die' than consent to 'their separation in his person' (Dixon, p. 254). He suffered severely from gout, and his health deteriorated sharply during the five years of his second term as Foreign Secretary. The climax came in January 1827, when he caught a severe chill attending the funeral of the Duke of York, when he quixotically lent his coat to the ailing Lord Chancellor, Lord Eldon, one of his fiercest cabinet opponents, and never really recovered.

Less than a month later, Lord Liverpool suffered the cerebral haemorrhage which led to his retirement from the premiership. The only serious candidates to succeed him, from within the cabinet, were Canning and a somewhat reluctant Wellington. After some vacillation, George IV invited Canning to take over the government, but immediately half the cabinet, including Wellington, announced their resignation, as did no fewer than 41 office holders. It was estimated that around half of them were opposed to Canning because of his championship of Catholic emancipation and the other half because they objected to him personally. It was immediately clear that Canning would be unable to form a purely Tory government, but he secured the King's permission to approach the Whigs to see whether they would be willing to participate in a coalition. The Whig leader, Charles Grey, now the 2nd Earl Grey, was firmly opposed. Despite his progressive views on such subjects as parliamentary reform, he declared himself unalterably opposed to having 'the son of an actress' as Prime Minister. Other Whigs, however, were more forthcoming, notably the 3rd Marquess of Lansdowne, the son of the former Prime Minister, Lord Shelburne. Protracted negotiations eventually led to Whigs taking over almost half the cabinet portfolios, with Lansdowne as Home Secretary, the Duke of Devonshire as Lord Privy Seal and Lord Lyndhurst as Lord Chancellor. Canning became Prime Minister, and Chancellor of the Exchequer, on 10 April 1827. His cabinet was not completed until 16 July. On 8 August, he died, after five days of intense pain caused by inflammation of the liver and lungs. He was 57 years old, and had served for only 119 days. Almost his entire premiership had been taken up with the formation of his government, though he did introduce a budget on 1 June, and was able to complete the parliamentary passage of the Corn Amendment Bill (somewhat liberalizing the Corn Law), which he had earlier introduced, and on which he made his last speech in the Commons, on 21 June. He was buried in Westminster Abbey, fittingly alongside Pitt, and his widow was made a Viscountess by a deeply grieving George IV.

Canning was, without doubt, one of the most gifted politicians of the nineteenth century. As a young man, he showed tremendous promise: a fine speaker, persuasive in argument, decisive in action, enormously intelligent, he lacked only patience and discretion. These came to him later in life, perhaps after he had missed his best chances of progressing to the top. Whether he would have made a great Prime Minister, we shall never know. As it is, he is principally remembered as one of our most effective foreign secretaries.

Works Consulted

Derek Beales, 2004, Article in *Oxford Dictionary of National Biography,* Oxford, Oxford University Press.
Peter Dixon, 1976, *Canning:Politician and Statesman,* London, Weidenfeld & Nicolson.
John Ehrman, 1996, *The Younger Pitt: The Consuming Struggle,* London, Constable.
Norman Gash, 1984, *Lord Liverpool,* London, Weidenfeld & Nicolson.
Denis Gray, 1963, *Spencer Perceval: The Evangelical Prime Minister 1762–1812,* Manchester, Manchester University Press.
Wendy Hinde, 1973, *George Canning,* London, Methuen & Co.
Lucille Iremonger, 1970, *The Fiery Chariot,* London, Secker and Warburg.
Wilbur Devereux Jones, 1967, *'Prosperity' Robinson,* London, Macmillan.
P.J.V. Rolo, 1965, *George Canning: Three Biographical Sketches,* London, Macmillan.

8

Frederick John Robinson, Viscount Goderich, 1st Earl of Ripon – Inadequate Stopgap

THE RIGHT HON.ᵇˡᵉ FREDERICK JOHN ROBINSON.

Chancellor of the Exchequer

Andrew Bonar Law, who was Prime Minister for barely seven months in 1922–3, was dubbed the 'Unknown Prime Minister'. A better candidate for this dubious honour might have been Viscount Goderich, who lasted a mere four months in 1827–8. He had the added handicap of relative anonymity. For most of his long life he was known either as Frederick Robinson or the Earl of Ripon. It was only for a six-year stretch, which included his premiership, that he was known as Goderich. He was born on 30 October 1782, the second of three sons of the 2nd Baron Grantham, and his much younger wife, Lady Mary Jemina Grey Yorke, daughter of the 2nd Earl of Hardwicke. Both Lord Grantham, who as Foreign Secretary had negotiated the peace terms with the American colonies in 1782, and his father had been cabinet ministers, and another kinsman, Lord Malmesbury, was also a prominent politician and diplomat. So, the young Frederick John Robinson came from a very well connected family, who were heirs to several titles and vast estates. Unfortunately, however, all these went to his elder brother, Thomas, even though there was only ten months between their ages. Robinson was to be one of the more obvious examples of younger sons deciding on a political career as their route to fame or fortune. (Of the 52 Prime Ministers to date, only 13 were only sons or the first born in a family).

Lord Grantham was a very fond father, and it was a devastating loss to Frederick and his brothers (the younger of whom was not to survive infancy), when he died, aged 41, shortly before Frederick's fourth birthday. From an early age, Frederick, whose first education was received at the hands of his parents, proved much more able than his brother, and was an excellent, but not outstanding scholar, both at Harrow School and at St. John's College, Cambridge, from which he graduated in 1802. An extremely amiable, popular and rather studious young man, he enrolled at Lincoln's Inn to study law, but did not persist for very long with his studies. The Peace of Amiens, in 1802, enabled Robinson to visit France in a party led by Lord and Lady Bessborough, a leading Whig couple who were family friends. Several members of the party were presented to Napoleon, but, his biographer recounts, 'whether or not Robinson met the man whose career he followed with a mixture of fascination and distaste is unknown' (Jones, p. 10). The following year, he had intended to go on the Grand Tour, but the resumption of hostilities made this impossible. Instead, he set off for Ireland, where his cousin, the 3rd Earl of Hardwicke, had become Lord Lieutenant in the Addington government. In his pocket, he carried a letter written by his brother, now the 3rd Lord Grantham. This explained that

> It was necessary to find him some 'proper occupation' pending the next election, when he would be returned to Parliament, and that he hoped ... 'some situation under you might present itself, which tho' at present rather subordinate, might be an extremely proper situation, for one with an inclination,

and I can say without vanity with abilities to appear in [the] future in a higher one. (Jones, p. 11)

Lord Hardwicke knew his family duty, and promptly appointed Robinson as his confidential secretary. Robinson was to spend more than two years working for Hardwicke, and acting as his personal representative in visits to ministers in London. He then, as his brother had predicted, became a Member of Parliament in the 1806 general election. None of the seats which his broader family controlled was vacant, so he had, perforce, to purchase a 'rotten' borough, the Irish constituency of Carlow near Dublin, under the control of the Earl of Charleville. The price he paid is unknown, and it is not clear who put up the money. He was 24 years old, and a very personable young man, with blue eyes and blond hair, though by no means as good-looking as his elder brother. Robinson did not appear to have strong political views at the time, and it was initially unclear which party he would support. He was, in fact, cross-pressured by his family connections – Hardwicke leaning towards the new Prime Minister, Lord Grenville, and the Whigs, while Lord Malmesbury was a strong Pittite. In fact, throughout his life, moderate without any deep partisan commitments, he would probably have preferred to pursue an independent line. Malmesbury, however, was ambitious for his kinsman, and when the Portland government was formed, in March 1807, managed to secure for him a nomination to the Admiralty Board. To no avail, as he recounted in his diary:

> In the morning I spoke to Fred. Robinson about his accepting the Admiralty; he doubtful, with no good reason, but influenced by the Yorkes, and his own family. Spoke to Lady Grantham; she irresolute, and, though not saying so, manifestly against his taking office, under an Administration she did not think would last. (Jones, p. 16)

Nevertheless, Robinson did throw in his lot, though very loosely, with the Tories, and his adherence was strengthened by his change of seat in the 1807 general election. He was elected for Ripon, a Yorkshire constituency which was to return him unopposed in eight further contests. It was controlled by his distant cousin, Elizabeth Sophia Lawrence, a strong Tory and a spinster, who was reputedly in (unrequited) love with his very handsome elder brother, Thomas. Robinson was not a frequent performer in parliamentary debates, but created a good impression as a relatively open-minded MP who spoke clearly and always with moderation. Then, in December 1808, he received a letter from the Leader of the House, Spencer Perceval, inviting him to move the address at the opening of Parliament in 1809. Robinson waited several days to reply, realizing that this would be tantamount to a formal declaration of support for the Portland government. He then wrote to Hardwicke saying that 'this step may possibly not meet with your entire approbation', and asking for his indulgence. Hardwicke's reply has not survived, but as he continued to correspond cordially with his cousin, it must be assumed that he was not too upset. Having thus finally nailed his colours to the mast, he soon acquired a powerful patron in Viscount Castlereagh, the Secretary for War and the Colonies, who invited him to become an Under-Secretary in his department, the following April. He remained in office for less than six months, until October 1809, when the Portland government resigned, and Castlereagh was excluded from the succeeding Perceval government. Perceval pressed Robinson to stay on, but both Hardwicke and his brother, Charles Yorke, who had been a supporter of Portland, advised him not to, as they believed that the new government would not long survive. Robinson followed their advice, but Yorke himself subsequently became First Lord of the Admiralty in Perceval's government, and offered him a post as one of the Lords of the Admiralty, with a salary of £1,000 a year, which Robinson gratefully accepted.

During this period Robinson became associated with a group of serious-minded youngish Tory MPs, who dined together at the Alfred Club, and were known as the Alfred Club Set. All of them came from an aristocratic or wealthy background, all represented pocket or rotten boroughs and most of them had been at university together, either at Oxford or Cambridge. Apart from Robinson, they included two future Prime Ministers – Sir Robert Peel and Lord Palmerston. They shared a common political outlook, but their unanimity (though not their friendship) was shattered, in 1812, when Canning successfully proposed a motion in the Commons advocating Catholic emancipation. Robinson was among those who voted in favour, despite the strong opposition of Malmesbury and of Miss Lawrence, to whom he wrote a careful letter of justification, explaining that emancipation would conciliate Ireland and yet would not 'endanger the perfect security of the Protestant establishment'. The vote was significant as perhaps the first sign that Robinson was following his own independent judgement, and was leaning towards the 'liberal' side of the Tory party. It did him no harm at all with Castlereagh, who shared his views, and hastened to bring Robinson into the Liverpool government, of which he was the most influential member, when it was formed after the assassination of Perceval. The post he obtained for Robinson was Vice-President of the Board of Trade, where he was immediately immersed in the minutia of waging economic warfare against the French. In lieu of a ministerial salary, Castlereagh secured two sinecures for him, though he apparently only drew the emoluments of one of them.

When Castlereagh left London, in December 1813, with plenipotentiary powers, to meet with the sovereigns of Russia, Prussia and Austria, in the closing stages of campaign against Napoleon, and to negotiate a peace treaty with the restored Bourbon government, he took Robinson with him, as a counsellor and friend, and the ties between them grew even stronger. At Liverpool's urgent request, Robinson returned in May, after the signing of the Treaty of Paris, to report back to Parliament, and to prepare for the visit of the crowned heads of Europe to London the following month. He received a rapturous welcome, something of the glory of the victory achieved after so many years of struggle was reflected upon him, and his popularity soared. Four months later, this 31-year-old impecunious bachelor surprised his family and friends by getting married, apparently after a whirlwind courtship. Ten years earlier, his brother, Thomas, had married the 'transcendently beautiful' daughter of the Earl of Enniskillen. Frederick Robinson was also to marry an earl's daughter, but she was notably devoid of either charm or beauty. She was, however, the sole heir to a very considerable fortune, and the world drew what seemed to be the appropriate conclusion. Lady Sarah Hobart was the daughter of the 4th Earl of Buckinghamshire, President of the Board of Control for India in Liverpool's government, and was also a kinswoman of Castlereagh. She was to prove a very serious handicap to Robinson, being demanding, neurotic and hypochondriacal, but the couple remained devoted to each other through all their vicissitudes, so perhaps the world was mistaken.

The first important parliamentary duty which Robinson was to perform after peace was restored was to move the adoption in the Commons of the famous 'Corn Law', the President of the Board of Trade being in the Lords. As Robinson was later to be credited, along with William Huskisson, as an architect of the free trade measures adopted during the final years of the Liverpool government, it is paradoxical that he was at least nominally responsible for the most notoriously protectionist measure to be adopted during the nineteenth century (see Chapter 6). In fact, Robinson seems to have been extremely lukewarm about the measure, carefully setting out both the case for, and the case against, during his parliamentary speeches. This did not save him from being a target of a London mob, furious at a measure which they believed would push bread prices through the roof. Fearing that his house in Old Burlington Street was about to be attacked, he evacuated his wife and himself to her father's residence, leaving his servants to protect his property, and their own lives, with the help of some soldiers supplied by the Home Secretary at Robinson's request. In the ensuing melee two unfortunate bystanders, one a widow, were fatally wounded, one at least of the shots being fired by Robinson's butler, James Ripley. A conscience-stricken Robinson subsequently recounted the incident in a speech in the Commons, but was so overcome by emotion that he burst into tears, earning him the nickname of 'the Blubberer'. He was unable to shake this off, as this was to be only one of a number of occasions when his emotions got the better of him. The effect on Robinson's wife, who was pregnant at the time, was a great deal worse. She was reported to have reacted 'in a most extreme manner', while W.D. Jones comments: 'Lady Sarah's fears seem to have grown gradually from morbid anxiety to positive obsession during the next decade, haunting, nagging fears, destructive to her own peace of mind, as well as that of her husband' (Jones, p. 64).

Robinson served as Vice-President for six years, but effectively was in charge of the department because the President, the Earl of Clancarty, took his duties extremely lightly. In 1818 he retired and Robinson took over, serving for a further four years, and joining the cabinet. He was thus responsible for trade policy over a full decade. During this period, he showed himself an effective administrator, and a true disciple of Adam Smith, whose works, and those of other economists, such as David Ricardo (who sat in the Commons on the opposition benches), he had closely studied. Conscious as he said, on more than one occasion, that Britain could not hope to sell its products in foreign markets if their traders were unable to export goods to Britain in return, he set his face against prohibitive tariffs, and was always on the look-out to reduce, or remove them, when the opportunity arose. He also worked hard to restore trading relations with the United States, which had been broken by the 1812–14 War, leaving a legacy of renewed bitterness between the two sides. The Americans were extremely touchy about negotiations, having long experience of condescension by British ministers, and were therefore delighted when both Robinson and Castlereagh showed themselves more forthcoming than their predecessors. The result was the Commercial Convention between the two countries, signed on 3 July 1815, and eight years later two Acts of Parliament, sponsored by Robinson, opening up a large number of harbours in the West Indies and Canada, as Free Ports, open to American ships and those of all other nations. The US Congress passed a reciprocal act in the following year. The US Ambassador in London, Richard Rush, a 'radical democrat', later left his impressions of the two British ministers with whom he had to deal. His verdict on Castlereagh was 'that he was dangerous to all the remaining liberties of England', but at the same time called him 'the British statesman who was most interested in promoting Anglo-American goodwill'. On Robinson, he wrote several years later: 'We are amongst those who think very favourably of Lord Goderich' He called him a 'clear-headed, diligent and efficient man of business', and especially noted his 'fine education' and 'admirable temper', concluding that Robinson was 'an intellectualised version of Lord Liverpool' (Jones, p. 86).

The suicide of Castlereagh. in August 1822, deprived Robinson of his patron, but in the subsequent government reshuffle, he was promoted Chancellor of the Exchequer. From this time onward, he was generally seen as a supporter of Canning, but did not enjoy particularly close relations with him. However, his role as Chancellor, at a time when Britain was strongly emerging from the post-war depression, established him as a major political figure, and one who, largely because of his great amiability, had virtually no enemies. He benefited from the budgetary policy of his predecessor, Nicholas Vansittart, who bequeathed him booming tax revenues. For the first time in many years, the budget was in surplus, and it continued to be until his final year at the Exchequer. In addition, he was the beneficiary of a large windfall, when Austria quite unexpectedly repaid an old debt of £ 2.2 million, which had practically been written off as a loss. The result was that for the first three years, he was able to deliver expansionary budgets, abolishing many of the more pernickety taxes, including those on 'windows, male servants, wheeled vehicles, occasional house servants, occasional gardeners, certain ponies and mules, horses and mules engaged in agriculture and trade, on clerks and shopmen of traders, and some other items of a similar nature' (Jones, p. 101). He flanked his tax cuts, with sweeping tariff reductions, which led to his being hailed as the author of the first real Free Trade budgets in British history. Some later scholars have questioned whether he was their true architect, suggesting that his contribution was less than that of William Huskisson, his successor as President of the Board of Trade. Nevertheless, it was Robinson who claimed the credit, and was rewarded with the nickname of 'Prosperity Robinson'. His stock rose very high, but was somewhat dented during his last year as Chancellor, when he was judged to have badly mishandled a financial crisis, and it seemed probable that Robinson's next budget would show a deficit. He became the object of unaccustomed criticism, though, as his biographer makes clear, it was of a far more gentle nature than another chancellor might have experienced. This was due, he recounted, to Robinson's popularity, on both sides of the House, which was 'the reward not only for his liberal policies , but for the essential kindness, honesty and integrity of his character, which made him a sort of special person whom the customs of the House protected from personal invective' (Jones, p. 122). Stories abounded of Robinson's geniality, lack of side and ability to laugh at himself. One famous incident, related by the political diarist and MP, John Wilson Croker, is quoted by W.D. Jones:

> Everyone knows the story of a gentleman's asking Lord North who 'that frightful woman was?' and his lordship's answering, that is my wife. The other, to repair the blunder, said I do not mean *her*, but that monster next to her. 'Oh!' said Lord North, 'that monster is my daughter'. With this story Fred. Robinson, in his usual absent enthusiastic way, was one day entertaining a lady whom he sat next to at dinner, and lo! the lady was Lady Charlotte Lindsay – the monster in question.

Nevertheless, Robinson found it hard to bear the strain of even mild criticism at a time of considerable upheaval in his private life. By this time his wife was suffering from severe mental illness, which led her to believe that she was dying, even though there was no objective reason for this belief. Her condition was then made much worse by the prolonged illness of their beloved daughter, Eleanor, who died, aged 11, in October 1826, their other child, a son, having died ten years earlier, aged only two days. Lady Sarah reacted from their loss by forming excessive fears about the health of her husband, being extremely reluctant to let him out of her sight As a result, Robinson wrote to the King, requesting permission to be absent from 'the approaching *early* session of Parliament', so that he could take his wife to their country estate in Lincolnshire. The King warmly responded in the affirmative, and Lady Sarah then aged 33, determined that they should have another child, who was to be born a year later, in October 1927. (Unlike his two siblings, George Frederick Samuel Robinson was to enjoy a long life, dying only in 1909, after a long and distinguished political career of his own). Two months later, in December 1826, Robinson wrote a further letter, this time to the Prime Minister, Lord Liverpool, in which he suggested that he should go up to the House of Lords, and occupy a less arduous position in the government. Liverpool replied that the government's position was extremely fragile, and that it was inexpedient to make any ministerial changes at that juncture, and Robinson agreed to carry on for the time being.

Liverpool was to suffer a cerebral haemorrhage, in February 1827, and shortly afterwards retired as Prime Minister. George IV momentarily considered Robinson as Liverpool's successor, in order to avoid having to choose between Canning and Wellington, but eventually decided on the former. Canning offered Robinson the post of Secretary for War and the Colonies, combined with leadership of the House of Lords, to which he was appointed as Viscount Goderich. Goderich served for too short a time to have a measurable effect in his department, but his leadership of the Lords left a great deal to be desired. It is doubtful if the Canning government enjoyed a majority in the Upper House – no confidence vote was called during its four months in office. What was soon apparent was that its enemies were more cohesive than its friends. Goderich had to face fierce attacks from right-wing Tories, who wanted nothing to do with Canning, and from the main body of Whigs, under Earl Grey, whose object was to replace his administration with a purely Whig government. A third element of dissension was a faction around Charles Stewart, the third Marquess of Londonderry, the half-brother of Castlereagh and a former friend of Goderich's. He now bitterly attacked him for having transferred his loyalties to Canning – Castlereagh's earlier foe – even though the two men had long since patched up the quarrel which had led to their duel many years earlier. Goderich never succeeded in imposing himself on the House and was humiliated when a government bill to ameliorate the worst effects the Corn Law was effectively shredded by a hostile amendment proposed by the Duke of Wellington. Goderich's short spell in the Lords cast serious doubts upon his leadership qualities, but George IV lost no time in sending for him to succeed Canning, when the latter died on 8 August 1827. Goderich, who was 44, would have been well advised to refuse the King's offer to form a government, particularly under the restrictive conditions which were imposed. He had already told colleagues that he doubted whether a coalition between liberal Tories and only a minority faction of the Whig party could long survive, or one which was not at liberty to proceed with Catholic emancipation.

Yet these were just the conditions on which George IV was insisting, and he also imposed a veto over the personnel of the Cabinet. Thus he declined to accept Lord Holland, Charles James Fox's nephew and political heir, who would have greatly boosted political support for the government, and insisted – against Goderich's advice – on the appointment of the ultra Tory, John Charles Herries, as Chancellor of the Exchequer. It is fairly clear that George IV had little confidence in Goderich, but chose him as a stopgap – to avoid, or postpone, a painful choice between appointing a Tory government under the Duke of Wellington or a Whig one under Lord Grey.

So, the government started on an uncertain note and never developed any rhythm. While there were some changes in personnel, its composition was similar to that of Canning's government, an uneasy coalition between moderate Tories and moderate Whigs, with the Prime Minister, the most moderate of them all, actively regretting the mere existence of party distinctions. His closest associate in the government was Huskisson, Secretary for War and the Colonies, but more importantly also leader of the House of Commons. Conscious that they would soon have to meet Parliament, they began preparing the draft of a King's speech setting out a government programme for the next session. One idea which Goderich was working on was for a new property tax which would replace a range of indirect taxes, and which in fact foreshadowed Sir Robert Peel's introduction of the first peace-time income tax in 1842. But ministers' attentions, and unity of purpose, were distracted by dramatic news which arrived from Greece. Before his death, Canning had negotiated a treaty with Russia and France that the three countries should jointly endeavour to secure a peaceful end to the struggle for Greek independence by attempting to secure a separation of the belligerent forces. On the Turkish side, this largely consisted of a force which had been sent from its vassal state of Egypt, under the command of Ibrahim Pasha, and which was currently terrorizing the Morea. A naval force, under the British Admiral Codrington, had been sent to the Aegean and was monitoring the Egyptian and Turkish fleets, which were lying in the harbour of Navarino. A dispatch was drawn up to send to Codrington urging him to act with great circumspection and not on any account to provoke hostilities. Due to the length of time it took to consult too many ministers and officials, there was a delay in sending it out, and, in the meantime, Codrington had taken affairs into his own hands and, on 20 October 1827, sailed his warships into Navarino, mooring them provocatively close to the Turkish and Egyptian vessels. It was never established who fired the first shots, but by the end of the afternoon 60 of the 89 Turco-Egyptian ships had been sunk, with a loss of 8,000 men, while the much smaller allied fleet had lost no ships and suffered no more than 200 casualties. The Battle of Navarino was to go down in history as the last major engagement between sailing ships. The steam age was about to emerge.

The cabinet was completely split on whether to proclaim Codrington a national hero or have him court-martialled, and there was considerable apprehension that the country would find itself in a totally unwanted war against Turkey. There were anguished discussions on how the issue should be handled when Parliament met in January 1828. At this stage a row broke out between ministers on a relatively trivial issue – the chairmanship of a finance committee to be set up in the Commons. After consulting several colleagues, Huskisson approached a Whig MP, Lord Althorp, to ascertain whether he would be willing to accept this post. Herries then protested, on the grounds that he, as Chancellor of the Exchequer, should be responsible for the nomination, but when the majority of the cabinet backed Huskisson appeared to acquiesce. Partly because of these quarrels, Goderich now determined that the cabinet must be strengthened before the beginning of the parliamentary session. Together with Huskisson and Lord Lansdowne, the leading Whig minister, he agreed that he should tell the King, when he met him on 8 December, that it was now essential to bring Lord Holland into the government and balanced this with the suggestion that the former Tory Foreign Secretary, Marquess Wellesley, should also be brought in. Goderich was under exceptional pressure at this time, not only because of the cabinet splits, but because of the mental state of his wife. She had successfully given birth to their second son, on 24 October, but was now suffering from an extreme form of post-natal depression and was behaving in a most unreasonable way towards her husband. Huskisson referred to this in a letter he wrote at this time, saying that Goderich was 'in a most pitiful state...his spirits are worn out...he has lost his powers of decision'. He attributed this not to the new cabinet crisis, but to 'constant worry in which he has been kept by his all but crazy wife' (Jones, p. 189). Goderich's interview with the King was far from satisfactory. George IV was quite happy to accept Wellesley, but refused point blank to have Holland. Goderich indicated that this would be unacceptable to his cabinet colleagues. The three men then wrote a formal letter to the King, stressing the need for more 'solid and united support', They proposed that the Duke of Wellington or Lord Hill should be made Master of the Ordnance, that Wellesley should become Lord President of the Council and that Holland should be brought into the Cabinet. The alternative, they implied, was resignation. Then, unknown to his colleagues, Goderich added a postscript to the letter, in the following terms:

> Lord Goderich cannot conclude this statement without venturing to add, how deeply he feels his own inadequacy to discharge the great duties of the situation to which your Majesty's far too favourable opinion called him. His own natural infirmities have been aggravated by a protracted state of anxiety during the last two years; his health is enfeebled, and above all he fears that the health of one dependent upon him for support and strength is still in a state of such feebleness and uncertainty as to keep alive that anxiety to a degree not easily compatible with the due discharge of duties which require the exertion of the energies of the strongest mind. (Iremonger, 1970, p. 80)

Goderich certainly did not intend this to be taken as a letter of resignation. It was merely a plea for more understanding from the King of the difficulties which he was in. George IV, however, construed it as such, sending a cold reply, which contained the words: 'The King can only regret that Lord Goderich's domestic calamities unfit him for his present situation, but over this the King unhappily has not control' (Jones, p. 19). He then sent for the Earl of Harrowby, a former Foreign Secretary and Lord President of the Council, and invited him to form a new government. Harrowby eventually declined, recommending the King to persist with Goderich. Goderich's reprieve did not, however, last long. Herries, possibly egged on by the King's private secretary, Sir William Knighton, who was anxious to see the back of the Goderich government, renewed his objection to the appointment of Lord Althorp to head the Finance committee of the Commons, and said that he would resign if the appointment went ahead. Huskisson thereupon declared that he would resign if it did not. The King, concluding that the Prime Minister was incapable of controlling his ministers, told Goderich when he saw him on 8 January 1828 that he considered the government as dissolved. According to one account, Goderich, very upset, dissolved in tears, and the King lent him his handkerchief. Two weeks later, Wellington accepted an invitation to form a government, in which the majority of Goderich's ministers retained their posts. Goderich had served for a total of 130 days, and his was the only government in modern British history not to present itself to Parliament.

Despite this humiliation, this was by no means the end of Goderich's ministerial career, which was one of the longest in British history. Altogether, he served for 30 years, 20 of them as a Cabinet minister. He was also to establish something of a record as to the number of different party labels under which he served. Starting off as a Tory, he was to join the Whig government of Lord Grey, in 1830, as Secretary for War and the Colonies, and later, as Lord Privy

Seal, becoming the Earl of Ripon in 1834. In 1841, he was back in Sir Robert Peel's Conservative government, for a further term as President of the Board of Trade, with the young Gladstone as his deputy. His final post , also under Peel, was as President of the Board of Control of India, in 1843–46. When the Conservative Party split over the abolition of the Corn Law, he became a Peelite. Living until 1859, he died at the age of 76. His wife, whose mental health was to recover remarkably quickly once he had left the premiership, outlived him by eight years.

Goderich was valued as a Cabinet colleague as somebody who was conscientious, reliable and easy to deal with. His very amiability, however, proved a fatal weakness as head of government. There was neither enough steel in his character to assert his will over awkward colleagues, nor enough firmness to enable him to deal effectively with a blustering but essentially weak-willed monarch. His career is an illustration of the 'Peter Principle', enunciated, in 1966, by the Canadian author Laurence J. Peter. He argued that, in any hierarchical organization, people are promoted until they reach their level of incompetence. In Goderich's case that level was very high indeed – the premiership.

Works consulted

Norman Gash, 1984, *Lord Liverpool*, London, Weidenfeld & Nicolson.

Wendy Hinde, 1973, *George Canning*, London, Purnell Book Services.

Lucille Iremonger, 1970, *The Fiery Chariot*, London, Secker & Warburg.

Wilbur Devereux Jones, 1970, *'Prosperity' Robinson: The Life of Viscount Goderich 1782–1859*, London, Macmillan.

Peter Jupp, 2004, Article in *Oxford Dictionary of National Biography*, Oxford, Oxford University Press.

9

Arthur Wesley (Wellesley), 1st Duke of Wellington – Military Hero, Political Misfit?

The war hero, who takes up politics and rises effortlessly to the top, is a familiar figure in American history. At least eight presidents – George Washington, Andrew Jackson, William Henry Harrison, Zachary Taylor, Ulysses S. Grant, Benjamin Harrison, Theodore Roosevelt and Dwight Eisenhower – conform to this stereotype. The only British Prime Minister to have followed a similar route is Arthur Wellesley, 1st Duke of Wellington, and even he is somewhat different, as he already had a fair amount of political experience before his military triumphs. Born Arthur Wesley, in Dublin, on 1 May 1769 (the same year as Napoleon), he was the fifth son and sixth child of nine children. His father, the 1st Earl of Mornington (in the Irish peerage), was a composer and Professor of Music at Trinity College, Dublin. His mother, the former Anne Hill, was the eldest daughter of the 1st Viscount Dungannon. Both of his parents were products of the Protestant ascendancy in Ireland. Arthur grew up a solitary child, closer to his father than his mother, and showed no promise whatsoever, either academically or at games, other than at playing the violin, at which he seems to have inherited something of his father's skill. (That is, if the first Lord Mornington was, indeed, his father. According to the historian L.G. Mitchell, Arthur later came to doubt his mother's fidelity, and believed his actual father may have been a gardener on the Wesleys' Irish estate – Mitchell, p. 183). The family moved to London, where they lived in rented rooms in Knightsbridge, Lord Mornington now being quite heavily in debt. When Arthur was 12, Lord Mornington suddenly died, and the following year, Arthur and his younger brother Gerald were sent to Eton by his eldest brother, Richard, nine years his senior and now the 2nd Lord Mornington. Richard had to mortgage the family estate in County Meath in order to pay the school fees. Richard himself had been a brilliant scholar at Eton and had gone on to win the Chancellor's prize for a Latin ode at Christ Church, Oxford, but neither of his younger siblings made any sort of mark at the school; the only memorable event being recorded by the school's historian was a fight Arthur had with Robert Smith, the brother of the well-known clergyman and wit, Sydney Smith.

After only three years, he was taken away from the school, in order to save money, by his mother, Anne, who not only did not lavish her son with love but seems to have actively disliked him. She took him to live in Brussels, where she hoped to live more economically than in London, and set him, with only mediocre results, to learn French. Yet Arthur showed little aptitude for this, and spent most of his time lounging around, his only interest being playing the violin, 'the only species of talent that the young man appeared to possess', according to a fellow lodger (Hibbert, 1997, p. 6). Anne soon returned to London, leaving Arthur to fend for himself in Brussels, but when her youngest son, Henry, decided to join the army, concluded that her 'ugly son Arthur', also, was 'good for powder and nothing more', and packed him off to a military academy for young noblemen at Angers, in western France. Here he learnt fencing and ballroom dancing, and how to sit properly on horseback. He also greatly improved his French, developed a taste for gambling, and most probably lost his virginity in a local brothel. He much impressed the academy's director, Marcel de Pignerolle, who was reported as saying that he had 'one Irish lad of great promise, of the name of Wesley' (Longford, 1969, p. 21). He returned to London, aged 17, in 1786, ready to take advantage of the patronage of his brother Richard, now an MP in the Irish House of Commons, and a Junior Lord of the Treasury in the government of the Younger Pitt. Shortly before his eighteenth birthday, he became an ensign in the 73rd (Highland) Regiment of Foot, and was soon promoted Lieutenant and appointed as aide-de-camp to the Marquess of Buckingham, the Lord Lieutenant of Ireland. His duties were extremely light, and it soon became apparent that his role was intended to be that of a courtier rather than filling any administrative or military function.

It was a lazy and corrupt court, and Lieutenant (later to be Captain, Major and Lt.-Colonel) Wesley, who periodically bought promotion with money advanced by his brother Richard, spent much of his time playing cards, getting into debt and visiting brothels, in one of which he was arrested and fined for assaulting a French client with a stick. There was a more serious side to him, however; he regretted not having been to a university, and a visitor to his home was surprised to find him reading John Locke's *Essay concerning Human Understanding*. In April 1790, he became a Member of the Irish House of Commons, for the family seat of Trim and was elected unopposed. He was not yet 21 and had to wait for two years before making his maiden speech. In 1792, he began courting Lady Kitty Pakenham, the 20-year-old daughter of the 2nd Earl of Longford, described both as a 'beauty' and 'bookish'. In 1793, he proposed marriage, only to be rejected because her elder brother, Thomas, soon to become the third Earl, considered that neither the income nor the prospects of a captain in the 18th Light Dragoons would be sufficient to keep his sister in the life to which she had become accustomed. Mortally offended, Arthur determined to turn his back on Ireland and go to war against the French, with whom hostilities had finally broken out four years after the storming of the Bastille. At the same time, he resolved to take his own life in hand, to exercise the maximum of self-discipline, to become a real professional soldier instead of a part-time dilettante. Gone would be the endless hours playing cards, gone his ineffectual entry into politics, gone his beloved music – he was to burn his violin with his own hands in the summer of 1793. Nevertheless, it was to be another year, before he was able to join the British army in Flanders, sailing from Cork in June 1794, as a Lieutenant-Colonel. Before he left, he wrote a final letter to Kitty, summarized in the first of two enthralling biographical volumes written by Elizabeth Longford, the wife of a lineal descendant of Kitty's brother, Thomas:

> He could not accept that all was over. As Lord Longford's decision was founded upon 'prudential motives', an improvement in Arthur's situation could alter everything. There followed a sentence of which the last phrase was decisively to alter Arthur's life. If something did occur to make Kitty and her brother change their minds – 'my mind will still remain the same'. To an honourable man, those seven words would be binding. (Longford, 1969, p. 36)

The campaign which Wesley was to join in Flanders was one of the least glorious in British military history. Commanded by the ineffectual Duke of York, the British troops were made mincemeat of by their much more motivated and better-led French adversaries. In Lady Longford's words, Colonel Wesley:

> saw the effects of a divided command, of a winter campaign in a bitter climate, of no properly organized food supply or winter clothing, of local inhabitants who preferred the enemy to their allies, and above all of a prolonged and undisciplined retreat. In short, as he told [the Earl of] Stanhope forty-five years later when his friend was suggesting that the Dutch campaign must have been very useful to him: 'Why – I learnt what one ought not to do and that is always something'. (Longford, 1969, p. 37)

Lieutenant-Colonel Wesley was, however, one of very few British officers whose reputation was enhanced by the campaign, being congratulated by headquarters on an action he had fought at Boxtel, in Holland, the first military engagement in his life, in which, thanks to the iron discipline which he imposed on his troops, they had repulsed a French charge. After returning to Dublin, Wesley then had to wait another dispiriting year before receiving command of the 33rd Regiment of Foot, with orders to sail to India. Still heavily in debt, he resolved to spend the long voyage out in self-improvement, purchasing a library of well over 100 books, including works on military history, law, economics, philosophy and theology. In the course of her voluminous research, Elizabeth Longford was able to establish that five of the books purchased by Wesley also appeared in the *Bibliothèque du camp* which accompanied Napolcon Bonaparte on his 1798 campaign (Longford, 1969, p. 44n.) After arriving in Calcutta, and later Madras, Wesley soon settled again into the desultory round of self-indulgent regimental life, which he had known in Dublin, embarking on numerous affairs, mainly with the wives of fellow officers. Of only medium height, with a too prominent nose, Wesley was neither blessed with the appearance of a matinee idol, nor did he possess any small talk. Yet his conversation was interesting, and by this time he exuded great self-confidence, and already a certain charisma which marked him out from his fellows. His position in India was transformed by the arrival a year later of his eldest brother, Lord Mornington, as Governor-General, accompanied by a younger brother, Henry, as his private secretary. Some years earlier, Mornington had abandoned the use of his surname, Wesley, in favour of an older spelling 'Wellesley', which sounded more aristocratic and removed any suspicion that he might be connected with the recently established religious movement of Methodism, of which the brothers John and Charles Wesley were the leading spirits. Colonel Arthur Wesley now followed suit, while Mornington was shortly advanced in the peerage and became known as Marquess Wellesley.

The governor-general's main objective in India was vastly to expand the territory under British control and to extirpate any French influence within the peninsula. Ignoring claims of military seniority, he blatantly used his brother as the main instrument of his ambitions, giving him successive military commands in campaigns against the Sultan of Mysore, Tipu Sultan, and then the powerful Maratha confederacy in central India. He won all his battles, with the exception of a night-time skirmish in woods outside the great fortress of Seringapatam, which he was able to reverse the following day. His greatest victory, against the odds, was at Assaye, in September 1803, when his 7,000 men defeated a 50,000-strong force of Marathas in a battle in which Arthur Wellesley had two horses shot from under him. The extent of his victories wiped out any criticism of his brother's favouritism, and he returned home in 1805, with a knighthood, the rank of Major-General and £42,000 in war booty to his credit.

He was now 36, appeared to have the world at his feet, but – encouraged by a mutual friend and would-be matchmaker – promptly fired off a renewed proposal to Kitty Pakenham, with whom he had had no contact in 12 years. The passing years had not enhanced her attractions. 'By 1802, Kitty had decided that the affair was over, became engaged to another man, broke it off, and suffered a nervous breakdown which destroyed her youthful charm and self-confidence' (Gash, 2004). She wrote back to Wellesley accepting his proposal, but suggesting that they should meet again before he finally committed himself. Wellesley demurred, and set in hand the arrangements for the marriage to be celebrated in Dublin on 10 April 1806. He was soon to regret his impetuosity, whispering at the altar to his brother, the Rev. Gerald Wellesley, who performed the ceremony, 'She has become ugly, by Jove!' (Iremonger, p. 89). Many years later, he explained to his friend, Harriett Arbuthnot, 'I married her because they asked me to, and I did not know myself. I thought I should not care for anybody again, and that I should be with my army, and, in short, I was a fool' (Ibid.). One does not need a Ph.D. in psychology to conclude that what motivated him was his injured pride: that he wanted to demonstrate to the Longfords that they had been grievously wrong in undervaluing him a dozen years earlier. It did not take long before both partners concluded that the marriage had been a mistake, finding that they had few interests in common and derived no pleasure from each other's company. Two sons were, however, born within the first two years; after that they spent a minimum of time together, and Wellesley did not once come home on a visit during five years he was away fighting the Peninsular War. Largely at the suggestion of Lord Grenville, the Prime Minister, who had replaced Pitt on his death in Janury1806, Wellesley now resumed his political career, though at a much higher level. He was elected to the House of Commons for Rye, in April 1806, and, the following year was appointed Chief Secretary for Ireland in the new government formed by the Duke of Portland. He accepted the post on condition that it should not be allowed to interfere with his army career. He proved himself brisk and efficient in the performance of his duties, and gained general respect, but his heart was not really in it. Later,when in the summer of 1808 an expedition was sent to Copenhagen to seize the Danish fleet, he successfully applied to participate, and was awarded the command of a division which routed a Danish force sent to relieve the siege of the capital.

Back in Dublin, he resumed his duties, but for less than a year, when, with the outbreak of the Peninsular War, he was put in temporary charge of an expeditionary force sent to resist the French invasion of Portugal. He sailed from Cork, with 9,000 men, landing in Portugal on 1 August 1808, and within three weeks had inflicted two crushing defeats on the French army led by Marshal Junot. The French sued for an armistice, but by then two more senior generals had arrived from London, who took over command from Wellesley, and negotiated ridiculously generous terms with Junot's representatives, the so-called Convention of Cintra. Wellesley was appalled, but counter-signed the agreement, which led to his being bracketed with his two seniors in a subsequent parliamentary enquiry, which exonerated him. A year later he was back in Portugal, in charge of the British army after the death of Sir John Moore. He was not to return to Britain until June 1814, following the apparent final defeat of Napoleon. The largest contributory factor to the Emperor's downfall was obviously his disastrous invasion, and subsequent retreat, from Russia, in 1812–13, but historians have generally attributed second place to the Peninsular War, known as 'Napoleon's Spanish ulcer'. In this, Wellesley had held down vastly superior French forces, depriving Napoleon of their use elsewhere, and had then – together with Spanish and Portuguese auxiliaries – succeeded in expelling them from the Peninsula. He pursued them into France, gaining a final military victory at Toulouse in April 1814, four days after Napoleon's abdication, news of which had not yet reached the south of France. Wellesley's command had gained him great renown, he won all the pitched battles which he fought, was created successively an earl, a viscount and finally Duke of

Wellington, and voted £400,000 by a grateful House of Commons, as well as being awarded estates in Portugal, Spain and the Netherlands by the monarchs of these newly restored countries. He used the parliamentary grant to purchase two imposing residences – at Stratfield Saye, in Hampshire, and Apsley House, at Hyde Park Corner in London.

But before he could enjoy them, he was called back for foreign service – as Ambassador to the restored Bourbon court in Paris. Arriving in August 1814, he cut a glittering social figure, with legions of attractive young women throwing themselves at his feet. Among his amours were at least two of Napoleon's former mistresses, one of whom was later to recall that 'M. le duc était beaucoup le plus fort' (Longford, 1969, p. 375). He also had at least one assignation with the famous courtesan, Harriette Wilson, with whom he had consorted more than a decade earlier in London, and who later tried to blackmail him, in exchange for expunging his name from her notorious memoirs. The Duke's response was immediate: 'Publish and be damned', he wrote to her egregious publisher. The unhappy Kitty, who belatedly joined her husband in Paris, with their two sons, was severely embarrassed by his conduct and was the recipient of many pitying glances. The Duke undoubtedly added lustre to the British representation, none of the Austrian, Prussian or Russian representatives being able to compete with his renown, but his many distractions left him little time to concentrate on serious diplomacy. This may have been one reason why, in February 1815, when Lord Castlereagh, the Foreign Secretary and Leader of the House of Commons, was recalled from the Congress of Vienna to resume his parliamentary duties, Wellington was sent to replace him. Another reason why Wellington was removed from Paris was a lively fear of assassination attempts by disgruntled Bonapartists. Within a month of his arrival in Vienna, however, Napoleon escaped from Elba, and the four principal powers represented at the Congress – Britain, Austria, Russia and Prussia – promptly appointed him commander-in chief of the allied armies, and Wellington set out for Brussels to prepare for the final showdown with the restored Emperor.

The climax was the battle of Waterloo, fought on 18 June 1815, which he was to describe as 'a damned close run thing…I was nearly beat'. On the day, he showed himself a better general than Napoleon, marshalling his forces more intelligently, showing greater flexibility and more actively inspiring his troops. Was Wellington a military genius? No, if measured against the achievements of Alexander, Julius Caesar, Frederick the Great or Napoleon. Yes, if 'genius' is defined, as it was by Thomas Carlyle, as the ability to take infinite pains, or, more vulgarly, 'nine tenths perspiration, one tenth inspiration'. Wellington was essentially a defensive general, and as such had few equals. No general took as much trouble as Wellington in securing logistical support and adequate weaponry and supplies for his troops, cultivating the goodwill of local inhabitants in foreign campaigns, spying out battlefields in advance, choosing the best defensive positions for his troops and actively directing the flow of battle by ceaselessly riding round from unit to unit during the course of a conflict. He also had a healthy respect for his opponents. He never met Napoleon in battle before Waterloo, but he was heard to say that if he learnt that the Emperor was about to take personal command of his troops it would be more fearful news than if 40,000 French reinforcements were on their way. By contrast, Napoleon was by no means in awe of his British opponent, blaming French defeats in Portugal and Spain on his marshals rather than on Wellington's skill. On the morning of Waterloo, he said to Marshal Soult: 'Just because you have been beaten by Wellington you regard him as a great general. I tell you that Wellington is a bad general, that the English are bad troops and that this battle will be a picnic. We have ninety chances in our favour and not ten against' (Hibbert, pp. 177–8). Wellington was a harsh disciplinarian, who became known as the Iron Duke, though he himself on several occasions showed scant respect for the orders of his superiors. Though often grumpy and short tempered, he was invariably straightforward and honourable in his dealings. He was popular with his troops and was customarily known as 'Nosey', a comment on his appearance rather than his curiosity. If Wellington had a fault as a general, it was in his reluctance to give credit to his subordinates. He mortally offended the family of his second-in-command at Waterloo, Lord Uxbridge, whose leg was shot off as he rode at Wellington's side, by giving him only the most perfunctory of mentions in the dispatch which he sent to the Secretary for War after the battle. He has subsequently been criticized for his alleged attempts to downplay the role of Marshal Blücher and his Prussian army, without whose timely arrival the battle would undoubtedly have been lost. That said, Wellington was far from glorying in his victory. 'Nothing except a battle lost can be half so melancholy as a battle won. I hope to God that I have fought my last battle', he told his friend, Lady Shelley, 'It is a bad thing to be always fighting' (Ibid., p. 185).

His wish was granted, but Waterloo was by no means the end of either his military or his broader public career. He returned to Paris, no longer as ambassador but commander-in-chief of the 150,000-strong allied army of occupation which was to remain in France until the defeated nation had paid off the reparations which had been imposed by the Congress of Vienna. After three years he was recalled to join the cabinet of Lord Liverpool's government. The attraction of this for Liverpool was obvious. His government was highly unpopular and going through a bad patch. Its standing could only be improved by the recruitment of so eminent a figure as the Iron Duke. Wellington was more hesitant: he did not wish to label himself as a party politician, though his Tory views were obvious enough. He consented to join only after being persuaded by Castlereagh, who had appointed him to his command in the Peninsular War, and supported him through thick and thin against his many critics. Even so, Wellington insisted on the condition that he should not be counted as a political supporter of the government and would be free to go his own way if it subsequently fell, without being committed to opposing any alternative ministry. The original plan was that he should be appointed as a minister without portfolio, but Lord Mulgrave offered to relinquish the post of Master-General of the Ordnance in his favour, which was regarded as a highly suitable post because of his military experience.

Wellington took great care over the running of his department, and showed himself an outstanding administrator, but played little part in general cabinet discussions for the first three to four years, until the death of Castlereagh, in 1822. He then played a significant role in persuading George IV to accept the appointment of George Canning as Foreign Secretary and leader of the Commons. The King was highly reluctant (see Chapters 6 and 7), but when Wellington added his great influence to that of Liverpool, he finally gave way. It was not long before Wellington regretted having helped bring Canning back on board. He gradually emerged during the succeeding five years as his main opponent within the Cabinet both on foreign and domestic affairs. In foreign policy, he unsuccessfully opposed, together with the ultra Tory peers, Canning's championship of independence for Spain's Latin American colonies and his opposition to the Holy Alliance (of Russia, Prussia and Austria) in Europe. On the domestic front, he was against Liverpool and Canning's Liberal Tory policies, and in particular Canning's determination to press for Catholic emancipation. This was to lead to a misunderstanding which was later to cost Wellington dear. Unlike the Tory ultras, he was not opposed to Catholic emancipation as such; his private views were little different from Canning's. What he was against was bringing the issue to a head at that particular time. The Tory ultras did not appreciate the difference, and he was decidedly their candidate for the succession when Liverpool's health broke down early in 1827. Wellington himself professed reluctance, and told the House of Lords that he 'felt disqualified from the post of prime minister and lacked the capacity to fill it', adding: 'My Lords, I should have been worse than mad if I had thought of such a thing' (Gash, 1990, pp. 122–3). In the event, George IV chose Canning, and Wellington and half of the Cabinet promptly resigned, leading Canning to seek Whig support in order to form an administration. In January 1827, Wellington had been appointed Commander-in-Chief of the army, on the death of the Duke of York. He resigned in a huff, in April, when Canning became Prime Minister, but he was persuaded to resume the post when Canning died, and was replaced as Prime Minister by Lord Goderich, in August 1827.

Goderich lasted barely four months before he was effectively dismissed by George IV, who, this time, unhesitatingly sent for Wellington as his successor. George IV was now determined to have a purely Tory government, having a marked aversion to the Whig leader, Lord Grey. Sir Robert Peel, the Tory leader in the Commons, who had been Home Secretary in the previous three govern-ments, would have been an obvious alternative, but the King did not like him either. Despite Wellington's earlier diffidence, he accepted without demur. He was 58 years old, and took office on 22 January 1828. There was an immedi-ate crisis due to Wellington's pigheaded determination to retain his post as commander-in-chief. He refused to see any constitutional impropriety in com-bining the two posts, and only backed down, with exceedingly bad grace, in the face of the opposition of his entire cabinet. George IV's hope was that Wellington would succeed in restoring the sort of balance within the Cabinet that Lord Liverpool had enjoyed. The Whigs were excluded, and the posts were divided up between the more traditional Tories, mostly peers, and those who were regarded as Liberal Tories or Canningites, of whom the most prominent was William Huskisson, the Secretary for War and the Colonies. The other Canningite ministers were Lord Palmerston MP, as War Secretary, Charles Grant as President of the Board of Trade and the Earl of Dudley as Foreign Secretary. The Chancellor of the Exchequer was Henry Goulburn, a far from assertive personality, who was described as having 'the self-effacing habits of a good civil servant'. Robert Peel returned to his earlier post as Home Secretary, which he combined with the leadership of the Commons, and was clearly the number two man in the government. On the question of Catholic emancipa-tion, the most divisive political issue of the day, the Cabinet was almost evenly divided, with seven pros and six antis, and a general agreement not to push the issue in the face of the King's known opposition. On parliamentary reform, of which the Duke himself was a resolute opponent, there was a clear majority against, though the Canningites were more sympathetic.

Although Wellington started off by enjoying the affection and goodwill of nearly all his colleagues, it was not long before difficulties began to arise. Naturally authoritarian by temperament, he had long grown used to having his decisions accepted unquestionably by his military subordinates, and he found it hard to accept any disagreement or criticism from his cabinet colleagues. The daily round of compromise and negotiation which was meat and drink to most politicians and senior officials was wholly alien to his character. He also did not appear to have any serious misgivings about his own abilities to lead. When the Princess Lieven, the wife of the Russian ambassador and a notorious intriguer, especially among the upper ranks of the ultra Tories, suggested to him that his lack of practice as a parliamentary speaker would be a handicap, he replied: 'No…to begin with, I can learn; if I want it, it will come back to me. And, even if I can't, the Duke of Portland had no more idea of speaking than I have, and yet he was at the head of the administration' (Gash, 1990, p. 125). Nevertheless, he confessed in a private letter to the Prince of Orange, immediately after his appointment, that it was an office 'for the performance of the duties of which I am not qualified, and they are very disagreeable to me' (Ibid., p. 119).

It was therefore predictable that he would have a bumpy ride, and in the process upset many of his supporters. The first to feel aggrieved were the ultra Tories, who did very badly out of the Duke's initial cabinet appointments; in particular, Lord Eldon, the former Lord Chancellor, was left out, much to his chagrin. Wellington's own family was also grievously disappointed. His eldest brother Richard, Marquess Wellesley, who had previously held the posts of Governor-General of India, Foreign Secretary and Lord Lieutenant of Ireland, had wrongly assumed that he would be included, while the second brother, William Wellesley-Pole, who had married into great wealth and was a former minister under Lord Liverpool, also had his hopes dashed.

The ultras were further put out by one of the earliest pieces of legislation introduced by the Wellington government. This was a long overdue measure to repeal the Test and Corporation Acts, excluding Protestant dissenters (that is, Quakers and members of nonconformist churches, such as Methodists, Congregationalists and Baptists) from holding various public offices. These acts had long been a source of vexation to important sections of the business community, even though they were seldom applied in practice. Wellington had not himself been in favour of repeal, but when the government was defeated in the Commons on a motion moved by Lord John Russell, he concluded –as a military man – that the government's position was untenable and that a healthy retreat was required. He therefore pushed through a government bill repealing both pieces of legislation. The ultras were horrified, not so much because of the minor damage which this did to the status of the Church of England, but because they saw it as the thin edge of the wedge for Catholic emancipation. They began to lose all confidence in Wellington. It was, however, the Canningites who were the first to withdraw their support, and this was due to the other major controversial issue – parliamentary reform. The trigger was a debate on the disfranchisement of two parliamentary boroughs on account of gross electoral corruption. These were the Cornish borough of Penryn and the Nottinghamshire seat of East Retford. The issue, so far as East Retford was concerned, was whether its representation should be transferred to the fast growing city of Birmingham, which had no parliamentary seats at all, or merely amalgamated with the neighbouring district of Bassetlaw. The government decided to choose the amalgamation option, but when a division was called in the Commons by the opposition, two government ministers, Lord Palmerston and William Huskisson, decided to abstain and remained in their seats. Peel, as leader of the House was totally unprepared for this, and, Joseph Planta, the Tory chief whip firmly admonished Huskisson for his 'disloyalty'. Huskisson, a proud and over-sensitive man, went home and wrote a letter to Wellington offering his resignation. He did not mean it to be accepted – 'his ill-conceived letter was meant as an *amende honorable* for his demonstration of the night before' (Gash, 1976, p. 99) – but Wellington and Peel took it at face value, and started to look for a successor. When alarmed Canningites sought to intervene on Huskisson's behalf, they were told that if he did not mean to resign he should formally withdraw his letter, which he was too proud to do. So, after five days, Wellington informed Huskisson that arrangements had been made to appoint a successor, and the other three Canningite cabinet ministers resigned in sympathy with him, as did William Lamb (the future Lord Melbourne), who was Chief Secretary for Ireland.

Wellington's stiff-necked response was a major political blunder, and fundamentally weakened his government over a very peripheral issue. Henceforth, it enjoyed no stable majority in the House of Commons, and had a greatly weakened front bench. It also, inadvertently, brought to a head the Catholic issue, which the government had vainly hoped to keep in abeyance. The government reshuffle did Wellington no good at all. In place of Huskisson, Palmerston, Dudley and Grant, he brought in, respectively, Sir George Murray, Sir Henry Hardinge, the Earl of Aberdeen and Vesey Fitzgerald. The first two were generals from the Peninsular War, which led to accusations that Wellington was inaugurating a military dictatorship, but the appointment which brought him real problems was that of Fitzgerald. He was MP for the Irish constituency of Clare, and in accordance with the law at the time was forced to resign his seat and fight a by-election before taking up his ministerial post. Normally such proceedings were a mere formality, with the retiring MP being returned unopposed or with a large majority after only token opposition. This time, however, the leader of the Catholic Association, the brilliant lawyer, Daniel O'Connell, caused a sensation by offering himself as a candidate, despite the fact that, as a Catholic, he would be ineligible to take his seat. The franchise in County Clare was wider than in many constituencies, being open to '40 shilling freeholders'. This meant that a large number of peasant farmers, most of them Catholics, could vote, and vote they did, returning O'Connell with 2,057 votes to 982 for Fitzgerald.

Once again, the old soldier concluded that he was in an indefensible position – that it would cause an uncontrollable wave of discontent in Ireland if O'Connell was deprived of his seat and Catholic emancipation was not granted.* He therefore determined finally to corner George IV and insist that the appropriate legislation should be tabled. This was far from being an easy task. The King, at

---

*In an interesting historical parallel, in 1961, the Labour MP, Tony Benn, who had inherited a peerage, successfully contested a by-election in his Bristol constituency, but was then unseated in favour of the Tory runner-up. The government, however, hastened to bring in a bill enabling hereditary peers to disclaim their titles, and the Tory MP subsequently graciously resigned his seat in Benn's favour.

best a slippery customer, was fast declining after a life of unrestrained excess. He was seriously ill, his mind wandering, so much so that there were serious fears that he would follow his father into insanity. Wellington had several audiences in his bedchamber, with the King anxious to discuss any issue except that of emancipation. He railed at Wellington, claimed that he himself had fought at the battle of Waterloo and earlier, at Salamanca, where he had led 'a magnificent charge of dragoons disguised as General Bock' (Hibbert, p. 271). George's resistance was stiffened by the presence of his younger brother, the Duke of Cumberland, normally resident in Hanover, of which he later was to become King, a fanatical anti-Catholic who threatened to put himself at the head of popular protest marches. Probably only Wellington could have persuaded the King to give way. He finally succeeded in doing so, though only after having threatened to resign if Cumberland was not sent back to Hanover.

Wellington's own thoughts on this episode, and on many others throughout his premiership, and generally in the period between 1820 and 1832 have been preserved for posterity in the political diaries of his *confidante* Harriett Arbuthnot, published only in 1950. The much younger second wife of Charles Arbuthnot, a senior Foreign Office official and later a cabinet minister, she and Wellington used to walk arm-in-arm together in Birdcage Walk and in St. James's Park, while he recounted to her all the details of the daily political round. It was widely assumed that she was his mistress, but this was apparently not the case. Charles was almost as close to Wellington as his wife, and when she died of cholera in 1834, at the age of nearly 41, he gave up his own home and went to live with Wellington in Apsley House for the following 16 years until his own death in 1850.

Wellington long had been anxious to resolve the Catholic issue, and in 1825 had submitted a memorandum to the Liverpool government, advocating a concordat with the Pope and the licensing of priests, who would in future receive a stipend from public funds, as a *quid pro quo* for admitting Catholics into Parliament. His memorandum, which was not published at the time, failed to win the approval of his ministerial colleagues, notably Peel, and it was Peel in particular who influenced the content of the Bill which the Cabinet put before Parliament in March 1829. It was to pass both Houses and receive the royal assent within six weeks. The Catholic Relief Bill differed greatly from Wellington's earlier proposal. It opened up the House of Commons, and all but a tiny list of senior public offices (of which the most important was the Lord Chancellorship) to Roman Catholics, provided for an amended parliamentary oath which they could take and balanced these concessions by two measures designed to promote security in Ireland and to limit the political influence of the Catholic majority. These were the banning of the Catholic Association as a subversive body, and the raising of the property qualification for voting in Irish constituencies to £10, rather than 40s.

The Bill's parliamentary passage was remarkably smooth, being supported by the opposition Whigs and Canningites, and opposed only by the Tory ultras. Daniel O'Connell was delighted with the result, and exclaimed to his wife: 'Who would have expected such a bill from Peel and Wellington!' (Quoted in Gash, 1990, p. 158). The ultras now, however, regarded Wellington as their bitter enemy, and he was grossly libelled by the Earl of Winchilsea. When he refused to withdraw his allegations, Wellington demanded satisfaction, and they met on Battersea Fields on the morning of 21 March 1829. Both deliberately shot wide, after which Winchilsea belatedly offered an apology, which was accepted by Wellington, who then calmly rode off, to report on the affair to Mrs Arbuthnot (Hibbert, p. 294).

George's health continued to decline, and few believed his death could be long delayed. In the early summer of 1830, Wellington, tiring of the wear and tear of office and the long working hours which he, a conscientious man and stickler for detail, imposed upon himself, drafted a memorandum to Peel. In this he suggested that the approaching end of the reign would be an appropriate moment for him to retire and for Peel to take over the premiership. But he never sent it off, perhaps suggests Norman Gash, 'because of the objections made by his over-partial friends the Arbuthnots' (Gash, 2004). But George's death, on 26 June 1830, at the age of 67, undoubtedly hastened Wellington's departure.

The ensuing general election, occasioned by William IV's accession, was largely fought on the issue of parliamentary reform, and produced substantial gains for the opposition Whigs and Canningites. It seemed likely that the government would be defeated on the first occasion that an issue of confidence was voted on. Some very tentative approaches were made to the Canningites to see whether they could be drawn back into the government, and Wellington himself travelled up to Liverpool, Huskisson's constituency, for the grand opening ceremony of the new Liverpool–Manchester railway line. Ensconced in a luxury carriage, Wellington was chatting amiably with Huskisson through the carriage window, when a warning went up that the famous steam engine, George Stephenson's *Rocket*, was approaching on the other track, where Huskisson was standing. He made a clumsy effort to get out of the way and was fatally struck by the engine; he died a few hours later. Wellington was ever after to have a visceral dislike of the railways, but the more immediate effect of the tragedy was to forestall a formal approach to the Canningites, of whom Huskisson was the undisputed leader. Wellington then effectively sealed his fate as Prime Minister by a rabidly anti-Reform speech, which he made – for no good reason – in the House of Lords, on 2 November 1830. This not only united the opposition, virtually driving the Canningites into the arms of the Whigs, but upset many on his own side, including senior ministers, who would have preferred to produce their own moderate Reform Bill to head off the prospect of a more radical measure being carried by their opponents.

Wellington might have hoped that the previously disaffected ultra Tories would be encouraged by his speech, in which he said in as many words that the existing system of electoral representation was as near perfect as could be devised by mankind, that he was not prepared to bring forward any measure of reform, and would 'always feel it my duty to resist such measures when proposed by others'. But their venom against him was now so strong that many of them were consumed by the desire to drive him out of office, whatever the issue involved. Virtually everybody else was dismayed by the evidence that Wellington was totally out of touch with a growing groundswell of opinion in the country (see Chapter 10) that the time had at last come to grasp the nettle of reform, which all governments had studiously avoided since the Younger Pitt's unsuccessful efforts in the 1780s.

The Whigs were preparing to propose a reform measure on 16 November, and it was widely expected that this would lead to a government defeat. There was already a sense of crisis in the air: Wellington, however, was utterly confident that he would prevail. He was cocooned in his own overwhelming self-confidence, reinforced by his inability to consult freely even with his most senior ministers. Peel was to tell the diarist Charles Greville that 'the Duke was never influenced by men, though he was by women and the silliest women at that' (Hibbert, p. 290). In truth, however, the government had lost control of the Commons, and, on the day before the Reform measure was to be debated, fell to an unexpected ambush, provoked by a Tory malcontent, on a vote on the Civil List, going down by 233 votes to 204, with 34 Ultras voting with the Opposition. Wellington, now seriously disillusioned with the experience of governing, took this as a cue to throw in his hand, and promptly resigned. William IV, who did not share his brother's aversion to Lord Grey, summoned him to form a new government. This he was able to do without difficulty, blending Whigs and Canningites, and even including the former Tory Prime Minister, Lord Goderich.

Wellington's government had lasted for two years and 298 days. Despite its shambolic demise, it was not without its achievements. Apart from Catholic relief, and the repeal of the Test and Corporation Acts, it had passed a Bill (largely the work of Robert Peel) establishing a Metropolitan Police Force for the first time and had amended the Corn Laws in a liberalizing direction. In foreign policy, it had veered away from the liberal policies pursued by Canning, withdrawing the British troops guaranteeing constitutional rule in Portugal and adopting a more pro-Turkish position in the Balkans. This did not, however, preclude the establishment of Greek independence in 1829. Following his resignation, the Duke retired to his Stratfield Saye estate in Hampshire, where he was Lord Lieutenant of the county, and energetically applied himself to the restoration of order in the county, which was much affected by the so-called 'Captain Swing' riots and nocturnal burnings of hayricks provoked by growing rural unemployment caused, it was believed, by the introduction of mechanization. He also involved himself more in family affairs, adopting the three abandoned children of his scapegrace nephew, William, and placing them in the care of his Duchess, Kitty. This led to a late reconciliation between them, and a revival of his affection for her. He was to care for her devotedly in her final illness (possibly cancer), which led to her death on 24 April 1831, at the age of 59. The Duke was to outlive her by 21 years. He was regarded as a highly eligible widower, but never married again, though there was no shortage of ladies who would have been only too happy to take Kitty's place. One of these was the famous philanthropist and banking heiress, Angela Burdett-Coutts, who actually proposed to him, when she was 30 and he, 76. He good-naturedly declined and preferred to keep her as one of several ladies, with whom he enjoyed an intimate and probably chaste friendship comparable to, but less intense than, his earlier relationship with Harriett Arbuthnot, who had died in 1834. Another such *confidante* was the young Lady Salisbury, mother of the future Prime Minister.

The somewhat undignified collapse of his government was not the end of Wellington's political career, though he had little appetite for opposition politics. He unsuccessfully attempted to form a second government in May 1832, when Grey resigned because of a dispute with the King over the Reform Bill, and Grey resumed office. Later, when William IV agreed with Grey to create a sufficient number of new Whig peers to carry the Bill through the House of Lords, Wellington persuaded enough Tory peers to abstain to make this unnecessary, even though he remained a fervent opponent of reform. Once again, this demonstrated the determination of a military man not to die in the last ditch when the battle was clearly lost. Then, in November 1834, on the fall of the Melbourne government (see Chapter 11), he again became Prime Minister, but only for three weeks before handing over to Peel, who had been away in Rome. He continued to serve, under Peel, as Foreign Minister, until the following April, when the government fell, and he was Leader of the Opposition in the Lords for the following six years. Returning to office in 1841, as Minister without Portfolio under Peel, he loyally stuck with his chief and helped to push the abolition of the Corn Laws through the Lords, in 1846, even though he did not agree with the policy. He had resumed his position as Commander-in-Chief in 1842, and held this office until his death ten years later, his last public role being to organize massive cover for the police during the last great Chartist demonstration in 1848, the 'year of revolutions'. To general relief, the demonstration passed off peacefully and the troops were not needed. He was to die four years later, at the age of 83, and was buried with great pomp in St. Paul's Cathedral, London. For the last three to four decades of his life, Wellington held a unique place in British society. He was regarded as the first subject of the monarch; indeed George IV treated him as a near equal, addressing him familiarly as 'Arthur'. His appearance was known to virtually the whole population, nobody's face appeared in more cartoons or prints during the first half of the nineteenth century, and once when he was approached in the street by a stranger, who said 'Mr. Jones?' he famously replied 'If you believe that, Sir, you'll believe anything'. (In fact, Wellington bore a marked resemblance to George Jones, the Keeper of the Royal Academy). He carried with him the aura of a 'Great Man', and even those who did not accept this valuation conceded that he was, at least a 'great character', if not a 'national treasure'. His views were widely regarded as anachronistic, or just plain wrong, but he was respected for the sincerity with which he held them. Above all, he was credited – justly – with acting out of a strong sense of duty. His earlier enormous popularity did not endure among all social classes. He was widely reviled for his opposition to Reform and his house was attacked more than once by London mobs, while there was some booing at his funeral. His political career, as a whole, cannot be counted as a success, but he had one great achievement to his name, somewhat in spite of himself, that of Catholic emancipation. This finally laid to rest a controversy which had festered and poisoned political life for the previous three decades.

Works consulted

Norman Gash, 1990, (ed.), *Wellington: Studies in the Military and Political career of the First Duke of Wellington*, Manchester, Manchester University Press.

Norman Gash, 2004, Article in *Oxford Dictionary of National Biography*, Oxford, Oxford University Press.

Christopher Hibbert, 1997, *Wellington: A Personal History*, London, HarperCollins.

Richard Holmes, 2002, *Wellington: The Iron Duke*, London, HarperCollins.

Lucille Iremonger, 1970, *The Fiery Chariot*, London, Secker & Warburg.

Elizabeth Longford, 1969, *Wellington: The Years of the Sword*, London, Weidenfeld & Nicolson.

Elizabeth Longford, 1972, *Wellington: Pillar of State*, London, Weidenfeld & Nicolson.

L.G. Mitchell, 1997, *Lord Melbourne 1779–1848*, Oxford, Oxford University Press.

Edward Pearce, 2003, *Reform!: The Fight for the 1832 Reform Act*, London, Jonathan Cape.

10

Charles Grey, 2nd Earl Grey – In the Footsteps of Fox

The Right Hon.ble Charles Earl Grey

If Earl Grey is a household name, it is less through his political accomplishments, than because a popular brand of tea has been named after him. Nevertheless, he must be reckoned as one of the more significant of Nineteenth-century premiers, as the architect of the 'Great Reform Bill', of 1832, an important staging post on the long road to parliamentary democracy. Charles Grey was born on 13 March 1764. He was the second of nine children, but effectively the eldest, as his elder brother Henry died a few days after his birth. His father, Sir Charles Grey, was a general, who distinguished himself as commander-in-chief in the West Indies during the American War of Independence, and a sizeable landowner in Northumberland, where the family had been established since the fourteenth century. His mother, Elizabeth Grey, was possibly a distant cousin of his father. Of great significance in young Charles's life was his uncle, Sir Henry Grey, a bachelor who made him his heir. He was Sir Charles's elder brother, and his estate, at Howick, was rather grander than the former's at Fallodon.

Very little is known about Charles's childhood. He was sent to a school at Marylebone in London, where he was apparently lonely and unhappy. His most traumatic experience as a child was inadvertently witnessing the public hanging of several forgers at Tyburn. This was to cause severe nightmares, which afflicted him periodically throughout his life. He went on to Eton, where he was to remain for eight years until 1781. He was not much happier there, forming no great affection for the school, and, like the Elder Pitt, declined to educate any of his own children at a 'public' school. He learned to write competent Latin verse, but, according to his own account, little else. He went on to Trinity College, Cambridge, where he lived an active and enjoyable social life, but left the University – like many other aristocrats at the time – without bothering to take a degree. He left for the Grand tour, but while he was away a vacancy occurred in the Parliamentary representation of Northumberland, due to Lord Algernon Percy inheriting a peerage. His Uncle Henry, a former MP for the county, lost no time in pushing the nomination of his 22-year-old nephew, who was returned unopposed in a by-election in July 1786. Sir Henry had promoted Charles as 'one who would follow in his own footsteps and who would be agreeable to the local country squires as a quiet backbencher of conservative instincts' (Smith, 1990, p. 9), fully expecting that he would be a loyal supporter of the Younger Pitt. Grey, however, an extremely handsome young man, very vain and with a high estimation of his own intellectual abilities, had other ideas. He soon fell in with the Whigs, captivated by the personality of Charles James Fox, and even more so by the leading Whig hostess, the glamorous Georgiana, Duchess of Devonshire. The daughter of the first Earl Spencer, and a collateral ancestor of Princess Diana, with whom she has been much compared, she and Grey soon became lovers and she bore him an illegitimate daughter. Her 'dull middle-aged husband' packed her off to the Continent, accompanied by his own mistress (and later second wife), Lady Elizabeth Foster, to give birth to the child, who was then entrusted to Grey's parents, who brought her up themselves, passing her off as Grey's much younger sister.

Grey's relationship with Georgiana did not last for more than a few years. His commitment to Fox, however, was to endure, as E.A. Smith recounts:

> Within a year, perhaps two at most, Grey had become what he was to remain for the rest of his life: a disciple of Fox's brand of liberal, populist yet basically conservative Whiggism, an advocate of 'civil and religious liberty all over the world', yet a political realist ever ready to temper idealism with expediency, a pragmatist who never lost sight of reputation and consistency, at once ardent and cautious, idealistic and calculating. (Smith, 1990, p. 10)

Highly ambitious, Grey was soon recognized as one of the finest speakers in the House of Commons, with an exceptionally clear style, though not quite able to match the oratorical heights of Pitt or Fox. He aspired to being recognized as Fox's chief lieutenant and collaborator; his principal rivals being the Irish-born playwright, Richard Brinsley Sheridan, a brilliant wit whose political judgement, however, left much to be desired, and, somewhat later, Fox's own nephew, the 3rd Lord Holland. Two years after the birth of his daughter, Grey, then aged 30, married the 18-year-old Mary Elizabeth Ponsonby, daughter of a leading Whig peer, in November 1794. It was a happy marriage, blessed with 16 children, and Grey became a devoted father, though this did not prevent him from having numerous affairs while he was away in London, including with Sheridan's second wife, Hecca, and, much later, when he was in his 60s, with Princess Lieven, the promiscuous wife of the Russian Ambassador and notorious intriguer at the court of George IV.

Grey's rise in the Whig hierarchy was hastened by the split in the party provoked by the French Revolution and its aftermath. The first to defect from Fox was Edmund Burke, the Revolution's fiercest critic, but two years after war broke out between Britain and France, the Duke of Portland, the nominal leader of the party, took almost half of its parliamentary strength with him in joining Pitt's government, in July 1794. In the much depleted ranks of the Foxites, Grey now stood out as the brightest star. He had already established himself as the party's chief advocate of parliamentary reform, launching a popular movement entitled the Society of Friends of the People, in April 1792. This sounded a more extreme body than it actually was. Grey, no supporter of democracy, rejected the Radical demand for manhood suffrage, and restricted himself to calling for the elimination of 'pocket' and 'rotten' boroughs, most of which were represented by Tories, and a modest extension of the franchise in borough constituencies. Nevertheless, Fox hesitated to support the new organization, fearing the loss of support by the more conservative Whigs, and only reluctantly backed his protégé's initiative. When Grey introduced a parliamentary motion in support of reform, in May 1793, it was defeated by 282 votes to 41. His second attempt, four years later, was again defeated, by 256 votes to 91, leading to the 'secession' from Parliament of Fox, Grey and their supporters, who boycotted the House for 18 months. Throughout the 1790s, Grey and Fox had stoutly resisted the Pitt government's repressive measures against dissidents, arguing strongly against the suspension of *habeas corpus* and the restriction of the rights of assembly and of the press, while advocating peace with France. This alienated them from 'respectable' opinion, and the Whigs lost more and more parliamentary and popular support. Grey took up the issue of Catholic emancipation as well as parliamentary reform and was a strong opponent of the Act of Union with Ireland, passed in 1800.

Two events in 1801 had a marked personal effect on Grey. His father accepted a peerage, without consulting him, becoming the first Baron Grey. Grey was furious, as he realized that he would have to give up his seat in the Commons, when his father died, and that this would be a setback to his political career. He was much happier at the decision of his uncle, Sir Henry Grey, to give up living at Howick and to offer it to Grey as a residence for his own family. Grey, who eventually inherited the property in 1808, came to love Howick, where he luxuriated in the company of his rapidly growing family, and became more and more reluctant to travel to London to carry out his parliamentary duties. When his father was promoted to an Earldom in 1806, Grey assumed the courtesy title of Viscount Howick, but continued to sit in the Commons.

Also in 1801, Pitt resigned as Prime Minister, following George III's refusal to agree to Catholic emancipation, and this had the effect of ending the isolation of the Foxites. Pitt's Foreign Secretary, Lord Grenville, a strong advocate of emancipation, refused to join the incoming Addington government, and rapidly became one of its strongest critics (see Chapter 2). This brought him into contact with Fox and Grey, and they began to co-operate closely in opposition. When Pitt returned to power in 1804, Grenville declined to resume office unless Fox was also admitted into the government, which George III vetoed. Grey and the other Foxites then refused to serve in the absence of their chief. Pitt's death in January 1806 left George III with little alternative but to appoint Grenville in his place, and to swallow his pride by accepting Fox as his deputy, as Foreign Secretary and Leader of the Commons. This enabled the Whigs to return to office, for the first time since 1783, as the leading element in Grenville's 'Ministry of all the Talents'.

In the new government, Grey was First Lord of the Admiralty, and, after Fox, the government's leading spokesman in the Commons. It was he who carried through the Commons the Bill abolishing the slave trade, the short-lived government's greatest achievement. At the Admiralty, he proved an energetic and effective minister, though he was over-ruled by his cabinet colleagues when he resisted pressure to authorize an attack on the Spanish colony of Buenos Aires, which – after initial success – proved a failure. After the death of Fox, in September 1806, he was preferred to Lord Holland (Fox's own choice) as Foreign Secretary and also became Leader of the Commons, and effective head of the Whig party. The government was swept from office when it tried to legislate to enable Catholics to achieve senior rank in the Army and Navy (see Chapter 3). George III forced the government to withdraw the Bill, and then insisted that no further measures of Catholic relief should be put forward during his lifetime, a pledge which the ministers were unwilling to give. The King then dismissed the government and replaced it, in May 1807, with a Tory administration, headed by the Duke of Portland. Grey, whose Foreign Secretaryship had lasted a mere six months, then suffered a further setback when Portland called an election, and he was unceremoniously removed from his Northumberland county seat, which he had represented for 21 years, by the Duke of Northumberland, who insisted on putting forward his own son, Lord Percy. An infuriated Grey regarded this as rank treachery by his previous friend and sponsor, and withdrew from the contest, having to make do instead with the pocket borough of Appleby, provided by his friend, Lord Thanet. Grey was now universally recognized as the leader of the opposition in the Commons, and made a powerful speech attacking the circumstances (a 'court intrigue') under which the Portland ministry had been brought to power, and pledging his continuing enmity. As the most talented debater in the House, he threatened to be a thorn in the government's side, but the death of his father a few weeks later removed him from the scene of all his earlier triumphs and condemned him to serve in what he regarded as the much less congenial atmosphere of the House of Lords. He wrote to his wife after his first speech in the chamber: 'What a place to speak in! With just enough light to make darkness visible, it was like speaking in a vault by the glimmering light of a sepulchral lamp to the dead. It is impossible I should ever do anything there worth speaking of' (Smith, 2004).

In the Lords, he largely deferred to Lord Grenville, who was now widely accepted as the notional leader of the Whig party, even though his parliamentary faction was much smaller than the Foxites, led by Grey. The two men were bracketed together in the public's perception as being joint leaders of the opposition, though no such post formally existed at that time. Thus began a dispiriting period of nearly a quarter of a century, during which the Whigs were to languish in opposition, and for the most part not offering a very inspiring alternative to the governments in power. For most of this time, the Whigs were badly led in the Commons, and neither Grey nor Grenville were consistent attenders in the House of Lords, preferring to spend the bulk of their time on their country estates. On several occasions – notably in 1809, when Portland resigned and was succeeded by Spencer Perceval – they muffed opportunities to return to government, insisting that a predominantly Whig administration should be formed, rather than being (as they perhaps wrongly assumed) merely junior partners in a coalition. Their hopes of achieving office when the Prince Regent assumed power in 1811 were to prove illusory. The Prince was initially forthcoming, but found their demands too exigent, and feared the reaction of his father if he were to return to sanity, and find out that he had ejected the Perceval government for no good reason.

Grey's subsequent career was to parallel Fox's to a remarkable extent, spending over 20 continuous years as Opposition leader, largely as result of his own insistence on maintaining the purity of his Whig principles. Like many other Whigs his attitude to the war against France was ambiguous. He no longer believed in peace at any price, seeing Napoleon as a dictator and aggressor, yet he was consistently pessimistic about the military prospects and downplayed Wellington's achievements in Spain. His earlier fierce ambition gradually waned, and for long periods he was inactive, springing back to life in 1820, when he emerged as one of the strongest and most effective opponents of George IV's attempt to divorce his wife, Queen Caroline. He made one of the finest speeches of his life, denouncing the Bill of Pains and Penalties in the Lords, and when the government dropped the Bill the new King's resentment against Grey was so great that there appeared little chance that he would ever again serve as a minister so long as George remained King. An opportunity did, however, arise, in 1827, when the already dying George Canning became Prime Minister in succession to Lord Liverpool, and was immediately abandoned by half the members of the Cabinet. With the permission of George IV, Canning applied to the Whigs to fill the vacant places, to be met with a blunt refusal by Grey, still the party leader (Grenville having given up in 1817). Grey regarded Canning as an unprincipled adventurer, but was apparently also influenced by his aristocratic disdain for his low birth, as the son of an actress. Other Whigs, led by Lord Lansdowne, were less fastidious, and agreed to serve (see Chapter 8), but the death of Canning after four months, and the dismissal of Lord Goderich's ministry after a similar period, led to the formation, in January 1828, of a purely Tory government under the Duke of Wellington.

Lord Grey was now 63 years old, and it looked as though his political career was gliding gently to its close. Yet three developments over the next couple of years enabled him to re-establish himself in the forefront of politics and to compensate for the many years of frustration by a final burst of achievement. These were the death, in June 1830, of George IV, and the succession of his brother, William IV, who had no ill-feelings towards Grey; the inability of Wellington to hold his government together, and the sudden surge of public opinion in favour of parliamentary reform. The surge had been long in coming. The Parliamentary system had remained virtually unchanged since the middle of the seventeenth century, and more and more anomalies had built up. These were well described by an American historian, Frank Woodbridge:

> There were rotten boroughs, in which the population had dwindled to little or nothing, and pocket (or nomination) boroughs, where one or very few men controlled elections, in effect appointing Members of Parliament. The Report of the Society of the Friends of the People indicated that 154 individuals sent 307 (out of 658) Members to the Commons. In the late 1820s, Croker, a Tory opposed to reform, concluded that at least 276 (out of 489) English Members were returned by patrons. There was a very uneven distribution of Members in relation to population. For example, more Members were elected in the two counties of Cornwall and Wiltshire than in the five counties of Middlesex, Somerset, Warwickshire, Worcester and Yorkshire, though the latter had a combined population of more than ten times the former. The franchise, with few exceptions, was very limited. Even in Westminster, generally considered a very democratic constituency, less than one quarter of adult males could vote. (Woodbridge, 1974, p. 344)

When Wellington resigned the premiership, in November 1830, William IV, who was himself convinced of the necessity of parliamentary reform, had no hesitation in sending for Grey, now aged 66. He would have preferred to lead a purely Whig administration, but in order to secure a parliamentary majority was compelled to appoint several Canningites and even one ultra Tory, the Duke of Richmond. It was an overwhelmingly aristocratic government, whose members, Grey was to claim, controlled more acres than any previous administration. In a letter to Princess Lieven, he justified his choices:

> In these times of democracy and Jacobinism it is possible to find real capacity in the high Aristocracy – not that I wish to exclude merit if I should meet with it in the commonality; but given equal merit, I admit I should choose the aristocrat, for that class is the guarantee for the safety of the state and of the throne. (Smith, 1990, p. 259)

His government was also well stocked with his own relatives and in-laws, no fewer than seven of whom, including his eldest son, Viscount Howick MP, held government posts, while Lord Althorp MP, the Chancellor of the Exchequer and leader of the Commons – a key figure – was the nephew of his long dead former mistress, Georgiana. Apart from Althorp, the most senior posts were held by Viscount Melbourne (Home Secretary), Viscount Palmerston MP (Foreign Secretary), Lord Lansdowne (Lord President of the Council) and Lord Durham, known as 'Radical Jack' and Grey's son-in-law (Lord Privy Seal). The colleague whom he had the greatest difficulty in placing was the leading

Whig lawyer and orator, Henry Brougham, whose views on Reform and other contentious issues were far more radical than his own. Grey feared he would dominate any proceedings in the House of Commons, to the embarrassment of the government, and to avoid this – after tricky negotiations – made him an offer he couldn't refuse. He became Lord Brougham and Vaux, and, by general consent, one of the greatest of Lord Chancellors. The government included a former Prime Minister, Lord Goderich, who became Earl of Ripon, and no fewer than four future ones – Melbourne, Lord John Russell, Edward Stanley (later Earl of Derby) and Palmerston.

Before it could get into its stride, the Grey government was faced by two urgent crises, one foreign, the other domestic. In August 1830, the Belgian uprising against Dutch rule posed a direct challenge to the postwar settlement agreed at the Congress of Vienna in 1815, and also to perceived British interests. Grey and Palmerston reacted promptly, determined that it should lead neither to international conflict nor to the re-absorption of Belgium by France, which was the evident desire of many French-speaking Belgians. They convened the London Conference, of December 1830–January 1831, attended also by Austria, France, Prussia and Russia. This recognized Belgian independence and guaranteed its permanent neutrality. At the same time, the British leaders applied strong pressure on the new French King, Louis Philippe, to withdraw the candidature of his second son, the Duc de Nemours, for the Belgian throne. Instead, the British successfully advanced the claims of Prince Leopold of Saxe-Coburg, the widower of Princess Charlotte, the former heiress to George IV, who had died in childbirth in 1817. Leopold then diplomatically proposed marriage to Louis Philippe's elder daughter, Louise-Marie, and the couple subsequently became the first sovereigns of the new Belgian kingdom. Grey's and Palmerston's success was to be hailed as a diplomatic masterstroke.

Nearer home was the problem of rural unrest, manifested by the wave of rick-burnings and destruction of agricultural machinery, sweeping southern England and known popularly as the 'Captain Swing' riots. Despite the consistent resistance of the Whigs to the repressive legislation brought in by Pitt in the 1790s, and by the Liverpool government after 1815, Grey and his colleagues, with Home Secretary Melbourne to the fore, did not hesitate to introduce the harshest measures to put down the disturbances. They set up special commissions to try the suspects, which handed down stern punishments – 644 imprisonments, 481 transportations and 19 executions (O'Gorman, 1997, p. 362). The tough line appeared to pay off – in little over a year the protest movement petered out.

Nearly four decades earlier, Grey had first proposed a parliamentary motion in favour of Reform, and his views had changed little in the intervening period. Then and now, he had been a moderate reformer, anxious to remove the anomalies in the existing system rather than to develop it radically in a democratic direction. An aristocrat to his finger-tips, he believed that the landed interest should be the predominant influence in Parliament and had no patience with those who were advocating universal (or even manhood) suffrage, annual parliaments or secret ballots. Yet he was convinced that it was dangerous to leave the rising manufacturing, trading and professional classes without an effective voice, fearing that this would drive them to make common cause with radical or even revolutionary forces. A judicious extension of the franchise, and the removal of the more indefensible and corrupt features of the electoral process would, on the contrary, effectively co-opt them to the governing class of, as he saw it, enlightened aristocrats.

One of Grey's first acts as Prime Minister was to establish a committee of four ministers, the most influential being Durham and Lord John Russell, not yet a member of the Cabinet, to draw up detailed proposals for Reform. Within a month, they produced three draft bills, for England and Wales, Scotland, and Ireland. Presented to the House of Commons by Russell, in March 1831, the Bills proposed the disfranchisement of 60 boroughs with populations of less than 2000, while 47 other boroughs with populations between 2,000 and 4,000 were each to lose one of their two members, while the borough of Weymouth and Melcombe Regis was to go down from four to two. Altogether, 168 seats were to be eliminated, but – in a smaller House of Commons – 105 of these were to be redistributed, mostly among English counties (55 seats) and 42 urban constituencies, including the previously unrepresented cities of Manchester and Birmingham, and four London boroughs, which were to receive two members each. Most people were taken aback by the scale of the proposed redistribution. There were few defenders of such ultra-rotten boroughs as Gatton (two electors) and Old Sarum (seven), but not many had anticipated that the overall clear-out would be quite so wholesale. The proposals concerning the franchise were much more limited in their scope. The previously widely differing voting qualifications in borough constituencies were consolidated in a single requirement – to be a male householder of property worth £10 a year. In the counties, the £10 copyholder and £50 leaseholder were to be enfranchised, in addition to the 40s freeholder. The net effect of these changes would have been to increase the overall number of qualified electors from around half a million to something over 700,000, or seven per cent of the adult population.

The provisions of the bills were very much in line with Grey's own views, and he remained closely in control of the parliamentary proceedings, even though – as a member of the upper house, he was not able personally to present the case to the Commons or to gauge the reactions of individual MPs. His first – and essential move – was to clear the proposals with the King, whom he visited in Brighton, on 30 January 1831. It proved more difficult to get the proposals through the House of Commons, which had been elected during Wellington's premiership and where the government enjoyed only the narrowest of majorities. After a furious debate, the English Bill passed its second reading by a single vote (302 votes to 301). Grey sought a dissolution in order to secure the election of a House more favourable to Reform, but the King refused. A month later, on 30 April, the Opposition carried a 'wrecking amendment' during the Committee Stage by 299 votes to 291. Grey then threatened resignation if he did not get a dissolution, and William IV reluctantly gave way. The resulting general election, in May 1831, was a triumph for Grey and a humiliating rout for the Tories. The Bill was reintroduced, in an only slightly modified form, and rapidly made its way through the House of Commons. It then went up to the Lords, which was to prove a much stiffer hurdle. The House had been stuffed with Tories, during the long first premiership of the Younger Pitt, who in 17 years persuaded George III to create no fewer than 140 new peers. It was they, or their inheritors, who now presented an almost insurmountable barrier to the Bill. On 8 October, despite a powerful speech by Grey, the Lords rejected the Bill on its second reading by 41 votes.

The Lords' action provoked widespread revulsion in the country, with huge protest meetings being held in many towns and cities. Most of these were entirely peaceful, but in several places order broke down. In Derby the army was called in to suppress a riot, in Nottingham the castle was burned down by a mob, while in Bristol a mob went on the rampage for three days. The Cabinet was divided about how to proceed, with Palmerston and Melbourne urging delay, and Durham – much the most radical minister – in favour of raising the stakes. Grey was firmly against any significant watering down of the Bill, but authorized negotiations with the more moderate Tories (known as 'the waverers') to see whether some minor amendments might reconcile the Lords to letting the Bill through. These came to nothing, and the question then arose of asking William IV to create a sufficient number of new Whig peers to force the measure through. The only precedent was in 1712, when Queen Anne created 12 new Tory peers to carry through the Treaty of Utrecht, which brought the War of Spanish Succession to a close. This time a much larger creation – of perhaps 60 new peers – might well be necessary in order to secure the passage of the Reform Bill. Grey discussed this tentatively with William IV, who was horrified at the prospect, and indicated that he would not wish to increase the size of the Lords by more than two or three, and that beyond that any new creations should be confined to the heirs to existing peerages, many of whom were currently in the Commons, which would create a rash of by-elections, something the government was anxious to avoid.

The government then withdrew the Bill, but reintroduced it, with only minor changes, into the Lords, who passed it on second reading by a majority of nine votes, in April 1832. A month later, in committee, it voted to postpone the most crucial clauses in the Bill, by 35 votes, and the Cabinet decided formally to ask

William IV to create sufficient peers to carry the Bill through. William refused, and Grey promptly submitted his government's resignation. William then summoned the Duke of Wellington, and asked him to form a government, with the objective of carrying a more moderate measure of Reform. Within a week, Wellington, after extensive consultations with his Tory colleagues, returned to tell the King that he had been unable to do so. This was mainly because of the determined refusal of Sir Robert Peel, the Tory leader in the Commons, to serve. The King then threw in the sponge, asked Grey to carry on, and finally agreed to create whatever number of new peers should prove necessary. In the event, Wellington absolved him of the need for such action. When the Bill came up for its third reading, on 4 June 1832, he left his seat in the Chamber, and followed by a hundred Tory peers, allowed it to pass by 106 votes to 22. Three days later, it received the royal assent.

Neither Grey nor any member of his cabinet (with the exception of Durham) saw the Reform Act as a forerunner of future legislation further enlarging the franchise. They saw it rather as a final settlement, removing the imperfections which had appeared in the constitutional arrangements bequeathed by the 'Glorious Revolution' of 1688–9. One of Grey's strongest supporters, Lord John Russell, who had pioneered a series of earlier unsuccessful attempts at Reform, earned himself the nickname of 'Finality Jack', when he declared, in 1837, that no further changes were necessary. In fact, the initial impact of the Act was rather modest. It increased the franchise only from around 5 to 7 per cent of the adult population, and though the amount of bribery and corruption was undoubtedly reduced, the failure to provide for a secret ballot meant that landlords and employers were still able to exert undue influence over their tenants and employees. The predominance of the 'landed interest' was to continue for at least another three or four decades. The Act's significance lay in the precedent it set for future legislation which, in Bills passed in 1858, 1867, 1872, 1883, 1884, 1911, 1918 and 1928, paved the way, in easy stages, to the eventual adoption of universal suffrage. Predictions that the adoption of the 1832 Bill would open the way to chaos or Jacobin revolution were wide of the mark, but, according to John Derry, 'the Duke of Wellington and Peel were right when they said that Grey's reform of Parliament was opening a door which there was no prospect of closing' (Derry, p. 192).

Grey's own contribution to the passage of the Bill was crucial. He showed a cool nerve, and great firmness, in that, while he was willing to be flexible over details, he was resolved not to tolerate any watering down of the central features of the Bill, insisting when the second and third drafts were produced that they should be no less 'efficient' in their effect than the original version. Probably only he could have persuaded a timorous and reluctant William IV to persevere with the measure, while his own highly respectable and conservative image undoubtedly reassured many doubters who might have shied away if the lead role had been taken by a more obviously radical figure, such as Brougham, Durham or, even, Lord John Russell. The Bill's large body of supporters outside Parliament, led by Francis Place, William Cobbett, 'Orator' Hunt and – most effectively – Thomas Attwood, whose Birmingham Political Union was the best organized and most widely supported of the many grass-roots organizations pressing for Reform (always spelled with a capital 'R'), would have liked a more radical measure, at least incorporating household suffrage. Yet, as John Derry emphasizes: 'the real alternatives to Grey's Bill were either a more limited bill ... or no bill at all ... there was no chance of a democratic measure being accepted by [a still unreformed] Parliament' (Derry, p. 185).

No sooner was the Act passed, than Grey moved swiftly to consolidate the government's position. He called a general election, in December 1832, and the enlarged electorate duly expressed their thanks, giving the Whigs a handsome majority. Together with their Radical and Irish allies, they secured no fewer than 479 seats, against 179 for the Tories. The government went on to introduce a series of measures on which is based its claim to be the first of the great reforming governments of the nineteenth century. These included, notably, the abolition of slavery throughout the British Empire (completing the work done by the 'Talents' ministry, in 1806, when Grey had played a leading part in the abolition of the slave trade). Another important measure was the Factory Act, of 1833, limiting the working hours of children and creating a factory inspectorate. The Poor Law Act, of 1834, was a less benign measure. It went some way to ameliorating rural poverty, but totally failed to tackle the more widespread misery in the towns, instituting a harsh regime of workhouses to replace the 'outdoor relief' for which paupers were previously eligible. Other new bills removed the trade monopoly of the East India Company, introduced elected local government into Scotland and reformed the banking system.

Yet, with Reform successfully accomplished, Grey undoubtedly felt a sense of anti-climax and – approaching his seventieth year – began to lapse into the 'despondent indolence' which, in the words of John Derry, had characterized his long years in opposition. He no longer possessed the energy or patience to deal with awkward and quarrelsome ministers, and was particularly vexed by disagreements on how to deal with Irish problems, which were still high on the political agenda, despite the granting of Catholic emancipation in 1829. Three interlocking issues dominated the debate – rural unrest, the privileged position of the Anglican Church and the continued campaign by Daniel O'Connell for the rescinding of the Act of Union of 1800 and the restoration of a separate Irish Parliament. A feud soon developed between Lord Anglesey, the Lord Lieutenant, and the Chief Irish Secretary, E.G. Stanley (later the 14th Earl of Derby). Anglesey, whom Grey had inherited from the Wellington government, was a pronounced liberal, sympathetic to Irish demands, while Stanley, who was a member of the Cabinet, was a strong advocate of coercion as well as being a diehard supporter of Church privileges. Anglesey threatened to resign on several occasions, and was eventually transferred to another post, but subsequently Stanley also resigned, and this effectively brought the government to an end. The point at issue was the payment of tithes, predominantly and unwillingly by Catholic farmers, to the Church of Ireland. An enquiry revealed that the revenues raised were far in excess of the legitimate needs of the Church, and Lord John Russell introduced a bill to apply the surplus to secular purposes, mainly for education. His action split the Cabinet down the middle, and four ministers – Stanley, the Duke of Richmond, the Earl of Ripon and Sir James Graham, the First Lord of the Admiralty – walked out of the government. Shortly afterwards, Lord Althorp MP (shortly to succeed his father, as the third Earl Spencer) resigned on another issue, which proved the last straw for Grey, who followed suit.

He relinquished the premiership on 9 July 1834, after serving three years and 229 days, giving one of his finest orations in his resignation speech in the House of Lords, which was widely applauded. William IV turned to the Tories to form a new government, but Wellington and Peel, whose supporters were only a small minority in the Commons, were unable to do so. William invited the Home Secretary, Lord Melbourne, to take over the reins from Grey, who would, in fact, have preferred to be succeeded by Althorp. He had lost all appetite for office, but had a strong desire to control the Melbourne government from the outside. Melbourne, a diffident man, deferred to Grey's advice in many of his early decisions, but with growing self-confidence became more independent and less inclined to seek guidance from his former leader. His government was short-lived, being turned out by William IV after four months (see Chapter 11). The succeeding Tory government, under Sir Robert Peel, did not last much longer, resigning in April 1835, after a series of parliamentary defeats, and William was obliged to turn back to the Whigs. Grey was strongly pressed to resume the premiership, or to serve as Foreign Secretary, but firmly declined, and Melbourne returned and remained Prime Minister for another six years. During this time, he received only lukewarm support from Grey, who grew more and more impatient at what he saw as his undue dependence on the Radicals, and, in particular, on Daniel O'Connell (whom he saw as a dangerous demagogue). He was also deeply offended that Melbourne had not appointed his eldest son, Viscount Howick MP, as Chancellor of the Exchequer, and had fobbed him off with a relatively junior Cabinet post. Grey became more and more conservative as he grew older, saying that he now had no significant differences with Wellington and Peel, for whom he had the greatest personal respect. When Howick finally resigned from the government, in 1839, Grey withdrew from politics altogether, ceasing to attend the House of Lords, and retiring to his beloved Howick, where he lived out a relatively tranquil old age, dying on 17 July 1845, aged 81.

Grey might well be compared with a Prime Minister of more modern times – Edward Heath. He also had a long but largely unsuccessful political career, crowned with one great achievement which offset all his failures – bringing Britain into the European Economic Community. Grey, however, was more lucky than Heath, in not being repudiated by his own party. He continued to be honoured by them for many years, both before and after his death. His greatest admirers were, perhaps, his fellow Northumbrians, who erected a large column on which his statue still stands, dominating the centre of Newcastle. According to Edward Pearce, the latest chronicler of the struggle to pass the Reform Bill, he is the only British civilian to be memorialized on a column.

Works consulted

John W. Derry, 1992, *Charles, Earl Grey: Aristocratic Reformer*, Oxford, Blackwell.

Frank O'Gorman, 1997, *The Long Eighteenth Century*, London, Arnold.

Edward Pearce, 2003, *Reform!: The Fight for the 1832 Reform Act*, London, Cape.

E.A. Smith, 1990, *Lord Grey 1764–1845*, Oxford, Clarendon Press.

E.A. Smith, 2004, Article in *The Oxford Dictionary of National Biography*, Oxford University Press.

George, Woodbridge, 1974, 'Earl Grey', in Herbert Van Thal, (ed.), *The Prime Ministers*, Vol. I, London, Allen & Unwin.

11

William Lamb, 2nd Viscount Melbourne – Mentor to a Young Monarch

Of Britain's 52 Premiers, two were undoubtedly born illegitimately. One – Ramsay MacDonald – was brought up in extreme poverty by his mother and grandmother, and had a fierce struggle to establish himself in life. The other – William Lamb – grew up in great luxury in an aristocratic home, was educated at Eton and Cambridge and inherited a peerage from a man who was certainly not his father. Yet he appeared to have suffered some psychological damage, and though gifted and highly intelligent he grew up chronically indecisive and directionless, which, among other things, led him into a disastrous marriage. Born on 15 March 1779, he was the second of six surviving children born to Elizabeth Lamb (née Milbanke), Lady Melbourne. Only the eldest of these – Peniston – appears to have been fathered by her husband Peniston Lamb, the First Viscount Melbourne (originally in the Irish peerage). A complaisant husband, he allowed all six to be brought up in the family home and did not openly question their parentage. The first Lord Melbourne was a pleasant nonentity, without ambition, speaking only once during his 40 years in Parliament. The only official post he ever held was as a Gentleman of the Bedchamber to the Prince of Wales. Lady Melbourne, the daughter of a wealthy Yorkshire baronet, was of sterner stuff. Intelligent, vivacious and beautiful, she established herself as a leading Whig hostess (third only to the Duchess of Devonshire and Lady Holland), and held regular soirées in Melbourne House, in Piccadilly (now the site of the Albany), which she had taken over from the Holland family, when they had moved to Holland Park. A highly ambitious and promiscuous woman, who was caricatured in Sheridan's play *The School for Scandal* as 'Lady Sneerwell', she had many lovers, including the Prince of Wales (the probable father of her fourth son, George). The identity of William's father is unknown, though he was generally believed to be George Wyndham, the third Earl of Egremont, the eccentric and immensely wealthy owner of Petworth House, in Sussex, one of the grandest of family seats. Egremont, a notorious roué, was certainly the longest-standing of Lady Melbourne's 'admirers', and evidently believed that William was his son. He was also probably the father of William's brother Frederick and his sister Emily.

So William was brought up in the heart of the high Whig aristocracy – clannish, worldly, amoral and united politically – by little more than by their belief that they were the natural rulers of the country and their enduring distrust of the monarchy. In William's case, this was complicated by close family ties with two successive monarchs, George IV and William IV. The former was the father of his favourite brother, George, while the latter's illegitimate son was married to William's half sister, an illegitimate daughter of Lord Egremont.

William had a happy childhood, being doted on by his mother, whose favourite child he was, and getting on very well with all his siblings. His relations with his nominal father were perfectly amiable and correct, but – not surprisingly – the first Lord Melbourne reserved his warmest feelings for his own son, Peniston. In addition to their London home, the Melbournes had an estate, Melbourne Hall in Derbyshire, and another seat at Brocket Hall, in Hertfordshire, which had been more recently built and where they stayed more often, while Lord Egremont allowed the children a pretty free run at Petworth, where they were frequent visitors. Bookish and highly intelligent, though not particularly hard-working, William was taught at home by a governess and a local clergyman until the age of nine, when he was sent to Eton (the almost *de rigueur* school for eighteenth- and nineteenth-century premiers). Here, he was reasonably happy, enjoying the freedom and the privileged status accorded to aristocrats and managing to survive without too much difficulty the endemic bullying. As one of his biographers was to note:

> William himself disliked any kind of rough and tumble tinged with malice, or brutality that so often among boys produced a fight about a trifle. Why get hurt unnecessarily for something quite unimportant? Fights could not always be avoided even by young William but, as he told [Queen] Victoria later, if he found he was getting the worst of it he gave up and walked away, deterred by no false shame, declaring that it was a silly business. (Marshall, 1975, pp. 8–9)

His behaviour as an adult followed the same pattern. 'Throughout his life Melbourne never confronted unpleasantness, but always fled before it' (Mitchell, 1990, p. 27). He early developed an extraordinary detachment, perhaps too easily seeing both sides of a question, and finding it hard to commit himself to any cause or course of action. William left Eton in 1796, without having obtained any particular distinction, though he was steeped in classical learning. At Trinity College, Cambridge, he had a thoroughly good time, but the University having declined, at that period, into little more than a finishing school for young aristocrats before they departed on the Grand tour, he did very little organized studying, though he continued to read widely, He did, however, win the University prize for an oration on 'The Progressive Improvement of Mankind', which, to his great satisfaction, was read by the Whig leader, Charles James Fox, and commended by him in a speech in the House of Commons. He left after two years, but the Grand tour was now out of the question because of the continuing war with France. Some family friends of the Melbournes suggested that he should, instead, round off his education by going for a couple of years to the University of Glasgow, which in contrast to Cambridge was then at its height as a centre of learning. So, with his younger brother, Frederick, William Lamb travelled north to board with Professor John Millar, one of the University's finest scholars and a disciple of two of Scotland's greatest seers, David Hume and Adam Smith. Here the two brothers were subjected to the discipline of long periods of hard work and study, but Lamb found time to write light-hearted verse and to lead an active social life, dining with the Earl of Minto, who described him as 'a remarkably pleasant, clever and well-informed young man' (Marshall, p. 13). Glasgow did not dramatically change him, but enlarged his fund of knowledge, and confirmed him in the sceptical rationalism which had already become one of his hallmarks. Intellectually, he was interested in religion, but was probably not a believer, though he always counted himself as supporter of the Church of England, telling his mother in a letter: 'If we are to have a prevailing Religion, let us have one that is cool and indifferent and such a one we have got' (Mitchell, 1997, p. 36).

Politically, he was a Whig, more out of tribal reasons than from intellectual conviction, though for a time at least he paraded fairly extreme views, including a marked sympathy for France in its war against Britain. At the age of 21, he returned to London and entered 'society', or more precisely, Whig society, becoming an *habitué* not only of his mother's functions, but also those at Devonshire House, Holland House and above all, Carlton House, the home of the extravagantly hospitable Prince of Wales. The Prince was at odds with his father, George III, and revelled at surrounding himself with the King's political enemies, above all Fox and his circle. Lamb soon became a popular figure – good-looking, amusing, and obviously attractive to women, though notably discreet in any affairs which he may have conducted. There seemed to be only one thing lacking: as a younger son, he had no money and little prospects. What was he to do with his life? Apart from appointment to a sinecure, which his mother's connections might conceivably have been able to secure, there were, in Dorothy Marshall's words, four options, 'the Army, the Navy, the Church and the Law' (Marshall, p. 17). The first three having no appeal to Lamb, he moved into Chambers in 1801, and was called to the Bar three years later, joining the Northern Circuit. He is recorded as having received only one brief, for which he earned precisely one guinea, before his life was transformed by the sudden death of his elder brother Peniston, at the age of 35. A distinctly unpromising young man, his father had purchased a parliamentary seat for him, at the age of 23, but his main interests in life were gambling and horse-racing. Lord Melbourne was devastated by his son's death, and unhappy that William was now his heir. He cut the allowance of £5,000 a year, which he had been paying to Peniston, to £2,000, but nevertheless set in train arrangements to send him into Parliament. In January 1806, at the age of 26, William Lamb was elected unopposed in a by-election for the Herefordshire constituency of Leominster, a 'pocket borough' which he represented by courtesy of the Scottish peer, Lord Kinnaird, an old school friend.

Already before his election, Lamb had taken another portentous step: in June 1805, he got married to the 19-year-old Lady Caroline Ponsonby. He had apparently already been in love with her for four years, but was unable to contemplate marriage before his prospects dramatically improved. The daughter of the

Earl and Countess of Bessborough, and niece of the famous Georgiana, Duchess of Devonshire, Caroline had had a wayward and undisciplined childhood, and was virtually uneducated, though she had a lively intelligence and undoubted charm. Views differed as to whether she was beautiful, with her androgynous figure, but she had little difficulty in attracting admirers. Highly strung and impetuous, she had, already at the age of 12, announced that she was in love with Fox, but a year later had transferred her adoration to Lamb. The marriage was to lead to one of the great scandals of the century, which is recounted with immense verve by Lord David Cecil in his brilliant book, first published in 1939, *The Young Melbourne*. Here we are concerned only with its effect on Lamb, whose life and career were blighted for over 20 years by this *mésalliance*, from which he never emotionally recovered. That, however, was some time in the future. At the beginning of his marriage Lamb was blissfully happy, and embarked on his life as a parliamentarian in good spirits. With his well established connections at the apex of the Whig world, he received the warmest of welcomes in the House of Commons, being already on terms of intimacy with Fox and other leading Whigs. When the Whigs joined the Grenville government, after nearly 23 years 'in the wilderness', in February 1806, only a week or two after his election, it was taken for granted that he would soon be considered for office. As a newly elected MP, however, he could hardly expect an immediate appointment.

In fact, Grenville's government lasted barely a year, before being turned out by George III and replaced by a Tory ministry under the Duke of Portland (see Chapter 3). So Lamb's early years in Parliament were spent mostly in opposition, though he was hardly a typical opposition MP. To the consternation of many of his Whig friends, he refused to toe a party line, and got into the habit of considering every issue which came up on its merits, which often led him into supporting measures proposed by the government, especially concerning the war effort, having long since abandoned his pro-French views in the face of Napoleon's growing despotism. In particular, he formed a growing admiration for the Tory Foreign Secretary, George Canning, which was ironic in view of the fact that some ten years earlier, while still at Cambridge, he had written and published a rebuttal, in verse, of a poem written by Canning attacking the Whigs for their alleged lack of patriotism (see Chapter 7). Now, he found much to agree with in Canning's progressive Toryism, and while retaining his Whig affiliation, privately came to regard himself as a Canningite, though he did not particularly like the man and did not have close relations with him. He dreamed of an inter-party coalition, preferably led by Canning, in which he could honourably participate, without abandoning the Whigs. When the Prince of Wales became Regent, in 1811, it looked for a time as if such an outcome might be possible (see Chapter 5), but the future George IV became disillusioned with his former Whig friends and confirmed the Perceval government in office. His personal wish, however, was to further Lamb's career and, in February 1812, he persuaded Perceval to offer him the post of a Lord of the Treasury. Lamb turned it down, probably out of loyalty to the Whigs, though it has been suggested (Mandler, 2004) that he felt insulted at the meanness of the offer. Had he been offered a cabinet post, he might well have been more tempted.

Difficulties in his marriage, however, were already upsetting Lamb, and perhaps sapping his political ambition. Four pregnancies in as many years had led to two miscarriages, a still-born daughter and the birth of an apparently healthy son, Augustus, who later turned out to be mentally handicapped. The strain on Lady Caroline Lamb, whose grasp of reality was slender at the best of times, was considerable, and she proceeded to act in a more and more irrational manner, with frequent tantrums and rages, often involving the destruction of much valuable crockery. William showed great patience, but his essentially passive nature and horror of facing unpleasantness made him ill-equipped to deal with the situation. Caroline, who had fantasized that her William was a strong and forceful figure, was deeply disappointed, and soon sought comfort elsewhere. She began a liaison with Sir Godfrey Webster, the son of Lady Holland by her first marriage, and then appeared to transfer her affections to his younger brother, Harry. The Holland family strongly disapproved, and their relations with the Lambs were strained, damaging William's political prospects. Adultery, even serial adultery, was readily condoned in Whig circles, but Lady Caroline seemed to go out of her way to flout the unwritten rules, which both her mother, Lady Bessborough, and her mother-in-law, Lady Melbourne, had scrupulously observed in their many amours. These were that affairs should be conducted with a measure of decorum, and above all that their spouses should not be subjected to public humiliation.

If Lady Caroline had been indiscreet in her relations with the Webster brothers, this was as nothing compared to her next adventure. At a ball, in April 1812, she met Lord Byron, fresh from the triumph of the publication of the first volume of *Childe Harold*, which made him the new darling of London society. She famously noted in her journal that he was 'Mad, bad and dangerous to know', but this did not prevent her the following day from throwing herself at him, and beginning a wild, passionate and very public affair which lasted for some 14 months, before ending with a terrible scene at another ball where she slashed herself with broken glasses. All three principals emerged with their reputations in threads: Byron was regarded as a cad, Caroline a slut and William Lamb a wimp (though that term was not yet in current usage). There were many (including Caroline herself) who thought that the least he could do would have been to challenge Byron to a duel, but this would have been wholly out of character, and the best he could manage was to present himself as a long-suffering husband. He was, however, deeply wounded, hardly able to bear the realization that he was mocked in every club and tavern as a cuckold, and wanting nothing more than to withdraw himself from society and hide away at Brocket Hall.

Subconsciously at least, this probably also influenced his decision not to contest the general election in October 1812, though there were certainly other reasons. One was his acute lack of money, his father still not having increased the £2,000 a year he had set seven years earlier. Lamb felt he could not afford the cost of buying and maintaining a parliamentary seat. Portarlington, for example, the Irish constituency which he represented from 1807 to 1812, had been purchased for £5,000. He felt inhibited from approaching his parents, currently struggling to pay off gambling debts, for assistance. He was also not willing to go cap in hand to Whig proprietors of pocket boroughs who would let him have a seat for nothing, but only if he undertook to vote in accordance with their wishes. He had some hopes that his friend, Lord Holland, might be able to use his great influence to find him a constituency with no strings attached, but Holland was currently upset with him and did not exert himself. So at the age of 33, after six years in the Commons, it looked as though his political career was over. If truth be told, it had not been a glorious one: he was a nervous and hesitant speaker, and a poor attender at the House, and his influence owed much more to his social position than to any other factor. Nevertheless, he felt the keenest disappointment, writing to his mother that: 'It is impossible that any Body can feel the being out of Parliament more keenly than I feel for myself. It is actually cutting my throat. It is depriving me of the greatest object of my life at the moment' (Mitchell, p. 109).

Outside the House, there was little respite from his marital troubles. Caroline continued to act in an unpredictable way, with fearful rows alternating with tearful reconciliations. She was dropped from respectable society and instead started to ingratiate herself with the intellectual world and with fringe figures who had also been excluded. She had a series of affairs with 'unsuitable' – and usually very young – men, including the young Bulwer Lytton and an illegitimate son of the Duke of Bedford, and was frequently drunk. Lamb's family took strongly against her, and put enormous pressure upon him to agree to a judicial separation, but at the last moment he could not bring himself to sign the papers. By 1816, just as he was beginning to feel that he had put the scandal behind him, Caroline published a *roman-à-clef*, in which the whole affair was regurgitated in the most sensational way. It was only in 1824, that Lamb finally agreed to a separation, though he continued to visit and correspond affectionately with her until her death, from dropsy, in 1828, aged 42. Lamb returned to Parliament in 1816, for the borough of Peterborough, switching to Hertfordshire in 1819. He carried on more or less as before, retaining his Whig affiliation, but frequently casting his vote in favour of government measures. This did not endear him to his colleagues. He had written to Lord Holland, already, in 1815 , declaring that he supported: 'The Whig principles of the [Glorious Revolution of 1688–89]...the irresponsibility of the crown, the consequent responsibility of ministers, and the preservation of the dignity of Parliament as constituted by law and custom. With the modern additions, interpolations, facts and fictions, I have nothing to do' (Ziegler, 1982, p. 70).

Lamb's mother died in 1818, and after that he seemed to drift on aimlessly, his ambition all but extinguished. He remained an insatiable reader, and spent his time thinking about the world, and eating and drinking well, while remaining faithful to Caroline, despite all her transgressions. He felt a nagging frustration at the emptiness of his life, and started to write a biography of Sheridan, whom he had known well, and who had died in 1816. Yet the effort seemed too great, and after a while he handed the project over to the popular Irish poet, Thomas Moore, who duly published a volume in 1825. The nadir of Lamb's fortunes came in 1826, when – accustomed to being returned unopposed in his parliamentary contests – he unexpectedly faced a Tory challenger in his Hertfordshire constituency. Lamb, who did not believe in democracy, and was at best a lukewarm supporter of Reform, found the whole business of canvassing for votes extremely unpleasant, and, when his opponent started to drag up the Byron-Lady Caroline Lamb affair, abruptly withdrew from the contest. Once again, outside of Parliament, it looked as though his political career was finally over. Then, it was rescued by a totally unexpected sequence of events. In early 1827, Lord Liverpool, who had governed for nearly 15 years, was incapacitated by a stroke, and George Canning, already a dying man, was appointed by George IV to succeed him (see Chapter 7). When half of Liverpool's cabinet, and many other Tories, refused to serve under him, Canning was desperate to find suitable people to fill a large number of government posts. He appealed to the Whig leader, Earl Grey, to join a coalition, but Grey refused, though other Whigs agreed to serve on an individual basis. Canning then offered Lamb the vacant post – outside the cabinet – of Chief Secretary for Ireland. Lamb accepted, and departed for Dublin, delighted that he now, at the age of 48, finally had a real job to do. (Canning was also able to find him a pocket borough – Newport, Isle of Wight – for which he was returned unopposed in a by-election in April 1827).

Lamb remained at his post until June 1828, under three Prime ministers – Canning, Goderich and Wellington. As L.G. Mitchell relates:

> In these fifteen months, he showed a capacity for hard work that surprised his family and may have surprised himself. By September 1827, he was writing letters that suggested a mastery of such Irish problems as tithes, education, customs, and land reform. Though there were topics like 'police, gaols, hospitals, penitentiaries' which he had 'little or no taste for', he worked away at them and modestly thought his situation 'enough for me, who have been for so long used to doing nothing'. (Mitchell, p. 113)

Lamb got on well with both the Lord-Lieutenants with whom he served, the touchy Marquess Wellesley and his successor, the more amiable Marquess of Anglesey, but his great success was with the majority Catholic community. Previous Chief Secretaries had mixed only with the Protestant Ascendancy, but Lamb, a great believer in religious toleration, refused to distinguish between the affiliations of those he met, and dined as often with Catholics as with Protestants, while making himself equally available to all-comers at his office, receiving a constant stream of visitors, without hiding behind secretaries or attendants. At this stage – but not later – he liked and admired Daniel O'Connell, the Irish nationalist leader, and had no difficulty with his campaigning for the rights of Catholics and tenants, so long as it was done peacefully. If, however, violence was threatened, he was determined to deal with it with a firm hand.

Lamb now regarded himself more than ever as a Canningite and this inclination was reinforced by family connections. His cousin, William Huskisson, was a leading Canningite minister, while his sister Emily, who was married to Lord Cowper, was the long-time mistress of Lord Palmerston MP, another Canningite, and was to marry him after her husband's death. When Huskisson resigned from Wellington's cabinet in May 1828 (see Chapter 9), the other Canningite ministers, including Palmerston, also left in sympathy with him. Lamb felt he should do the same, though he did not agree with Huskisson over the issue on which he resigned, and returned from Dublin with his reputation as a serious politician largely restored. His nominal father died a month later, aged 83, leaving him a large fortune and extensive estates. As the second Viscount Melbourne, he was now at last a man of substance, and was to cut a rather more impressive figure in the House of Lords than he ever had in the Commons. It was thus no surprise that Earl Grey sought to include Melbourne in the government he formed in 1830, essentially a coalition between Whigs and Canningites, with a mandate to introduce electoral reform. What had not been expected, however, was that he should be offered so senior a post as Home Secretary. The probability was that Grey wished to balance the appointments of radical figures such as Lord Brougham, the Lord Chancellor, and Lord Durham, his son-in-law and Lord Privy Seal, with somebody of more conservative views. Apart from the ultra Tory, the Duke of Richmond, who became Postmaster-General, no member of the new government was more conservative than Melbourne.

Melbourne remained at the Home Office throughout Grey's ministry of nearly four years. Of chief interest are his attitudes and actions concerning two policy areas – the Reform Bill, and law and order, for which he had overall Cabinet responsibility. On Reform, he was, in L. G. Mitchell's words: 'virtually invisible. He spoke on the issue rarely, had no part in drawing up the measure, and had to be carried along like a dead weight by his more enthusiastic colleagues' (Mitchell, p. 130).

Melbourne's difficulty was that, though he recognized the necessity of the Bill, in view of the state of public opinion, he found it highly distasteful. In his view, politics was a matter to be determined by men of property and taste, not by the broad masses, and he had a particular dislike for those likely to benefit from the Bill. 'I don't like the middle classes', he was recorded as saying, 'the higher and lower classes, there's some good in them, but the middle class are all affectation and conceit and pretence and concealment' (Cecil, 1954, pp. 161–2). So he was never more than a lukewarm supporter of the Bill, and with Palmerston, was in favour of shelving it when it was first defeated by the Lords. He was particularly opposed to swamping the House of Lords with new members in order to get the Bill through, and only ten days before its final passage threatened to resign if this should be resorted to. As recounted in Chapter 10, it proved unnecessary due to the mass abstention of Tory peers, led by the Duke of Wellington, at the conclusion of the Third Reading debate.

On law and order, Melbourne was very firm in insisting that laws should be obeyed, but he was extremely reluctant to extend the scope of the law, especially (in this respect, being a good Whig) if this would curtail the liberties of citizens. Thus he cracked down hard on the 'Captain Swing' disturbances of 1830–31, involving a great deal of arson and destruction of farm machinery, setting up commissions to try the offenders, who imposed heavy sentences, including 227 of death, all but 19 of which were commuted to imprisonment or transportation. Nevertheless, he refused impassioned appeals from landowners for the widespread use of troops to protect their estates and for even more coercive laws to be passed, taking the view that their best protection would be to act as model landlords and employers, which very few of them were.

He took the same attitude during the protests provoked by the defeat by the House of Lords of the first version of the Reform Bill. He refused to legislate against the creation of 'political unions' campaigning for a more extreme reform measure, or against the holding of mass demonstrations – both of which – he said were perfectly legal, and would be tolerated if they did not break the existing law. He used his own influence to mediate with protest leaders, such as the Chartist William Place, who had once worked for him as a tailor, to ensure that their followers were law-abiding. He regarded the demands of certain Tory peers for more extreme measures as hysterical, writing to the Duke of Buckingham, saying that 'it is impossible to guarantee any one against broken windows'. The ultra-Tory Duke of Newcastle, whose property was destroyed during riots in Nottingham, received an even dustier reply: 'Melbourne refused to put him on a commission to try the rioters, thought his claim for damages exorbitant, since his house was nothing but an 'old ruin' anyway and resolutely refused to allow him the use of arms' (Mitchell, p. 129).

Equally, Melbourne declined to re-impose restrictions against the forming of trade unions, which had been repealed in 1824, though he regarded unions as pernicious organizations, inevitably doomed to failure. When ten Dorset agricultural workers, known to history as the Tolpuddle Martyrs, broke the law in 1834, by administering oaths, he refused to intervene against the sentences of transportation passed on them by local magistrates. They were shipped to New South Wales, but two years later, when Melbourne was Prime Minister, they were allowed to return after mass protests on their behalf.

Grey soon became dissatisfied with Melbourne's performance, regarding him as indolent, and, in 1831 proposed to move him to a less senior post. He was dissuaded by Lord Holland, who argued that his apparently casual ways were deceptive, and that he was, in fact, a hard-working and assiduous minister, who carefully read his briefs and replied promptly to his correspondence. If, in any particular matter, Melbourne decided not to take action it was because in his view it could only make matters worse and that inactivity was the better option. So Melbourne remained in place, though Grey was not really convinced. When Grey resigned in July 1834 – he did not see Melbourne as a likely successor – his own preference would have been Lord Althorp MP, who had been his Chancellor of the Exchequer and Leader of the Commons. Melbourne too did not have any expectation of succeeding, or any evident desire to do so. The choice was made by King William IV, who wanted to appoint a Tory, but in deference to the situation in the House of Commons, went for the next best thing, a highly conservative Whig, which was how Melbourne was then seen. This was acquiesced in by Melbourne's cabinet colleagues because, in the words of Lord Durham, the very radical Lord Privy Seal, 'he was the only one of whom none of us would be jealous'. Melbourne himself expressed no enthusiasm, as recounted by the diarist, Charles Greville:

> When the King sent for him he told Young [his private secretary] 'he thought it a damned bore, and said he was in many minds what he should do – be Minister or no'. Young said, 'Why damn it, such a position never was occupied by a Greek or Roman, and, if it lasts only two months, it is well worth to have been Prime Minister of England.' 'By God that's true,' said Melbourne; 'I'll go'. (Hibbert, ed., 1981, p. 120)

So, he became Prime Minister, on 16 July 1834, at the age of 55. He reappointed all the members of Grey's cabinet, adding only his brother-in-law, Viscount Duncannon MP, as his own successor as Home Secretary. With some difficulty, he persuaded Lord Althorp MP, who had just resigned as Leader of the Commons, to stay on. The death of Althorp's father, the second Earl Spencer, whose title and seat in the House of Lords he inherited, sounded the death knell of the government only four months later. Melbourne travelled down to Brighton to discuss with William IV a replacement for Althorp, having in mind Lord John Russell MP, who happened to be the King's *bête noire*. William said he would sleep on the matter, and invited Melbourne to stay overnight. In the morning, he abruptly dismissed the government, and said that he would invite the Duke of Wellington to form a Tory administration. Wellington demurred, in favour of Sir Robert Peel, who was away in Italy, but acted as Prime Minister for three weeks until Peel's return. William IV was taking a gamble in dismissing a government which still enjoyed a majority in the Commons, something which his father, George III, had done several times, but which was now widely seen as a constitutional outrage. Peel called a general election within two months, and tried to gild his party's colours by renaming it the Conservative Party, and indicating that it now fully accepted the Reform Act, as well as Catholic emancipation. He made extensive gains, but not enough to achieve a parliamentary majority. When, inevitably, he was defeated on a major parliamentary vote a few months later, in April 1835, he immediately resigned, and the king was forced to swallow his pride and send again for the Whigs. Since then no monarch has ever dared to turn out a government with a Commons majority.

The Whigs were angry with Melbourne for having given up office without a fight, and strongly appealed to Grey to come back as Prime Minister, which he firmly refused. Melbourne was then invited to form a government, but this time he insisted on making his own ministerial appointments, and – to their great chagrin – excluded the two most radical members of Grey's government, Lords Brougham and Durham. He also wished to move Palmerston, whose brash conduct of foreign affairs had annoyed many foreign rulers, but he refused to accept any other post. Melbourne then, most reluctantly, reappointed him as Foreign Secretary. Russell now became Home Secretary and leader of the Commons, while Thomas Spring-Rice was Chancellor of the Exchequer and Lord Holland (the acknowledged 'keeper of the Whig conscience') returned to his former post as Chancellor of the Duchy of Lancaster. The Marquess of Lansdowne was Lord President of the Council, and Melbourne's deputy as leader of the House of Lords. The general expectation was that Melbourne's second government would not last long. In fact, it managed to stagger on for nearly seven years. The main reason for this was Melbourne's lack of ambition. He had few objectives other than keeping his government together, which meant that he seldom took political initiatives, and proposed a minimal amount of legislation, which limited the possibilities of defeat.

There were objective reasons for Melbourne's caution. The King was hostile, while his government was in a small minority in the House of Lords, where the Tory majority had little hesitation in blocking government bills or hamstringing them by wrecking amendments. In the Commons, the Whigs (who had by now successfully incorporated the Canningites, apart from those who, led by E.G. Stanley, had defected to the Tories in 1834) were far short of being a majority. They could only survive with the support of the Radicals and/or the

Irish nationalists led by Daniel O'Connell. Melbourne heartily disliked both factions, and was most unwilling to treat with them, but they reluctantly kept him in office solely to keep the Tories out. Even the Tories, themselves, led by Wellington and Peel, were for long in two minds about the desirability of defeating Melbourne. In order to form a government of their own, they knew that they would have to include a large swathe of 'ultras' determined to put the clock back, both on Reform and Catholic emancipation. For them also, at least until 1839 or thereabouts, a Melbourne government was the lesser of two evils.

Melbourne's team was by no means homogenous. It included strong and mutually unsympathetic characters, who were only kept together by Melbourne's charm and his resolute determination to avoid the taking of unpleasant decisions. Each minister was left in virtually unchallenged control of his own department; cabinet meetings were infrequent and parliamentary recesses long. The reforming era ushered in by the Grey government was stopped short in its tracks. The only important reform for which Melbourne was prepared to fight was the Municipal Corporations Act of 1835. This provided for triennial elections by ratepayers in 178 boroughs and cities, each of which was to have a mayor, alderman and councillors. They replaced a largely corrupt system of self-perpetuating corporations, most of which were Tory controlled, perhaps a reason why Melbourne promoted the measure, which was a logical consequence of the 1832 Reform Act. A minor but useful measure was the Registration of Births, Deaths and Marriages Bill, which for the first time provided for secular records to be kept of matters which had previously been left in the hands of parish clergy, who carried out this duty with widely varying efficiency.

Although he might appear to have been a 'do nothing' premier, Melbourne was by no means idle. He was conscientious to a fault in such matters as recommending the appointment of bishops, despite his own absence of religious beliefs. He was anxious to ensure that only able nominees were chosen, being careful to exclude those too infected with sectarian enthusiasms. He also kept up his voracious reading habits, amazing acquaintances with the breadth of his knowledge in a wide range of fields and continued to be an enthusiastic diner-out, particularly, but by no means exclusively, at the table of Lord and Lady Holland. He refused to move into 10 Downing Street, preferring to remain in his house in South Street, Mayfair, which he had bought in 1828, after selling off Melbourne House. Melbourne's emotional life was fairly bleak, and was not improved by the death of his backward son Augustus, on whom he had lavished much care, in 1836. Yet he was not lacking in female company, having a number of (mostly married) women friends, with whom he consorted, but without forming deep attachments. He had the misfortune to be cited in court cases by two aggrieved husbands, the first of whom, Lord Branden, he managed to pay off, but the second actually came to court while he was Prime Minister, causing a sensation. The plaintiff was George Norton, the blackguardly husband of Caroline Norton, the beautiful and intelligent grand-daughter of Sheridan, who succeeded precariously in maintaining herself, and supporting her young family, by novel-writing. There was no doubt that Melbourne had been highly indiscreet, but when the case came to court he was dismissed from the action due to lack of convincing evidence. After these scrapes, Melbourne cold-heartedly refused any further contact with the two women concerned, though he continued to support them financially, and remembered both of them in his will. His biographer, L.C. Mitchell, had little doubt of the cause of the older Melbourne's inability to form a deep relationship:

> He had loved and trusted Caroline Lamb, and the result had been such public humiliation and misery, that he had been forced into terrible introspection. He determined never to love or trust anyone again. ... women were to be taken on as friends only on terms. He much prized their company, but he wanted nothing more. (Mitchell, p. 231)

If there was one exception to this, it could only have been the young Queen Victoria. Certainly, his association with her gave him a new purpose in life, and for three to four years he gave every indication of being a happy and fulfilled man. She succeeded her uncle, William IV, on 20 June 1837, when she was barely 18. Her father, Edward, Duke of Kent, had died when she was less than two, and she had been brought up in semi-seclusion by her mother, the former Princess Victoria of Saxe-Saalfeld-Coburg, with whom she was on bad terms. She suspected her mother of scheming with the Comptroller of her Household, Sir John Conroy, to take control of the monarchy, reducing her to a mere puppet. Her first action on becoming Queen was to summon the Prime Minister to tell him that she had no intention of changing any of her ministers, and Melbourne, 'handsome and resplendent in full court dress' (Marshall, p. 126) kissed hands on his re-appointment. That night the Queen recorded in her journal that her first minister was 'straightforward, clever, honest and good'. This was the first of a long series of flattering references to her 'good friend', whom she rapidly came to accept as the father she had never had. He was, in fact, the first adult who had taken her seriously and given her good, disinterested advice, with the partial exception of her Uncle Leopold, the King of Belgium, who wrote her encouraging letters, but for the most part was far away in Brussels. On his part, Melbourne was fascinated to have this young, lively, naïve, yet alert and strong-willed girl – forty years his junior – hanging on his every word, as he endlessly recounted the ups and downs of his life and of politics and society over the previous half-century. He told her a great deal about such characters as Fox, Pitt, Liverpool and Canning, and about her grandfather, George III, and her two regal uncles George IV and

William IV, while imparting to her a straightforward Whig account of history and injunctions over how a constitutional monarch should behave. It was not long before he became her private secretary, as well as Prime Minister, and got into the habit of spending nearly all his time at the court, either at Windsor or Buckingham Palace.

Nearly always he gave her good advice, with two notable exceptions. One was over the Lady Flora Hastings affair, concerning a lady-in-waiting of the Queen's mother, whose stomach became swollen and rumours swiftly travelled round the Court that she was pregnant, by – evil tongues suggested – no other than Sir John Conroy. This she vehemently denied, but Victoria insisted that she should submit to a medical examination, which revealed that she was a virgin. She died soon afterwards, and the post-mortem revealed that the swelling had been caused by an enormous liver tumour. Melbourne was at fault in not deterring the Queen from forcing Lady Flora to submit to humiliation, and also for trying to cover up the affair, when her brother, Lord Hastings, vehemently objected. Victoria emerged with her reputation damaged. The other occasion occurred in 1839, when Melbourne's government resigned, after its parliamentary majority fell away to a mere five votes in a parliamentary debate over a rebellion in the colony of Jamaica. Victoria was distraught to lose her Prime Minister, but, on Melbourne's advice, sent for Sir Robert Peel to form a new government. This Peel agreed to do, but in submitting his list of proposed appointments, included nominations of some Tory women to replace the Ladies of the Queen's Bedchamber, all of whom had been Whigs. The Queen was flabbergasted, and consulted Melbourne, who advised her that she could insist that these were personal appointments, and that she could not agree to Sir Robert's proposals. Melbourne's action was undoubtedly unconstitutional – as he had resigned as Prime Minister he had no business in offering advice on appointments. When Sir Robert heard the Queen's response, he said that the Tories were unwilling to form a government under such conditions, and Melbourne resumed as Prime Minister, somewhat shame-facedly, as he almost certainly realized that he had erred in proffering advice.

The diarist Charles Greville has left a graphic description of how Melbourne's daily routine was dominated by his attendance on the Queen:

> He is at her side for at least six hours every day – an hour in the morning, two on horseback, one at dinner, and two in the evening…Month after month he remains at the Castle, submitting to this daily routine…he is always sitting bolt upright; his free and easy language interlarded with 'damns' is carefully guarded and regulated with the strictest propriety, and he has exchanged the good talk of Holland House for the trivial, laboured, and wearisome inanities of the Royal circle. (Hibbert, pp. 163–4)

Melbourne could only spend so much time with the Queen by grievously neglecting his duties as Prime Minister, and effectively abdicating from any supervision of his ministers. In particular, Lord Palmerston, who had recently become Melbourne's brother-in-law on marrying his sister Emily, established himself as the absolute ruler of the Foreign Office. In 1840, this almost led to a disastrous war with France, for which the nation was utterly unprepared. The occasion was the rebellion of the ruler of Egypt, Mehemet Ali, against his Turkish overlords. Strongly encouraged by the French government, led by Adolphe Thiers, he had seized Syria and Palestine, and was threatening to march on Constantinople. Palmerston reacted with extraordinary belligerence, to the horror of several of his cabinet colleagues, notably the pro-French Lord Holland. Melbourne failed to take energetic steps to restrain him, and it was only the downfall of the Thiers government, and his replacement by the anglophile François Guizot, which prevented hostilities from breaking out (see Chapter 15).

Melbourne's position at Court was transformed in February 1840 by the marriage of the now 20-year-old Queen to Prince Albert of Saxe-Coburg-Gotha, after a whirlwind courtship. Albert took over the role of Victoria's secretary, and though he continued to have close access to her as Prime Minister, her emotional dependence on him quickly faded, so besotted was she with her new husband. The political difficulties of his government now also greatly increased. The Tories had made further gains in the 1837 general election, and Peel – now the most effective debater in the Commons – began to press the government much harder, particularly on financial and economic issues, with the government seemingly unable to control a mounting budget deficit. Relations between ministers began to deteriorate – the chief would-be reformer, Lord John Russell became increasingly frustrated; while, in September 1839, Earl Grey's son, Viscount Howick MP, who had constantly been threateningly to resign, finally did so. His replacement as War Secretary was T.B. Macaulay, who proved to be far less effective as a politician than as a historian. Against his better judgement, Melbourne was forced to dismiss another cabinet minister, Lord Glenelg, the Colonial Secretary, after several other ministers had threatened to leave unless he did so. The government was deeply split over two political issues which were assuming increasing importance – the Corn Laws and the secret ballot. Agitation to repeal the protectionist Corn laws (see Chapter 12), led by two Radical MPs, Richard Cobden and John Bright, built up strongly during 1839, and Melbourne, who was personally opposed to repeal, had to agree that it would be regarded as an 'open issue', with Cabinet ministers free to argue on either side, though he was adamant that there was no immediate possibility of legislation. On the secret ballot, of which Lord John Russell was a strong advocate, Melbourne refused to budge, not even to the extent of allowing this also to be recognized as an open issue. The government appeared increasingly care-worn and ineffective, and there was little surprise when it went down to defeat in the 1841 general election, of which the result was:

Conservatives   368
Whigs and allies   290.

Melbourne resigned soon after, on 30 August 1841, with evident feelings of relief. The only thing he regretted was the loss of his close proximity to the Queen. Despite increasingly clear hints from Albert and others that they were unwelcome, he continually bombarded Victoria with letters proffering advice on a wide range of questions. The Queen responded in a kindly way, but her replies became more and more infrequent, and Melbourne was forced to the sad conclusion that he had outlived his usefulness to her. In Mitchell's view, his ultimate rejection by 'the young Victoria, who became a surrogate daughter' was almost on a par with his betrayal by Lady Caroline Lamb, and gave a 'bitter edge to his last years' (Mitchell, p. 276). He survived his premiership by some seven years, but after suffering a stroke, in October 1842, his health sharply deteriorated, and he was confined mostly to Brocket Hall. Despite devoted care by his sister Emily, whose Palmerston family estate was nearby, his brother Frederick and his young Austrian wife and the widow of his brother George who had died in 1834, after having served under Melbourne as Under-Secretary at the Home Office, he was lonely and miserable, finding it difficult to accept that Russell had now effectively replaced him as leader of the Whigs. He died on 24 November 1848, at the age of 69.

As Prime Minister, Melbourne's performance was, at best, mediocre. As guide, counsellor and friend to the young queen, he excelled himself. It would be idle to contend that she invariably showed wisdom and good judgement throughout her long reign. Yet without his gentle tutelage, it is highly improbable that she would have coped as well as she did in treading the difficult and unfamiliar path of being a constitutional monarch in an age of unprecedented upheaval.

Works consulted

Lord David Cecil, 1948, *The Young Melbourne*, London, Pan Books.
Lord David Cecil, 1954, *Lord M: The later life of Lord Melbourne*, London, Constable.
Christopher Hibbert, 1981, (ed.), *Greville's England: Selections from the diaries of Charles Greville 1818–1860*, London, The Folio Society.
Lucille Iremonger, 1970, *The Fiery Chariot*, London, Secker & Warburg.
Peter Mandler, 2004, Article in *The Oxford Dictionary of National Biography*, Oxford, Oxford University Press.
Dorothy Marshall, 1975, *Lord Melbourne*, London, Weidenfeld & Nicolson.
L.G. Mitchell, 1997, *Lord Melbourne 1779–1848*, Oxford, Oxford University Press.
Philip Ziegler, 1982, *Melbourne*, New York, Athenaeum.

12

Sir Robert Peel – Arch Pragmatist or Tory Traitor?

Robert Peel came from a different social background from all his predecessors as Prime Minister and, for that matter, from nearly all his successors. His father and grandfather, both also called Robert, were northern manufacturers, self-made men who rose from the yeoman class.

His grandfather, who had started life as a dealer in linen, opened up a small calico printing factory at Oswaldtwistle in Lancashire in the early 1760s, together with two associates who put up most of the capital. They had the good fortune to employ James Hargreaves, the inventor of the spinning jenny, whose invention he was able to exploit. Known as 'Parsley' Peel, because of his success in marketing a simple parsley leaf design, within a few years he became one of the leading figures in the Lancashire cotton industry. His son Robert chafed at working at his father's side and, in 1772, at the age of 22 was given £500 to set up on his own. Within a very few years, he had outstripped his father, and by 1784 was employing at least 6,800 people, directly or indirectly, which by the end of the century had increased to 15,000. By then, he had far outgrown his Lancashire roots, transferring much of his manufacturing activity to Staffordshire, where he bought an estate, Drayton Manor, from the Marquess of Bath, in the vicinity of Tamworth, for which he became MP in 1790, and served for 40 years. A loyal supporter of the Younger Pitt, he was made a baronet in 1800.

In 1783, he had married Ellen Yates, the much younger daughter of his business partner, and, on 5 February 1788, their eldest son, Robert, was born. He was the third of eleven children, having five brothers and five sisters, the two youngest of whom were to die in childhood. Sir Robert Peel, Bart, was ambitious for all his children, though initially he had the highest hopes for his second and third sons, William and Edmund. Nevertheless, it was to Robert that he – only semi-jocularly – remarked, as the latter was to recall late in life, 'Bob, you dog, if you are not prime minister some day, I'll disinherit you' (Gash, 1976, p. 6). He was determined that they should grow up to be 'gentlemen' rather than merely mill-owners like himself and his father. The young Robert was duly enrolled at Harrow, where he arrived in 1800, at the age of 12.

At Harrow, Robert, who was initially looked down upon by his aristocratic schoolfellows as a rough provincial (he was to retain a Lancashire accent throughout his life) became something of a solitary. He avoided organized games, preferring to roam alone the ten-mile stretch of open country between Harrow and the metropolis, carrying his shot guns, and often returning with rabbits for the cooking pot. He was a first-class shot. Apart from a thrashing from a senior pupil for whom he refused to fag, Peel avoided being bullied, being a large, well-built young man, who looked as though he was well able to take care of himself. Nevertheless, he was extremely sensitive, and became more so after a tragedy befell his family, when he was 15, with the sudden death of his mother, at the age of 37. His father almost immediately remarried – to a woman to whom he had proposed and been rejected over 20 years earlier, before his first marriage. This second marriage was a total failure, and soon broke up, leaving a vacuum in the household, instead of the loving stepmother that Sir Robert had hoped to provide for his children. Robert grieved deeply over his mother, and it may be significant that almost the only close friend he made at Harrow was the young Lord Byron, his exact contemporary at the school, who had lost his father at a very young age. Academically, he was an ideal pupil, more than fulfilling his father's ambitions for him. His tutor, Mark Drury, was in the habit of saying to his classmates, to Robert's deep embarrassment, 'You boys will one day see Peel Prime Minister' (Iremonger, p. 99). He avoided unpopularity among his fellows, by being extremely generous in helping the less gifted with their exercises.

Robert left Harrow at the end of 1804, aged nearly 17, and spent several months living at his father's London house, preparing to go up to Oxford the following October. He often went to the House of Commons to listen to debates, and his father introduced him to the Prime Minister, William Pitt, though the highlight of this visit was to listen to one of the finest speeches ever made by his great rival, Charles James Fox. It was on Catholic emancipation, and over 20 years later he was to recall that 'he had never heard a speech which made a greater impression on his mind than that delivered by Mr Fox during that debate' (Gash, 1976, p. 9). At Oxford, he came under the supervision of Cyril Jackson, the famous Dean of Christ Church, through whose hands had earlier passed two other future prime ministers – Charles Jenkinson (Lord Liverpool) and George Canning – as well as Henry Fox (Lord Holland), the nephew of Charles James Fox and his political heir. He was heard to remark that 'Harrow has sent us up at least one scholar in Mr Peel', and Robert was not to let him down, exceeding all his other students in his achievements. The Oxford degree curriculum had recently been divided into two separate schools – *Literae Humaniores* and Mathematics – and students had to choose between them when being examined for their degree. Peel chose to do both, and was the first person ever to achieve a double First Class result, a tribute not only to his intelligence, but the enormous hard work he had put in. According to his brother William, he read 'eighteen hours in the day and the night. I doubt if anyone ever read harder than Robert for the two or three terms before he passed his examinations' (Gash, 1976, p. 11). He had a more rounded time at Oxford than at Harrow, abandoning his solitary ways and taking part in such sporting activities as rowing and cricket. He also became quite a popular figure, with his handsome physique, and dressing for a while in a dandyesque way. He made a number of good friends, the closest being Henry Vane, later Earl of Cleveland.

His father, now an enormously wealthy man, lost no time in rewarding him for his tremendous effort. Robert left Oxford in March 1809, having just passed his twenty-first birthday. Within a month, he was to become Member of Parliament for the Irish pocket borough of Cashel, his father having already begun negotiations to purchase the seat, through the good offices of General Sir Arthur Wellesley (later the Duke of Wellington), who was at the time the Chief Secretary for Ireland. He joined his father in the House, and like him aligned himself with the Pittite faction, who were by now generally recognized as Tories. The elder Peel had already made his mark as a respected and active MP. His large fortune derived, at least in part, from the exploitation of child labour, and he now sought to make amends by improving the employment conditions in his own factories, and by carrying through Parliament the first piece of factory legislation – 30 years before the Factory Act of the Grey government. This was the Health and Morals of Apprentices Act of 1802, which was far from pleasing to most of his fellow Lancashire manufacturers. The younger Peel was not yet definitely set on a political career. With his father's encouragement, he had taken chambers at Lincoln's Inn, and began studying for the Bar. But the decision was soon taken out of his hands. His maiden speech, seconding the reply to the King's Speech, on 23 January 1810, was a triumphant success, prompting the Speaker to declare that it had been the best maiden speech since the Younger Pitt's.

Four months later, Lord Liverpool, the Secretary of State for Colonies and War, and one of the leading figures in the Perceval government, snapped him up to be one of two under-secretaries in his department. Liverpool, a fellow alumnus of Christ Church, had picked him out as the most promising of the newer pro-government MPs. At just over 22, he was beginning his ministerial career even younger than William Pitt, who became Chancellor of the Exchequer at the age of 23. His post, which he was to hold for two years, gave him excellent administrative and parliamentary experience. The other under-secretary was responsible for military matters, while Peel was left to deal with the whole range of colonial issues, in which Liverpool took little interest and left him largely a free hand. These covered everything, 'from Botany Bay to Prince Edward Island' as he himself put it. He was also responsible for the administration of secret service money. Moreover, as the only minister in the department in the Commons, he was responsible for answering in Parliament for all questions concerning the war effort, including the ongoing campaigns in the Iberian peninsula, and was thus one of the government's most frequent spokesmen in the lower House. He worked hard, mastered his briefs with little difficulty, and spoke with great confidence in the House. He was soon seen as a rising star, and when Liverpool became Prime Minister, after Perceval's assassination in 1812, there was little surprise when he rewarded Peel with a senior post. This was as Chief Secretary for Ireland.

He was there for six years – an exceedingly lengthy incumbency for this post – and made his mark on the island as it did upon him. The position was an exceptionally testing one for a young politician. He virtually acted as Prime Minister of Ireland (with the Lord Lieutenant effectively playing the role of a constitutional monarch). Peel was formally responsible to the Home Secretary, Lord Sidmouth, who took little interest in Irish affairs. Peel, who crossed the Irish Channel no fewer than 15 times during his period in office, acted as his own chief spokesman in the House of Commons, where, he once remarked, 'Most MPs knew as much about Ireland as they did of Kamchatka' (Gash, 1976, p. 39). On arrival, he was extremely depressed by what he saw, particularly as he ventured out from Dublin. He was shocked at the level of poverty, the chronically bad relations between the (often-absentee) Protestant landowners and their Catholic tenants, the high level of violence and disorder, the low quality of the local administration and the prevalence of corruption and jobbery. He set himself to reform the Dublin administration, weeding out inefficient officials and ensuring, as far as he was able, that their successors were chosen on merit. He sadly concluded that it was impossible to achieve anything comparable at local level – the powers of patronage of the country landowners were so entrenched that there was no means of over-riding them without enraging the entire Protestant ascendancy, on which the British government depended for the maintenance of the union with England. Nevertheless, despite the feeble implements at his disposal, Peel soon acquired a reputation as a first-class administrator. His work methods are well described by his principal biographer, Norman Gash:

> Few things are more striking in his dealings with his Irish subordinates than his insistence on precise, factual information, a commodity not easy to obtain in Ireland. Facts to Peel were the basis of sound administration; facts were the best arguments to lay before the legislature. 'There is nothing like a fact' he observed '... facts are ten times more valuable than declamations'. In administration this was an admirable attitude; in politics, where much depends on appearances, it was not always to be so infallible a guide. (Gash, 1976, p. 445)

Peel was well aware of what was expected of him during the two general elections which occurred during his time in Ireland. This was, as he delicately put it, 'to secure the Government's interest if possible from dilapidation, but still more to faint with horror at the mention of money transactions' (Gash, 1976, p. 20). He was able to secure a handful of net gains during the 1812 election, and rather more in that of 1818, when it was estimated that 71 of the 100 Irish Members elected were Tory supporters. Peel was resistant to the claims of the Catholic majority, both as regards to emancipation and the repeal of the 1800 Union Act. He fell out badly with Daniel O'Connell, the leader of the Catholic agitation, with whom he traded notable insults, leading, in 1815, to a challenge to a duel, which the participants agreed should be held on the neutral ground of Ostend. This could have had the most disastrous consequences, as both men were first-class marksmen, and O'Connell had already killed an opponent in another duel earlier the same year. Word of the projected duel got round, however, and on his way to Belgium O'Connell was arrested in London, eventually sending Peel a formal apology nine years later. Peel claimed not to have any animosity to Catholics as such, and 'appears to have felt that in the long run the best hope for the country would be that popery was something which a more prosperous people would grow out of' (Prest). He privately felt contempt for the Ulster Protestants, but publicly was seen as their champion, and the nickname of 'Orange' Peel, which O'Connell had bestowed on him, stuck. Even more so, after the great debate on Catholic emancipation, which took place in the Commons on 9 May 1817, on a motion tabled by the Irish Whig Henry Grattan. The pro-Catholics had been expected to carry the day, and that they did not do so was attributed almost entirely to a rumbustious speech by Peel – long regarded as one of the greatest of his parliamentary orations – winding up the debate. He became an instant hero to the many Anglicans who were fundamentally opposed to emancipation. Nowhere was the Church of England interest stronger than at the University of Oxford, one of whose prestigious seats in Parliament was currently vacant. It had been kept warm for George Canning, but – as a pro-Catholic – his supporters now abandoned him and approached Peel instead. Canning withdrew his name, and Peel was returned unopposed on 10 June 1817, giving up his Chippenham constituency, to which he had transferred from Cashel in 1812. Now, whether he liked it or not, Peel was seen as an arch Protestant, which was to have portentous consequences in his later career.

In Ireland, he made no reputation as a reformer, but as a firm and fair administrator. Two achievements in his final two years there ensured, however, that he would leave the country (to which he would never return) with an enhanced reputation. One was his energetic response to the failure of the Irish potato crop in 1817, when he exerted himself to obtain money and alternative supplies of food, which probably saved the country from widespread famine. The other was the creation of the beginnings of a national police force for Ireland, foreshadowing his action ten years later in creating the Metropolitan Police. His purpose was to minimize the use of troops in responding to disorder, and though his embryo force, nicknamed the 'Peelers', left a great deal to be desired, it was undoubtedly an improvement on what went before. Peel worked exceptionally hard during his six years as Chief Secretary, taking only one holiday – in 1815, when he visited Paris and dined with the Duke of Wellington, who gave him a first-hand account of his recent victory at Waterloo. By 1818, he felt exhausted, and submitted his resignation, spending the next three-and-a-half years as an influential backbencher. As such, he was chosen as the chairman of a high-powered House of Commons committee, including all the senior ministers in the lower house, to consider the complex question of whether Britain should return to the 'gold standard', after having printed a substantial amount of paper money during the course of the Napoleonic wars. Peel tackled the task with his customary assiduity, and eventually produced a magisterial report which argued in favour, largely on the grounds of curbing inflation. His recommendations were immediately accepted by the Government.

His period out of office was marked by two events of great significance in his private life. On 8 June 1820, he got married to Julia Floyd, daughter of General Sir John Floyd, who had been the commander-in-chief of the British army in Ireland during his Chief Secretaryship. He was then 32, and his bride 24. Beautiful and warm-hearted, but – according to Wellington – 'not a clever woman', she had little interest in politics or intellectual pursuits, but she was utterly devoted to Peel, and he to her, and their marriage appears to have brought total satisfaction to both parties. It produced seven children, several of whom went on to have distinguished careers of their own, three serving as government ministers, one of them finishing up as Speaker of the Commons, while another son was to win a VC in the Crimean War. The other development was that Peel, who had an acute artistic sense, began to build up his fine art collection, which gave him immense satisfaction throughout the remainder of his life. Backed by his father's wealth, he made a number of shrewd acquisitions, starting with a Rembrandt, which he picked up at a sale in Dublin for a mere 59 guineas, but culminating in Rubens' magnificent portrait 'Chapeau de Paille', which cost him the considerable sum of £2,725. Peel became a trustee of the National Gallery, which was established in 1824, when he was Home Secretary, and at his death he bequeathed to it his entire collection of over 300 works.

Liverpool was keen to bring Peel back into his government, as indeed was the King, but the only vacant Cabinet post which he had to offer was President of the Board of Control (of Indian affairs), which Peel twice declined, in 1820 and 1821. A proposal to appoint him as Chancellor of the Exchequer, which Peel would almost certainly have accepted, was blocked by the already ailing Lord Castlereagh MP, who feared that Peel's presence would undermine his own position as leader of the House of Commons. So Peel had to wait until January 1822, when a general reconstruction of the government included the retirement of Lord Sidmouth as Home Secretary, a post which Peel was happy to accept. Eight months later, the suicide of Castlereagh led to another reconstruction, which brought Canning back into the government to take over both of Castlereagh's functions, as Foreign Secretary and leader of the House. Peel, who might well have staked a claim to the latter post, declined to do so, in the interest of restoring harmony to the Cabinet, and of easing Canning's return (see Chapter 6).

The reconstructed Cabinet was a finely balanced affair between 'liberal Tories' open-minded about reform measures, generally in favour of free trade and sympathetic to nationalist and liberal movements in South America, the Iberian peninsula and Greece, and the 'ultras', highly protectionist, opposed to all reform measures and in favour of aligning British foreign policy with the authoritarian governments of the Holy Alliance powers – Russia, Prussia and Austria. The first group consisted largely of the ministers sitting in the House of Commons, led by George Canning, and including Fredrick Robinson (later Lord Goderich), the Chancellor of the Exchequer, and William Huskisson, the President of the Board of Trade. Peel, who was the senior minister in the Commons, after Canning, naturally gravitated to this group, which also normally received the support of the Prime Minister, Lord Liverpool. The 'ultras' were concentrated in the House of Lords, where their most influential representative was the Duke of Wellington, but their intellectual leader was the Lord Chancellor, Lord Eldon. The other divisive issue within the Cabinet was over Catholic emancipation, which was treated as an 'open question'. The majority, pro-Catholic faction was led by Canning, but on this issue Peel found himself in general agreement with the 'Ultras', along with Liverpool. Indeed, he and the Prime Minister were the most fervent opponents of emancipation within the government.

Peel served as Home Secretary, under Liverpool, for nearly five years, until April 1827, and then, again, from January 1828 to November 1830, under Wellington, seven and a quarter years in all, and according to a later Prime Minister, Harold Wilson, 'was undoubtedly the greatest reforming Home Secretary of all time' (Wilson, 1977, p. 45). His two most notable achievements were the complete re-codification of English criminal law (with the purpose, he said, 'of simplification, consolidation and mitigation') and the establishment of the Metropolitan Police Force. The first exercise involved the examination of thousands of separate laws, some dating as far back as the thirteenth century. Altogether, 278 Acts were repealed, and the remainder consolidated into eight statutes. Peel was especially concerned to cut down on the number of offences for which the death penalty was prescribed (more than 200 in all, including for stealing a lamb), and to substitute lesser and more realistic penalties, as many criminals were being let off scot-free because juries were becoming more and more reluctant to convict. The immediate result was not a reduction in the number of criminals hanged (that had to wait until the return of more merciful Whig governments in the 1830s), but a marked increase in the rate of convictions, as punishments such as transportation, whipping, the treadmill and prison sentences of varying length were imposed. Peel's Act of Parliament establishing the Metropolitan Police, passed in 1829, created for the first time a reliable and efficient police force for the capital city, without – as had been feared – opening the way to an oppressive means of political control, such as had occurred in Paris and other continental cities. As in Ireland, a decade earlier, the members of the force became known as 'Peelers' or more commonly, 'Bobbies', after the first name of their founder.

Peel was in many ways the outstanding member of Liverpool's cabinet from 1822 onwards, even though Canning was more prominent. Extraordinarily hard-working, always the master of his brief, he dominated all the parliamentary debates in which he participated. His principal worry was the mounting discontent in Ireland, for which he now had governmental responsibility, and which, unlike many previous Home Secretaries, he took extremely seriously. His task was made no easier by the new Lord-Lieutenant of Ireland, the haughty, lazy and uncommunicative Marquess Wellesley, elder brother of the Duke of Wellington. Peel was disconcerted by the growing demand for Catholic emancipation, which not only affected Ireland, but increasingly British public and parliamentary opinion and also his Cabinet colleagues. He began to have private doubts as to whether continued resistance was realistic, but he was seen as the principal government advocate for the status quo, and was put up to speak as such whenever the question was aired in Parliament. In March 1825, a Bill proposed by the Radical MP, Sir Francis Burdett, passed the Commons. Peel felt his position was untenable and offered his resignation, but the Lords rejected the Bill, and Liverpool persuaded him to stay on. A year later, it looked as though Burdett's bill would again pass the Commons, this time with an increased majority, and both Peel and Liverpool proposed to resign if this happened, leaving the King with no alternative but to appoint a Whig government, or one led by Canning, to carry the measure through. Yet, on 17 February 1826, Liverpool was incapacitated by a stroke (though he did not resign until 9 April), and when, in March, Burdett's resolution came up before the House, where it was debated for two full nights, it was to general surprise defeated by the narrow margin of four votes – 276 to 272. This owed much to a brilliant speech by Peel.

Nevertheless, he was to resign a month later, when Liverpool gave up the premiership, and George IV asked Canning to succeed him. As recounted in Chapter 7, half the Cabinet – the ultra Tories – refused to serve under the new premier. Peel, who on most policy issues was extremely close to him, might have been expected to stay on, but advanced his own opposition to Catholic emancipation as his reason for refusing to serve. This was a fateful decision: Peel was essentially a natural 'Canningite', and had he stayed with him he would very probably have ended up in the Liberal Party, like most of the other Canningites, and eventually become its leader. As it was, he was to become leader of the Tories, a party with which he had little in common, and for whose natural supporters, the country squires, he felt only contempt.

Peel sat out Canning's government, and also that of Lord Goderich, each of which lasted a mere four months, but returned as Home Secretary, and also as leader of the House of Commons, when Wellington formed a purely Tory government in January 1828. He was now clearly the number two man in the government and was extensively consulted by Wellington about its composition. Peel wanted it to be a centrist coalition, and insisted that all the leading Canningites should be included, and that several of the hard-line Tory 'ultras', such as Lord Eldon, should be left out. It was thus as much Peel's construction as Wellington's, but the whole balance of the government was destroyed, when Wellington clumsily provoked the resignation of the Canningites in May 1828 (see Chapter 9). The subsequent reconstruction of the government inadvertently brought the issue of Catholic emancipation to a head, resulting in the fall of the government and gravely damaging Peel's already bad relations with the 'ultras'. One of the Canningites who resigned was Charles Grant, the President of the Board of Trade, and Wellington nominated as his successor William Vesey Fitzgerald, a Protestant Irish landowner who, under the law at the time, was required to resign his parliamentary seat and fight a by-election before taking up his post. Fitzgerald, a popular figure in his constituency of County Clare, where he was regarded as a model landlord, and who was personally in favour of Catholic emancipation, had every expectation of being returned unopposed. Yet, Daniel O'Connell, the leader of the Catholic Association, decided to contest the seat, even though, as a Catholic, he was disqualified from sitting in the House of Commons. The electorate was made up predominately of Catholic farmers, who were insistently urged by their priests to vote for O'Connell. He was triumphantly returned with more than two-thirds of the vote. Peel immediately concluded that the game was up, so far as further resistance to emancipation was concerned. In his view, civil war in Ireland could only be averted by the taking of early steps to enable O'Connell to take up his seat in the House. Yet he did not want to be the instrument for bringing forward a reform which he had resisted so tenaciously for so long. He resolved to urge his Cabinet colleagues, and King George IV, of the necessity of acting without delay, but fully intended to resign from the government so that he should have no responsibility for the legislation which would be brought in. Wellington, also a long-term opponent of emancipation, though not so publicly associated with the Protestant cause as Peel, had drawn the same conclusions from O'Connell's triumph. He set himself to persuade the ailing and highly reluctant King that there was no alternative to ceding the Catholics' claim, which he only succeeded in doing by threatening the resignation of the whole Cabinet. The Duke, however, felt incapable of carrying the necessary Bill through Parliament without the help of Peel, who out of loyalty to a chief whom he profoundly admired, though their personal relations were never close, very reluctantly agreed to carry on. It was thus he who was responsible for introducing the Bill in the Commons and carrying it though all its stages, until it finally received the Royal Assent on 13 April 1829. In Gash's words: 'A more prudent, a more timid, a more selfish man would have left Wellington to deal with the situation as well as he could; Peel chose to remain' (Gash, 1976, p. 123).

The personal consequences for him were considerable. He was vigorously criticized by some of his Oxford University constituents, and felt constrained to resign his seat and seek a vote of confidence in a by-election. In this, he was humiliatingly defeated, in a poll in which it was reported by the diarist Charles Greville that 'an immense number of parsons' had taken part. The government could not afford his absence from the House and immediate steps had to be taken to find him a new seat, the Member for the pocket borough of Westbury, Sir Manasseh Lopez, being induced to make way for him. Many of the ultra Tories openly treated Peel as a 'traitor', one of them declaring that he should henceforth be known not as 'Orange' Peel, but as 'Lemon' Peel because of the bitterness his action had caused. Some of them did not have to wait long before seeking revenge on him and on Wellington. The accession of William IV, the following year, led to a general election, in which the opposition (of Whigs and Canningites) improved their position, without gaining a majority in the House. They hoped to defeat the government over the issue of parliamentary reform, for which public support was sharply rising, encouraged by the July Revolution in France, which brought down the authoritarian Bourbon monarchy. Even before the Commons voted on a motion for Reform, however, the government was defeated, on 16 November 1830 in a division on the Civil List, in which 29 ultra Tories voted with the opposition to bring the government down (see Chapter 9). Wellington immediately resigned and the King called on Earl Grey to form a Whig government. This marked the end of Peel's long period as a departmental minister, which had occupied all but five of the 21 years of his parliamentary career so far. He was to serve for another 20 years, all but five of them in opposition, and the only ministerial post in which he was to serve was as Prime Minister. The year 1830, during which he celebrated his forty-second birthday, was a watershed in one other important respect. His father, the first Sir Robert Peel, died on 3 May, aged 80, and Peel inherited the baronetcy, an income of £40,000 a year, and the estate of Drayton Manor, where he proceeded to build a new and much grander house, incorporating every modern innovation. He also took over his father's parliamentary seat of Tamworth, which he was to represent for the rest of his life.

With the installation of Lord Grey's government, Peel became leader of the opposition in the Commons. His first challenge was how to respond to the Reform Bill which the government introduced early in 1831. Peel was personally a moderate supporter of Reform, believing that limited steps should be taken to remove the most obviously corrupt features of the existing system. But he was quite unprepared for the sweeping proposals included in the new Bill (see Chapter 10), and concluded that the only course open to him, and his party, was to seek its total defeat. He almost succeeded, when, on 22 March 1831, it passed its Second Reading by a single vote (302–301). He lost his temper (a rare event for such a well disciplined man) in a subsequent debate when the Government had successfully sought a dissolution in order to get a popular mandate for the Bill, and engaged in a shouting match with the Speaker. This was only concluded when the King arrived to announce the dissolution in person. The subsequent general election, which produced a strong majority for the Whigs, convinced Peel that further resistance to the Bill would be fruitless, but he refused to take steps to facilitate its passage. A year later, when the Lords had defeated the Bill, and the King had refused Grey's request to create sufficient new peers to force it through, the government resigned. The King invited Peel to form a government with the object of bringing in a more limited measure, but Peel declined, saying that it would be far preferable for the Whigs to carry through the Reform which they had demanded. After his experience with Catholic emancipation, he refused to do his opponents' work for them. The King then made the same proposal to Wellington, which he was willing to attempt, but the firm refusal of Peel and other leading Tories in the Commons to join his government meant that he was unable to proceed. The King then recalled Grey, and gave him the assurance which he had previously refused. As recounted in Chapter 10, the leading Tory peers, led by Wellington, then abstained on the Third Reading vote, and the Bill was finally passed, on 4 June 1832, by 106 votes to 22.

In the subsequent general election, the Tories suffered their worst ever defeat, and Peel found himself leading a much-depleted group of 179 Tory MPs against 479 Whigs, Radicals and Irish followers of Daniel O'Connell. It looked as though the Tories would be condemned to many years in opposition, but only two years later they once again had an opportunity to govern. This was in November 1834, when Peel had taken his wife and elder daughter to Italy for a rare holiday. William IV peremptorily dismissed Lord Melbourne's Whig government, only four months after he had succeeded Lord Grey, and determined instead to install a Tory administration (see Chapter 11). He had Peel in mind as Prime Minister, but in his absence offered the post to Wellington who, however, accepted only on a temporary basis, pending Peel's return. When Peel returned, three weeks later, he realized that he had no choice but to accept the premiership, but he made two conditions. One was that he should not be restricted to known Tories in proposing his Cabinet, the other was that he should be granted dissolution in order to bid for a parliamentary majority. His primary target for new recruits was the Stanleyite group of former Canningites, who had resigned from Grey's government, in June 1834, on the issue of Irish tithe reform. He therefore invited both Edward Stanley (the future 14th Earl of Derby) and his close associate, Sir James Graham, to join the Cabinet. Both were sympathetic, but they were not yet ready to throw in their lot with the Tories, so Peel had to make do with what was effectively a rerun of the Wellington cabinet of 1827–30, with the Duke now acting as Foreign Secretary. Even before the general election, Peel had to present himself again to the electors of Tamworth to confirm his nomination as Prime Minister, and he took this as an opportunity to re-make the image of the Tory Party, whom he now renamed the Conservatives. He issued his famous 'Tamworth Manifesto', formally an appeal for support from his constituents, but intended as a programme on which Conservative candidates could fight the general election – an unprecedented step.

The manifesto made it clear that the Conservatives had finally accepted both Catholic emancipation and the Reform Act as irreversible, and henceforth saw themselves as the representatives of 'that great and intelligent class of society...which is far less interested in the contentions of party, than in the maintenance of order and the cause of good government'. He pledged a 'careful review of institutions, both civil and ecclesiastical and the correction of proved abuses and the redress of real grievances'. Caution and good sense were the keynotes of Peel's manifesto, which was an accurate reflection of his own longstanding attitudes. It was meant to convey reassurance to the new body of electors enfranchised by the Reform Act, and its initial impact was largely favourable. The Conservatives made substantial gains in the general election, becoming the largest party in the House of Commons. They remained in a minority, however, only because of the success of Daniel O'Connell's followers who swept up the great bulk of the Irish seats. Within a few weeks of the general election the O'Connellites linked up with the Whigs and Radicals to defeat the government and, on 18 April 1835, Lord Melbourne was able to return to office at the head of a Whig government, to the humiliation of William IV. Peel, now aged 47, had been in office for a mere 119 days.

For the next six years, Peel was again leader of the opposition, and proved to be the dominant figure in the House of Commons. Shy and often awkward in his personal contacts, he was a fluent and authoritative public speaker, and the larger the audience the more confident he became. A tall, imposing figure, the contrast between him and the diminutive Lord John Russell, the leader of the Commons, and his frequent opponent in debate, was striking. He was less successful in establishing warm relations with his followers, a natural reserve being reinforced by his acute sensitivity abut his social inferiority. He was always over-anxious that he should be seen to act like a gentleman, but was quick to take offence, and on more than one occasion was only dissuaded from fighting duels with other politicians by the good sense of their 'seconds'. Nevertheless, Peel showed great patience in marshalling his forces, particularly in the House of Lords, where the ultra Tory element was still strong and he could not always rely on Wellington to keep them under control. He had to fight hard to prevent the Lords, where the Tories had a large majority, from throwing out the Municipal Corporations Act of 1835, which he regarded as an essential measure of local government reform. Otherwise, the Lords effectively put an end to the timid reforming instincts of Melbourne's government, voting down several other measures including the Irish Tithes Bill, which would have expropriated the excess revenues of the Anglican Church in Ireland for educational purposes. Peel continued to woo the Stanleyites, but refused to countenance any moves to co–operate with the Radicals or O'Connellites in what he regarded as premature efforts to dislodge the government. He was wary of any repeat of his experience in 1834–5, of trying to govern without a majority of his own, while the accession of the openly pro-Whig Queen Victoria, in June 1837, removed any possibility of preferential treatment by the monarch. Even so, he came near to resuming office, in May 1839, when Melbourne resigned after his parliamentary majority fell to five votes in a division arising over the rebellion in Jamaica. As recounted in Chapter 11, Melbourne advised the deeply unhappy Queen to send for Peel, whom she received in a foul temper, making 'it clear that she would not agree to a dissolution of parliament, that she wished Wellington to be a member of the new administration, and that she intended to continue her friendship with her late prime minister' (Gash, 1976, p. 186).

Peel, always awkward in the presence of women and lacking Melbourne's easy charm, was taken aback by the abrupt manner of his 20-year-old sovereign, but meekly agreed to her conditions. He did, however, emphasize the difficulty of his parliamentary position and asked the Queen for some public sign of her confidence, suggesting that this might be shown by *some* changes in her Household appointments, all of which were currently held by Whig women, some of them the wives of prominent Whig politicians. Victoria was incensed, telling Melbourne untruthfully that Peel had demanded the dismissal of *all* the Ladies of the Bedchamber. Melbourne, no longer Prime Minister, should have refrained from offering advice on the matter, but nevertheless suggested to her that she should tell Peel that these were personal appointments, not subject to governmental decision. Victoria thereupon informed Peel that she would make no changes to her Household, and the incoming Cabinet decided that in these circumstances it could not take office. The outcome of the 'Bedchamber episode' as it became known, was that a delighted Victoria was able to reappoint Melbourne, who remained in office for a further two years.

During this time the economic situation in the country deteriorated, and the government seemed quite unable to prevent a sharp rise in the budget deficit. Peel, whose grasp of economics was formidable, regularly worsted ministers in debates on these issues, and the government's standing fell sharply. In the general election of 1841, Peel's patience received its reward, the Conservatives securing an overall majority of 77 seats. It was a truly historic victory: the first time in British history that 'a party in office enjoying a majority in the

Commons had been defeated in the polling booths by an opposition previously in a minority' (Gash, 1976, p. 207). At last, Peel's hour had come, and he embarked on what is widely regarded as his great administration. Even before the election, the ground had been laid for Peel's accession to power by a private initiative of Prince Albert. He sent his private secretary, George Anson, to see Peel to suggest a discreet compromise over Household appointments, in order to avoid any repetition of the 'Bedchamber affair'. This was to the effect that the three leading Whig ladies, and any others to whom Peel took objection, should be privately persuaded to resign, and that the Queen herself should announce the appointment of their replacements, although Peel would communicate to her the actual names. Thus began an increasingly close and warm relationship between Peel and Albert, who in the course of time succeeded in thawing out the *froideur* of his wife towards her new Prime Minister. It was not long before their relations became perfectly amicable, though there was none of the intimacy which she had shown to Melbourne. Peel led a 12-man Cabinet, of whom two were widely seen as 'passengers', appointed for reasons of political balance. These were the Duke of Buckingham, as Lord Privy Seal, and Sir Edward Knatchbull, as Paymaster-General. The former was regarded as representing the agricultural interest, the latter the ultra Tories. Both Edward Stanley, as Secretary for War and Colonies, and Sir James Graham, as Home Secretary, agreed to join the government, signifying their integration into the Conservative Party, while Lord Aberdeen became Foreign Secretary and Henry Goulburn, Chancellor of the Exchequer. Wellington joined the Cabinet as Minister without Portfolio, but also resumed his earlier post as Commander-in-Chief. The Earl of Ripon, who had been Prime Minister, as Lord Goderich, in 1827–8, became President of the Board of Trade, with the young William Gladstone as his deputy. Among the many disappointed office-seekers was Benjamin Disraeli, MP for Shrewsbury, who wrote him an obsequious letter, which Peel ignored, to his later cost.

Peel himself took a close interest in foreign policy, refusing to allow the mild-mannered Aberdeen anything like the autonomy which Palmerston had enjoyed under Melbourne. The main external distractions during the course of his government were strained relations with the United States and France, and problems in India. The Governor-General, Lord Ellenborough, nominally employed by the East India Company, pursued a forward policy, leading to a hazardous military campaign in Afghanistan, and the annexation of the Sind, neither of which were in accord with Peel's wishes. Ellenborough, difficult to control at such a distance, then added to his misdemeanours by writing directly to Victoria, suggesting that she should proclaim herself Empress of India, a proposal which Peel strongly deprecated, though it was to be adopted by Disraeli over 30 years later. When, in 1844, Ellenborough proceeded to yet another unauthorized annexation, that of Gwalior, he was eventually dismissed, and

Sir Henry Hardinge, a cautious old soldier, and a trusted intimate of Peel's, was sent out in his place. With both the United States and France, Peel insisted on pursuing a firm but conciliatory policy. This eventually led to a settlement of the long-standing border dispute with the United States, with the signing of the Oregon treaty, retaining British control of Vancouver. With France there were numerous quarrels, including disputes over Tahiti, Morocco and Syria, and naval rearmament, but the main British concern was to forestall French dynastic ambitions in Spain, where Louis-Philippe was suspected of designs to marry off one of his younger sons to the adolescent Queen Isabella. He was eventually dissuaded, though the Duc de Montpensier did in fact marry the Queen's younger sister, Lucia, after Peel had left office, to the great dissatisfaction of the British court and government.

Yet Peel's main concern was with 'the Condition of England', as it was described in a famous pamphlet by Thomas Carlyle, published in 1840. This described the misery caused by one of the worst depressions of the nineteenth century, with widespread unemployment and poverty, particularly in towns such as Bolton and Paisley, where starvation was barely kept at bay. The nation was in tumult, with mass meetings by the Chartists and the Anti-Corn Law League constantly threatening public order, while the ten-hour day campaign by Lord Ashley (later the Earl of Shaftesbury) was infuriating industrialists. Meanwhile the accumulated national deficit had grown to £7½ million, an unprecedented level in peacetime. Peel came to power with two clear objectives. One was to create a budget surplus. The other – closely allied – was to reorganize the taxation system so as to permit a progressive transition to free trade, lowering the price of food and raw materials, which would both ease poverty and stimulate demand, thus giving an upward push to economic growth. To achieve a surplus, he suggested what no previous government had dared since 1816, when the temporary wartime income tax introduced by Pitt had been swept away by a backbench revolt in the Commons. He proposed a rate of 7d in the pound, for incomes over £150, to run for a three-year period. He probably had a shrewd idea that this period would be extended, and so it has proved, with income tax being the mainstay of the government's revenue ever since. It took some doing to persuade the Cabinet, with Stanley and Graham being particularly sceptical, but he gradually won them round, and the tax formed the central element in the budget which Peel personally introduced in March 1842, the Chancellor, Henry Goulburn, having deferred to him. Much of the surplus obtained through the tax was disbursed through a large range of tariff reductions, focussed on food and other essential items. Peel would have liked to remove all duty from corn, but fearful of the strong agricultural lobby, extremely well represented on the government benches largely peopled by country squires, he proposed instead only a marginal liberalization of the Corn Laws. Even this was too much for his Lord Privy Seal, the Duke of Buckingham, who was President of the Agricultural Protection Society. He resigned after only five months in office.

Within a year or two, Peel's tax policies were clearly having an effect, with employment rising, the budget showing a healthy surplus and the level of public discontent sensibly easing. Before this happened, though, there was continuing fear of public disorder, and even of revolution, with both the Chartists and the Anti-Corn Law League stepping up their activities. There was great alarm in January 1843, when Peel's Private Secretary, Edward Drummond, was assassinated while walking down Whitehall, and it was evident that he had been mistaken for the Prime Minister. There was some relief, however, when it appeared that the assassin was a man of unsound mind, pursuing a private grievance, rather than being politically motivated. With his government getting into its stride, all now seemed set fair for Peel, when the failure of the Irish potato crop in 1845 led to the greatest crisis of his political career. Estimated to have caused over a million deaths, and massive emigration to the United States and elsewhere, Peel immediately realized that it would be necessary to suspend the operation of the corn laws in order that cheap grain, mainly from Canada, could be imported in large amounts. He also concluded that it would be politically impossible to re-impose the laws once they had been suspended, and decided that the only honest thing to do was to repeal them altogether. He found it impossible, however, to persuade his own Cabinet, only three of whom, including the Home Secretary, Sir James Graham, initially supported him. In the meantime, the leader of the opposition, Lord John Russell, had launched a stirring call for abolition, in an open letter issued in Edinburgh. Peel composed no less than five memoranda arguing the case to the Cabinet, in the period between 31 October and 4 December 1845, and when the Cabinet met on that date, two members, Stanley and the Duke of Buccleuch, declared that they would resign rather than back Peel's proposal, for which he received only lukewarm support from the majority of his other colleagues. Peel then decided to resign, recommending that Lord John Russell should be invited to form an administration to carry through the policy which he had publicly recommended.

The Queen promptly summoned Russell, who tried to form a government, but failed due to the inability of his leading colleagues to agree on the allocation of ministerial posts, in particular whether Palmerston should be permitted to resume the Foreign Secretaryship. Peel would much have preferred Russell to have succeeded, so as to prevent a re-run of the events of 1829, when he had had to carry through, with Whig support, a measure (Catholic emancipation) of which the great majority of his fellow Tories disapproved. Yet, when the Queen appealed to him not to abandon her, he readily agreed to resume as Prime Minister. His decision was welcomed by his Cabinet, with the exception of Stanley, who insisted on resigning, and Buccleuch, who asked for time to consider his position, but eventually agreed to carry on. Peel was greatly encouraged by Wellington's strong support, even though the Duke had pre-viously been a supporter of the Corn laws. Gladstone was promoted to fill Stanley's position as Secretary for War and Colonies.

On 27 January 1846, Peel introduced his Bill to repeal the Corn Laws, allow-ing three years before the Bill would take full effect. He was spectacularly aban-doned by the great bulk of his own party, only 112 Conservative MPs voting for the second reading, and 231 against. His opponents were rallied by Lord George Bentinck, a younger son of the Duke of Portland and a prominent member of the Jockey Club, who had sat for 20 years as a silent MP, but: 'who now brought to the Protectionist cause the ruthless determination and single-mindedness which he had formerly shown in hunting down dishonest trainers and crooked jockeys on the Turf. Violent and unscrupulous by temperament, he made up for his political inexperience by tenacity and force' (Gash, 1976, p. 275).

If Bentinck provided the organizational drive for the Protectionists, it was Benjamin Disraeli, still bitter at his exclusion from office by Peel, who supplied the debating skill, launching a series of merciless attacks on the Prime Minister, which greatly wounded him. When Peel expostulated that Disraeli had begged to be included in his government, Disraeli brazenly denied it, gambling on the probability that Peel would not have his letter to hand – he did not. Disraeli effectively knocked the stuffing out of Peel, whose only desire now was to get the Bill through as quickly as possible, with Whig support, and then to insist on resigning. On 25 June 1846, the Bill was finally passed by the House of Lords. On the same day the government was defeated in the Commons on its Irish coercion bill, and Peel resigned four days later. His party was irremediably split, the majority eventually choosing Stanley (later the 14th Earl of Derby) as their leader. The minority, who included most of the more able figures, became known as Peelites, most of whom, including Gladstone, later joined with the Whigs, who, under Russell, united with the Radicals to form the Liberal Party.

On the day he resigned, Peel went down to the House of Commons and made was what probably his greatest ever speech. The peroration was long remembered, and acted as his political epitaph:

> I shall leave a name execrated by every monopolist who … clamours for pro-tection because it accrues to his individual benefit; but it may be that I shall leave a name sometimes remembered with expressions of goodwill in the abodes of those whose lot it is to labour, and to earn their daily bread by the sweat of their brow, when they shall recruit their exhausted strength with abundant and untaxed food, the sweeter because it is no longer leavened by a sense of injustice. (Wilson, p. 60)

Peel's hope was handsomely fulfilled: he remains the only Conservative peacetime leader to be widely revered by the working class. By contrast, the

Conservative Party, of which he was the founder, has largely airbrushed him out of its history, blaming him rather than Bentinck or Disraeli for the 1846 split in the party, which condemned it to spending the best part of a generation in opposition. It has preferred to regard either the Younger Pitt or Disraeli as its true source of inspiration. Peel's offence was his pragmatic response to the Great Irish famine, choosing, as in 1829, to do what the situation clearly demanded, rather than to follow the prejudices of the mass of his party colleagues. The question remains whether he could have achieved his objectives without losing their support. A less arrogant, less prickly, more clubbable man might have pulled it off, it is sometimes suggested, but this seems highly unlikely. Yes, he might have been able to win round a few more of his opponents if he had shown more tact and made more of a personal effort, but the size of the majority against him in his party strongly suggests that any such effect would have been marginal. Peel's intensely unflattering assessment of the mass of his fellow Tory MPs is a sufficient explanation of why he disdained to make a more serious attempt to woo them:

> How can those who spend their time in hunting and shooting and eating and drinking know what were the motives of those who are responsible for the public security, who have access to the best information, and have no other object under Heaven but to provide against danger, and consult the general interests of all classes! (Hilton, 1998, p. 147)

In the general election of 1847, Lord John Russell's Liberals, and their Irish allies, won 323 seats against 321 Conservatives, though the latter were divided between around 225 Protectionists and just under 100 Peelites. There was thus no question of the Liberal government being defeated, and it was not long before it became clear that there would be no healing of the Conservative split. Peel, though only 59, concluded that his ministerial career was over, and made no effort to organize a parliamentary opposition, regarding himself henceforward as an elder statesman, and confining himself to occasional, well thought-out speeches on major issues. His last speech, on 28 June 1850, was a magisterial critique of Palmerston's aggressive foreign policy, provoked by the storm created by the Don Pacifico affair (see Chapter 16). The day after, while riding his horse on Constitution Hill, it stumbled, throwing its rider and then falling on top of him. Peel suffered fatal injuries, from which he died at his London home in Whitehall Gardens four days later. He was 62, and had been Prime Minister, taking his two terms together, for a total of five years and 57 days. For those who put party loyalty above all other considerations, he was the object of scorn and derision. Others have rightly regarded him as one of, if not *the* greatest of Nineteenth-century Premiers.

Works consulted

Norman Gash, 1961, *Mr Secretary Peel: The Life of Sir Robert Peel to 1830*, London, Longman.

Norman Gash, 1972, *Sir Robert Peel: The Life of Sir Robert after 1830*, London, Longman.

Norman Gash, 1976, *Peel*, London, Longman.

Christopher Hibbert, 1981, (ed.), *Greville's England*, London, Folio Society.

Boyd Hilton, 1998, 'Robert Peel' in Robert Eccleshall and Graham Walker, (eds.), *Biographical Dictionary of British Prime Ministers*, London, Routledge.

Douglas Hurd, 2007, *Robert Peel: A Biography*, London, Weidenfeld & Nicolson.

Lucille Iremonger, 1970, *The Fiery Chariot*, London, Secker & Warburg.

John Prest, 2004, Article in *Oxford Dictionary of National Biography*.

Harold Wilson, 1977, *A Prime Minister on Prime Ministers*, London, Weidenfeld & Nicolson.

13
Lord John Russell, 1st Earl Russell – from Whig to Liberal

THE RIGHT HON^{BLE} LORD JOHN RUSSELL, M.P.

It is an open question whether Lord John Russell should be considered the last of the Whigs or the first of the Liberals. He has an equal claim to both distinctions. His upbringing could hardly have been more Whiggish. The third son of the 6th Duke of Bedford, he was brought up to believe that Charles James Fox (whose life he was later to write in three volumes) was the fount of all wisdom. He was the first person to describe his party as Liberal rather than Whig, and he should perhaps be regarded as the first Liberal Prime Minister, though Palmerston is usually accorded this honour. Born on 18 August 1792, two months prematurely, John Russell was a sickly child, who was to remain unhealthy and short of stature throughout his life, never quite reaching five foot, five inches. His father, then known as Lord John Russell, was a Whig MP, who later rose to be Lord-Lieutenant of Ireland. He was the younger brother of the 5th Duke of Bedford, and unexpectedly succeeded to the title in 1802, when his still unmarried brother was killed in a riding accident. Young John's mother, Georgiana Elizabeth Byng, was a daughter of the 4th Viscount Torrington, and had already borne her husband two sons. Her new-born baby was undoubtedly her favourite, and she lavished care and attention upon him, delighting in his early signs of maturity, writing to her husband:

> It is not in my power to express the merits of that child. His sense, his cleverness, his quietness, and the sweetness of his temper and disposition surpass all I've ever witnessed. His attentions to me are those of a grown person of superior sense. His active mind makes him attempt everything. (Scherer, 1999, pp. 13–14)

This included teaching himself Latin, while still in his infancy, and reading *Plutarch's Lives* to his mother, before he was belatedly sent to school for the first time, at the age of eight. This was what he later described as 'a very bad private school at Sunbury', and a year later he was devastated by the death, on 11 October 1801, of his mother – from unknown causes – though she had been an invalid more or less continuously since his birth. Soon afterwards his Uncle Francis died, and his father succeeded to the dukedom, moving into the grand family seat of Woburn Abbey, which now became his home. Young John was now known as Lord John, and in June 1803 his father married again, once more to a Georgiana. This was Lady Georgiana Gordon, a 21-year-old daughter of the Duke of Gordon. She tried to be a good stepmother to John, but as she went on to have seven sons and three daughters of her own, she had little time to spare for him. John was forced more and more into the company of his two elder brothers. The elder of these, Francis (known as Lord Tavistock and, much later, the 7th Duke), treated him with condescension, but the middle brother, William, two years his senior, became a close companion. When he was 11 he was sent to Westminster School, traditionally patronized by the Russell family, but life there was soon regarded as being too boisterous for such a frail child, and – at his stepmother's suggestion – he was withdrawn from the school in July 1804, and privately tutored for six months by the chaplain at Woburn, Dr Edmund Cartwright, the inventor of the power loom. He was later sent to a small private boarding school, run by a clergyman in Kent, where he remained until he was 15. Here he made a number of close friends, including Lord Clare, who shared with him the handicap of being under-sized, and for whom he felt a great deal of empathy. The school's curriculum was undemanding, but Lord John was a voracious reader.

His father achieved high office in the 'Ministry of All the Talents', led by Lord Grenville, in 1806–1807, being appointed Lord-Lieutenant of Ireland, and the young Lord John met many leading Whig politicians who visited their home, or the Vice-regal lodge in Dublin, nearly all of whom were impressed by his intelligence and precocity. The Duke of Bedford lost office in March 1807, when George III dismissed Grenville's government, and he decided to spend more time with his children, particularly Lord John. He took John, together with his wife, on a three-month tour of Scotland, and in the autumn of that year, John left school for the last time, after Lord Holland, the leading Whig peer, had offered to take him with him on a tour of Spain and Portugal, where the Peninsular War was now raging. The visit lasted until August of the following year, and proved a hazardous venture, Holland's party being caught up in a British retreat against superior French forces, while John caught a fever which delayed their return. During the visit he met most of the leaders of the Spanish revolt against the French, and grew very close to Holland, and, particularly his wife, who 'became virtually a second mother to Lord John' (Scherer, p. 17).

On his return, he was anxious to go up to Oxford or Cambridge, but Bedford, dismayed that his eldest son, Tavistock, had learnt nothing at Cambridge beyond becoming a playboy, insisted that he should instead go to Edinburgh, which he regarded as a far more serious university. This proved a wise decision, and though Lord John declined, like many other aristocrats at the time, to take a degree, he had a thorough grounding, particularly in more 'modern' subjects, such as mathematics, chemistry and physics. His tutor, Professor Playfair, described him as 'one of the most promising young men I have ever met with' (Scherer, p. 17). A valuable experience for Russell, which helped to prepare him for a political career, was his membership of the Speculative Society, whose 30 elected members met every week to read essays and conduct debates. He thoroughly enjoyed his time at Edinburgh, and made frequent visits to the city throughout his later life. He left in 1812, and instead of the Grand Tour, made impossible by French occupation of most of Western Europe, departed with two friends for a tour of the Mediterranean. He left them for a while, to visit his brother, Lord William, who was fighting in Spain, and had been wounded at the Battle of Talavera. It was a dangerous trip, in which he narrowly avoided capture by French forces, but he rejoined his friends and sailed with them to Majorca, intending to go on to Greece, Egypt, Palestine and Syria. But word reached him there that, on 4 May 1813, he had been elected unopposed to Parliament in a by-election in the 'family seat' of Tavistock, caused by the death of the sitting member, Richard Fitzpatrick. He was not yet 21, and only took his seat several months later, when he had come of age.

Russell was later to be regarded as a great parliamentarian, but his first term in Parliament was distinctly patchy. He revealed himself immediately as an 'advanced Whig', particularly strong on libertarian issues, devoting his maiden speech, on 12 May 1814, to attacking the decision in the peace settlement to transfer Norway from Danish to Swedish rule, against the wishes of the Norwegians, and to cede Parga, on the Greek Adriatic coast and formerly ruled by Venice, to the Turks. But his attendance was fitful – he took part in only three divisions out of 32 –, and spent much of his time travelling on the Continent, including a visit to Elba, where he had an interview with Napoleon. Later, after Napoleon's escape, he attacked the decision to renew the war against France, describing it as 'impolitic, unjust and injurious...' (Scherer, p. 26). He soon lost interest in debates dominated by the large Tory majority, and, in 1817, announced his withdrawal from Parliament, accepting the Chiltern Hundreds. He later changed his mind, and stood for re-election at Tavistock, in the 1818 general election, though for the next few years he devoted most of his time to writing, turning out a biography, a novel, a five-act play in verse and a history of the English constitution, all during a three-year span. It was only in the early 1820s that he started seriously to devote himself to politics, taking up the issue which was later to bring him lasting fame – parliamentary reform. He had felt strongly about the issue for a long time. When he was barely 18, in August 1810, he had written to Lord Holland, complaining at the lack of 'zeal', which the Whig leader, Earl Grey, was displaying on the question of reform. He scathingly commented: 'He still seems to think of himself as a Whig, and I am afraid the Tory Opinions which he wears under that cloak will bring the name into great discredit' (Prest, 1972, p. 12).

Nobody could make the same complaint about Lord John. He seized on the issue like a terrier, raising it on every possible occasion, and giving greater thought to the practical details than any other politician. His first initiative came in the 1820–21 session, when he proposed the disfranchisement of Grampound, a rotten borough, for 'gross corruption', and that its two seats be transferred to the (unrepresented) city of Leeds, or another large town. Grampound duly lost its seats, but – at the government's insistence – they were transferred instead to the county of Yorkshire, which henceforth returned four members. He returned to the charge in 1822, when he proposed a motion in favour of a more comprehensive reform measure, proposing that one member should be taken away from each of 100 small boroughs, and that 60 of these seats should be transferred to the counties and 40 to the large towns. In a stirring speech, which made his reputation as a parliamentary orator, he asserted: 'At the present period the ministers of the crown possess the confidence of the House of Commons, but the House of Commons does not possess the esteem and reverence of the people' (Prest, 2004).

The House divided, largely upon party lines, and Russell's motion was defeated by 269 votes to 164, and when he tried again, four years later, he was defeated by a wider margin. He had more success with a motion to curb bribery in elections, which he won, by the Speaker's casting vote, after a tied division in the Commons. This, however, led indirectly to a personal setback, when he lost his seat in the ensuing general election, of June 1826. Together with his brother, Lord Tavistock MP, he high-mindedly resolved not to do any canvassing, or to spend money on entertainment or the transportation of voters. The money which ordinarily would have been devoted to election expenses was instead donated to local charities. This had a disastrous effect on their election results. Tavistock held on to his seat, but came in second in a contest in the 'family borough', where he would normally have been expected to head the poll, while Russell was defeated in Huntingdonshire, to which he had transferred in 1820. He was out of Parliament for six months, until December 1826, when he was returned unopposed in a by-election for the pocket borough of Bandon.

By now, Russell was recognized as one of the most forceful and active MPs on the Whig side of the House. In February 1828, he tabled a resolution to repeal the Test and Corporation Acts, which restricted the civic rights of members of nonconformist churches. He succeeded in winning over 15 of the ultra-Tories, and his motion was carried by 237 votes to 193, leading the Wellington government to introduce its own repeal measure (see Chapter 9). Earlier, Russell had taken the lead in pressing for Catholic emancipation, urging his fellow Whigs to join the short-lived Canning and Goderich governments in exchange for a pledge for early action on this issue. It was at this time that Russell began to take a close interest in Irish affairs, and he became a long-term advocate of measures to appease the grievances of the Catholic majority. Despite his high level of parliamentary activity, Russell continued to be a frequent visitor to the Continent, and maintained his prolific literary output, publishing three major historical works in the decade after 1822 – the two-volume *Memoirs of the Affairs of Europe from the Peace of Utrecht* (1824, 1829), *Establishment of the Turks in Europe* (1828) and *Causes of the French Revolution* (1832). He also spent much time in the company of writers, including the Irish poet Thomas Moore (whose letters he was later to edit in an eight-volume collection), Lord Byron, Sir Walter Scott and Charles Dickens. As his latest biographer comments: 'Far from their equal as an author, Lord John was nevertheless a skillful writer for a full-time politician. He continued to publish a substantial quantity of work throughout his career' (Scherer, p. 36).

If Russell made steady progress, both as a politician and an author, during the 1820s, his private life was a series of embarrassing setbacks. He was painfully shy, and physically unprepossessing, and – despite his advanced views – was vain of his Russell ancestry, and very much aware of his position as the son of a duke. He was, however, a younger son, which did much to diminish both his financial and matrimonial prospects. Moreover, he lacked social graces, and many young women were put off by his over-intellectualized approach. He was to remain unmarried until after his fortieth birthday, which led his friend Lady Holland to lament to her son, Henry Fox, that 'he was making himself almost ridiculous by his frequent proposals' (Scherer, p. 23). The first of these had been back in 1817, when, aged 25, he had proposed to the society beauty Elizabeth Rawdon, only to discover that she had become engaged to his brother William just a few hours before. This was a lucky escape, as William was to find her a most unsatisfactory wife. Lord John was to be turned down by a long list of other aristocratic ladies during the 1820s, and he settled instead for a long-running affair with a married Italian lady, Louise Durazzo, which greatly impressed young Henry Fox, who wrote in his journal: 'I was extremely delighted with the beauty, pretty manners, simplicity and agreeable conversation of Madame Durazzo. Little Johnnie Russell has made an excellent choice. I never saw a woman more calculated to captivate one than she is...M. Durazzo (her husband) is a little, sulky disagreeable man' (Scherer, pp. 44–5).

Other women known to have attracted Russell during this time, included Henry Fox's sister Mary and Lady Elizabeth Vernon, with whom the entire Russell family was reputed to have been in love at one time or another. In his biography, John Prest suggests that he proposed in 1829 to the 19-year-old Lady Emily (known as 'Minnie') Cowper, but that she turned him down in favour of the Tory peer and factory reformer Lord Ashley, later the Earl of Shaftesbury (Prest, 1972, p. 71). Scherer disputes this, and suggests that there may have been a confusion with another 'Emily', one of three daughters of Nelson's captain at Trafalgar, Sir Thomas Hardy, two of whom Lord John is known to have wooed unsuccessfully a year or two later.

So Lord John was still a bachelor in 1830, when Earl Grey formed a Whig government, and he began his ministerial career, at the age of 38. He was appointed Paymaster-General of the Forces – to his great disappointment, outside the Cabinet. Yet, because of his long interest in the subject, he was immediately co-opted, to a committee of four, appointed by Grey to prepare a Reform Bill. Russell was to go on to a long and distinguished political career, during which he was twice Prime Minister, but this was undoubtedly his finest hour. He was the dominant member of the committee, providing, according to his own estimate, 90 per cent of the input into the draft Bill, which followed – though on a much more ambitious scale – the principles of the Bill which he had twice unsuccessfully introduced while in opposition. It provided for a wide-ranging cull of 'pocket' and 'rotten' boroughs, without any provision for financial compensation for their 'proprietors', in contrast to the million pounds which the Younger Pitt had proposed in his unsuccessful measure of 1785 – the last serious attempt at Reform. In addition, Russell proposed a modest extension of the franchise, particularly in borough constituencies

The long and complicated story of the eventual passage of the Bill is summarized in Chapter 10, but here we are concerned primarily with Lord John's role, which was second only to that of the Prime Minister's, Earl Grey. It was Russell who set out the full details of the Bill, in a marathon speech on 1 March 1831, which stunned the House by the unexpected ambition of the government's proposals, and made an instant hero of Lord John, in all but the most conservative ranks of the Whig party, as well as among the small group of Radicals in the House. For the remaining 15 months until the Bill's final adoption in June 1832, he was the principal spokesman for the government in all the lengthy debates in the Commons, which dominated the timetable of the House. He effectively became the joint-leader of the House, with Lord Althorp MP, who was a vital ally in piloting the bill through. Within the Cabinet, which he joined in June 1831, he was, together with the Radical, Lord Durham, the strongest advocate for pressing ahead, when fainter hearts were tempted to compromise or abandon the Bill altogether. In the process, he deeply upset the King, William IV, by strongly pressing the demand, which William eventually conceded with great reluctance, to create as many new peers as necessary to overcome the veto of the House of Lords. In the general election which followed the passage of the Bill, in which the Whigs, with their Radical and Irish allies, won an overwhelming majority, Lord John was returned for the new county constituency of South Devon.

In the new Parliament, while retaining his portfolio as Paymaster-General, which was little more than a sinecure, he greatly expanded the range of his interests, in particular taking up the question of Irish grievances, which soon brought him into conflict with his cabinet colleague, Edward Stanley, the Irish Chief Secretary, who was much more interested in introducing coercive measures than in taking constructive steps to remove the causes of discontent. Stanley, a scion of an ancient Whig family, and heir to the Earldom of Derby, was seen as a rising figure in the party, being one of its most effective parliamentary performers, described by Edward Bulwer-Lytton as 'the Rupert of debate'. He was regarded by many as the future party leader, and this may well have sharpened Russell's sense of rivalry, as his own ambitions ran in the same direction. The issue which split them apart was the payment of tithes to the Church of Ireland (the Anglican church), which claimed the allegiance of only 10 per cent of Irishmen, the remainder being either Catholics or Presbyterians, who bitterly resented being forced to pay. Despite Earl Grey's strong discouragement, Russell insisted on backing a proposal to expropriate the 'excess' proceeds of the tithe system for general educational purposes in Ireland, to which Stanley, as a fanatical Anglican, was fundamentally opposed. When a majority of Whigs supported a Bill proposed by Russell, Stanley, together with three other cabinet ministers resigned, and stormed out of the party, joining the Tories several years later. (Whether by design, or otherwise, Lord John had got rid of a dangerous rival, though his Bill was to be defeated in the House of Lords). This episode indirectly led to Grey's resignation, two months later, his place being taken by Lord Melbourne, the Home Secretary.

Melbourne took over the Grey government, with only minimal changes, but the death of Lord Althorp's father, Earl Spencer, four months later, in November 1834, led to his elevation to the House of Lords leaving a vacancy in the leadership of the House of Commons. As related in Chapter 11, Melbourne proposed to William IV that Russell should be appointed to the post. The King, whom Lord John had grievously offended, took this as an opportunity to dismiss the Melbourne government, appointing a Tory administration in its place. The incoming Prime Minister, Sir Robert Peel, sought to win a majority in the subsequent general election, in January 1835, but though he made extensive gains, he fell short of the combined total of seats won by the Whigs, Radicals and Irish Nationalists, and he was forced to resign three months later, when – largely at Lord John's initiative, the three opposition groups came together and inflicted repeated defeats on the government in parliamentary divisions. Lord John had had little difficulty in defending his seat, and during the course of the campaign met the recently widowed Adelaide, Lady Ribblesdale, who was living in Torquay. Aged 27, the mother of four young children, she and Lord John, now aged 42, were immediately attracted to each other, and were married three months later, at St. George's, Hanover Square, in London. Adelaide was generally acclaimed as being 'pretty, charming, amiable' and 'clever' and shared with Russell the attribute of being diminutive. As Lord John's friend, the cleric and wit, Sydney Smith, put it, no doubt with some exaggeration, 'she was about three feet high; his late love Miss Hardy was seven feet'. 'To the surprise of many', his biographer records: 'Russell made an excellent husband and father. He was extremely devoted to his stepchildren, and retained their love and respect throughout their lives' (Scherer, p. 80).

A week into his marriage, Russell (who acquired a new nickname as 'The Widow's Mite') became a minister again, but this time at a much more senior level. Melbourne, who became Prime Minister for the second time, on Peel's resignation after a series of defeats in Commons' votes, appointed him both Home Secretary and Leader of the House, effectively the number two man in the Government. He was generally seen as the only realistic choice within the Whig party, though many – including his father, the Duke of Bedford – doubted whether his health would stand the strain, and regretted the appointment. In the event, he was to lead his party in the Commons for over 20 years, a record only rivalled in the post-Reform Bill period by Clem Attlee, who led the Labour Party from 1935 to 1955. During the six years of Melbourne's second government, from April 1835 to August 1841, Russell was easily the most dynamic minister, and was the moving force behind its relatively few successes. He was constantly prodding the Prime Minister into attempting new reform measures, despite the continual obstruction of the Tory-dominated House of Lords, which threw out a series of Bills passed by the Commons, especially those relating to Ireland, where Russell's repeated attempts to 'appropriate' the surplus yield of tithes for secular purposes were given short shrift. Russell, however, was able to use his executive authority, as Home Secretary, to implement a wide range of measures which did not require legislation. These included the recruitment of Catholics into the police force, the appointment of Catholics to public offices, including the judiciary, and ceasing the practice of using troops to collect the tithe, which effectively meant it was not paid at all in many areas. The result of Russell's efforts was a marked improvement in law and order, and a sharp reduction in the intensity of the agitation to end the Union. Daniel O'Connell (whom Russell had unsuccessfully urged Melbourne to appoint to the Cabinet) warmly approved of his decisions, and his followers gave consistent support to the government in the Commons, where the Whigs were in a minority, and depended on them as well as the Radicals to keep themselves in power.

As Home Secretary, he proved himself a vigorous law reformer, carrying a series of bills drastically reducing the large number of crimes for which the death penalty was imposed. Henceforward, only treason, murder and arson against buildings or ships with persons inside, were subject to capital punishment. He also gave a sharp forward push to the development of state support for education by forcing through an Order in Council providing financial support for teacher training and apprenticeships programmes after he had been forced to abandon a more general education bill due to Anglican hostility.

In November 1838, Russell suffered a grievous blow with the death of his wife, Adelaide, shortly after having given birth to their second daughter, after less than four years of marriage. He was to re-marry, three years later, to Lady Frances Elliot, daughter of the Earl of Minto, and 23 years his junior. Described by the Cambridge historian Jonathan Parry, as 'his protective, unworldly and cloyingly religious second wife' (Parry, p. 155), she was to present him with three sons and a daughter, and helped to bring up his own two children and four step-children. Russell appeared to be happy with her, though her health was bad, and she lacked the self-confidence and skills to act as a political hostess, tending to cut him off from his political associates, which undoubtedly had a deleterious effect on his later career. Already, while leader of the House, he had offended many of his own MPs by his cold and distant attitude towards them. His father, the Duke of Bedford remonstrated with him in a letter, in August 1838: 'You give great offence to your followers...in the H. of Commons by not being *courteous* to them, by treating them superciliously or *de haut en bas*, by not listening with sufficient patience to their solicitations, remonstrances, or whatever it may be' (Prest, 1972, p. 134).

Bulwer Lytton wrote of him, in his political poem, *The New Timon*:

> Like or dislike, he does not care a jot.
> He wants your vote, but your affection not.

Russell's insouciant attitude to his followers was partly due to his personal shyness, but many people detected in him the traditional haughtiness of the Russell family, who, according to a later Duke, the 13th, 'have always thought themselves rather grander than God' (John Robert Russell, 1959, p. 17). In 1839, while retaining the leadership of the Commons, he swapped jobs with the Colonial secretary, Lord Normanby. His main achievement in his new office was to settle the future constitutional arrangements for Canada, following the rebellions of 1837 and the short but stormy governor-generalship of Lord Durham, the irascible Radical peer. Durham's influential Report, following his impetuous resignation, is often credited with paving the way for future Canadian independence, but it was Russell who was the architect of the short-term programme of reforms, which were ably implemented by the new Governor-General Charles Poulett Thomson (later Lord Sydenham). When the Melbourne government finally resigned, following its defeat in the 1841 general election, it was Russell who emerged with the greatest credit from its six-year span of office. He had been responsible for almost all the reforms which it had been able to carry through, despite the unrelenting hostility of a Tory-dominated House of Lords, and – in the Commons – he had successfully kept both the Radicals and the Irish followers of Daniel O'Connell in line, despite their impatience with Melbourne's lack of reforming zeal. Few now doubted that if a new Whig administration were to be formed in the foreseeable future it would be led by Lord John. Any doubt on this point was removed in October 1842, when Melbourne suffered a severe stroke, and it was obvious to everyone (apart from Melbourne himself) that his political career was over.

Now Russell became once again leader of the opposition in the Commons, and given Peel's large majority and his commanding presence in the House of Commons, it looked as though he would have a long wait before returning to office. Then – in 1845 – came the Irish famine, and what appeared to Peel to be the imperative need to repeal the Corn Laws, despite the resistance of the bulk of his own party. In November 1845, without consulting his own followers, Russell launched a stirring appeal for complete free trade in an open letter sent from Edinburgh, where he was on a visit, to his constituents in the City of

London, which he had represented since the 1841 election. When Peel, within a few days, failed to persuade his Cabinet to back a Bill repealing the laws, he submitted his resignation to Queen Victoria, who promptly called upon Russell to form a new government (see Chapter 12). Russell, accepted, and then – humiliatingly – was forced a few days later to report that he could not do so. This was because he was unable to impose himself on his potential cabinet colleagues. Several of them, led by Lord Howick, son of the former Prime Minister Earl Grey, refused to serve if Lord Palmerston MP was reappointed as Foreign Secretary, after having effectively pursued his own personal foreign policy throughout the period of the Melbourne government. For his part, Palmerston obstinately refused to accept any other post, and Russell felt – given the minority position of the Whigs and their allies in the Commons – that he would not be able to take office without him.

This episode perhaps foreshadowed that when he subsequently did become Prime Minister he would be weak and ineffective, and incapable of fulfilling his earlier promise. There were a number of reasons for this. One was his inability, as already mentioned, to develop a warm relationship with his followers. Second, his lack of stature, compared to the commanding presence of Peel. When colleagues such as Henry Fox could casually refer to him as 'little Johnnie Russell', it hardly suggests that they saw him as a figure of authority. Third, Russell regarded himself, in a phrase later made famous by Margaret Thatcher, as 'a conviction politician'. Not for him, an earnest search for consensus: when a problem arose he was in the habit of asking his conscience what was right, and reacting precipitately without bothering to consult his followers. All too often, they refused to follow where he led, and he was forced to backtrack.

He did not have to wait that much longer, however, before moving into 10 Downing Street. As recounted in Chapter 12, Peel carried the repeal of the Corn Laws, with Whig support, but against the votes of the majority of his own party, and he was almost immediately afterwards defeated on a vote on the Irish Coercion Bill. He resigned on 26 June 1846, and Russell took office four days later, leading a minority government, but in the hope that Peel and his followers would support him in crucial parliamentary votes. He had some difficulty in forming his cabinet, but Howick (now the 3rd Earl Grey, on the recent death of his father) withdrew his earlier objection to Palmerston's resumption of the Foreign Office and accepted the post of War and Colonial Secretary. The other leading posts were filled by Sir George Grey as Home Secretary, Sir Charles Wood as Chancellor of the Exchequer and Lord Lansdowne as leader of the Lords. Russell also found room in his Cabinet for his father-in-law, the Earl of Minto, who became Lord Privy Seal. It was noted how beholden Russell felt towards the Grey family, as Sir George was the new Earl Grey's cousin and Sir Charles was his brother-in law. Of this trio, only Sir George really pulled his weight, and Russell embarked on his first premiership at the head of a weak and quarrelsome team. It was almost immediately to be faced with the most painful challenge of any government during the century, when, one year after the failure of the Irish potato crop in 1845:

> there was a second and even more complete failure, and the cereal crops, which had been good in 1845, were poor all over Europe. Peel had got out just in time. In bare outline, a population of ten millions faced the winter, spring, and early summer of 1846–47 with no more than four-fifths of their normal food supply. Within that population, 2m were normally unem-ployed, and one-third lived off their potato patches at subsistence level. These groups were already enfeebled by the first failure, and had no reserves to face the second successive dearth. The truth will never be known, but in round figures 1m or more people perished in the two years after Lord John took office, and another 1m emigrated between 1847 and 1850. It was 'an evil unknown in the history of modern Europe', or as Lord John said in a famous phrase, it was like a famine of the thirteenth century acting on a population of the nineteenth century. (Prest, 1972, pp. 234–5)

Russell, whose sympathy with the Irish masses was long-standing, was anguished by the human suffering involved, and took what steps he could to ameliorate the situation. These included an easing of the Irish poor law, public works programmes, the provision of soup kitchens, assisted emigration and very limited government purchase of food supplies. His efforts were, however, inhibited by adherence to the prevailing doctrines of *laissez-faire*, obstruction by Treasury officials and by the presence in his Cabinet of major Irish absen-tee landlords, such as Lord Lansdowne and Lord Palmerston MP, who actively sought to defend their own class interests. Scherer concludes:

> There is no reason to lavish praise upon the Russell government for its handling of the Irish famine. The Treasury, which controlled most relief efforts, was doctrinaire, harsh, and parsimonious. Nevertheless, the Whigs did about as well as an average government of the time would have done, limited by the attitudes of its era. (Scherer, p. 175)

In his domestic programme, Russell did rather better, attempting to con-tinue with, and expand, the range of reform measures for which he had been responsible during the Grey and Melbourne governments. He was inhibited by his lack of a parliamentary majority, in either House, but succeeded in passing a very important Public Health Act, repealing the navigation laws, which were a severe inhibition on free trade, introducing further educa-tional reforms, including a long overdue review of Oxford and Cambridge universities, legislating to enable practising Jews to sit in Parliament (though this was blocked by the House of Lords) and granting self-government to the Australian colonies. Russell's firm but sensitive handling of the last great Chartist demonstration in 1848 was credited by some observers with having saved Britain from the wave of revolutions which swept across Europe during that year.

Despite these successes, Russell himself steadily lost support among his fellow Whigs, while being unable to recruit the leading Peelites into his government, though, in 1851, he managed to persuade Peel's second son, Frederick, to accept an under-secretaryship. He upset the more conservative Whigs by his continuing zeal for reform, by his constant efforts to remove disabilities from Dissenters, Catholics and Jews – to the chagrin of many of his fellow Anglicans – and by a number of serious misjudgements. One of these concerned his appointment to the vacant bishopric of Hereford of Dr R.D. Hampden, the Regius Professor of Divinity at Oxford, who was widely accused of heresy. This uniquely succeeded in simultaneously upsetting both the High and Low Church factions. Then, in 1850, he grievously offended his previously loyal Irish supporters (who contributed substantially to his parliamentary strength) by his intemperate reaction to a Papal Bull creating 12 Roman Catholic bishops in Britain, and allocating them territorial titles. Russell roundly condemned this in a widely publicized letter to the Bishop of Durham, and he promptly introduced the Ecclesiastical Titles Act, which made it a criminal offence for Catholic priests to accept geographical titles. For a man who had previously been regarded as a beacon of religious toleration, it was a sad aberration, which later cost him dear.

At about the same time, Lord John, who in 1838 had won himself the nickname 'Finality Jack' for declaring that the 1832 Reform Act had settled the suffrage question for all time, became convinced that it was now essential for an extension of the franchise to take in a much larger proportion of working class voters. Yet he had great difficulty in persuading his cabinet and MPs to act.

Lord John's final misfortune was to fall out seriously with his Foreign Secretary, Lord Palmerston MP. The fault was almost entirely Palmerston's, but it was Russell who was ultimately to be more damaged by their quarrel. Palmerston had grown used to running the Foreign Office, with virtually no control by the Prime Minister, in his earlier stint under Lord Melbourne, and he continued to do so under Russell. An imperious character, he treated foreign governments, and even monarchs, with little concern for diplomatic niceties, which Russell deprecated but which caused consternation to Queen Victoria and Prince Albert. Russell attempted to shuffle him out of the Foreign Office, by offering to go up to the Lords himself and making Palmerston leader of the Commons. This he flatly refused to discuss – his public and parliamentary reputation having been greatly boosted by the Don Pacifico affair (see Chapter 16) – but he reluctantly acquiesced in the Queen's demand that he should in future submit all proposed actions and dispatches for her approval before implementing them. Then, in December 1851, he went too far, by publicly endorsing Louis-Napoleon's *coup d'etat*, over-throwing the Second French republic, after the government had agreed to take a neutral stance. Russell's patience finally snapped, and he peremptorily dismissed Palmerston, who got his 'tit-for-tat' two months later, in February 1852, when he moved a hostile amendment to the government's Militia Bill, securing its defeat in a parliamentary vote, which led to its immediate resignation. The Queen called on the Tory leader, Lord Stanley (who had recently succeeded his father as the 14th Earl of Derby), to form a new government.

Russell went into opposition, confident that he would soon be back, correctly surmizing that Derby's government would not last long. Derby secured a dissolution, and the ensuing general election brought substantial Tory gains and Peelite losses, but still left him short of a majority. After less than 10 months in office, he was forced to resign, and, in December 1852, his government was replaced by a coalition of Whigs and Peelites. Russell had assumed that, as the Whigs greatly outnumbered the Peelites, he would be Prime Minister, but he had become so unpopular in his own party (and especially among his former Irish supporters) that they were unwilling to push his claim. The Queen's first choice was Lord Lansdowne, the Whig leader in the Lords, but he declined, and the choice then fell on the Earl of Aberdeen, a former Foreign Secretary, who had led the Peelites since Peel's death in 1850.

Russell was now 60 years old, and his health being poor, he might have been well advised to retire from politics altogether or at least go to the Lords as an elder statesman. He chose, however, to battle on for another 14 years, during which he was to serve twice as Foreign Secretary and for a second period as Prime Minister, but his achievements were slight, and – if anything – subtracted from, rather than added to, his reputation. Russell's ambivalent attitude towards the Aberdeen government did nothing to further his own influence or popularity. Deeply resentful at being supplanted by someone he clearly regarded, with justification, as his inferior, he failed to develop a considered view on whether he really wanted to serve in the government, or if so, in what post. In the end, he accepted the Foreign secretaryship, only to renounce it after two months in favour of leading the Commons, without a department of his own. The government lasted for just over two years, and proved deeply frustrating for Lord John. He was, nominally, the number two man, but his influence was largely disregarded, and his continued efforts to persuade his colleagues to agree to the introduction of a new Reform Bill came to nothing, as they appealed neither to the more conservative Whigs nor to most of the Peelites.

Aberdeen's government was dominated by the Crimean War (see Chapters 15 and 16). It was an unwanted and unnecessary conflict, largely caused by the failure of Aberdeen and Palmerston (now Home Secretary, but retaining his proprietorial interest in foreign policy) to agree on the so-called Eastern Question. The crisis was provoked by Russian demands on Turkey to oversee the Holy Places in Palestine, and, more generally, to be accepted as the guarantor of the rights of Christians throughout the Ottoman Empire. Tsar Nicholas I ordered his troops to occupy the two Romanian principalities of Moldavia and Wallachia, in October 1853, and refused to withdraw them unless the Turkish sultan accepted his claims. Aberdeen favoured appeasing Russia and pressurizing the Turks to give way, while Palmerston argued for a robust support of Turkey, threatening war on Russia if it did not withdraw from the two principalities, which were under Turkish suzerainty. Either policy, if consistently followed, might have brought peace, but Britain wavered between the two, and eventually, in March 1854, the Turks declared war on Russia, and Britain and France followed suit. Russell, who tended to support Palmerston, found that his views were virtually ignored. Aberdeen's shortcomings as a war leader were soon apparent, and in January 1855, Russell resigned, rather than defending his conduct of the war in a parliamentary debate. This precipitated Aberdeen's own resignation, and he was succeeded as head of the coalition by the more warlike Palmerston.

Russell did not initially rejoin the government, but was sent by Palmerston to a conference in Austria, whose purpose was to seek a compromise peace with Russia, in view of the bloody stalemate which had developed before Sebastopol, or – alternatively – to induce Austria to enter the war on the allied side. Russell showed great patience as a negotiator, despite the apparent intransigence of the Russian delegate, Prince Alexander Menshikov, and considered that a reasonable settlement was possible, but neither the French, who still hoped for a military victory, nor Palmerston, now in hock to the fervour worked up by a jingoistic press, was prepared to accept the terms available. Nor were the Austrians prepared to join in the war, so the conference ended in failure. Russell, who had accepted the post of Colonial Secretary, returned to London, but did not stay long in office, resigning in July 1855, after he had been widely attacked for his alleged willingness to accept a humiliating settlement at Vienna. Palmerston's government managed very well without his services, and won a greatly increased majority in the 1857 general election, benefitting from Palmerston's war leadership and the eventual capture of Sebastopol, which brought the Crimean War to a victorious conclusion. Yet the government was dominated by the most conservative elements of the Whig and Peelite parties, and Russell gradually reclaimed his popularity with their younger and more progressive supporters by his continued advocacy of reform. Meanwhile, parliamentary support for Palmerston began to crumble, following the Indian mutiny and the Orsini plot, planned in London, to assassinate Napoleon III (see Chapter 16). Palmerston responded by introducing the

Conspiracy to Murder Bill, to mollify French anger, but this was defeated in the Commons, on 18 February 1858, and the government resigned, leaving the way open for the Earl of Derby to form a Conservative administration for the second time. In opposition, the Whigs, Peelites and Radicals, together with their Irish supporters, finally agreed to amalgamate, forming the Liberal Party, at a meeting, in June 1859, attended by 274 MPs.

Russell was the main architect of the new alignment, and would probably have been its first choice for Prime Minister, if a vote had been taken. Yet when the Derby government, having done badly in the 1859 general election, resigned shortly afterwards, Queen Victoria sent for Lord Granville, the Liberal leader in the Lords, and when he failed to form a government, sighed that she would have to choose between the 'two terrible old men'. Inevitably, she picked Palmerston, as Russell's views were much too radical for her liking. Russell and Palmerston were now thoroughly reconciled to each other, and Russell demanded and received the Foreign secretaryship. Thus began a partnership of more than six years, during which their relations remained remarkably good. Russell accepted an earldom in 1861, and Palmerston, now well into his seventies, unexpectedly left him a remarkably free hand, intervening only on major issues, and, even then, often deferring to his colleague's views. Four issues dominated – Mexico, the US Civil War, Italian unity and Denmark (the Schleswig-Holstein question). These are discussed in some detail in Chapter 16, but here it may be noted that the first three were handled relatively well, producing outcomes which were generally acceptable from a British point of view, but the fourth resulted in public humiliation (partly because of unwanted interference by Queen Victoria).

In July 1865, Palmerston, almost 82 years old, again led the Liberals to a general election triumph, but he did not live to face the new House of Commons, dying the following October, after having caught a chill while out driving. Victoria had no real choice, but to ask the 73-year-old Russell to take over the leadership of the government, which he did with great enthusiasm, feeling that the time had at last arrived to complete his mission of again reforming the British electoral system. He made very few ministerial changes, confirming the former Peelite, William Gladstone, as Chancellor of the Exchequer, and appointing him also as leader of the Commons and effective deputy premier. Lord Clarendon, who had been Foreign Secretary in 1853–8, now replaced him in that post. Russell lost little time in introducing his Reform Bill, which provided for a substantial widening of the franchise, though falling well short of manhood suffrage. It was vigorously attacked by the Tory opposition, supported by many right-wing Liberals (dubbed the 'Cave of Adullum' by the arch-reformer John Bright), and to Russell's great chagrin was defeated by 11 votes in a crucial division during the Committee Stage. The government resigned, in June 1866, after 240 days in office, and Lord Derby became Prime Minister for the third time. Despite this defeat, Russell was the moral victor, as the new momentum he had created for Reform proved unstoppable. A year later, the 1867 Reform Bill, designed by Disraeli 'to steal the Whigs' clothes while they were bathing', and going substantially further than Russell's own measure, was passed. It gave the vote to all heads of households in borough constituencies (see Chapter 17).

Russell lived another 12 years, declining office in Gladstone's first government formed in 1868, but continuing to be active in the House of Lords almost until his death, aged nearly 86, on 28 May 1878. Undoubtedly the smallest of the nineteenth-century Prime Ministers, 'Little Johnnie Russell' made a bigger impact than most. Almost single-handedly, he enlarged the objectives of the Whig Party from a narrow desire to curb the prerogatives of the monarch and to protect ancient liberties, into a much wider social concern, and a mission to subject not only Parliament but all elements of public life to critical scrutiny and reform. 'Above all', in the words of one of his biographers, 'he was absolutely without fear of change (only of no change)' (Prest, 2004). Despite not commanding a parliamentary majority, and much obstruction from the House of Lords, the legislative record of his first government, in 1846–52, surpassed that of any other administration between Gray's government of 1830–34 and Gladstone's of 1868–74, though he could undoubtedly have done more had it not been for the conservatism of many of his own supporters. His legacy was a Liberal Party which, under the leadership of Gladstone, and later of Campbell-Bannerman, Asquith and the younger Lloyd George, was prepared to lead the nation in new and more radical directions. Another gift he left to posterity was his grandson, Bertrand Russell, whose restless mind reflected that of his distinguished ancestor.

Works consulted

J.B. Conacher, 1968, *The Aberdeen Coalition 1852–1855*, Cambridge, Cambridge University Press.

Lucille Iremonger, 1970, *The Fiery Chariot*, London, Secker & Warburg.

Jonathan Parry, 1993, *The Rise and Fall of Liberal Government in Victorian Britain*, New Haven, Yale University Press.

Jonathan Parry, 1998, 'Lord John Russell, First Earl Russell', in Robert Eccleshall and Graham Walker (eds.), *Biographical Dictionary of British Prime Ministers*, London, Routledge.

John Prest, 1972, *Lord John Russell*, London, Macmillan.

John Prest, 2004, Article in *Oxford Dictionary of National Biography*.

John Robert Russell, 1959, *A Silver Plated Spoon*, London, Sphere Books.

Paul Scherer, 1999, *Lord John Russell*, Selinsgrove, Susquehanna University Press.

14

Edward Stanley, 14th Earl of Derby – 'The Brilliant Chief, Irregularly Great'

THE EARL OF DERBY, K.G.

Chancellor of the University of Oxford.

From the original Picture at Knowsley Hall, Lancashire.

Lord Derby was the first person ever to become Prime Minister three times, but he failed to live up to his early promise, and his posthumous reputation is shadowy, being almost entirely eclipsed by those of his principal opponents and by his leading follower, and successor, Benjamin Disraeli. Born Edward George Geoffrey Smith Stanley, on 29 March 1799, he was the scion of an ancient Whig family, whose title dated back to 1485. His father, the 13th Earl, was mostly known for the impressive zoological collection which he built up at the family seat of Knowsley Hall, in Lancashire. He had married his cousin, Charlotte Hornby, a clergyman's daughter. Edward was their first child, and they went on to have two other sons and four daughters.

The young Edward was little influenced by his father, who sat for many years as an inactive and ineffective Whig MP, but from his mother he inherited a strong devotion to the Church of England. The dominant figure in his early life was his grandfather, the 12th Earl, an ardent Whig and a close friend and admirer of Charles James Fox. A widower, he married a second time to a young actress, Elizabeth Farren, and their children were of a similar age to Edward. Indeed, one of Edward's contemporaries at Eton was his uncle, James Stanley, who was a year younger than himself, and who was to die at the age of 17. Edward was to be noted at Eton as 'clever' and 'scholarly' and 'full of self-assurance'. From Eton, he went on to Christ Church, Oxford, where he distinguished himself for his classical scholarship, winning the Chancellor's prize for Latin verse. He disgraced himself one night by leading a drunken group of undergraduates, who pulled down from a plinth in the college's Great Quadrangle a figure of Mercury, erected in 1695, but he was generally seen as a figure of great promise, though wilful and resentful of personal criticism. According to one biographer, his 'precocity was so rare among members of his class that Stanley was some-times mentioned as the only 'brilliant eldest son produced by the British peerage for a hundred years' (Jones, 1956, p. 6). His family was immensely wealthy, being major territorial magnates in Lancashire, and owning estates in several other English counties, as well as in Limerick, Ireland.

Leading Whigs came to see him as a potential 'great catch' for their party, and his grandfather was induced to buy a 'pocket borough' for him, at the age of 23. The sitting MP for Stockbridge, duly made way for him, and he was returned unopposed in a by-election in July 1822. He waited nearly two years before making his maiden speech, on the unpromising subject of the Manchester Gas Light Bill, but – despite feeling an acute sense of failure when he sat down – was astonished to find that his speech was widely hailed as an oratorical triumph. Three months later, he decided to take a prolonged leave of his parliamentary duties, sailing for New York for a nine-month tour of the US and Canada, and shortly after his return, in May 1826, got married, at the age of 26, to Emma Bootle-Wilbraham, the 20-year-old daughter of a Tory MP, who later became the first Lord Skelmersdale. Little is known about their courtship, but it was apparently a successful marriage, which produced two sons (one of whom, later the 15th Earl of Derby, was himself to serve as both Colonial and Foreign Secretary) and a daughter. Emma acted from time to time as Stanley's secretary, and became an active political hostess.

It was not long before Stanley came to be seen as the finest speaker in the House of Commons, with no rival after the death of Canning in 1827. A political opponent, Lord Campbell, wrote of him that: 'Stanley is a host in himself. He has a marvellous acuteness of intellect and consummate power in debate. There is no subject which he cannot master thoroughly and lucidly explain. His voice and manner are so good that no one can hear him without listening to him' (Jones, p. 51).

Campbell's verdict was typical of many of his contemporaries, including Daniel Webster, reputedly the greatest of American orators, who heard him speak in the Commons in 1839, and declared it to be the best speech he had ever heard. He was not, however, without his critics. Many MPs regarded him as a most appalling snob, who treated his non-aristocratic colleagues with undisguised disdain, while others – noting his independent views – came to doubt the orthodoxy of his Whiggism. Stanley was one of the first Whigs to rally to the support of George Canning, when many leading Tories refused to join his government in April 1827. Canning appealed to the Whigs to fill the vacant places, and – despite the discouragement of the Whig leader, Earl Grey – several took up the offer, including Stanley, who became a junior Lord of the Treasury, and went on to serve as under-secretary for the Colonies in Goderich's equally short-lived government of 1827–8. When Earl Grey formed his Whig government, in 1830, Stanley, now aged 31, obtained the important post of Chief Secretary for Ireland, initially outside the Cabinet.

Stanley then suffered the first setback in his promising political career. In order to be confirmed in his new post, he had to resign his seat at Preston, to which he had transferred at the 1826 general election, and fight a by-election. He was disconcerted to be challenged by Henry 'Orator' Hunt, the radical campaigner who had been the speaker at the 'Peterloo massacre' meeting, in 1819, and Hunt succeeded in winning the seat, by 3,392 votes to 3,370. There followed a desperate search to find Stanley another seat, and the new King, William IV, came to his rescue by offering the pocket borough of Windsor, which he personally controlled. He was returned unopposed nine weeks later, after the sitting MP was bought off by being appointed Commander of the Forces in Ireland. Stanley embarked on his new duties with enthusiasm, but before he could give Ireland his undivided attention, he was much in demand as a parliamentary speaker during the long series of debates on the Reform Bill. Grey and most of his senior ministers were in the Lords, and Lord John Russell, who was in charge of the Bill in the Commons, badly needed debating support in the Lower House. Stanley was hardly a born reformer, and he was reported to have roared with laughter when he first heard the details of the Bill, which went so much further than he or most of his colleagues had expected. But he buckled down, and in a series of brilliant speeches swept the floor with his Tory opponents.

His record as Irish Secretary was a mixed one. He promoted a number of reforms, notably the Irish Education Act of 1832, which provided for secular schools open to children from all religious denominations. Yet he was determined to give over-riding priority to the restoration of law and order, and the protection of private property, and introduced a number of coercive measures, which upset several of his cabinet colleagues, who thought it more expedient to concentrate instead on removing Irish grievances. He also made a bitter enemy of Daniel O'Connell, dubbed 'the Liberator' for his successful leadership of the campaign for Catholic Emancipation, who was now himself ensconced in the House of Commons, and became his most intransigent critic. Stanley joined the Cabinet in June 1831, and was a close ally of Grey in opposing his more radical colleagues, but during his entire time in Ireland was at loggerheads with the Lord Lieutenant, the Marquess of Anglesey, who, as Lord Uxbridge, had been Wellington's second-in-command at Waterloo, where he had lost a leg in the battle. Anglesey was a pronounced liberal, and his relations with Stanley became so bad that, in 1833, Grey decided to shift both of them out of their jobs. Stanley was promoted to Secretary for War and the Colonies, and Anglesey was replaced by Marquess Wellesley, elder brother of the Duke of Wellington.

The outstanding event during the 14 months that Stanley spent in his new post was the abolition of slavery in the British Empire, a logical sequel to the legislation carried, in 1806, by the predominantly Whig government of Lord Grenville, which brought an end to the slave trade. Stanley was responsible for the Bill, which provided for compensation of some £20 million for the slave-owners, and laid down a fixed seven-year apprenticeship for adult slaves before they would be finally freed. The Bill was opposed by the West Indian 'planters', whose influence in the House of Commons, where they had controlled many 'pocket boroughs' was greatly diminished by the Reform Act, and by Radical MPs who objected to the scale of the compensation and the compulsory apprenticeships, but Stanley's action was generally applauded, and his reputation soared. Many years later, Disraeli was to recall an intriguing conversation he had had at this time with Lord Melbourne, then Home Secretary, from whom he had sought advice about promoting his own nascent political career. He brashly mentioned his ambition to become Prime Minister, and Melbourne replied: 'No chance of that in our time. It is all arranged and settled...Nobody can compete with Stanley...you must put all these foolish notions out of your head; they won't do at all. Stanley will be the next Prime Minister, you will see' (Cromwell, 1998, p. 163).

Melbourne was wrong: it was he, himself, who unexpectedly succeeded Grey as Prime Minister, in 1834, but it might well have been Stanley (then 35) if he had not disagreed with his colleagues over Ireland, and resigned from the government a few weeks earlier. All would have been well, if Stanley had not continued to take a close interest in Irish affairs after taking up his new post. However, he put himself at the head of the opposition to the move by Lord John Russell to expropriate, for secular purposes, the excess yield of the tithes paid to the Anglican church in Ireland (see Chapter 13). For Stanley this was an intolerable attack on the perquisites of the Church, and, in June 1834, when Russell obtained cabinet approval to introduce a bill, he abruptly resigned from the government, saying 'Johnnie has upset the coach' He took with him, the Earl of Ripon (Lord Privy Seal, and a former Prime Minister, as Lord Goderich), Sir James Graham (First Lord of the Admiralty) and the Duke of Richmond (Paymaster-General). Their departure destabilized the Grey government, and while not the proximate reason for the Prime Minister's own resignation a month later, was undoubtedly a contributory factor.

Stanley still considered himself a Whig, but on policy issues felt far closer to Sir Robert Peel, who was about to relaunch the Tories as the Conservative Party. When Peel formed his first government, in December 1834, he was anxious to include both Stanley and Graham, but they were not yet willing to break their ties with the Whigs, and declined to serve. In the general election which followed, in January 1835, the Stanleyites put up a significant number of candidates, hoping to win the balance of power between Whigs and Tories and form the basis of a new centre party. The results were a great disappointment to them, only about half a dozen of Stanley's supporters were elected, and the Whigs were returned by a substantial majority, though smaller than in 1832. Peel's government resigned shortly afterwards, and Melbourne, who had been arbitrarily dismissed by William IV (see Chapter 11), triumphantly returned to power.

It was at this time that Stanley first became afflicted with gout, a disease which seemed to be hereditary in the Derby family, and which periodically incapacitated him throughout the remainder of his life. His biographer comments that 'with the onset of this illness, Stanley became increasingly cautious in political affairs, and the impetuousness of his youth rapidly became a fading memory' (Jones, p. 71). Stanley's little group, contemptuously referred to by O'Connell as 'the Derby Dilly, carrying six inside',* tried for some time to maintain an independent existence, but in 1838 both Stanley and Graham formally joined the Conservative Party, and Stanley became one of Peel's leading associates. When Peel formed his second government, following the Conservative victory in the

---

*The reference was to a poem by Canning describing the Derby Dilly (or diligence carriage) making its way through the Derbyshire hills.

1841 election, both took senior posts, Graham as Home Secretary, and Stanley as Secretary for War and the Colonies and effectively the number two minister in the Commons. The Earl of Ripon also joined the government, as President of the Board of Trade, with the young William Gladstone as his deputy, and, two years later, successor. Scowling on the government backbenches was Disraeli, bitterly disappointed to have been left out of the government, despite the passionate plea he had made to Peel to be included (see Chapters 12 and 17).

Peel regarded Stanley as his most able colleague, but they never became personally close, perhaps because Peel, acutely sensitive about his relatively humble origins, sensed the scarcely concealed superiority which the proudly aristocratic Stanley felt towards him. As War and Colonial Secretary, Stanley had to confront a wide range of issues. These included winding up the first 'Opium War' with China, which led to the annexation of Hong Kong, about which he was personally unenthusiastic; the negotiation, in conjunction with the Foreign Secretary, Lord Aberdeen, of the Webster-Ashburton treaty with the United States; demarcating the boundary between Canada and the state of Maine, the passage of the Canadian Corn Bill; allowing preferential imports from Canada; the annexation of Natal and Sind, and troubles arising from the recent establishment of the colony of New Zealand, for which the governor was largely to blame but for which Stanley was much criticized. In November 1844, he accepted a peerage, becoming Lord Stanley of Bickerstaffe. This was at his own request, following a renewed attack of gout, and he thought he would have a more relaxing time in the Upper House. It was also the case that the Duke of Wellington, the Tory leader in the Lords, was badly in need of additional debating power on the government side. Peel, who may always have felt a trifle uneasy about sitting side by side with him in the Commons, was probably somewhat relieved, but it is highly doubtful if the change was in Stanley's own long-term interest, even though he was bound to end up in the Lords on the death of his father. This did not, however, occur until seven years later.

Within a year of joining the Lords, Stanley was faced with the most difficult choice of his entire career, when Peel, faced by the Irish famine, determined to repeal the Corn Laws to permit the importation of cheap foreign grain (see Chapter 12). Stanley was not oblivious of the need to assist the Irish, but was adamantly opposed to Peel's decision. He regarded the landed interest as the bedrock of British society and was not prepared to put its prosperity at risk by allowing it to be undercut by foreign suppliers, which he felt would have a devastating effect on the English countryside. He also felt that Peel and his government had been elected on a Protectionist mandate and that it would be a betrayal of their own supporters for them to act in this way. If the Corn Laws were to be repealed, Stanley thought, it would be far better to make way for a Whig government to do the dirty deed. 'We can't', he said, 'do this as gentlemen' (Jones, p. 114). He therefore insisted on resigning, even though the rest of the Cabinet, including even the Duke of Buccleuch, who led the Scottish landed interest, agreed to support Peel, although most of them had initially been opposed to him.

Peel felt he could not continue in the face of Stanley's resignation, and the opposition of the majority of Tory MPs, and submitted the government's resignation to the Queen. He considered recommending her to send for Stanley to try to form a protectionist government, but thought that he would be unable to succeed, and that public opinion would not tolerate an aristocratic government deliberating forcing up food prices. So he suggested that Lord John Russell, the opposition leader, should be appointed instead, and promised his full support in carrying the repeal. When Russell failed to form a government, he unhesitatingly accepted to carry on, determined to push the measure through in the teeth of his own party's resistance. Stanley was saddened that Sir James Graham, formally his own closest supporter, was foursquare behind Peel, and equally committed to repeal. When Graham came to see him to try to talk him round, he was cut to the quick by a remark of Graham's which he took to imply that he was opposing Peel in the hope of replacing him as Premier. This may sub-consciously have been true, and certainly accorded with the wishes of his wife Emma, but Stanley was never prepared to admit it, and his friendship with Graham abruptly ceased.

So far from aspiring to the premiership, Stanley gave some indication at that time that he was thinking of giving up politics altogether. Writing to his former cabinet colleague, Lord Ellenborough, at Christmas 1845, he said: 'Though it is difficult to foresee the future, my own opinion is that my official life is over, and I am well content that it should be so. The political current seems steadily setting in a direction which leaves me high and dry on the beach' (Stewart, 1971, p. 55).

Had he still been in the Commons, Stanley would have faced irresistible pressure to put himself at the head of the protectionist forces, and his biographer Wilbur Devereux Jones speculated that his great debating power might have been sufficient to ensure the defeat of the Repeal Bill. As it was, he found himself 'in the wrong house of Parliament' (Jones, p. 107), and the leadership of the protectionists fell into the unskilled hands of Lord George Bentinck, with Disraeli as his main lieutenant (see Chapter 12). They secured the backing of two-thirds of the Tory MPs, but with Whig support the Bill was carried through. After much hesitation, Stanley agreed to oppose it in the Lords, and made a fine speech in the second reading debate which won the support of a majority of the peers in the Chamber. But the Duke of Wellington, who decided to back Peel despite his own opposition to repeal, had succeeded in collecting enough proxy votes to carry the day. The Bill was finally passed on 25 June 1846. Four days later Peel resigned, his government having been defeated in the Commons on the Irish Coercion Bill, when many of the protectionists voted with the Whigs, leading to the formation of a new Whig government under Lord John Russell.

Stanley was chosen as leader of the Conservative peers, and later succeeded Bentinck as the overall leader, and his main concern now became to prevent the split in the party from becoming permanent. He took a moderate stance in the 1847 general election, and afterwards declared that the electorate had clearly given a mandate for free trade, as a majority had voted either for the Whigs or the Peelites. He therefore saw the question as settled, at least for the time being, and saw no reason why the Conservative Party should not now be reunited. He was disconcerted by the continuing hostility of Peel's main supporters, who included nearly all the most able figures of the party. When he himself had left the Whigs, he had continued to have good personal relations with his former colleagues, notably Lord John Russell, and throughout his life maintained that political differences should not be allowed to take precedence over friendly intercourse (at least between social equals!). He was amazed at the depth of hostility which arose between former party allies. Disraeli narrowly avoided fighting a duel with Peel's brother Jonathan, while Peel himself was only restrained from challenging Bentinck, when Lord Lincoln threatened to call in the police. Lincoln himself, a leading Peelite, became totally estranged from his father, the 4th Duke of Newcastle, because of their opposing views over protectionism, and they were only reconciled on the Duke's deathbed in 1851.

Bentinck resigned the Tory leadership in December 1847, dying the following year at the early age of 46, and Stanley exerted himself to prevent the election of Disraeli as the new Tory leader in the Commons. He wanted to ensure that he would be fully consulted on tactics in the Commons, and he disapproved of Disraeli on social grounds, regarding him as an opportunistic *parvenu*. He also feared that Disraeli's leadership would forestall any possibility of reunion with the Peelites, who had been appalled by the vehemence of his attacks on Peel. He therefore agreed with Bentinck that the new leader should be the Marquess of Granby MP, an unexceptional Tory aristocrat, and he was duly elected by the protectionist MPs. But Granby was lacking in self-confidence, and refused to serve, which meant that for the whole of the 1848–9 session, the party was leaderless in the Commons. Despite the fact that Disraeli was, by a wide margin, the most able of the MPs (and, by an even wider margin, the most ambitious!), Stanley continued to look elsewhere, and proposed John Herries, a veteran ex-civil servant, who had briefly served in Peel's 1834–5 government. Yet Herries, too, was diffident about assuming the leadership, and Stanley eventually acquiesced in an agreement that the party should be led in the Commons by a triumvirate of Granby, Herries and Disraeli. The latter, however, comported himself as if he were the sole leader, and the other two quietly effaced themselves, but it was only late in 1851 that Stanley was prepared to accept him as leader, and another two years before he brought himself to invite him to a house party at Knowsley Hall, where other leading protectionists had been regular visitors over a long period. Despite this unpromising beginning, Stanley and Disraeli were to work together, as respective party leaders in the two Houses, with surprising harmony for the best part of two decades.

Stanley insisted that the Protectionist party should resume the name Conservative Party against the wishes of most of his leading colleagues, who preferred to be known as Tories. Because of his high social standing, and his unmatched oratorical abilities, his own leadership was unchallengeable in a party largely made up of country squires, but he was to be constantly criticized for his apparent lack of commitment and the self-described tactic of 'masterly inactivity' with which he opposed a series of Whig or coalition governments, preferring to wait for them to make mistakes. He absented himself for long periods to Knowsley Hall, where he was a fanatical hunter and shooter, but his main interest was in horseracing, and he was a familiar figure at racetracks throughout the country. He regularly left the impression that he would rather win the Derby (a race named after his own family) than be Prime Minister. He never did, but it was a great day in his life when, in 1848, he became Steward of the Jockey Club. Some years later, a Tory backbencher, Lord Henry Lennox, was to write to Disraeli complaining that 'as a leader of a party, [Stanley] is more hopeless than ever!! Devoted to whist, billiards, racing, betting, & making a fool of himself with [the Ladies]...' (Blake, 1966, p. 369). Some of his many interests were more intellectual: he was to publish a translation of *The Iliad*, which was widely admired in its day. The writer and Tory MP, and much later minister in Derby's third government, Sir Edward Bulwer-Lytton, summed up both his virtues and shortcomings in his political poem *The New Timon*:

> The brilliant chief, irregularly great,
> Frank, haughty, rash, the Rupert of Debate.

He was drawing on a parliamentary speech of Disraeli's, in 1844, when, referring to Stanley, he had said: 'The noble lord in this case, as in so many others, is the Prince Rupert of parliamentary discussion; his charge is resistless; but when he returns from pursuit he always finds his camp in the possession of the enemy' (Hansard, 24 April 1844).

The first occasion on which Stanley seriously disappointed his followers was in February 1851, when Russell's government resigned, after being defeated in a parliamentary vote on electoral reform. Painfully aware of the lack of potential ministerial talent among the Tories, Stanley made strenuous attempts to recruit leading Peelites to his team, and even put out feelers to Palmerston, whom he correctly identified as the most conservative of the Whigs. He had particular hopes of attracting Lord Aberdeen, who was personally very friendly to him and who he hoped to make Foreign Secretary, and Gladstone, to whom he offered the choice of any other post in the government. Both, however, declined, as did all their colleagues, partly because of the continuing Tory commitment to reimpose tariff duties on corn, even though these would be at a moderate level. It was still open to Stanley to form a minority government, but after reviewing the talent available to him, and particularly when Herries proved reluctant to take the Chancellorship of the Exchequer, he threw in his hand, and the Queen invited Russell to resume power.

Four months later, Stanley's father died, aged 76, and on 30 June 1851, he became the 14th Earl of Derby. He was now 52, and within eight months he unexpectedly became Prime Minister for the first time. The opportunity arose, as described in Chapter 13, because of Lord Palmerston's action in turning out Russell's government, following his own dismissal as Foreign Secretary. This time Derby realized that he must take office, even without Peelite support, but he had high hopes of recruiting Palmerston to his colours, though negotiations with him proved abortive. As for the Peelites, of whom Gladstone seemed the most likely to join up, there were two insuperable objections. One was the lingering Tory commitment to protectionism, which Disraeli was quite ready to abandon, but which Derby could not bring himself to do, at least until he had fought another election on the issue. The other Peelite objection was to Disraeli's leadership of the Commons, but Derby, having reluctantly accepted him in that role a year earlier, was not prepared to let him go at the first sign of trouble. So he had to make do with the meagre talent available to him in his own party. Disraeli became Chancellor of the Exchequer and leader of the Commons, and the second Earl of Malmesbury, his favourite shooting companion at Knowsley, Foreign Secretary, but most of his other appointees were virtually unknown. Indeed, the government became known as the Who? Who? Government, after the hard-of-hearing Duke of Wellington had repeatedly queried the unfamiliar names when a list of the cabinet members was read out to him. Derby had to put up with a great deal of ridicule about some of his more obscure choices. Lady Clanricarde, the wife of a rather raffish Whig peer, asked him at a dinner party: 'Are you sure, Lord Derby, that Sir John Pakington [the new Colonial Secretary] is a *real* man?', and was disconcerted when he coolly replied 'Well, I think so – he has been married three times.'

So Derby became Prime Minister on 23 February 1852. It was a minority government, but Derby was reasonably confident that – given the serious dissensions within the ranks of the opposition – it would not be turned out in a hurry. His objective was to govern calmly in a non-controversial manner, in the hope of building up confidence with the electorate and winning a majority at the subsequent general election, to which he was committed during the summer of 1852. The election was duly held in July, and the Conservatives made numerous gains, largely at the expense of the Peelites but remained in a minority. In a memorandum to Prince Albert, Derby analysed the membership of the new House of Commons, as follows: '286 Conservatives, 150 Radicals, 120 Whigs, 50 in the Irish Brigade, and 30 Peelites'. A major effort was now mounted to recruit the Peelites, with particular attention being paid to Lord Aberdeen and William Gladstone, who had pursued a policy of benevolent neutrality towards the government prior to the election. Derby now made the grand gesture of renouncing protectionism. Speaking in the House of Lords, in November 1852,

> Derby admitted that a very large majority of the British people, including many from agricultural districts, no longer sought a reimposition of the Corn Laws, and that he himself saw there might be advantages to the nation as a whole in retaining Free Trade. Derby added: 'on the part, then, of myself and my colleagues, I bow to the decision of the country'. (Jones, p. 173)

Derby's concession came too late. The Peelites were no longer interested in reuniting the Conservative Party. They had received a better offer from the Whigs – of a coalition government – in which they would secure the Prime Ministership and almost half the cabinet seats. This, to the chagrin of the former Whig Prime Minister, Lord John Russell, who found himself forced to play second fiddle to Lord Aberdeen. The government was duly defeated on a vote on Disraeli's budget, and resigned on 17 December 1852, after a mere 292 days in office.

Derby was replaced as Prime Minister by the Peelite leader, Lord Aberdeen, but might well have had a second innings two years later, when Aberdeen resigned after losing what amounted to a confidence vote on his conduct of the Crimean War. There were widely seen as three possible candidates for the succession – Derby, Russell and Palmerston. It was, perhaps, Derby's misfortune that the Queen sent for him first. Ignoring the earnest plea of his colleague, Lord Ellenborough ('Don't leave the room without kissing hands'), Derby temporized, and said that because of the strong public support for Palmerston it would be necessary to include him in the government. He declined to accept office until he had discussed the situation with Palmerston and the leading Peelites, but finding them unco-operative returned the next day to tell the Queen that he could not proceed. The probability is that Derby was confident that neither Russell nor Palmerston would be able to form a government, and that the Queen would then turn to him again, as a last resort. Victoria then summoned Russell, who – as predicted – failed to assemble enough support, but, against all expectations, the much older and frailer Palmerston succeeded in reconstructing the previous coalition, minus Aberdeen and the 5th Duke of Newcastle (formerly Lord Lincoln), who had been War Secretary. To the ill-disguised fury of Disraeli, the Conservatives were condemned to continue in opposition, with no likely early prospect of a return to power.

Over the next three years, Derby, isolated in the House of Lords from the main forum of political combat, grew more and more conservative in his outlook. He fiercely opposed any whisper of parliamentary reform, concentrating his energies on ecclesiastical affairs and the protection of the rights of hereditary peers, and strongly discouraging efforts by Disraeli (aided and abetted by Derby's much more liberal eldest son, Edward) to find common cause with the Radicals in harassing the government. Derby still considered the Peelites as the only acceptable source of additional support. He again began to woo Gladstone (who had resigned from the Palmerston government in March 1855), but nothing came of it, and the Peelites were virtually wiped out in the 1857 election, which was a triumph for Palmerston. So far from winning new recruits, Derby nearly lost one, when Palmerston offered his son, Edward, the Colonial secretaryship. Lord Stanley, as he now was, hastened to consult his father, and then declined, explaining in a letter to Disraeli that 'I shall never during my Father's public life, connect myself with a party opposed to his' (Jones, p. 214).

Then, quite unexpectedly, the Palmerston government collapsed, due to the dissastisfaction of its Radical supporters and manouvring by Lord John Russell, still smarting from his displacement as leader of the Whigs. The occasion was the attempted assassination of Napoleon III, in January 1858, by an Italian republican, Felice Orsini, who had plotted his conspiracy in London, where he had acquired the bomb with which he killed many bystanders, but not the Emperor. The French government sent an insultingly provocative note demanding that the British government took steps to prevent a recurrence of the outrage, and Palmerston, normally quick to repulse any foreign interference, meekly introduced the Conspiracy to Murder Bill, which was explicitly designed to meet the French protest. The Radicals, deeply disappointed in Palmerston because of his indifference to Reform, put down a no confidence motion, which was backed by Russell. Derby and Disraeli, sensing that the government was in danger, ordered their troops to vote in favour of the motion, which was carried by 19 votes.

Derby went on to form his second government, taking office on 20 February 1858, with substantially the same personnel as the first, though they were now older and more experienced, and appeared more authoritative. Lord Stanley now became Colonial Secretary, and Peel's younger brother, General Jonathan Peel, served as War Secretary, though none of the leading Peelites responded to Derby's approaches. They passed several important bills, notably the India Act, which took over the government of the sub-continent from the East India Company, following the suppression of the Indian Mutiny, and they supported measures to remove the property qualification for MPs and to allow practising Jews to sit in the Commons. Yet the centrepiece of their legislative programme was a Reform Bill, Derby having finally been convinced that a moderate measure, slightly enlarging the franchise, would forestall the introduction of a much more democratic Bill by his opponents. The gamble did not come off: 40 ultra conservatives, including two ministers who resigned from the Cabinet, declared their opposition, while the Bill did not go nearly far enough to attract much support from the other side of the House. The Bill was sunk, when a hostile motion moved by Lord John Russell, on 1 April 1859, was carried by 330 votes to 291. Derby immediately sought a dissolution, and the Conservatives gained seats in the subsequent general election, but still emerged as a minority, with 306 seats. Before the new Parliament met, the Whigs, Peelites and Radicals came together to form the Liberal Party (see Chapter 13), and on 10 June 1858 defeated the government on a no confidence motion by 323 votes to 310. Derby immediately resigned; his second government had lasted rather longer than the first: one year and 111 days.

There followed eight dispiriting years in opposition, during which his health gradually declined and he appeared increasingly elderly and out of touch. Periodically he thought of retiring from the leadership, but declined to do so, as he saw no generally acceptable candidate for the succession. The only two possibilities were Disraeli and his own son, Edward. Yet the former was widely distrusted, and the latter was regarded as too liberal in his views to be acceptable to the mass of Tory supporters. So he ploughed on, and these years saw a late blossoming of his social conscience. He had always prided himself on being a good landlord, but his sympathies broadened out to include the entire working class of his native Lancashire, when the US Civil War, which cut off cotton supplies from the South, had a devastating effect on employment in the textile industry which dominated the county. Derby threw himself with great vigour into the relief effort, serving as chairman of the Lancashire Relief Committee to which he devoted at least a day a week of his time, contributing generously to its funds and persuading other wealthy aristocrats to do the same.

He had the slenderest hopes of returning to the premiership, but it was the reform issue which created the opportunity for Derby's third and last government. In 1866 Lord John – now Earl – Russell, and Prime Minister for the second time, sought to crown his own career by passing a more radical Bill, but could not carry all his Whig supporters who, as recounted in Chapter 13, joined with the Tories in voting it down. The Queen invited Derby to form a new administration, and this time he accepted without hesitation, though again seeking to enlarge his parliamentary support by recruiting ministers from outside the Tory Party. On this occasion, he targeted the 'Adullamites', the right-wing Liberals who had voted against Russell's Reform bill, but they declined to serve, and Derby formed an entirely Conservative government. It was, however, stronger than its two predecessors, including some promising newcomers, notably Lord Cranborne, a future Prime Minister as the Third Marquess of Salisbury, while Lord Stanley became Foreign Secretary.

He took office on 28 June 1866. There now occurred the most extraordinary transformation in his attitude. Having been a fervent long-time opponent of parliamentary reform, he now decided that it had become imperative to pass a Bill, and moreover that it had to be more radical than Russell's abortive measure if it was to have any hope of settling the issue for the foreseeable future. Russell had proposed reducing the property qualification for voters in borough constituencies from £10 to £7 a year, while his more Liberal supporters wanted to go down to £6. Derby brooded on the question, asking himself whether he should propose £5 or some lesser sum, but finally concluded that the only logical conclusion was household suffrage, that is, that every head of household should have the vote whatever his income. His experience in dealing with the unemployed in Lancashire had convinced him that, so far from being potential revolutionaries they were, on the whole, moderate and reasonable men. Moreover, his friend Lord Malmesbury had concluded that, whereas the better off members of the working class were more likely to be Liberal voters, the really poor tended to be deferential to the wealthy, and were thus an untapped source of Tory support. Lord Cranborne, however, did some rapid calculations, and concluded that if Derby's proposal was implemented, it would give the working class a 2:1 majority in the electorate, and that this would pose an unacceptable risk. Derby then came up with what he regarded as a masterstroke, proposing a plurality of votes for the wealthier and better educated.

Disraeli, who later got the credit for what became the 1867 Reform Act (see Chapter 17), was extremely sceptical at the outset, but hastened to do his master's bidding. He was in charge of the Bill in the Commons, under close direction by Derby until the later stages when the Prime Minister's health began to fail, while Derby himself steered it through the Lords, with assistance from Malmesbury. During the parliamentary passage the plurality proposals were defeated, but Derby determined to persist with the Bill, despite a Cabinet revolt which led to the resignation of Cranborne, the Secretary of State for India, and two other ministers, the Earl of Carnarvon and General Peel. It led to a very large extension of the electorate, from 7 to 16 per cent of the adult population, a far bigger enlargement than the more famous measure of 1832. Derby gave his own summing up at the conclusion of the Lords' debates:

> No doubt we are making a great experiment and 'taking a leap in the dark', but I have the greatest confidence in the sound sense of my fellow countrymen, and I entertain a strong hope that the extended franchise which we are now conferring on them will be the means of placing the institutions of this country on a firmer basis, and that the passing of this measure will tend to increase the loyalty and contentment of a great portion of Her Majesty's subjects; (House of Lords Hansard, 6 August 1867)

With the passage of the Bill concluded, Derby had no thoughts of early retirement, but successively severe attacks of gout gradually weakened him, and the following February he made way for Disraeli, whom he nominated as his successor. He lived on until October 1869, making one last spirited speech in the House of Lords, in June 1869, in defence of his beloved (Anglican) Church of Ireland, which the newly elected Gladstone government was determined to disestablish. He failed, and predicted that this would herald the end of the Union with Ireland. For some 20 years, he had led the Conservative Party, most of the time in opposition, but for rather less than four years, in total, in government, always in a minority. He had been a dignified and usually moderate leader, who had always commanded respect, but it is doubtful whether his long tenure of the leadership did his party much good. He failed to secure a re-union with the Peelites and did little to improve the electoral prospects of his party. The elements that he represented most strongly – the landed interest and the Church of England – were in relative decline, and he failed to make much impact on the rising industrial and middle classes, or the nonconformist churches. Only his belated conversion to parliamentary reform provided the opportunity for extending the Tories' appeal to newly enfranchised sections of the electorate, and it was left to his successors, Disraeli and Salisbury, to reach out to what became an essential element in Conservative electoral success over the next 100 years – the deferential working-class voter.

Works consulted

Robert Blake, 1966, *Disraeli*, London, Eyre & Spottiswoode.

James Chambers, 2004, *Palmerston: The People's Darling*, London, John Murray.

J.B. Conacher, 1968, *The Aberdeen Coalition 1852–1855*, Cambridge, Cambridge University Press.

Valerie Cromwell, 1998, 'Edward George Geoffrey Smith Stanley, 14th Earl of Derby', in Robert Eccelshall and Graham Walker (eds.), *Biographical Dictionary of British Prime Ministers*, London, Routledge.

Angus Hawkins, 2004, Article in *Oxford Dictionary of National Biography*, Oxford University Press.

Christopher Hibbert, 2005, *Disraeli, A Personal History*, Harper Perennial, London.

Wilbur Devereux Jones, 1956, *Lord Derby and Victorian Conservatism*, Blackwell, Oxford.

Robert Stewart, 1971, *The Politics of Protection: Lord Derby and the Protectionist Party 1841–1852*, Cambridge, Cambridge University Press.

15
George Gordon, 4th Earl of Aberdeen – Failure or Scapegoat?

Lord Aberdeen is unusual among Prime Ministers in never having been a Member of the House of Commons. Many other peers became Prime Minister, but nearly all of them had served an earlier apprenticeship in the Lower House. During the past two centuries, only Aberdeen and Lord Rosebery spent their entire political careers in the House of Lords. It is perhaps no accident that they have long been regarded as being among the least successful of British premiers.

George Gordon (later Hamilton-Gordon) was born on 28 January 1784, to a life which was to be repeatedly marked by tragedy. He came from a long line of Scottish aristocrats who had been the largest landowners in Aberdeenshire for several centuries, though his belief that he was a direct descendant of Bertrand de Guerdon, whose fatal arrow had killed Richard the Lionheart at the siege of Chalus in 1199, was probably erroneous. Less fanciful was the literally shotgun marriage contracted by his grandfather, the 3rd Earl. He seduced a blacksmith's daughter, who, when he visited her a second time, produced a loaded pistol and threatened to shoot him unless he married her. The eldest son of this union was Lord Haddo, who at the age of 18 married Charlotte Brand, the sister of a Scottish general. George was the eldest of seven children (one born posthumously) that Haddo fathered before dying, aged 27, in a riding accident. Charlotte soon quarrelled with her father-in-law and took her seven children off to London, where she herself died four years later.

George, aged 11, was now the heir to a large fortune and estate, which his grandfather was busy diminishing by making generous provisions for his many mistresses and illegitimate children. Together with his six siblings, he was now taken into the London household of one of his father's friends. This was no other than Henry Dundas (later Lord Melville), the most powerful politician in Scotland, and a close friend and associate of the Prime Minister, William Pitt, in whose government he was to serve as Home Secretary and War Minister for over a decade. George and his brothers were sent to Harrow School, where he was a contemporary of two other future Prime Ministers, Palmerston and Goderich. At the age of 14, under Scottish law, he was permitted to nominate his own guardians. He chose Dundas and Pitt, and lived alternately with them. 'In a sense', wrote his biographer, 'his whole later political career sprang from those critical years' (Chamberlain, 1983, p. 26). Indeed, it seems improbable that he would have gone into politics at all if it had not been for the strong influence on him of his two guardians. There was no recent political tradition in his family; he had a poor temperament for politics, and strong intellectual and artistic interests which would most likely have led him into different directions if it had not been for these circumstances.

Despite his grandfather's expressed desire that he should be educated in Scotland, George (now known as Lord Haddo) proceeded from Harrow to St. John's College, Cambridge, in 1800, his fees possibly being paid by Pitt.

Here he proved to be a dedicated scholar, immersing himself in Renaissance and classical studies, and falling in with a set of like-minded friends, all with literary ambitions. In August 1801, his grandfather died, and he became the 4th Earl of Aberdeen (in the Scottish peerage), though he was unable to take charge of his estates until his coming of age four years later. He did, however, travel up to Scotland, and was appalled at their run-down condition, and the considerable debts which his grandfather had incurred in providing for his illegitimate progeny.

Like other aristocrats at the time, he left Cambridge without taking a degree, and in 1802 embarked on the Grand Tour, which was made possible by the Peace of Amiens, which provided a break of 14 months in the long-running war with France. Pitt provided him with letters of introduction to many eminent personages, and he dined with Napoleon (who impressed him very much) at Malmaison, and with the widow of Bonnie Prince Charlie, the Young Pretender, in Florence. But the highlights of his journey were his visits to Greece and Constantinople, during which he participated in important archaeological excavations, bought several valuable artefacts which are now in the British Museum, and made extensive notes which he hoped to write up later for publication. He hoped to buy the 'Elgin marbles' from the Parthenon, but found that he had been pre-empted by his fellow Scottish peer. In Constantinople, he accompanied the British ambassador, William Drummond, who became a close friend, in an interview with the Sultan, but formed a very low opinion of the way that the Ottoman Empire was governed. This undoubtedly influenced his later attitude to the recurring 'Eastern question', both as Foreign Secretary and Prime Minister. The war with France having resumed, Aberdeen, now aged 20, returned to England in the summer of 1804, via Venice, Vienna and Berlin. Back in London, he was instrumental in founding the Athenian Society, and subsequently contributed a learned article about Troy, the probable site of which he had visited, for the *Edinburgh Review*. He was to establish a reputation for himself as an authority on antiquity, but was referred to, sarcastically, in a poem by his cousin, Lord Byron (whom he physically strongly resembled) as 'The travell'd thane, Athenian Aberdeen'.

Aberdeen came of age in January 1805, and hastened north to take possession of his estates, and the splendid, if neglected, Palladian mansion, Haddo House, which was his country seat. He immediately set in motion schemes to pay off the accumulated debts, to establish new and improved leases with his tenants, who, with their families included, came to over a thousand, to introduce modern methods of farming, and to renovate and modernize his home. He then repaired to London, where he effectively entered society for the first time, becoming an habitué at the endless series of receptions given by the Duchess of Devonshire, Lady Holland, and the Marquess of Abercorn. The latter, a Tory peer with vast estates in Ireland, held court at Bentley Priory, a mansion some distance from central London, at Stanmore, in Middlesex. He was immediately seen as a highly eligible bachelor, and the Duchess of Gordon marked him out as a likely suitor for her daughter Georgina. But Aberdeen showed no interest, and she was married off instead to the widowed Duke of Bedford, becoming, at the age of 20, stepmother to the young Lord John Russell. Aberdeen set his cap at the Duchess of Devonshire's daughter, Harriet, who played hard to get, and was then mortified when Aberdeen took up with Lady Catherine Hamilton, the beautiful and spirited eldest daughter of Lord Abercorn. They fell deeply in love, and were married a few months later, in July 1805, both aged 21.

Under the influence of Dundas and Pitt, Aberdeen was convinced that he should follow a political career, and Pitt, who resumed the premiership in 1804, promised to recommend him for an English peerage, which would enable him to enter the House of Lords (Scottish peers did not have an automatic right to do so, and were precluded – unlike Irish peers – from standing for the House of Commons). Before Pitt could make good on his promise, however, he died, in January 1806, at the age of 46. Aberdeen, who was very fond of Pitt, was deeply distressed, and not only because he was bereft of the launching pad for his intended career. Nevertheless, he was determined to obtain entry to the House of Lords, and decided to offer himself for election as one of the 16 Scottish representative peers, who were chosen in each Parliament by the whole body of Scottish peers, who then numbered 57. In the 1806 election, the 'Government of all the Talents', led by Lord Grenville, from which the Tories were excluded, put up its own slate of 16 peers. This did not include Aberdeen, who was nevertheless encouraged to run by Dundas, now Lord Melville, and his father-in-law, Lord Abercorn. Aberdeen established himself in Edinburgh, and began energetically canvassing, offering to trade his own votes with several other nominated candidates, and succeeded in coming out in fifteenth place, the only candidate not backed by the government to be elected.

Aged 22, Aberdeen made a far from glorious début in the upper house. The government bill to abolish the slave trade deeply divided the opposition, but Aberdeen decided to support it in his maiden speech. Yet when the time came for him to rise from his place, his nerve failed him, and he left the Chamber. He finally spoke some months later, on the occasion of the installation of the new Tory government, under the Duke of Portland, when he declared his support, and attempted to justify the action of George III in turning out the 'Talents' government, even though it maintained its Commons majority (see Chapter 3). It was a badly delivered speech, and throughout his long career Aberdeen failed to master the art of speaking in the Lords, and always dreaded doing so, though he was apparently able to speak passably well at other venues. Despite this poor effort, Portland offered Aberdeen a minor post in his government, a Lordship either at the Treasury or the Admiralty. Palmerston, a newly elected MP, received a similar offer, and accepted it with alacrity, but

Aberdeen declined, apparently believing it was too junior for somebody of his rank. He hoped, instead, to receive an ambassadorial appointment, but for this too, he was extremely choosy, and had to wait for several years before being made an acceptable offer. He twice turned down the ambassadorship to Russia, and prevaricated over the post of British Minister to Sicily, hoping instead to be offered Constantinople, which was not then available, though he turned it down several years later. Over the next six years, he devoted himself mainly to running his estates, and to his scholarly pursuits, being elected a Fellow of the Royal Society in 1808, and President of the Society of Antiquaries in 1812. Three daughters, on whom he doted, were born in successive years, but in November 1810, the long-awaited son died less than an hour after his birth. His mother, Catherine, was to survive him for just over a year, succumbing to tuberculosis, in February 1812. Aberdeen was totally devastated: he wore mourning for the rest of his life, and transferred his perhaps extravagant devotion to his three daughters, all of whom were, in turn, to follow their mother to their graves before reaching their twentieth birthday.

In 1813, he finally accepted a diplomatic appointment, proposed by his friend, Lord Castlereagh MP, the Foreign Secretary. This was to go to Vienna, to re-establish diplomatic relations, which had been broken off in 1809, and to persuade the Austrians to join Russia and Prussia in a renewed war against Napoleon, following his retreat from Moscow. He had some doubts whether to accept, and did not want to stay away from his daughters (who were left in the care of his sister-in-law, Maria) for more than a short time, but decided to go, at least partly because it had been hinted to him that if he succeeded in his mission an English peerage would surely follow.

Before Aberdeen could reach Austria, the Emperor Francis I had already taken the plunge, and declared war on France. Putting himself at the head of his armies, he had established himself at Teplice, in northern Bohemia, where he had been joined by Tsar Alexander and Frederick William III, the King of Prussia. Aberdeen hastened there, via Berlin and Prague, travelling at full speed, his coach overturning one night, and he suffered from concussion, which he blamed for the recurrent headaches which plagued him for the rest of his life. On arrival, he soon succeeded in ingratiating himself with the Austrian Emperor, and with his Foreign Minister, Prince Metternich, so much so that he was later to be criticized for falling under the spell of this master of intrigue. His own position at the allied camp was awkward, as he was – much to his chagrin – technically junior to two British army officers, Lord Cathcart and Sir Charles Stewart (Castlereagh's half-brother), who were the ambassadors at the Russian and Prussian courts. As the three of them had widely diverging views, it was difficult for any of them to present a coherent view of British policy. However, Aberdeen largely succeeded in preventing the three allied powers from presenting a purely 'continental' peace proposal to Napoleon's unofficial emissary, which ignored British interests in the Low Countries and the Iberian Peninsula, and her maritime interests. Even the document finally agreed was less than totally satisfactory from a British point of view, but Napoleon, still confident of his eventual success, rejected the terms with disdain. Shortly afterwards, in October 1813, the combined armies of Austria, Prussia, Russia and Sweden, who outnumbered the French by two-one, inflicted a comprehensive defeat, in the three-day battle of Leipzig, on Napoleon, who withdrew his forces to the Rhine in great disorder. Aberdeen, who witnessed the aftermath of the battle, was appalled by the extent of the slaughter, writing to his sister-in-law, Maria:

> For three or four miles the ground is covered with bodies of men and horses, many not dead. Wretches wounded unable to crawl, crying for water amidst heaps of putrefying bodies. Their screams are heard at an immense distance, and still ring in my ears... Our victory is most complete. It must be owned that a victory is a fine thing, but one should beat a distance. (Chamberlain, 2004)

Apart from Wellington, Aberdeen was the only British Prime Minister of the nineteenth century to witness war at first hand. This did not make him a pacifist, as some have suggested, but may well account for the pacific approach which he consistently brought to foreign policy issues, in sharp contrast, for example, to Palmerston. Following Napoleon's retreat, the allied powers established themselves at Frankfurt-am-Main, where again peace proposals were drawn up, and communicated to Napoleon through the brother-in-law of the French foreign minister. Aberdeen again did his best to temper the document to take account of British interests, with only partial success. It offered France the prospect of keeping its 'natural' frontiers of the Rhine, the Alps and the Pyrenees, rather than having to withdraw to its pre-war boundaries of 1793. Once again, the over-confident Napoleon turned it down, and the final campaign to overthrow his regime began, with Wellington entering France from the south, and the Austrians, Prussians and Russians from the east. At Christmas 1813, Castlereagh, fed up by the perpetual bickering between the three British ambassadors, hastened to join the three eastern monarchs at their new headquarters at Langres, in the Champagne country, and take personal charge of the negotiations. Aberdeen's last task was to attend the conference at Chatillon-sur-Seine, in the spring of 1814, which was meant to draw up the final peace terms to be imposed on the soon-to-be defeated French. The conference was terminated by a sudden collapse of the French resistance, and the abdication of Napoleon on 11 April 1814, and Aberdeen accompanied Castlereagh to Paris, where he seconded him in negotiating the first Treaty of Paris, which, so they believed, brought the War to an end. Aberdeen declined

Castlereagh's offer to accompany him to the Congress of Vienna, and instead returned to London, carrying with him the first copy of the Treaty. He had been away for nearly a year, more than enough for him, and he desperately wanted to rejoin his daughters, following the death, in January 1814, of his sister-in-law Maria, who had been looking after them. Like her sister, and – later each of the three children – she died from tuberculosis, which also cost the life of her brother, Lord James Hamilton, Abercorn's son and heir, whose death followed soon after.

Aberdeen's debut as a diplomat took place in difficult and frustrating, and even dangerous, circumstances, and on the whole he acquitted himself well. An English viscountcy, which guaranteed him a permanent place in the House of Lords, was duly bestowed on him, providing a firmer basis for his political career. This, however, trod water for more than a decade, as he concentrated his energies on family affairs, his intellectual pursuits and the running of his estates. It was not until 1828, when he was appointed Chancellor of the Duchy of Lancaster in the Duke of Wellington's government, that he again held public office. Muriel Chamberlain, in her definitive biography of Aberdeen, describes the ten months of his diplomatic mission as by far the most important formative influence in his career.

Aberdeen had decided some time earlier that he should marry a second time, partly, at least, to provide an acceptable stepmother for his daughters. He was attracted by Anne Cavendish, a niece of the Duke of Devonshire, but wooed her in a very low-key and spasmodic manner, perhaps because her parents disapproved of the match. He was also paying court to Susan Ryder, the very young daughter of his friend, Lord Harrowby, a leading minister in Lord Liverpool's government, but it was his father-in-law, Lord Abercorn, who acted as matchmaker. He suggested to Aberdeen that he should instead wed his daughter-in-law, Lady Harriet Hamilton, the 23-year-old widow of his only son, who had been left with three young children, including Abercorn's heir, the young James Hamilton. Abercorn thought that Aberdeen would be a most acceptable stepfather to his grandchildren, and that Harriet could perform a similar function for Aberdeen's daughters. Despite the fact that he had once described Harriet to his brother Alexander as 'certainly one of the most stupid persons I have ever met' (Iremonger, 1978, p. 95), Aberdeen fell in with the plan, and they were married in July 1815, a year after the death of Harriet's first husband. To symbolize the union, Aberdeen now hyphenated his surname to Hamilton-Gordon. It was not a happy marriage, though it produced four sons and a daughter (who was to die aged 16). Harriet was intensely jealous of Aberdeen's continued mourning for his first wife, and what she regarded as his excessive devotion to his daughters, one of whom was to die in 1818, aged ten, and another, in 1824, aged 17. She disliked living at Haddo House, and after four years she refused to go there anymore, insisting on renting a house in Brighton, where Aberdeen spent two miserable summers. She shared none of his intellectual interests, and from 1819 onwards they began to spend much of their time apart.

Aberdeen attended the House of Lords fairly regularly, but seldom spoke. He often felt out-of-step with his fellow Tories, and, according to Muriel Chamberlain, had 'a completely cross-bench mind' (1983, p. 184). It might be more apposite to suggest that he was a natural Whig, who had finished up in the wrong party, due to the early influence on him of Pitt and Dundas, which was reinforced by Lord Abercorn, who was a Tory through and through. Despite his unorthodoxy, it seems likely that Aberdeen was invited to join Liverpool's government when it was reshuffled in 1822, perhaps as Under-Secretary to Canning, at the Foreign Office. If so, he turned the offer down, though there is no record of this. When Wellington became Prime Minister, in 1828, however, he became Chancellor of the Duchy of Lancaster, and effectively number two to the Foreign Secretary, the Earl of Dudley, whom he succeeded in this post after six months. Aberdeen was to prove himself an effective administrator and, unlike Dudley, capable of standing up to Wellington when their views differed. This was to be the case over the Eastern question, which was the most important issue to come up during his term of office. The Wellington government had inherited from Lord Goderich's administration an extremely sensitive situation, following the 'accidental' sinking of the Turco-Egyptian fleet, at Navarino, by combined British, French and Russian forces, in October 1827 (see Chapter 8). War was now threatened between Turkey and Russia, and Britain was determined not to be involved in it, but to secure a negotiated end to the War of Greek Independence, which had been raging since 1821. Wellington, whose fear of Russian aggrandizement was great, and who thought that any Greek government would be likely to become a Russian 'satellite', was determined to appease the Turks, and was in favour of a settlement which would secure Greek independence within very restrictive borders, not including Athens, and its surrounding area. Aberdeen, much more sympathetic to the Greek cause and highly critical of Ottoman rule, sought a more generous territorial settlement, and with aid of events on the ground, largely had his way, though throughout he treated Wellington's views with great respect and deference. During his period as Foreign Secretary, the last of his three daughters, by Catherine, Alice, with whom he had spent two long periods in the south of France in a desperate effort to improve her health, died in his arms, in April 1829, at the age of 19. Utterly desolate, he shut himself away in his office for several days, and refused to attend to any business.

Tragedy had not yet finished with Aberdeen. His second wife, Harriet, was to die in August 1833, and he greatly missed her despite their many differences, while their daughter, Frances, was to follow her mother to her grave only eight months later, aged 15. Aberdeen's brother Charles, died of a cerebral haemorrhage the following year, and all but one of his six younger siblings were to pre-decease him, including notably, his brother Alexander, Wellington's ADC, who had been killed at Waterloo, aged 29.

Aberdeen went into opposition, when Wellington's government resigned in November 1830, but returned, briefly, to office, in December 1834, as War and Colonial Secretary in Sir Robert Peel's first government, which lasted barely four months. In 1841, when Peel formed his second government, he was again appointed Foreign Secretary. Personally close to Peel, he was left a relatively free hand, though the Prime Minister occasionally intervened to insist on a rather firmer stance, in relations with France, in particular. Aberdeen's predecessor, Palmerston, had left him with a difficult hand to play, with dangerously deteriorating relations with both France and the United States, and with disastrous wars in progress against both China and Afghanistan. The Afghan War soon came to an end with an inglorious British retreat, and the 'First Opium War' with China was terminated by the Treaty of Nanking, in August 1842, which ceded Hong Kong to the British, an annexation about which Aberdeen was less than enthusiastic.

Aberdeen's over-riding objective was to prevent war with either France or the United States, and, indeed, to seek to turn these rival powers into friends and allies. In 1842, he despatched Lord Ashburton to Washington in a serious attempt to settle festering boundary disputes which had poisoned relations between the two countries. A treaty signed later that year incorporated an adjustment of the boundary between Canada and the state of Maine, which represented a reasonable, and enduring, compromise between the two countries' claims. A further treaty signed, in 1846, in the dying days of the Peel government, settled the boundary between Canada and the Oregon territory, largely in favour of the United States, though it did ensure British control of Vancouver island. Relations with France were more difficult, with war narrowly avoided in crises over Morocco and Tahiti. Yet Aberdeen, drawing on his friendship with François Guizot, a former French ambassador to London, who was now Prime Minister, forged the first *entente cordiale* (a phrase coined by Aberdeen) with France, cemented by a visit by Victoria and Albert to the court of Louis Philippe, in the autumn of 1843. The *entente* did not long survive the end of the Peel government, and the return of Palmerston to the Foreign Office. It collapsed, in September 1846, with the Spanish Marriages affair (see Chapter 13), when a son of Louis Philippe married the Spanish Queen's sister, and heir presumptive, despite earlier assurances to the British government (which had favoured the candidature of Prince Leopold of Coburg, a cousin of Prince Albert).

When Peel first announced his intention of repealing the Corn Laws, in November 1845, Aberdeen was one of only three cabinet ministers who supported him. He remained a very close and loyal supporter of Peel's, over the next five years, and when his chief died, in a riding accident, in July 1850, he became the acknowledged leader of the Peelites, with Sir James Graham heading the now greatly reduced contingent in the Commons. Aberdeen regarded himself as a 'Liberal Conservative', and still wished to see the Conservative party reunited, but not at any cost. He, together with Gladstone, was repeatedly canvassed by Lord Stanley (later Derby), but they were unwilling to join up unless the Protectionists specifically renounced any intention to reimpose the Corn Laws. Aberdeen gradually came to the conclusion that it would be better to fuse with the Whigs, but was adamant that he would not serve in any coalition government in which Palmerston was restored to the Foreign Secretaryship. This was not only because he coveted the post for himself, but because he regarded the highly belligerent Irish peer as likely to draw the country into unnecessary wars – a prescient judgement – as it turned out. When the minority Derby government was defeated over Disraeli's budget proposals, in December 1852, it soon became clear that it would be succeeded by a coalition of Whigs and Peelites, with parliamentary support from the Radicals and 'the Irish brigade'. As there were some 270 Whigs, and only 30 Peelites, in the Commons, it might have been expected that the Whig leader, Lord John Russell, would resume the premiership. Yet Russell had made himself unpopular in his own party, and particularly among the Irish, through having brought in the Ecclesiastical Titles Act, of 1850 – an anti-Catholic measure – and so Aberdeen was chosen instead. Very popular with his fellow politicians, as well as at Court, he was seen as a kind, patient and conciliatory man, who could be expected to do a good job in holding together a government which included several awkward individuals with mutually conflicting views. Already nearly 69, he accepted in the belief that he would serve for only a short time, and would relinquish the premiership to Russell once the government was established, and when Russell's unpopularity, which he judged was only a passing mood, began to fade.

Aberdeen's cabinet, which consisted of six Peelites, six Whigs and one Radical, was initially seen as a very strong and talented team. It included Russell, as Foreign Secretary and Leader of the Commons, Gladstone as Chancellor of the Exchequer, Palmerston as Home Secretary, Sir James Graham as First Lord of the Admiralty and Sir George Grey as Colonial Secretary. Its balance was soon upset, however, when Russell decided to give up the Foreign Secretaryship after less than two months, and was succeeded by the Earl of Clarendon. Nevertheless, it made an impressive start. Gladstone's first budget, in April 1852, which he presented in a much-admired five-hour speech, set the tone for a reforming government, and measures for overhauling the Indian administration, penal reform and the admission of Jews to the House of Commons, were soon carried, though the last measure was overthrown by the Lords. A thorough-going overhaul of the educational system was projected, and Russell drew up a Reform bill, but these were pre-empted by the outbreak of the Crimean War, which shortly brought Aberdeen's administration to a humiliating end.

The origins of the Crimean War have already been briefly sketched in Chapter 13. It was originally provoked by the desire of the newly crowned French Emperor, Napoleon III, to enhance French influence in the Near East. He strongly backed the claims of Catholic monks to extend their control over the 'Holy Places' in Turkish-controlled Palestine, which led the Russian Tsar, Nicholas I, to intervene on behalf of their Orthodox rivals, and indeed to insist that he should be recognized as the guarantor of the rights of Orthodox Christians throughout the Ottoman Empire. To reinforce his claim, he sent his troops into the two principalities of Wallachia and Moldavia (essentially modern Romania), which were under Turkish suzerainty, and refused to withdraw them until his demands were met. The British reaction to the clear threat of war between Russia and Turkey was bedevilled by sharp disagreements within the cabinet. Aberdeen strongly favoured efforts to seek a diplomatic solution to the crisis, but was highly critical of the Turks, and believed that, in the last resort, they should be pressured to concede to Nicholas's demands. Palmerston, the most vigorous and assertive of his ministers, by contrast, was determined to resist the Russians at all cost, and believed that they could be forced to back down by making it clear that Britain, along with France, would join in on Turkey's side if war broke out. In Muriel Chamberlain's view: 'Either policy, carried through consistently, might have brought success. What was to prove fatal was the mixing of the two' (Chamberlain, 1983, p. 478).

Public opinion, still inflamed against Russia by its role in suppressing the Hungarian revolution of 1848, was largely on Palmerston's side, and Aberdeen's own position within the cabinet was a weak one. The Turks, confident that Britain and France would come to their aid, declared war on Russia, in October 1853, after it had refused to withdraw from the two principalities. Aberdeen still hoped to keep Britain out of the war, but his position became untenable when a Turkish naval squadron was sunk by a Russian fleet at Sinope, in the Black Sea, and he was forced to agree to the dispatch of a British fleet, and the sending of an ultimatum to the Russians to withdraw to their base at Sebastopol, in the Crimea. When the Russians declined to do so, Britain and France declared war on 28 March 1854. It would have been far better for Aberdeen, who had no appetite – or aptitude – to be a war leader, to have resigned at this stage, but he still hoped to prevent the actual outbreak of hostilities, particularly after Russia, under pressure from neutral Austria, agreed to hand over control of the two principalities. But Britain's new French allies, and a majority of the cabinet led by Palmerston, were adamant that a military campaign should be launched against the Russians, and after considering other possibilities, they settled on an attack on Sebastopol. Aberdeen argued, in vain, that a naval bombardment of the port would suffice to deter the Tsar from any further aggressive actions against the Turks. Accordingly, in September 1854, some 64,000 allied troops landed in the northern Crimea, in the confident expectation that a quick march on Sebastopol would soon settle the issue. Three bloody battles were fought – at Alma, Balaklava and Inkerman – over the next two months, and the allied troops then became bogged down outside the gates of the fortified city, as the Russian winter set in.

Meanwhile, the invention of the telegraph, and the presence in the war zone of newspaper correspondents, notably W.H. Russell, of *The Times,* enabled the British public to read – as they never had before – first-hand accounts of the horrors of war. The effect was comparable to that on US viewers of the television coverage of the Vietnam War a century later. They learnt of appalling administrative confusion, the absence of effective equipment, winter clothing and adequate medical attention for the wounded troops, and of serious strategic and tactical errors by the British and French commanders. The government was subjected to a barrage of criticism, in which the Tory leader, Lord Derby, played a leading role, making a series of highly effective speeches in the House of Lords. Aberdeen, who had never overcome his deficiencies as a speaker in the upper house, was pathetically incapable of mounting an effective defence. The Radicals joined with the Tories in attacking the government, and one of their number, John Arthur Roebuck, the MP for Sheffield, tabled a motion calling for a committee of enquiry into the state of the army before Sebastopol. At this point, Lord John Russell, who had retained the post of Leader of the Commons, decided to abandon ship, and resigned from the government, rather than defend its position in the ensuing debate. The motion was carried by a majority of 157, leaving Aberdeen no option but resignation. He had served for two years and 42 days, and the government, which had begun with so much promise, collapsed in ignominy.

Aberdeen's reputation was in tatters, and so it remained until, and long after, his death, aged 76, in 1860. Other ministers, particularly Palmerston, were more to blame for the British involvement in the Crimean War, while the responsibility for the lack of preparation of the British army lay primarily on other shoulders – those of its leaders over the preceding decades – not least the Duke of Wellington, who had been Commander-in-Chief for 10 years up to 1852. Yet Aberdeen was a convenient scapegoat, and very few of his colleagues rallied to his defence. Indeed, it soon became the norm to assume that he had performed inadequately throughout his career, and his achievements both as a diplomat and during his two terms as Foreign Secretary were consistently undervalued. Aberdeen was sadly aware of this, but felt he had nothing to be ashamed of, and was confident that he would be exonerated by posterity. He had carefully preserved and filed correspondence covering the whole of his career, and believed that in the hands of a skilled biographer the record would be set straight. He entrusted the task to his youngest son, Arthur Gordon, later Lord

Stanmore. Yet, because Arthur was still young and relatively inexperienced, he appointed two prominent politicians (and former ministerial colleagues) as his literary executors, with the right of veto. One of these was Sir James Graham, who died soon after him. The other was William Gladstone, who, it must be said, grossly abused the trust which Aberdeen had placed in him. Gladstone prided himself on his reputation as a reformer; Arthur's proposed text revealed (correctly) that, within the cabinet, he had strongly resisted proposals for parliamentary reform, both in 1852 and 1857, and Gladstone, on whom Arthur Gordon's own political prospects depended, refused to allow his biography to appear. It was only in 1893 that he was able to bring out a much attenuated version in a popular series of short lives of Victorian Prime Ministers, which did little to restore his father's reputation.

Nor did Aberdeen have any better luck with Lady Frances Balfour, the granddaughter of his young protégé, the Duke of Argyll, who published a two-volume life, based on random selections from his correspondence, in 1922 – a very slipshod affair. It was only in 1982, that a full-length biography appeared that did justice both to Aberdeen's achievements and his shortcomings. Muriel Chamberlain's life, one of the very best biographies of Nineteenth-century premiers yet to appear, shows not a great man, and certainly not a great prime minister, but an able, conscientious and wise man, who could fairly claim, like Othello, to have done some service to the state, even though he was temperamentally ill-fitted for politics. Chamberlain concludes her study by mentioning that, ten years after his death, some of Aberdeen's admirers erected a plaque in Westminster Abbey, comparing him to Aristides the Just. Aristides, she explains, 'stood as the type of the good man, who was not also a good politician'.

Works consulted

Muriel Chamberlain, 1983, *Lord Aberdeen*, London, Longman.
Muriel Chamberlain, 2004, Article in *Oxford Dictionary of National Biography*.
J.B. Conacher, 1968, *The Aberdeen Coalition 1852–1855*, Cambridge, Cambridge University Press.
Lucille Iremonger, 1978, *Lord Aberdeen*, London, Collins.
Lucille Iremonger, 1970, *The Fiery Chariot*, London, Secker & Warburg.

16

Henry John Temple, 3rd Viscount Palmerston – Master Diplomat or Playground Bully?

With the apparent exception of Disraeli, Lord Palmerston was the most colourful of nineteenth-century Prime Ministers, and the first to build up a mass political following. A man of enormous vitality, he drove himself extremely hard, working long hours, yet still finding time to indulge his large gastronomic and sexual appetites until almost the end of his long life. An Irish peer, he spent the whole of his long political career (58 years) in the House of Commons. He was born 20 October 8, 1784, Henry John Temple (known as Harry), the eldest of four children of the 2nd Viscount Palmerston, and his second wife, Mary Mee, the daughter of a wealthy Dublin merchant.

The second Viscount (who claimed descent from Lady Godiva) possessed extensive estates in both Ireland and England, including the Palladian mansion of Broadlands, in Hampshire, which later passed into the hands of the Mountbatten family. Pleasure-loving, but highly cultivated, he sat as an MP for 40 years without making much impact. He was a Whig and friend of Charles James Fox, but defected to the Younger Pitt, in the wake of the French Revolution, of which he was a partial witness when, in 1792–4, he took his young family off on a twoyear trip to the continent, while his London house was enlarged and renovated. When they reached Paris, in August 1792, the 2nd Lord Palmerston and his wife were received at the Tuileries Palace by Louis XVI and Marie Antoinette in one of their last audiences before the palace was stormed by revolutionary troops and the royal couple was carted off to prison. Sensing the danger, Lady Palmerston insisted that they should leave Paris immediately, and take the road to Switzerland. Their party left in four coaches, in the first of which the seven-year-old Harry travelled with his parents; the younger children followed in three other coaches with a bevy of servants. The first coach arrived at Charenton, some three miles down the road, when it was realized that the other three coaches had not been following them. They had been stopped, and the occupants arrested, by a local revolutionary committee, who submitted them to a frightening interrogation. They were only released through the intervention of a sympathetic militia commander, and reached Charenton after several hours' delay. The party then proceeded at full speed to Switzerland, where they were happy to relax in the company of Edward Gibbon at his beautiful villa at Lausanne. They then went on to Naples where they spent the ensuing two winters, as part of large group of aristocratic English friends centred round the elderly British ambassador, Sir William Hamilton, and his young wife Emma, shortly to succumb to the fatal attractions of Lord Nelson.

When Harry returned to England, shortly before his tenth birthday, in October 1794, he spoke excellent French and Italian, which was to be a major asset in his future career. Soon afterwards, he was enrolled at Harrow School, then the most fashionable choice for aristocrats, temporarily having put Eton in the shade. Coming from a happy family background, clever, good-humoured, handsome, and excelling at games and in his studies, he was popular both with the masters and his fellow pupils. His housemaster, Dr Bromley, described him as 'a most charming boy and very quick at his books', while his 'fag', Augustus Clifford, recalled in old age, when he was a retired Rear-Admiral, that 'he was reckoned the best-tempered and most plucky boy in the school, as well as a young man of great promise' (Chambers, 2004, pp. 19–20). Harry's father withdrew him from the school at the age of 16, believing that it had already taught him all it could, and proposed to send him to a university to prepare for a career in diplomacy. Yet he was too young to go to Cambridge – his first choice – and he was sent instead to Edinburgh, at that time a more distinguished centre of learning. He spent three fruitful years there, studying a wide range of subjects, and was particularly influenced by the lectures on political economy given by his tutor, Dugald Stewart, the biographer of Adam Smith, the author of *The Wealth of Nations*, whose free trade views he strongly reflected. He was an assiduous student, and showed great self-discipline, abstaining from the riotous drinking habits of most of the other aristocratic students. He led an active social life but took no part in the debates of the Speculative Society (the equivalent of the Oxford and Cambridge Union societies), a remarkable omission, as it was to be a training ground for all of the other distinguished future statesmen who passed through the university at this period. Generally, however, Palmerston kept his views – if he had any – on current political issues to himself. Perhaps he was inhibited by being a nominal Tory in a generally Whiggish *ambience*, but – more likely – he had yet to develop a taste for politics.

When he had been at Edinburgh for nearly two years, in April 1802, his father died suddenly of cancer, aged 62. Devoted to both his parents, Harry took his loss very hard and also that of his mother, who died three years later, at the age of 50. At the age of 17, he inherited both the title and a sizeable amount of debt from his father, and two guardians, the Earls of Malmesbury and Chichester, were appointed to look after him. The former, a distinguished ambassador, and close associate of the Younger Pitt, guided Harry's early career path, ensuring that he enrolled, as his father had intended, at St. John's College, Cambridge, to complete his studies. Before going up, he returned to Edinburgh for a third year, and then made a tour of the Scottish Highlands and Wales, where he fell in love for the first time. Apart from the fact that she was a redhead, little is known of the affair. At Cambridge, where he got to know scions of all the main political families, he was – as a nobleman – not supposed to take any examinations, being assured an honorary MA at the end of his course. Yet he insisted on taking them, obtaining first class results in each of his three years there, from 1803–1806. He led a very active social life, having numerous affairs, but his favourite pursuits were riding and hunting. In the face of the threatened French invasion, in 1805, he joined the local militia in Hampshire, as a Lieutenant Colonel. Under Malmesbury's influence, he also became more interested in politics, and when Pitt, who was one of the two MPs for Cambridge University, died in January 1806, he was pressed by Malmesbury, and by his college tutor, to offer himself as the Tory candidate in the ensuing by-election. He was 21, and had only just ceased to be an undergraduate, but had some hopes of success as the Whig vote was split. Both his opponents were recent Cambridge men, and only a little older than himself, but both were already MPs, anxious to exchange their 'pocket' boroughs for the more prestigious Cambridge University seat. The official Whig candidate was Lord Henry Petty, aged 25, who had just become Chancellor of the Exchequer in the 'Government of all the Talents', while the Radical candidate was Viscount Althorp, aged 24, son of Earl Spencer, who was Home Secretary in the new government. Althorp's chances were discounted, and it was generally reckoned (including by Lord Byron, then a Cambridge undergraduate, who wrote a mocking poem on the subject) that the contest would be between Petty and Palmerston. In the event, Palmerston was pushed into third place, the 600 or so Cambridge graduates who participated dividing their votes as follows:

Petty	331
Althorp	145
Palmerston	128

Lord Malmesbury lost no time in seeking another seat for Palmerston to fight at the general election which followed later in the year, and hit on the constituency of Horsham, supposedly in the gift of Viscountess Irwin, to whom Palmerston paid £1,500, plus the promise of an extra £3,500 if he was elected. Much to Palmerston's (and the Viscountess's) consternation, however, another local landowner, the Duke of Norfolk – a leading Whig – moved in and presented two candidates of his own, who finished up winning more votes than the two Tories. The returning officer refused to discriminate between two local grandees, and declared all four candidates elected, leaving it to the (now Whig dominated) House of Commons to decide to whom to award the seats. So it was back to square one for Palmerston, but the indomitable Malmesbury quickly found him another pocket borough, Newport, Isle of Wight, for which he was returned seven months later, in the 1807 general election, on condition that he paid £4,000 and promised never to set foot in the constituency. At the same time, Palmerston had another go at Cambridge, where – this time – he lost by only three votes, after honourably insisting that his supporters (each of whom had two votes) should not renege on a mutual agreement with his fellow Tory candidate not to 'plump' their votes.

So – after an unexpectedly bumpy ride – Palmerston became an MP, at the age of 22. He had already become a junior member of the Duke of Portland's government, having been appointed a month earlier as a Lord of the

Admiralty. He was to continue in this post – the duties of which were fairly nominal – for over two years, until October 1809, when the Duke retired, and Spencer Perceval was appointed in his place. The new Premier astonished Palmerston by offering him the post of Chancellor of the Exchequer – not such an important post as it later became, as the Prime Minister's duties as First Lord of the Treasury were still considerable – but still a very great promotion. Palmerston turned it down – not through lack of ambition, but through fear of tripping up in a post for which he had few qualifications, and probably remembering that the young Lord Henry Petty's short term in that office a few years earlier had badly damaged his reputation. Instead, he accepted the post of War Secretary, outside the Cabinet, in the belief – backed by Malmesbury – that if he performed well he would 'soon' win more merited promotion. Had he known how long he would stay in this post – over 18 years – it is doubtful if he would have accepted it. He was not the minister primarily responsible for defence – that was the Secretary of State for War and the Colonies, currently Lord Liverpool – who was his departmental superior. Palmerston's role, according to his latest biographer, was to act as 'the government's auditor' – a tedious and time-consuming job, which Palmerston carried out with heroic thoroughness, poring over some '40,000 regimental accounts in arrears, some of them dating back as far as the end of the War of American Independence in 1783' (Chambers, p. 62). Palmerston was soon seen as a first-class administrator, but his parliamentary performances were very variable. Highly authoritative when he kept to his script, he was ponderous and stilted when he had to ad lib. He also exhibited immense will-power, insisting on having his way in dealings with colleagues, and fighting a successful battle to establish the point that, as a civilian minister, he was senior to the Commander-in-Chief, who for much of the time was no other than the prickly Duke of York, the favourite son of George III.

Palmerston had been seen for several years as a highly eligible bachelor, but had skillfully avoided committing himself, though he continued be a great social success with the ladies, some respectable, others rather less so. He was soon dubbed 'Lord Cupid', but fell deeply in love with Lady Emily Cowper (formerly Lamb), sister to William Lamb (later Lord Melbourne), and a flighty society beauty. They had become lovers probably as early as 1809, and while Emily's first son, born in 1805, was almost certainly sired by Earl Cowper, her boring, drunken and neglectful husband, nobody doubted that Palmerston was the father of her three later children, one of whom was stillborn. Despite their mutual devotion, their association was by no means an exclusive one. In 1816, Palmerston fathered another child on a Mrs Emma Murray, whom he had set up in a flat in Piccadilly. He was called Henry John Temple Murray. Palmerston had earlier conducted simultaneous affairs with another society beauty, Lady Jersey, and probably also with Princess Lieven, the highly promiscuous wife of the Russian ambassador. Emily openly flaunted other lovers, including an Italian count, who for four years vied publicly with Palmerston for her affections, but the issue was finally decided in Palmerston's favour in 1818, when he survived an assassination attempt by a deranged ex-soldier, with a grievance. Palmerston suffered only superficial wounds, and taking pity on his penniless assailant, paid for the services of a lawyer to defend him in his trial. Clearly mad, he escaped the death penalty, but was committed to Bedlam 'during His Majesty's pleasure'.

When Spencer Perceval was assassinated, in 1812, he was succeeded as Prime Minister by the Earl of Liverpool, whose place as Secretary for War and Colonies was taken by Earl Bathurst, who remained Palmerston's superior throughout the 15 years of Liverpool's premiership. Palmerston was unlucky not to be promoted during all this time, but his relations with the Prime Minister were not good. His views were more liberal, and during the period, roughly between 1815 and 1822, when the government imposed a range of repressive and reactionary measures, he kept his head down, and refrained from supporting them in public. Also, on the divisive issue of Catholic emancipation, he took the pro-Catholic side, which did not commend him to the stoutly Protestant Prime Minister. In 1822, Liverpool tried to get rid of Palmerston, by offering him successively, an English peerage coupled with an appointment as Commissioner of Woods and Forests, and then the glittering post of Governor-General of India, but Palmerston declined, and chose to remain in his relatively junior government post. Yet he was not happy in this role; his former genial self became more and more abrasive, and he spared neither his ministerial colleagues nor his officials in his constant stream of acerbic remarks. The former 'Lord Cupid' became known as 'Lord Pumicestone'. His private life too did not give him much pleasure: possibly tiring of Emily's constant infidelities, he twice proposed marriage in 1823 and 1825, to Lady Georgiana Fane, the younger sister of Lady Jersey. Not willing to tie herself to one of her sister's castoffs, she turned him down both times. Then, in 1826, the more right-wing and anti-Catholic members of the government, with Liverpool's scarcely concealed connivance, intrigued to deprive him of his parliamentary seat. This was at Cambridge University, where Palmerston had finally succeeded in getting elected in 1811, and which he had represented ever since. The Tories nominated two new candidates, both fervent anti-Catholics, for the seats at the general election that year, and depended on the large number of clergymen who were Cambridge graduates to vote against Palmerston, whom they labelled a 'Papist'. Palmerston was only saved from imminent defeat by the decision of the Whigs not to put up any candidates of their own, and indeed instructed their supporters to vote for Palmerston. He survived, and may well have concluded that, as most of his best friends were Whigs, and his mistresses the wives or daughters of Whigs, he was perhaps in the wrong party. There were, however, other 'Liberal

Tories', including Canning, who had become Foreign Secretary and leader of the Commons in 1822, and for whom Palmerston felt a growing affinity.

When Canning succeeded Liverpool as Prime Minister, in 1827, he renewed the offer of the Indian Governor-Generalship, which Palmerston again declined, but then appointed him to the cabinet, retaining the post of War Secretary, and he was also appointed as acting Commander-in-Chief, following the death of the Duke of York. When Canning died four months later, the new Prime Minister, Viscount Goderich, wanted to appoint Palmerston as Chancellor of the Exchequer, but George IV objected, and Palmerston remained at the War Office, and carried on when the Duke of Wellington succeeded Goderich after another four months. Yet, in May 1828, when the 'Canningite' ministers resigned (see Chapter 9), Palmerston quit with them, and went into opposition. Now, for the first time, he had the opportunity to shine in the House of Commons. Instead of speaking on 'dry' subjects, such as the purchase of military supplies or the details of army organization, he was able to let his imagination fly, and he made a series of masterly orations criticizing the foreign policy of the Wellington government, castigating it for its failure to stand up for Greece in its struggle against Turkey and for its appeasement of the Miguelite regime in Portugal, which had temporarily overthrown the more liberal administration of Queen Maria. Palmerston's speeches were warmly received by the Whigs, but were heard in stony silence by Tory MPs. He was the first politician to make a practice of sending his speeches to the newspapers in advance, which greatly extended his audience. Normally they read far better in the papers than they sounded, for Palmerston's delivery was often poor, and his reputation in the country became far higher than in the Commons.

When, in November 1830, Wellington's government was defeated, in a division in which the Canningites joined with the Whigs, it was no great surprise that the incoming Whig Prime Minister, Lord Grey, made Palmerston his Foreign Secretary. He was not the first choice – this was Lord Henry Petty (now the Marquess of Lansdowne), his former rival for the Cambridge University seat. But Lansdowne declined, advising Grey to appoint Palmerston, whose claims were also strongly pressed by Princess Lieven, now an intimate friend of Grey's.

He was now 46, and could be seen as a 'late developer' in politics. But, having belatedly arrived in the front rank he remained there, for the next three and a half decades, serving three times as Foreign Secretary, once as Home Secretary and twice as Prime Minister, dying in office two days short of his eighty-first birthday, just after having been triumphantly re-elected. He has the all-time record for service as a minister – 48 years, a total unlikely ever to be exceeded. Having been among the most liberal Tories, Palmerston soon showed himself to be among the most conservative Whigs. Only a lukewarm supporter of the Reform Bill, he was one of the most strenuous advocates of compromise within the government, when it ran into fierce opposition from the House of Lords. When compromise failed, however, and he sensed that public opinion was overwhelmingly in favour of the passage of the Bill, he switched his position, and formally proposed in the cabinet that the King should be pressed to create enough new peers to assure its passage. Throughout his subsequent career, Palmerston was careful to keep public opinion on his side, and seldom failed to modify his policies if they encountered widespread opposition. Palmerston's support for Reform, however moderate, cost him his seat at Cambridge University in the 1831 general election, in the face of strong Tory opponents, who denounced him as a turncoat. He quickly returned to Parliament for a pocket borough (Bletchingly) in Surrey, but when this seat was abolished by the Reform Bill, switched to the South Hampshire constituency, which included his own country seat, at Broadlands. (He was to lose this constituency three years later, but then transferred to Tiverton, which he held for the remainder of his long life).

As Foreign Secretary, Palmerston soon revealed himself to be a worthy successor to two great predecessors – in Castlereagh and Canning. Like them, he vigorously pursued what he regarded as British interests, and set himself to counter the influence of the three 'Holy Alliance' powers, Russia, Austria and Prussia, who were bent on restoring absolutist rule throughout the European continent. By contrast, Palmerston strongly backed liberal or nationalist movements in Spain, Portugal and Greece. His attitude to France was equivocal, seeing her as a potential rival and military and naval threat, but also, on occasion as a useful ally, and believing that, under the Orleanist monarchy, she had much in common with Britain as a constitutional monarchy based on parliamentary institutions. Conversely, though he feared Russian expansionism, he was on occasion perfectly prepared to co-operate with the Tsar's government in curbing French pretensions. He famously justified his attitude in a speech in the House of Commons, in March 1848, declaring: 'We have no eternal allies and we have no perpetual enemies. Our interests are eternal and perpetual, and those interests it is our duty to follow' (Hansard, 1 March 1848).

His first challenge was to chair the London conference, attended by Holland and the five great powers of Europe – Britain, France, Austria, Prussia and Russia – to seek a settlement, following the Belgian rebellion against Dutch rule in 1830. Palmerston showed himself a master of diplomacy and intrigue, playing on the hopes and fears of all the participants, with whom he constantly played hot and cold, in order to achieve his own objects. These were to prevent a French takeover of Belgium, to avert a Dutch reconquest of the territory, and to prevent the three eastern powers from intervening on behalf of the Dutch King. He succeeded in all these objectives, by a judicious mixture of promises and threats. When the Belgian Parliament chose Louis Philippe's younger son, the Duc de Nemours, as their King, he put enormous pressure, with a none too subtle threat of war, on his father to withdraw the nomination, and he then successfully pushed a British nominee, Leopold of Saxe-Coburg, the widower of the former heiress to the British throne, Princess Charlotte. The French were appeased by the marriage of Leopold to Louis Philippe's daughter, Louise-Marie. The Dutch anger was then placated by compelling the Belgians to withdraw from the Grand Duchy of Luxembourg and the eastern part of Limburg province, which were restored to the Dutch king. It took nine years for Palmerston to achieve a generally acceptable settlement, but when he did so it was almost universally applauded as a diplomatic triumph – perhaps the greatest achievement of his whole career. The Treaty of London, finally signed in 1839, established the Kingdom of Belgium as 'an independent and perpetually neutral state', under the collective guarantee of Britain, France, Austria, Prussia and Russia. It was Germany's breach of this guarantee, in 1914, which brought Britain into the First World War, or, at least, was the justification claimed by the British government at the time.

Palmerston was also successful in preventing the Holy Alliance powers from intervening in the Iberian Peninsula. In both countries the relatively liberal legitimate monarchs – Isabella II in Spain and Maria de Gloria in Portugal – were challenged by male pretenders who wished to restore authoritarian rule. Palmerston persuaded the two governments to join with Britain and France in the Quadruple Alliance, of 1834, which successfully prevented any foreign intervention on behalf of the rebellious claimants. In 1834, Earl Grey, who had insisted on being kept fully informed of Palmerston's activities, resigned and was succeeded by Lord Melbourne, who tended to leave him to his own devices. This was partly because he was lazy, but also because he was chary of obstructing his sister Emily's lover. Lord Cowper died in 1837, and Palmerston, immediately proposed to her. They were finally married two years later, and still appeared a very handsome and youthful-looking couple, though he was 55, and she, 52. The snobbish Melbourne felt that Emily, the widow of an Earl, was lowering herself by marrying a mere Viscount (and an Irish one at that), but acquiesced in the match, and was now even less inclined to interfere with his brother-in-law's decisions, much to the chagrin of other cabinet ministers, who regarded the Foreign Secretary as a dangerous law unto himself.

Within the Foreign Office, Palmerston proved more forceful and more imperious than any of his predecessors. He issued exemplarily clear instructions to all his subordinates and expected them to be carried out with the utmost diligence. Working exceptionally long hours himself, he required his officials, who had grown used to 'knocking off' at teatime, to remain in the Office until late in the evenings, playing havoc with their social lives. Chronically unpunctual himself, he cheerfully turned up late at royal functions, and thought nothing of keeping such important visitors as the French ambassador, Talleyrand, waiting for hours before he condescended to see them.

It was not surprising that he was highly unpopular with his staff, and the only colleagues whom he treated with any pretence of equality were his ambassadors in Paris, Vienna, St.Petersburg and Constantinople, all of whom came from the highest social circles. Talleyrand had considerable respect for Palmerston, writing in his memoirs, that he 'is certainly one of the most able, if not the most able, man of business that I have met in my career'. However, he added:

> One feature in his character dissipates all these advantages, and prevents him, in my opinion, from ranking as a real statesman. He feels passionately about public affairs, and to the point of sacrificing the most important interests to his resentments. Nearly every political question resolves itself into a personal question in his eyes, and in appearing to defend the interests of his country, it is really the interests of his hate and vengeance that he satisfies. (Ridley, pp. 120–1)

The wily French diplomat may just have been lamenting that Palmerston's cynicism was not equal to his own, but his criticism – though exaggerated – was, perhaps, not all that far from the mark.

There was a short break in Palmerston's foreign secretaryship in November 1834, when Melbourne's government was dismissed by William IV, but he was back five months later when Melbourne returned to office, and – if anything – proved even more independent than before. He also grew more reckless, unjustifiably – in the eyes of many of his colleagues – risking war with both the United States and France, and actually getting into wars with China and Afghanistan. In the words of one biographer, 'He tried to pursue the policy which is now known as "brinkmanship" by going as far as he could with impunity, but no further' (Ridley, p. 96).

The gravest risks that he ran were with France, particularly over the affair of Mehemet Ali. An Albanian adventurer, who became the Ottoman Sultan's viceroy in Egypt, in 1805, he showed great military ability, and built up the strength of the Egyptian forces to such an extent that he effectively became independent of his Ottoman overlords. In 1833, he invaded Syria, and the Sultan was forced to cede the province to him. In 1839, the Sultan unwisely resumed the war, and Mehemet Ali's son Ibrahim decisively defeated the Ottoman Army at the Battle of Nezib. At this point, Sultan Mahmud II died, and his successor – the youthful Abdul Mecid I, fearing that Mehemet Ali would advance on Constantinople and take over the whole empire – appealed to the European great powers for assistance. The French refused any help, and – anxious to expand their own influence in the Middle East and North Africa – actively encouraged Mehemet Ali. Palmerston, however, took the lead, and resolved not only that Mehemet Ali should be prevented from taking Constantinople, but should be forced to give up Syria, and retire back to Egypt. He signed a treaty with Austria, Russia and Prussia to use whatever force was necessary to expel Mehemet Ali from Syria. The French government was furious, and threatened war, and many of Palmerston's Whig colleagues – traditionally pro-French – were aghast, and tried in vain to get Melbourne to curb Palmerston, or switch him to another post. Palmerston held his ground, but the French King, Louis-Philippe, lost his nerve and sacked his bellicose Prime Minister, Louis Thiers. He was replaced by the less belligerent and more pro-British François Guizot. Mehemet Ali was left in the lurch, and was – humiliatingly – forced to withdraw, his army being repatriated to Egypt by the British fleet. The only sop he received was to be granted the hereditary 'pashalik' of Egypt, his heirs continuing to rule the country, first as Khedives later as Kings, until 1952, when King Farouk was forced to abdicate. Palmerston was jubilant: he had been utterly convinced that there would be no war, telling the British consul in Alexandria that:

> France would, indeed, oppose a hostile coalition of [the Great Powers] if those Powers were to threaten to invade France, to insult her honour, or attack her Possessions; but France will not go to war with the other Great Powers in order to help Mehemet Ali, nor has she the means of doing so. (Ridley, p. 235)

He would, no doubt, have made a great poker player. In his time, Britain was not a first-rank military power, but her assets included an invincible navy and the strongest economy in the world. On this basis, Palmerston almost invariably played an aggressive hand – not least in his dealings with non-European powers. He was an arch exponent of gunboat diplomacy, provoking the first Opium War with China, in 1835. When Chinese officials seized and destroyed opium belonging to British merchants, which they were endeavouring to smuggle into China, he made extravagant demands for compensation, which the Chinese refused to meet. Palmerston promptly dispatched a fleet which bombarded Canton and occupied the island of Hong Kong, which was ceded to Britain, under the Treaty of Nanking, in 1842, negotiated by Melbourne and Palmerston's Tory successors, after they had left office the previous year. The Tories were also left to clear up the mess of the first Afghan War, which began in 1838, when Palmerston – in a pre-emptive strike – sent a British army to Kabul to dethrone the pro-Russian Emir and replace him with a British puppet. Despite initial success, the expedition proved a total disaster, only a tiny handful of survivors of the 4,500 troops (and their 12,000 camp followers) making it back to India when the retreat was ordered in January 1842.

The widespread fear that Palmerston might provoke war with the United States – a much more formidable potential opponent – was almost certainly greatly exaggerated, but there was no doubt that relations between the two countries became extremely bad towards the end of the 11 years of his first period as Foreign Secretary. The still unresolved border disputes continued to fester, and when the United States arrested, and put on trial for murder, a drunken Canadian, who falsely claimed to have participated in a raid on US territory in which an American citizen had been killed, he instructed the British minister in Washington to warn the US government that his execution: 'would produce war, war immediate and frightful in its character, because it would be a war of retaliation and vengeance' (Chambers, p. 199).

Fortunately, the man was acquitted, and was whisked back to Canada before a lynch mob could get at him. But by now a new, and more serious, dispute had arisen, as a result of Palmerston's laudable attempt to suppress the slave trade. Following the abolition of slavery in British territories in 1834, Palmerston had energetically pursued a policy of using the British navy to prevent other nations from trading in slaves and had negotiated treaties with several other maritime states permitting the British navy to stop and search vessels flying their flags to ensure that there were no slaves on board. No such treaty had, however, been signed with the United States, and slave traders from other countries were escaping detection by the unauthorized use of the American flag. In his usual forceful way, Palmerston demanded that the US government should agree to a 'right of visit' by British naval captains to boats carrying their flag, and when the US authorities temporized, he sent an impatient note to the American minister in London saying that it was unacceptable 'that a merchantman can exempt himself from search by merely hoisting a piece of bunting with the United States' emblems and colours upon it'. To refer to 'Old Glory' as a 'piece of bunting' caused great offence in Washington, but on the very day that Palmerston sent the note, Melbourne's government resigned, and Palmerston was out of office. His Tory successor, Lord Aberdeen, hastened to patch up the quarrel, and went on to negotiate a treaty settling the border between Canada and the state of Maine (see Chapter 15). Palmerston was furious, and attacked the treaty in the Commons, regretting that the conduct of foreign policy was left to a 'flock of geese'. His words were coolly received on both sides of the House, and several leading Whigs resolved that he should never again hold the post of Foreign Secretary.

This resolve was put to the test in December 1845, when Sir Robert Peel's government resigned, as he was unable to convince his colleagues to repeal the Corn Laws. The Whig leader, Lord John Russell, was invited to form a government, but the 3rd Earl Grey (son of the former Prime Minister), and several other potential cabinet ministers, refused to serve unless Palmerston was switched to a different portfolio. Palmerston adamantly refused any other post, and in the circumstances Russell was unwilling to risk forming a minority government, and Queen Victoria then invited Peel to resume office (see Chapter 12). Six months later, however, when Peel's government was defeated, and Russell was again invited to become Prime Minister, Grey and his colleagues meekly accepted the posts which they were offered, even though Palmerston again became Foreign Secretary, holding the position for a further five-and-a-half years.

In 1848, the 'year of revolutions', Palmerston actively encouraged liberal forces in Italy, Germany, Poland and Hungary, but refused to lift a finger to help them when they were crushed by Austrian and Russian military intervention. In France, he welcomed the February revolution, and the subsequent election of Louis Napoleon Bonaparte, an anglophile, as President, and in Switzerland he succeeded in discouraging Austrian intervention on the Catholic side in the brief civil war, which started in November 1847. Whether Palmerston, if left with a free hand, would have done any more to help the beleaguered revolutionaries, is doubtful, but he was, in any event, constrained by his cabinet colleagues, and by the royal couple, who sought constantly to clip his wings. Queen Victoria had first formed a low opinion of Palmerston some years earlier – in 1839 – when he was a house guest at Windsor Castle and at dead of night had crept into the bedroom of one of the Ladies in Waiting, Mrs Brand. Fearing rape, she had raised the alarm, and Palmerston rapidly retreated. The more worldly-wise Prince Albert assumed that he had made an assignation with another lady, and had, in the ill-lit corridors of the Castle, blundered into the wrong room, but Victoria was deeply shocked, and it required all the tact of the Prime Minister, Lord Melbourne, to persuade her to cover up the incident. Both Victoria and Albert were abashed at the high-handed way in which Palmerston conducted the country's foreign policy, and sought to curb him by insisting that all his dispatches should be submitted to the Queen before they were sent. Palmerston reluctantly agreed, but in practice kept only spasmodically to his undertaking. The Prime Minister, Lord John Russell, made ineffectual attempts to persuade Palmerston to exchange his post for another senior position in the government (see Chapter 13), but he refused to consider the matter.

Palmerston's critics, both royal and political, were waiting for an occasion when he would over-reach himself, and that moment seemed to have arrived in 1850, with the Don Pacifico affair. A Portuguese Jew, born in Gibraltar, and thus a British subject, his house in Athens had been burnt down in an anti-Semitic riot, with police standing idly by. Don Pacifico, a businessman with a more than shady reputation, sued the Greek government for an excessive amount of compensation and appealed to the British government for support. Palmerston promptly ordered a naval squadron to blockade the Greek coast, until the government paid up, provoking strong protests from the French and Russian governments which, with Britain, were guarantors of Greek independence. Palmerston was formally condemned by the House of Lords for his impetuosity in risking war over a comparatively trivial amount of money owing to a man whose claims on British protection were negligible. When a confidence motion was put to the House of Commons, Palmerston was faced by a concerted attack from the finest speakers in the House – Peel, Gladstone, Disraeli and the leading Radical, Richard Cobden – and it seemed all was up for him. Rising to heights of oratory of which he had never previously shown himself capable, Palmerston spoke for four hours with hardly a note, and made a rumbustious defence of his actions, culminating in a much quoted peroration, asking the House to decide:

> whether, as the Roman, in days of old, held himself free from indignity when he could say *Civis Romanus sum*; so also a British subject, in whatever land he may be, shall feel confident that the watchful eye and the strong arm of England will protect him against injustice and wrong. (Hansard, 25 June 1850)

Large numbers of MPs, led by a phalanx of Radicals (but not by Cobden and John Bright), rose to applaud Palmerston with enthusiasm, and at the end of the debate, the Government had a comfortable majority of 46. Palmerston's speech was extensively reported in the press, and met with overwhelming approval from his readers. His brash patriotism struck a chord with the public at large, and henceforward he was by a wide margin the most popular politician in the country. Victoria and Albert, who had been unsuccessfully pressing Russell to dismiss his Foreign Secretary, were discomfited, but 18 months later got their way, in December 1851, when Palmerston rashly congratulated Louis Napoleon Bonaparte on his *coup d'Etat*, which destroyed the Second Republic and paved the way for his proclamation as Emperor. The government was officially neutral, and several other ministers, including Russell himself, approved of Louis Napoleon's action. But Palmerston had acted without authority from either the cabinet or the Queen, and Russell took the opportunity to rid himself of an over-mighty colleague, softening the blow by offering him the Lord-Lieutenancy of Ireland. This, Palmerston politely declined, quietly preparing his revenge. This came only two months later, when he moved an amendment to the government's Militia Bill. Many Radicals joined with the Tories in defeating the government, by 13 votes, and Russell promptly resigned. Palmerston coolly wrote a letter to his brother, saying 'My dear William, I have had my tit-for-tat with John Russell, and I turned him out on Friday last' (Ridley, p. 401).

Palmerston was now in the anomalous position that – in a period in which no political party enjoyed a majority in the House of Commons – only his presence could ensure stability for any government that was formed, given his enormous popularity. Yet most leading politicians – and the royal couple – were determined that he should not again be Foreign Secretary. When the Earl of Derby was invited to become Prime Minister, following Russell's resignation, he tried long and hard to persuade Palmerston to join his minority Tory government as Chancellor of the Exchequer and leader of the House of Commons.

Palmerston was tempted, but was not willing to break his ties with the Whigs, and declined. Derby had to make do with Disraeli instead, and his government did not last long, resigning when Disraeli's budget was rejected by the Commons in December 1852, less than ten months after taking office. It was replaced by a coalition of Whigs and Peelites, led by Lord Aberdeen, in which Palmerston was offered any post he chose...other than the Foreign Office. Now 68-years-old, he was persuaded to accept the Home Office, explaining in a letter to his brother that: 'I should, in any case, much prefer the Home Office to going back to the immense labour of the Foreign Office' (Chambers, p. 349).

At the Home Office, Palmerston again proved himself to be a hard worker, and a moderate social reformer, influenced by his son-in-law, the Tory factory reformer, Lord Shaftesbury, who had married Lady Minnie Cowper, Emily's daughter by Palmerston. Yet one reform to which Palmerston was adamantly opposed was any extension of the electoral franchise, and Palmerston submitted his resignation, when Lord John Russell proposed to introduce a Reform Bill. Within a week, he was persuaded to withdraw the resignation, and Russell watered down the Bill, which was later withdrawn after the outbreak of the Crimean War.

The origins of this war are described in Chapter 15. Palmerston, who felt no inhibition whatever about intervening in foreign affairs, insisted from the outset that a robust attitude should be taken to the Russian demands on Turkey, and argued forcefully that a British and French fleet should be sent to the Black Sea as a deterrent. His colleagues did not, at first, agree, but his angry interventions undermined Aberdeen's patient attempts to find a peaceful settlement, and when the Russians sank a Turkish fleet at Sinope, in November 1853, Palmerston persuaded the cabinet, against Aberdeen's wishes, to adopt a more aggressive stance. This inevitably led to war with Russia, which was declared by both France and Britain in March 1854. Palmerston now effectively took over the direction of the war, urging an attack on the Russian naval base at Sebastopol, simultaneously with a naval blockade in the Baltic, leading to the seizure and destruction of a Russian base in the Aaland Islands. His initial war aims were boundless, including the liberation of both Finland and Poland from Russian control, but he eventually restricted them to neutralizing her influence in the Black Sea area and propping up the Ottoman Empire, which he improbably argued was now 'a more enlightened and reformed country than Russia' (Chamberlain, 1998, p. 181).

Palmerston was not directly to blame for the disastrous conduct of the war in its initial stages, and when Aberdeen was forced to resign, in January 1855, after losing a confidence vote in the Commons, Queen Victoria was forced by the overwhelming pressure of public opinion to appoint her *bête noire* as his successor, after both Derby and Russell had failed to form an administration. Palmerston had great difficulty in forming a cabinet, as all the leading Peelites refused to serve, out of loyalty to Aberdeen. The Queen herself then pleaded with Aberdeen to talk them round, to which the pliable ex-Premier agreed. So Palmerston took over the previous government with minimal changes, excluding only Aberdeen and the War Secretary, Lord Newcastle, though within a few months Gladstone and two other Peelites resigned and were replaced by Whigs. Palmerston initially intended to include his Tory son-in-law, Lord Shaftesbury, in the government, but changed his mind, and when he later renewed the offer, the ever hesitant Christian evangelist made such a meal out of his struggle with his conscience over whether to accept that the post was eventually given to someone else. Lord John Russell was at first excluded, and sent instead as a delegate to an abortive peace conference convened by Austria, but later became Colonial Secretary, only to resign in a huff five months later.

Palmerston's great popularity owed much to his consistent wooing of the press, which gave him the affectionate nickname of 'Pam'. He thought nothing of leaking sensitive information to sympathetic newspapers, and often wrote anonymous articles himself which they were delighted to print. Several newspapers were effectively in his pocket, including the *Morning Post, The Globe, the Morning Advertiser, The Daily News* and the newly launched *Daily Telegraph.* Only *The Times* remained impervious to his appeal, and, under its formidable editor, John Delane, was a fierce critic for many years. Palmerston owed much to his marriage. The still beautiful Lady Palmerston inherited a large fortune from her brother, Lord Melbourne, in 1848, which – together with some shrewd investments which Palmerston had made – enabled them to move from their relatively modest home in Carlton Gardens to the magnificent no. 94 Piccadilly, formerly owned by the Queen's uncle, the Duke of Cambridge. Here Lady Palmerston held receptions every Saturday during the parliamentary sessions, to which the flower of London's social and political life flocked. Lady P introduced a significant innovation, which no other hostess had ever attempted. Her receptions were thrown open also to 'the gentlemen of the press' to the horror of the bulk of high society, but not wishing to be left out, the great majority held their noses and continued to come. Among the grateful journalists who received invitations was John Delane, who, greatly flattered, and impressed by Palmerston's jingoistic appeal during the War, finally succumbed, and added his newspaper to the new Prime Minister's circle of friends.

Palmerston assumed office on 6 February 55. At 71, he was the oldest person to become Prime Minister for the first time. Despite this, he was able to inject a new energy into the prosecution of the war. His insistence led to a great improvement in the provision of logistical support for the troops, and he strongly backed the efforts of Florence Nightingale (a near neighbour to his Broadlands estate) to improve the rudimentary medical services. Yet it was Britain's French allies that brought the war to a successful conclusion, when they stormed the

Malakoff fortress in September 1855, and the Russians abandoned the city of Sebastopol, after setting fire to it. Palmerston was eager to continue the War, but the French – having secured their moment of glory – had had enough. The new Russian Tsar, Alexander II, who had succeeded to the throne after his father, Nicholas I, had caught a fatal chill while inspecting his troops in the rain, was more than ready to settle.

A peace treaty was signed in Paris, in March 1856. The terms were far worse than Palmerston had hoped, but he presented them as a great triumph to a grateful Queen and Parliament, and was rewarded with the Order of the Garter, whose sash he proudly wore at his wife's weekly receptions. Britain did not remain long at peace, due to Palmerston's customary aggressive response to provocations from weaker states, and the second Opium War was success-fully waged against China in 1856, while an army of 7,000 men was sent into Afghanistan to defeat a Persian force which had occupied the province of Herat. Palmerston was defeated in a parliamentary vote over his China policy in 1857, but promptly called a general election, which was effectively a referendum on his conduct of affairs. It was a major success, the Whigs and their allies making a net gain of 50 seats.

Yet an improved position in Parliament did not yet constitute a stable major-ity, and Palmerston fell to an ambush in the following year. An assassination attempt on Napoleon III by Italian nationalists, who formulated their plot and acquired their weapons in London, led to a demand from the French to tighten British laws against international conspirators. Palmerston considered the request reasonable, and promptly introduced the Conspiracy to Murder Bill, which made it a felony, instead of a misdemeanour, to plot in England to kill somebody abroad. He was taken aback when he was fiercely attacked by his Radical allies for surrendering to French pressure. Disraeli, prompted by Lord Derby, sensed an opportunity to defeat the government, and when a division was called on a hostile amendment, took his followers into the division lobby along with the Radicals, and the amendment was carried by 234 votes to 219. Palmerston was completely wrong-footed, and was too proud, or too misad-vised, to resort to the expedient of calling a vote of confidence, which he would most probably have won. Instead, he promptly resigned, and Lord Derby, for the second time, took office at the head of a minority Tory government.

Derby did not survive for long, despite calling a general election, in which the Tories gained 26 seats – not enough to give them a majority. Disraeli's budget was duly defeated, and Derby resigned after 15 months in office. In the meantime, the Whigs, Radicals and assorted allies had come together to form the Liberal Party, and Palmerston and Russell had made up their lengthy quarrel, each agreeing to serve under the other if invited by the Queen to do so. Victoria was not anxious to choose either of 'these terrible old men', and instead approached Lord Granville, the Liberal leader in the Lords. When he failed to form a government, she gritted her teeth and invited Palmerston back to office. So, now aged nearly 76, he returned to power with a more cohesive government than he had had before, with Russell at the Foreign Office and Gladstone at the Exchequer.

During his second term, which lasted for more than six years, the emphasis of his government was almost entirely on foreign affairs, the amount of legislation passed being minimal. Palmerston imposed an absolute block against any measure of parliamentary reform, and other reform measures were distinctly thin on the ground. Indeed, almost the only significant measure passed in either of his premierships was the Matrimonial Causes Act of 1857, which abolished the jurisdiction of ecclesiastical courts and established secular divorce courts in their place. (Six years later, it caused a sensation when Palmerston himself, then aged 79, was cited as a co-respondent in a divorce case, and his popularity undoubtedly increased in many quarters, while Lady Palmerston was vastly amused. When the case came to court, however, it was an anti-climax. The petition was dismissed on the grounds that the plaintiff, a journalist called O'Kane, was unable to establish that he was legally married to his wife, and it transpired that he had tried to blackmail Palmerston for £20,000 not to bring the action. The lady concerned then acknowledged that she had never slept with the Prime Minister).

Apart from yet another war against China, in which an Anglo-French force captured Peking and burned down the Emperor's summer palace, the main issues of contention concerned the struggle for Italian unification, the US Civil War and the Schleswig-Holstein dispute. Palmerston and Russell worked closely on each of these, and had remarkably few disagreements. The balance of their successes and failures was, at best, a narrow one. Over Italy, Palmerston was broadly supportive of the Nationalists. As he himself put it, the problem was essentially one of getting the Austrians out, without letting the French in. In this aim, he was only very partially successful. Austria was driven out of Lombardy in the bloody war which it fought against Sardinia and France in 1859–60, but was left in control of Venetia, as Napoleon III, sickened by the appalling bloodshed at the Battle of Solferino, negotiated an armistice, to the disgust of the Sardinians, before the job was fully done. The French, nevertheless, acquired Savoy and Nice, and ended up with a garrison in control of Rome, protecting the Pope's diminished domains. It was left to the Prussians to complete the work of unification, after Palmerston's death, by their defeats of Austria, in 1866, and of France, in 1870.

In the US Civil War, Palmerston – like most of the British ruling class – was sympathetic to the Confederates, and two disputes with the Federal side involving naval actions might well have led to hostilities. The first involved the stopping by a US warship of the British vessel *Trent*, which was carrying two Confederate diplomatic representatives on their way to France and Britain, and their forcible removal. They were subsequently released by the US government, but only after the British threatened war. The second incident involved the *Alabama*, a privateer secretly built in Britain for the Confederates, which was allowed to leave Liverpool by the port authorities, and later sank or captured no fewer than 93 Federal ships, mostly merchantmen. Palmerston and Russell haughtily rejected American claims for compensation, but eventually they were referred to arbitration, and Britain finished up by paying $15.5million in gold, long after Palmerston's death.

The Schleswig-Holstein affair was singularly complicated – Palmerston himself famously said that there were only three people who had ever understood it – the Prince Consort, who was dead, a Danish politician who was in an asylum, and himself, who had forgotten about it. Yet there was no mystery about the outcome – it was the most staggering humiliation that he ever suffered. The two duchies had been governed by Kings of Denmark, as their Duke, since the Middle Ages, though the majority of their inhabitants were German. When the Danish King, Frederick VII, died in 1863, his successor, Christian IX, was descended through the female line, and was thus ineligible to rule over the duchies, which came under the Salic Law. Under this law, the rightful heir to the dukedoms was the Duke of Augustenburg, and his claims were backed by the two leading Germanic states, Prussia and Austria. Christian, however, refused to accept this, and took steps to incorporate the territory into his kingdom. When Austria and Prussia threatened war, Palmerston declared in the House of Commons that if it came Denmark would not fight alone, which gave the Danes the confidence to reject the Prusso-Austrian ultimatum. The Prussian Chancellor, Otto von Bismarck, promptly called Palmerston's bluff, and Prussian and Austrian troops crossed the frontier. Apart from Queen Victoria, who was – as ever – strongly pro-German, British opinion was predominantly on the Danish side, and pro-Danish feeling was strengthened by the arrival in London of the popular Danish Princess Alexandra to marry the Prince of Wales. Yet, Palmerston knew that he had been outsmarted by Bismarck, and

> That there was nothing that he could do to help Denmark. For four hundred years, Britain had not fought a war in Europe except as the ally of a major European power; and there was now no such ally available to help her in a war against Austria and Prussia. (Ridley, p. 527)

A formal appeal from Denmark for help received no answer, and in two short campaigns the Danish resistance was overwhelmed, Austria annexing Holstein and Prussia, Schleswig. (Two years later the victors fell out over the spoils, and Prussia claimed both duchies after defeating Austria at the battle of Sadowa). Palmerston was now extremely vulnerable, and was censured in a House of

Lords debate. The Commons looked like following suit, General Peel, the son of the former Prime Minster, saying: 'Is it come to this, that the words of the Prime Minister of England, uttered in the Parliament of England, are to be regarded as mere menaces to be laughed at and despised by foreign powers?' (*Hansard*, 8 July 1864).

Palmerston's back was to the wall, but he was not too proud to call in favours, and scrambled for votes in all corners of the House, where he could hope to find them. Finally, it was the pacifist section of the Radicals, led by Richard Cobden, which came to his rescue, and he saw off the Opposition censure motion by 313 votes to 295. He was looking his age now, pushing 80, and his health was beginning to fail, but he had not lost his appeal to the voters. He called a general election in July 1865, and the Liberals were triumphantly returned with an increased majority. He did not, however, live long enough to meet the new Parliament, when it was summoned in October 1865. He caught a chill while out driving earlier in the month, and died on 18 October, two days short of his eighty-first birthday. The legend that his last words were 'Die, my dear Doctor, that's the last thing I'll do' is unfortunately not true.

Palmerston was a controversial figure in his day, and has remained so ever since. He was the object both of extravagant praise and of intense denigration. Often described as a Liberal abroad and a Tory at home, he was also categorized as a bully to the weak and a coward to the strong, reflecting the many occasions in which he had reacted in a violent way to petty provocations from smaller states, while backing off when confronted by one or more of the great powers. The only occasion when he was prepared to go to war with one of these was in the Crimea, where he was assured of the support of France and, at least, the benevolent neutrality of Austria, while the Russians were without any potential allies. As a diplomat, he had shown great resource and subtlety during his earlier periods as Foreign Secretary, but as he grew older, and his self-confidence and public support grew, he began to lose his touch, and emerged all too often as a loud-mouthed braggart. For many years he was seen in the chancelleries of the three great absolutist powers of Russia, Austria and Prussia as a dangerous demagogue and revolutionary. Yet his support for the nationalist movements which they oppressed, in Germany, Italy, Poland and Hungary, was confined to gestures, and he extended no practical help to the revolutions of 1848, or the successive uprisings of the Poles against their Russian masters. Nor, though he had welcomed the French revolutions of both 1830 and 1848, did he oppose the actions of Louis Napoleon Bonaparte, when he overthrew the democratic republic which had been established, by his *coup d'Etat* in 1851. Indeed, he went so far as to congratulate him, which led to his own removal as Foreign Secretary.

The one common thread which linked every action of Palmerston, both as Foreign Secretary and as Prime Minister, was his extreme patriotism. He regarded England as the best country in the world, and the best governed, and always put the interests of England, as he perceived them, first. Gladstone, a powerful critic of Palmerston in his day, in his own old age, summed up his basic attitude in an anecdote, which is recorded in most of the many biographies which have appeared. 'A Frenchman', he recalled in a letter to a friend: 'thinking to be highly complimentary, said to Palmerston: "If I were not a Frenchman, I should wish to be an Englishman"; to which Pam coolly replied: "If I were not an Englishman, I should wish to be an Englishman"'.

Works consulted

Muriel Chamberlain, 1998, 'Lord Palmerston' in Robert Eccleshall and Graham Walker, (eds.), *Biographical Dictionary of British Prime Ministers*, London, Routledge.

Muriel Chamberlain, 1987, *Lord Palmerston*, Cardiff, University of Wales Press.

James Chambers, 2004, *Palmerston: The People's Darling*, London, John Murray.

Jasper Ridley, 1970, *Lord Palmerston*, London, Constable.

Donald Southgate, 1966, *The Most English Minister ... The Policies and Politics of Palmerston*, London, Macmillan.

David Steele, 2004, Article in *Oxford Dictionary of National Biography*.

A.J.P. Taylor, 2000, 'Lord Palmerston' in *British Prime Ministers and other essays,* London, Penguin Books.

17

Benjamin Disraeli, Earl of Beaconsfield – Climbing 'the Greasy Pole'

The two best known Prime Ministers of the nineteenth century were probably Benjamin Disraeli and William Gladstone. They were notable opponents, and very dissimilar characters, but they had one thing in common – both of them switched their party affiliation. Gladstone started off as a Tory, but went on to become the most distinguished of Liberal Prime Ministers. Disraeli launched his political career as an 'Independent Radical', but it was as a Conservative that he achieved fame and fortune, and he is still revered today as one of the party's most formative influences.

Very little in his background and early life would have pointed to such a destiny. Disraeli (or Dizzy, as he became universally known) was without a doubt the most improbable character ever to have become Prime Minister. Indeed, when one considers the various obstacles which he had to overcome – some due to the accident of birth, but mostly erected by his own youthful folly – it seems a miracle that he ever managed to climb to the top of 'the greasy pole', as he himself described it. Benjamin Disraeli was born in London on 21 December 1804, the second child and eldest son of Isaac D'Israeli and his wife, Maria Basevi. Isaac was a scholar and dilettante, who, as a result of receiving a legacy while still a young man, had sufficient means to spurn a business career and devote himself to the literary life, spending much of his time in the British Museum Reading Room, and consorting with writers, artists and publishers. His speciality was collecting literary gossip and anecdotes, and his most successful work, *Curiosities of Literature*, first published in 1791 and going through 12 editions, was much admired by Lord Byron, Sir Walter Scott and the publisher, John Murray, all of whom became his friends. The young Benjamin loved and admired his father, but nursed a lasting grievance against his mother, whom he felt withheld the affection from him which she lavished on his younger brothers. He greatly embroidered his father's lineage in later accounts, maintaining that he came from an aristocratic line of Sephardic Jews, who left Spain in 1492 and established themselves in Venice for several centuries, before Isaac's father emigrated to England in 1748. Actually the family, originally known as Israeli, almost certainly came from the Levant, and went not to Venice but to Cento, a minor town in the Papal States. Ironically, his mother (unknown to Benjamin, but established by modern scholarship) had comparable antecedents to those which he attributed to his father. She was a direct descendant of Isaac Aboab, the leader of the Jewish community in Castille, who in 1492 led 20,000 followers into exile in Portugal (Blake, p. 7). Her family had lived in England since the seventeenth century.

Isaac D'Israeli was a member (but an inactive one) of the Bevis Marks Sephardic synagogue in London, and was disconcerted when he was elected a Warden of the synagogue. When he refused to serve, he was fined £40, which he refused to pay. He later resigned from the congregation, and – though not converting himself – had his three sons and his daughter baptized into the

Church of England. Benjamin was 12 at the time, and his father's action had a crucial effect on his later career. Jews were not eligible to sit in the House of Commons, and this disability was not removed until 1858. It is scarcely conceivable that Disraeli would ever have become Prime Minister if he had had to wait until late middle age before entering Parliament. As it was, he undoubtedly suffered from anti-Semitic prejudices at various stages in his life, and he remains the only person of Jewish descent to become prime minister.

Benjamin was deeply interested in, and immensely proud of, his Jewish heritage, which he had a strong impulse to glamourize. Despite the evident affluence of his father, which enabled him to grow up in a spacious and comfortable home, with a fair number of servants at his beck and call, Benjamin's education was badly neglected. Not only was he – apart from Wellington – the only nineteenth century Premier not to have gone to a university, but the only one not educated at a 'public' school. Instead, he was sent to a 'dame school' in Islington, and then to two little known private schools run by clergymen, in Blackheath and Walthamstow. This, despite the fact that his two obviously less intelligent younger brothers were both enrolled at Winchester. At the age of 15, Benjamin left school and spent the next couple of years luxuriating in his father's well-stocked library, reading widely, but in an undisciplined fashion, and acquiring a good stock of Latin tags, with which, as was the custom of the day, he later embellished his parliamentary speeches, but he had no solid knowledge of the classics. Some idea of Disraeli's schoolboy experiences may be gained from his two thinly-disguised autobiographical novels, *Vivien Grey* and *Contrarini Fleming*. From these it appears that he felt a profound sense of difference between himself and his fellow pupils, whom he felt to be both less intelligent and less sensitive than himself. As Robert Blake commented: 'It is certain that throughout his adult life he was conscious of dwelling apart from other men and it is probable that this awareness first came upon him when he was a schoolboy ... To the end of his days he remained an alien figure' (Blake, p. 17).

Part of the difference was no doubt due to his physical appearance; he did not look a typical Anglo-Saxon, as most of his schoolfellows probably did. Benjamin may not have gone to a 'public' school, but he did not miss out on at least some of the experiences usually associated with them. He appears to have fallen deeply in love with one of his fellow pupils at Walthamstow, though whether the relationship was physically consummated is not clear. Disraeli certainly had feminine traits in his character, and may perhaps have been bi-sexual. One of Disraeli's biographers refers to 'the latent homosexual element in Disraeli's friendships with younger men' and refers specifically to Lord Henry Lennox, an amusing but essential frivolous younger son of a duke who was unsuccessful both as a politician and as the would-be husband of an heiress, once lamenting to Disraeli that 'It is always the same thing; either the lady has too little money or I am too old'. Disraeli for long appeared to be besotted with Lennox, whom he habitually addressed as 'beloved' in his many letters, and once wrote 'I can only say I love you'. Even so, Sarah Bradford concludes that 'the relationship was almost certainly not physical' (Bradford, pp. 215–219).

Benjamin was allowed to sit in at his father's regular dinner parties, and he impressed the guests with his intelligence, precocity and gift for repartee, though not all of them accepted his self-evaluation as a genius. John Murray, in particular, took Benjamin very seriously, and began to send him manuscripts which he was considering for publication for his opinion, which elicited sharp, witty and pertinent comments. When he was 17, Isaac suggested that he should go to Oxford, but Benjamin demurred, and he was instead articled to the solicitors' firm of Swain, Stevens, Maples, Pearce and Hunt. One of the partners, Maples, was a close friend of Isaac's, and it seems to have been agreed between the two families that Benjamin and his daughter should eventually be married. Nothing came of this arrangement, and – though he appeared to give satisfaction to his employers, and made many useful contacts through his work – Benjamin's desire to become a solicitor soon waned. It was generally agreed that he should aspire to higher things, and in November 1824, not quite 20, he was admitted to Lincoln's Inn to read for the bar. Even then, Disraeli – who had by now dropped the apostrophe from his name – did not give the impression of having his heart set on the law. He had already sent Murray the draft of a novel which he had written, but when he received no early response, concluded that Murray was too embarrassed to tell him that it was no good, and so sent him a message to burn it. Now he set out self-consciously to present himself as a Bohemian, dressing in a very dandyish style, modelling himself on Byron, while attempting to build a quick fortune by gambling on the stock exchange, with money he didn't have. He drew friends, including Murray, into his speculations, particularly in South American mining shares, and though their value soared precipitately, they later collapsed, and all of them were out of pocket. Despite this, Murray responded enthusiastically to a proposal from his 20-year-old friend to launch a new newspaper, as a rival to *The Times*, for which Murray agreed to put up 50 per cent of the capital, the remainder to be supplied equally by Disraeli and a merchant called Powles. Disraeli promptly left for Scotland, with a laudatory letter of recommendation from Murray, to seek support from Sir Walter Scott, and – if possible – to recruit his son-in-law as editor of the new paper which, on Disraeli's suggestion, was entitled *The Representative*. Disraeli made extravagant – and quite unrealistic – promises to them, and to many others whom he sought to associate with the paper. It was launched two months behind schedule, in January 1825, was a total failure from the start, and crashed the following June, leaving Murray £26,000 the poorer, Powles on his way to bankruptcy and Disraeli with debts, which he had still not fully discharged a quarter of a century later. Desperate to make some money – *any* money – Disraeli now embarked on writing – at double-quick speed – a *roman-à-clef*, in which he mercilessly satirized his leading collaborators in the affair, including the long-suffering Murray. The novel, entitled *Vivien Grey*, appeared anonymously, but with the false suggestion that its author was a leading figure in high society. It was, initially, a *succès de scandale*, but when its true authorship emerged, it attracted universally hostile reviews, and the lasting enmity of Murray and of many others, who felt they had been duped by Disraeli. He made £750 from the book, but the whole episode had done him enormous damage, as Blake recounts: 'He acquired a reputation for cynicism, double-dealing, recklessness and insincerity which it took him years to live down' (Blake, p. 48).

Disraeli responded by having a nervous breakdown, from which he partially recovered through making a short 'grand tour', on borrowed money, to France, Switzerland and Italy. He was still feeling low, however, on his return, and Isaac D'Israeli thought a spell of country air would do him good, and moved the whole family to a beautiful Queen Anne house at Bradenham, near High Wycombe. Here Benjamin remained for some time, making only occasional furtive trips to London, fearful of running into creditors who would dun him for his debts. He continued his legal studies, but only fitfully, and soon embarked on another novel – one of his slightest – *The Young Duke*, which was moderately well received, and earned him £500. He then embarked, together with his sister Sarah's fiancé, William Meredith, on a far more ambitious foreign journey, which took him to Spain, Malta, Albania, Turkey, Palestine and Egypt. Altogether, he was away for 16 months, and it would have been longer if it had not been for the tragic death of Meredith, in Egypt, which prompted him to return home to comfort his sister, who henceforth devoted her life almost exclusively to her brother's interests. For Disraeli, this encounter with 'the gorgeous east' fired his imagination, reawakened all his fanciful dreams about the exotic origins of his family and installed a lasting prejudice in favour of the Turks and against the Greeks, which was to be reflected in his later policies as Prime Minister. He lapped up the luxury and the indolence of the Turkish court, writing home:

> To repose on voluptuous ottomans and smoke superb pipes, daily to indulge in the luxury of a bath which requires half a dozen attendants for its perfection; to court the air in a carved caique, by shores which are a perpetual scene; this is, I think, a far more sensible life than all the bustle of clubs, all the boring of drawing rooms, and all the coarse vulgarity of our political controversies... I mend slowly but I mend (Hibbert, 2005, p. 53)

His general health and sense of well being did indeed improve markedly during the journey, with one unfortunate exception. On his return, he had to undergo painful treatment for a venereal infection. He soon published two further novels, finally renounced the bar, and began to form political ambitions, beginning the slow process of trying to re-ingratiate himself with respectable society. He suffered the indignity of being blackballed by several London clubs, including the Athenaeum and the Travellers', but his friend and fellow novelist Edward Bulwer-Lytton invited him to several of his wife's receptions, where he enjoyed only partial success, repelling many by his exotic dress, especially his penchant for 'green pantaloons'.

By this time, Disraeli had convinced himself that the route to the great future to which he aspired lay through the House of Commons. He resolved to present himself as a candidate for High Wycombe, where his new family home, Bradenham House, was situated. His main problem was to decide in which political interest he should stand. He had formed a marked aversion to the Whigs, but otherwise had no settled political convictions. As the latest of his many biographers put it:

> Realising that it might prove fatal to attach himself to a falling star, he shied away from the Tories, whose influence was rapidly waning; and he made up his mind to present himself as a Radical. 'Toryism is worn out', he told [a friend], 'and I cannot condescend to be a Whig... I start in the high Radical interest'. (Hibbert, 2005, pp. 66–67)

Disraeli fought High Wycombe twice in 1832, once in a by-election, and the second time in the general election following the passage of the Reform Bill, which greatly enlarged the electorate. Each time he was defeated by Whig opponents, whom he confidently expected to beat, flattering himself – no doubt justifiably – with being a vastly better orator, and certainly possessing a great deal more chutzpah. He was to try again, in 1835, still as an 'Independent Radical', when he came no closer to winning. By now it had occurred to Disraeli that, if he was to prosper in politics, he needed to find a powerful political patron, and with this in mind, he began to penetrate the lower reaches of society, gradually moving up the scale as he received invitations to more and more grand houses. His progress was mixed; for every one who was charmed by his conversation and impressed by his vitality there were others who were appalled by his brashness and conceit. He made more impression on women than on men, and one of these was Lady Henrietta Sykes, a young married woman with three children and a complaisant husband. Disraeli began a passionate affair with her, later memorialised in his novel, *Henrietta Temple*. It was through her that he met Lord Lyndhurst, a veteran Tory politician, who was to be three times Lord Chancellor. Lyndhurst took him up, and was repaid when Disraeli readily agreed to share Henrietta's charms with him, and later passed her on to him when his own ardour began to cool. He now proclaimed himself as a Tory, for the first time, joining the Carlton Club, and fighting a by-election at Taunton, in April 1835, where he was soundly beaten by the Whig, Henry Labouchere. One person who reacted angrily to Disraeli's switch from Radical to Tory was the Irish nationalist Daniel O'Connell. He had written a letter of commendation to him when he had fought High Wycombe, and now read a newspaper report which alleged that Disraeli had branded him as 'an incendiary and traitor'. In fact, Dizzy was not giving this as his own opinion, but was citing an earlier accusation of the Whigs, who had now formed a parliamentary alliance with O'Connell. O'Connell reacted with extreme violence, describing Disraeli at a meeting in Dublin as 'a vile creature', 'a living lie', 'a miscreant' and 'a reptile'. He continued:

> His name shows that he is of Jewish origin. I do not use it as a term of reproach; there are many most respectable Jews. But there are as in every other people some of the lowest and most disgusting grade of moral turpitude; and of those I look upon Mr Disraeli as the worst. (Blake, p. 125)

Disraeli felt he had no alternative but to challenge O'Connell to a duel, but the Irishman had once killed an opponent and had vowed never to fight another. So Dizzy challenged his son, Morgan O'Connell, instead, and added the provocation of publishing an open letter to his father returning all his insults with interest. Morgan was not at all anxious to fight, but the police intervened and Disraeli was arrested and bound over to keep the peace. He seemed very pleased with himself, writing in his diary 'Row with O'Connell in which I greatly distinguished myself' (Blake, p. 126).

Disraeli went on to write his first political book, entitled *A Vindication of the English Constitution in a Letter to a Noble and Learned Lord* [Lord Lyndhurst], by 'Disraeli the Younger', an action which delighted his father, Isaac. He also wrote a series of articles, notable for the venom with which they attacked leading Whigs, under the pseudonym, *Runnymede*, which appeared in *The Morning Post*. He continued these in *The Times*, and – while he unconvincingly denied authorship – his fame spread and also his approval rating with the Tories. He lived extravagantly, contemplating moving into Byron's former chambers in The Albany, but he was always only one step ahead of his creditors, his debts now exceeding £20,000 (perhaps £600,000 in today's money). He was in daily dread of being thrown into a debtors' prison, and once had to hide down a well when a sheriff's officer came to arrest him, and on another occasion bribed the officer to go away. He importuned many of his friends and acquaintances for help, with varying degrees of success, and more than once called on his father to bail him out, while concealing the full extent of his debts. Then, in 1837, King William IV died, precipitating a general election, and he received a large number of invitations to stand as a candidate for the Conservatives. From at least nine possibilities, he chose Maidstone, which turned out to be an inspired choice. The other Tory candidate was one of the retiring members, Wyndham Lewis, a wealthy landowner, who was entranced by Disraeli, and took him under his wing, paying the bulk of his election expenses. Mrs Wyndham Lewis was even more impressed, describing him in a letter to her brother as 'one of the greatest writers and finest orators of the day – aged about 30' (Hibbert, p. 106). He was actually 32. The result, in a two-member constituency, was:

Lewis (Con)	707
Disraeli (Con)	616
Thompson (Radical)	412

Disraeli lost no time in making his maiden speech, and was determined to take the House by storm. It did not work out like that, being described by the diarist Charles Greville in the following terms: 'Mr Disraeli made his first exhibition the other night, beginning with florid assurance, speedily degenerating into ludicrous absurdity, and being at last put down in inextinguishable shouts of laughter' (Hibbert (ed.) 1981, p. 49).

Disraeli's first mistake was in the choice of subject matter. MPs normally chose non-controversial subjects for their first appearance, but Disraeli was determined to pursue his vendetta against O'Connell, who was the immediately preceding speaker. He launched into an elaborate assault on the electoral malpractices of the O'Connellites in the general election, accusing them of 'majestic mendicancy', and it was hardly surprising that he was soon the object of 'hisses, hoots, laughter and catcalls' from a claque of O'Connell's supporters. So extravagant was Disraeli's rhetoric and so bizarre his attire, that the bulk of the House soon joined in the merriment, and Disraeli could no longer make himself heard. He abruptly broke off his speech, with the defiant words: 'Though I sit down now, the time will come when you will hear me' (Blake, p. 149).

This has gone down as one of the most famous – if least successful – maiden speeches in history. It was not quite a total disaster: some good came from it in the shape of sage advice which was given to Disraeli by R.L. O'Shea, a veteran Irish MP, who was not one of O'Connell's men. 'Now, get rid of your genius for a session', he said: 'Speak often, for you must not show yourself cowed, but speak shortly. Be very quiet, try to be dull...and in a short time the House will sigh for the wit and eloquence which they know are in you' (Blake, p. 150).

Disraeli was sensible and humble enough to agree to follow O'Shea's counsel. Within a month or two of this fiasco, however, an event occurred which had a profound effect on his future prospects – the unexpected death, in March 1838, of his fellow Member for Maidstone, Wyndham Lewis. Lewis left his widow, Mary Anne, a life interest in his London home, in Gloucester Gate, and an income of £5,000–6,000 a year. A good-natured, but ill-educated woman, who was a notorious chatterbox, she was – at 45 – Disraeli's senior by 12 years, yet within four months he proposed to her. He was on record as having said that 'I may commit many follies in my life, but I shall never marry for "love"' (Hibbert, p. 79), and it was almost universally believed that his motive was pecuniary. He made no very strenuous effort to deny this, but it was also evident that he was genuinely fond of her, and may well also have been look-ing for a mother-substitute. Mary Anne insisted on waiting a year until after her husband's death before giving him an answer, but they were duly married at St. George's, Hanover Square, on 28 August 1839. Against expectations, it turned out to be a successful marriage; they became a devoted couple, and Disraeli was devastated when she died nine years before him. This, however, had not prevented him from embarking on a number of extra-marital affairs, and he appeared to have fathered two illegitimate children during the 1860s (Weintraub, pp. 419–36). As for her money, it turned out not to be enough to set-tle all of Dizzy's debts, though Blake estimates that, altogether, she shelled out some £13,000 to his creditors (Blake, p. 161). This, at least, considerably eased the pressure on him, while as an MP he was now safe from arrest for debt.

In the 1841 general election, Disraeli switched his constituency, and was elected for Shrewsbury. The election was a triumph for Sir Robert Peel's Conservatives, and when Lord Melbourne subsequently resigned, he became Prime Minister. Disraeli wrote him an obsequious letter begging to be included in the new government, saying that to be left out would be 'an intolerable humiliation'. Unknown to him, Mary Anne had written an equally sycophan-tic letter on his behalf. Peel, who was besieged by similar importunities from many other MPs, wrote back civilly, saying he regretted that he was not in a position to: 'meet the wishes that are conveyed to me by men whose co-operation I should be proud to have, and whose qualifications and pretensions for office I do not contest'.

There is some slight evidence, however, that Peel would have been ready to include Disraeli, had it not been for the objections of his leading colleague, Lord Stanley (later the 14th Earl of Derby). Stanley had a long-standing quar-rel with Disraeli, concerning a scrape in which his brother had been involved, and which he – probably unjustifiably – blamed on Dizzy. Stanley is cited as having declared that: 'If that scoundrel [were] taken in [he] would not remain [himself]' (Hibbert, p. 148).

Bitterly disappointed, Disraeli took himself and Mary Anne off to Paris, where (at least in his own account in a sheaf of letters to his sister), they were the stars of 'the season', being taken up by leading politicians such as Guizot and Thiers, writers such as de Tocqueville and Victor Hugo, Count Walewski (Napoleon's illegitimate son, and a future Foreign Minister), and not least by King Louis Philippe, who spent long hours with him, regaling him with stories of what he called his 'life of great vicissitude' (Hibbert, p. 155). It cannot be doubted that Disraeli responded with the diet of treacly flattery, which he later used with such effect on Queen Victoria.

Back home, he applied himself with energy to rebuilding his political career. Hitherto, he had been widely (and largely justifiably) seen as a brilliant, but unprincipled opportunist, with no abiding political philosophy. He now set out to formulate one, based on a deeply romantic view of the historic role of the aristocracy, which he came to see as the receptacle of all that was noble and generous in British society. He combined this with a total disdain for the money-grubbing middle class and sympathy for the poor and the workers. He discerned a community of interest between the landed and labouring classes, and – by extension – between the Tories and the Radicals, which justified his own peregrination between these two parties, which others saw as mutually contradictory. His elevated view of aristocrats was not just theoretical, but was based on actual models, in the shape of a small band of youthful MPs, all of whom had been educated together at Eton and Cambridge, known as Young England, which would – in modern terminology – be best described as a left-wing Tory pressure group. The three stalwarts of this group were Alexander Baillie-Cochrane (later Lord Lamington), MP for Bridport, the Hon. George Sydney Smythe, MP for Canterbury, and Lord John Manners, MP for Newark and son of the Duke of Rutland. All three were extremely attractive and congenial young men. Initially, they may have looked upon Disraeli as a *parvenu*, but they were deeply impressed by his gifts, and he was welcomed into the group, and soon recognized as its effective leader.

Disraeli now embarked on writing the trilogy of political and social novels – *Coningsby, Sybil (or The Two Nations),* and *Tancred* – which appeared between 1844 and 1847, and on which his reputation as a literary figure essentially rest. He attempted to weave his own political ideas into the novels, in which the Young England trio and many other political figures appear in scarcely disguised forms. It was in *Sybil* that the famous passage occurs:

> 'Two nations between whom there is no intercourse and no sympathy; who are ignorant of each other's habits, thoughts, and feelings, as if they were dwellers in different zones or inhabitants of different planets; who are formed by a different breeding, are fed by different food, are ordered by different manners, and are not governed by the same laws'. 'You speak of-' said Egremont hesitatingly, 'THE RICH AND THE POOR'. (Penguin Books edition, 1954)

Disraeli was to say 'My works are my life' and that anyone wishing to know him would find him there. The first two volumes in particular, sold extremely well, and were highly popular. By this time, too, his parliamentary reputation had soared, and he was seen as one of – if not the very best – speakers in the House of Commons. He was at his most impressive in the debates on the repeal of the Corn Laws in 1846 (see Chapter 12). Although the Tory Party revolt against Sir Robert Peel's initiative had been led by Lord Stanley in the Lords, and Lord George Bentinck in the Commons, it was Disraeli who made much the most effective – and personally wounding – attacks on the Prime Minister. Without his passionate interventions, which provoked enormous enthusiasm among the serried ranks of country squires who made up the bulk of Conservative MPs, it is unlikely that a large majority of them could have been mobilized to vote against their hitherto greatly respected Prime Minister, or to turn him out of office, at the first opportunity after repeal had been carried, with the assistance of Whig, Radical and Irish votes.

Disraeli was never a hard-line supporter of protectionism as such: he based his opposition to Peel on the necessity of political parties not betraying their principles, and as most Conservative MPs had been elected on a platform of maintaining the Corn Laws, it would be dishonourable, he argued, for them now to support repeal. He backed this up with a fierce defence of the landed interest, which he asserted was the backbone of the country's constitution and of its prosperity. There can be little doubt, however, that the bitterness of his invective against Peel was inspired – at least in large part – by his disappointment that he had not been rewarded with office. Peel had previously been cowed by the ferocity of his repeated onslaughts, but after Disraeli had said, during the third reading debate, that 'his whole life had been one of political larceny', he rose in his place to enquire why, if this was so, he had been 'ready, as I think he was, to unite his fortunes with mine in office?' (*Hansard*, 15 May 1846). With breathtaking audacity, Disraeli angrily denied that he had ever sought office. Peel, who, according to his colleague, Lord Lincoln, actually had Disraeli's letter of 1841 in his dispatch-case (Blake, p. 239), was too fastidious or too honourable to reveal the contents of a private letter, and Disraeli escaped unscathed from what would have been a highly damaging and humiliating revelation. The Conservative Party, which was fatally split by the Corn Law issue, has chosen to blame it retrospectively on Peel, who was promptly dropped from its pantheon of heroes. More objective observers, however, might conclude that Disraeli carried a greater responsibility, not only for the split in 1846, but for the fact that it led to a permanent fracture of the party.

Disraeli's performance in 1846 was the determining event of his whole career. It had two momentous consequences. It was to be another 28 years before a Conservative government was again elected with a clear majority in the House of Commons, and – by driving out virtually all the other MPs with ability – he greatly increased the chances that he himself would eventually become leader of the Conservative Party. As recounted in Chapter 14, it took some time before Stanley (now Lord Derby) could bring himself to accept

Disraeli as the undisputed Tory leader in the House of Commons. Yet by 1850 Disraeli was firmly in place, but not before he had adjusted himself to the role of frontbench spokesman, projecting a gravitas which had previously eluded him. Gone was his flamboyant attire: from now on 'he wore a suit of impeccable black, instead of the gorgeous colours of the past, and he spoke in a more weighty manner, avoiding the extravagance, the vituperation, and the imagery of his great philippics' (Blake, p. 256).

Moreover, this quintessentially urban figure attempted to turn himself into a country gentleman, exchanging his Shrewsbury constituency for the county seat of Buckinghamshire in the 1847 general election, which he went on to represent for the next 29 years, and buying a country house and estate in the county, Hughenden Manor. This cost £35,000 – far more than Mary Ann could afford, and much more than the legacy he received from his father, Isaac, who died in January 1848. He accepted a generous loan of £25,000 from the wealthy Bentinck and his two brothers, probably believing that he would never be called upon to repay it. But Bentinck was to die suddenly, within a year, and in 1857, his eldest brother, Lord Titchfield, who had become the Duke of Portland, suddenly called the loan in, putting Disraeli in severe difficulties and having to resort again to extortionate money-lenders to keep himself afloat. Relief finally came in 1863, when an elderly political admirer, Mrs. Brydges Williams, died, leaving him a legacy of £40,000, on condition of being buried in his vault at Hughenden. A wealthy widow, of Jewish descent, both Disraeli and his wife had been carefully cultivating her for years, in the apparent hope of eventually benefiting from her friendship.

For the best part of two decades, Disraeli was to lead the Tories in the Commons, under the tutelage of Derby, who came to value him highly, despite his initial misgivings. They had plenty of disagreements along the way, though Dizzy always treated him with deference, and conceded with good grace whenever the 14th Earl insisted on having his way. A frequent cause of contention was on the tactics to be pursued in trying to unseat the Whig, coalition or Liberal governments, which were in power for the bulk of this period. Disraeli was keen to make common cause with the Radicals, and even the Irish (after O'Connell's death in 1847) in parliamentary ambushes, which Derby frequently vetoed. He was much keener on effecting a reunion with the Peelites and was constantly wooing Lord Aberdeen and Gladstone, as well as Palmerston, whom he correctly identified as the most conservative of the Whigs. He might well have succeeded, had he been willing to abandon protectionism at an earlier stage than he actually did (in 1852), but the presence of Disraeli as his deputy acted as a severe deterrent to the Peelites. They hated him almost to a man because of the savage way in which he had attacked Peel in 1846–7. Disraeli was also widely unpopular for other reasons. He had not entirely lived down his earlier unsavoury reputation, was looked down upon by many aristocrats in his own party, as well as among the Peelites, and also suffered from anti-Semitic prejudices, which were only exacerbated by his strong support for the removal of the disqualification of Jewish MPs. One of Disraeli's severest critics in his own party was a future Prime Minister, Lord Robert Cecil MP (later the 3rd Marquess of Salisbury), who described him as 'an adventurer, a mere political gangster...without principles and honesty' (Hibbert, p. 231).

That he was able to maintain his position as Tory leader in the Commons throughout this period was due to three factors: the support of Derby, the absence of any plausible rival and – above all – his effectiveness. He was a master of parliamentary tactics, and dominated the House in debates, his only rival as an orator being Gladstone, who was certainly his superior as a platform speaker but perhaps not quite his equal as a parliamentary debater. In each of Derby's short premierships – in 1852, 1858–9 and 1866–8 – he served as Chancellor of the Exchequer and Leader of the Commons, and each time he was the key figure in the government. When Derby became Prime Minister for the first time, leading a minority government of almost unknown faces, Disraeli was far from keen to take the chancellorship, telling Derby that he had no knowledge of the subject. Derby brushed his misgivings aside, saying: 'You know as much as Mr Canning did. They give you the figures'.

The Treasury did indeed give Disraeli the figures, but when he came to prepare his budget, in the autumn of 1852, he did not much like what he saw. He had a tricky exercise to prepare, and – if he were to provide for a budget surplus, which was regarded as essential – he had very little margin of manoeuvre. His first priority was to satisfy his own supporters on the Tory benches, who were crying out for tax reductions favouring the landed interest, which had suffered as a result of the repeal of the Corn Laws. In order to do this, he would have to put up other taxes or cut public spending, which would not be popular. Yet he also needed to make other concessions which would appeal to the Radicals, whose votes he also needed to secure a Commons majority. He managed, with considerable ingenuity, to put a package together which might just conceivably have reconciled these conflicting objectives, when he was presented with a last-minute increase in the defence estimates, occasioned by a war scare with Napoleon's III's France. The adjustments he then had to make to bring in extra revenue destroyed the balance of his proposals, and when he presented them to the House, it soon became clear that he would not be able to win many votes from the Opposition benches. His discomfiture became complete when, after he had given what he thought would be the closing speech in the budget debate, William Gladstone rose to his feet. In a masterly oration, he coolly dissected all the inconsistencies in Disraeli's proposals, delivered a magisterial rebuke to him for the intemperance of his remarks, and staked his own claim for the chancellorship, to which he was duly appointed by Lord Aberdeen a few days later. When Gladstone sat down, the House divided, and the government was defeated by 305 votes to 286. Derby immediately resigned, and the government came to an end after less than a year in office. The date was 17 December 1852, and this also marked the effective beginning of the long rivalry between Disraeli and Gladstone, which was to dominate British politics for the next 28 years.

Disraeli, who had loved being in office, now faced the prospect of many more dreary years in opposition. He was furious with Derby, who had been summoned to the premiership by Queen Victoria in 1855, on the resignation of Aberdeen during the Crimean War, and had declined to take office, when Palmerston refused to serve under him. Then, quite unexpectedly, in 1858 Palmerston was forced from office as a result of Count Orsini's assassination attempt on Napoleon III (see Chapter 16), and Dizzy again became Chancellor and Leader of the Commons, in Derby's second government. This government was regarded as a distinct improvement on that of 1852, and lasted a little longer. Disraeli appeared more on top of his job as Chancellor, but shone more as Leader of the House, through which he successfully piloted the India Bill, which – following the suppression of the Indian mutiny – effectively wound up the East India Company, transferring its functions to the Viceroy and his administration. The principal piece of legislation presented, however, was a Reform Bill, carefully drafted by Disraeli to ensure that its effects would be more favourable to the Tories than their opponents. Its main provision was to equalize the franchise between borough and county constituencies, with a property qualification of £10 a year. It also introduced a system of plural voting (or 'fancy franchises', as they were called by the Radical leader, John Bright), giving additional votes to 'those who had an income of £10 a year from the Funds [government bonds], on possession of £60 in a savings bank; on persons receiving government payments of £20 a year; on doctors, lawyers, university graduates, ministers of religion, and certain categories of schoolmasters' (Blake, pp. 399–400).

It all seemed a bit too clever by half, and many Tories were alarmed by how far their party seemed to be prepared to enter into what had previously been regarded as Whig or Radical territory. The Liberal leader, Lord John Russell, cleverly moved an amendment which could be supported equally by those who felt the Bill had gone too far, as well as those who thought it did not go far enough. It was carried by 330 votes to 291, and, instead of resigning, Derby asked the Queen for a dissolution. The election – held in April 1859 – was won by the newly created Liberal Party. Lord Palmerston, who had politely rejected an extraordinary offer put privately to him by Disraeli, that he should assume the leadership of the Conservatives, with both Derby and Disraeli bowing out in his favour, became Prime Minister for the second time, serving for over six years until his death in 1865.

By this time, Disraeli, now aged 55, beginning to feel his years, much affected by the death of his sister Sarah, in December 1859, and irritated by continuing criticism from the more traditional Tories, momentarily thought of retiring from the fray. Yet there was no viable successor in view, apart from Derby's son, Lord Stanley MP, who was by now his closest collaborator in the Commons. But Stanley was mistrusted by many Tory MPs because of his left-wing views, and his father was not keen to promote him as his deputy. So Dizzy carried on, and was still leading the Tories in the Commons when Russell (now in the House of Lords) again became Prime Minister, on Palmerston's death in October 1865. Russell was determined to round off his political career by carrying a Reform Bill, which would lower the property qualification for voters (see Chapters 13 and 14). Disraeli skillfully led the opposition to the Bill in the Commons, and succeeded with the aid of right-wing Liberals (known as the Adullamites), in securing its defeat, which led to the resignation of Russell's government in June 1866. For the third time, Derby became Prime Minister of a minority government, with Disraeli as Chancellor and Leader of the House. Stanley became Foreign Secretary.

It was the Prime Minister, Lord Derby, who decreed that the first priority of his government would be to introduce a reform bill of its own, which went beyond that which had just been defeated (see Chapter 14). Disraeli, at first sceptical, was given the task of steering it through the House of Commons, where the government was in a minority of some 70 seats. His challenge, given that there were sure to be some rebels on his side of the House, including notably Lord Robert Cecil (now Lord Cranborne), was how to attract rather more than 70 votes from among the Liberals and Irish Members, to carry the Bill, whose principal provision was to extend the vote to all householders in borough constituencies, irrespective of their income. The Bill was heavily amended during its passage, notably by the exclusion of all the 'fancy franchises', on which Derby had insisted, in order to dilute the influence of the large number of working-class voters who would be added to the electorate. But Disraeli showed immense tactical skill in organizing *ad hoc* majorities for each of the Bill's other main provisions, leaving him with a clear majority of MPs who were prepared to support the bill as a whole, when it emerged from its Committee Stage.

During the later stages of the Bill's passage, Derby (who shepherded it through the Lords) suffered increasingly from ill-health, and in February 1868 submitted his resignation, advising the Queen to appoint Disraeli (now 63), rather than his own son, Lord Stanley, as his successor. Victoria was happy to do so, despite once having described him as 'detestable, unprincipled, reckless and not respectable', while Prince Albert had said that there was 'not one single element of the gentleman in his composition' (Hibbert, p. 269). Yet that had been long ago, and Dizzy had subsequently worked long and hard to win her favour, beginning with his tribute to Albert on the Prince Consort's death. This greatly surpassed all others, and brought much comfort to the stricken Queen.

Now as Prime Minister, he set out to consolidate his relationship with her. He took more time and trouble over his daily reports to her of parliamentary proceedings than any of his predecessors, seeking to turn them into minor literary masterpieces, and to entertain as well as inform his monarch. He followed to the full the advice which he gave to Matthew Arnold that 'Everyone likes flattery, and when you come to Royalty you should lay it on with a trowel'. When she published her *Leaves from the journal of our life in the Highlands,* in 1868, he delighted her by saying 'We authors, Ma'am'.

Disraeli made few changes to Derby's cabinet, replacing himself as Chancellor of the Exchequer with George Ward Hunt, a little-known barrister. He tried to lure Cranborne (the future Lord Salisbury), who had resigned over the 1867 Reform Bill, back into the government, but to no avail. His government was to last for 278 rather uneventful days, the main controversies being over a small war in Abyssinia (Ethiopia) and the proposal to endow a Catholic University in Ireland. Gladstone, now leader of the opposition, attacked this with great ferocity, coupling it with a demand to disestablish the (Anglican) Church of Ireland, to the great delight of the Non-Conformist churches. Disraeli called a general election in November 1868, hoping that the large number of new working-class voters enfranchised by the 1867 Act would show their gratitude by voting Tory. He was disappointed; the election produced a majority of over 100 for the Liberals, and Disraeli resigned without waiting to be defeated in a Commons vote. Victoria was mortified by having to accept Gladstone, whom she abominated, as Disraeli's successor, and was anxious to show her appreciation of her retiring Prime Minister by bestowing an important honour on him. He declined to accept, but asked instead for a peerage for his wife, who became Viscountess Beaconsfield.

For the next six years, Disraeli had a frustrating time, while his great rival Gladstone, presided over one of the great reforming governments of the nineteenth century. Mary Ann's health rapidly declined, and she died in December 1872, aged 80. Disraeli felt bereft, and paid her a heartfelt tribute, saying: 'There was no care which she could not mitigate, and no difficulty which she could not face. She was the most cheerful and the most courageous woman I ever knew'.

With her death, he also lost her private income and their London home at Gloucester Gate, which reverted to her first husband's heirs. For a year, he moved into a suite in Edward's Hotel, telling his friends that living in lonely hotel rooms was like 'a cave of despair'. He later acquired a small house in Whitehall Gardens. Many years before her death, Mary Ann had written to Disraeli a letter urging him to re-marry, and not to live alone. He was more than ready to follow her advice. 'At the age of sixty-eight he fell head over heels in love with Lady Bradford, who was fifty-four and a grandmother' (Blake, p. 531). Unfortunately, Lady Bradford was married to a Tory peer, so Disraeli proposed instead to her elder sister, Lady Chesterfield, then over 70 years of age, and recently widowed. 'She refused him, of course, well aware that he would have asked her sister instead, had not Lady Bradford been married already' (Hibbert, p. 298). Disraeli was to pursue the two sisters for the last eight years of his life, constantly seeking their company, and bombarding them with letters (some 1,100 to Lady Bradford and 500 to her sister). These were published in two volumes in 1929, and have been a major source for all his recent biographers. They were kind and sympathetic to him, but – though several other aristocratic ladies made it fairly clear that they regarded him as an eligible widower – neither of these sisters saw him in this light.

In the early 1870s, Disraeli, to general astonishment, resumed his career as a novelist, publishing *Lothair*, in 1870, the first novel written by a former Prime Minister. It was a great success, leading his publisher – Longman's – to produce a collected edition of Disraeli's novels some of which – notably the semi-autobiographical *Vivien Grey* and *Contrarini Fleming* – Dizzy had bowdlerised, in order not to reopen ancient controversies. Altogether, Disraeli made some £10,000 from the exercise – a welcome addition to his now diminished income. After his wife's death, he absorbed himself more and more in politics, showing a renewed dedication , and throwing off the lethargy induced by Mary Anne's long terminal illness, and his own bouts of ill-health. He instituted a thorough overhaul of the Conservative Party, establishing the National Union of Conservative Associations, ensuring that there was a functioning branch of the party in every single constituency, equipped to appeal to the greatly increased electorate created by the 1867 Act. This effort bore fruit in 1874, when Gladstone unexpectedly called a general election one year ahead of time. Disraeli fought the election largely as a stout defender of the Anglican Church, but the result – a majority of more than 50 for the Conservatives – was much more due to 'reform fatigue' induced by the great burst of legislative action by the Liberal government (see Chapter 18). Like other reforming administrations, it found that while the majority who benefited from its reforms took them for granted, those who had been disadvantaged were spurred into furious opposition, determined to defeat the government which had dared to challenge their privileges.

The government which Disraeli formed, on 20 February 1874, was markedly stronger than his administration in 1868. Lord Cranborne (now the 3rd Marquess of Salisbury) was induced to overcome his distaste for the new Prime Minister, and resumed his former post as Secretary for India, Sir Stafford Northcote became Chancellor of the Exchequer and Lord Stanley (now the 15th Earl of Derby) was again Foreign Secretary. The new Lord Derby, formerly a close associate of Disraeli, was now often at odds with him, his increasingly left-wing views making him seem to have more in common with the Liberal Party (to which he was later to defect, in 1880). As Home Secretary, Disraeli appointed a middle-class protégé of Derby's, R.A. Cross. 'Disraeli was a ceremonious, slightly remote, but patient and unassertive chairman of cabinet, which conducted its business with laxity' (Parry). He concerned himself mainly with foreign affairs and matters concerning the monarchy, and it was Derby and Cross who took the initiative in promoting the domestic legislative programme. They were determined to carry on the reforming policies of Gladstone's government, to prevent the Conservative Party being seen, once again, as a reactionary force, and to increase its appeal to centrist opinion. It was due to them that, during 1875, a whole host of social reform measures were carried, including two Trade Union Acts, the Public Health Act, the Factory Act, the Sale of Food and Drugs Act and the Conspiracy and Protection of Property Act, which legalized peaceful picketing. Disraeli's posthumous reputation as a social reformer owes much to the efforts of these two colleagues. He took little interest in the passage of these Bills, and Derby complained in his diary that he 'detests the class of business which he is apt to call parochial' (Parry, 2004).

In May1876, Disraeli performed his supreme act of flattery to Queen Victoria, by having her proclaimed as Empress of India, despite widespread parliamentary opposition. Three months later, she returned the compliment by creating him Earl of Beaconsfield, and he subsequently led the government from the Lords, his health no longer permitting him to spend the long hours in the Commons to which he had become accustomed. At about the same time, Gladstone announced his own retirement as leader of the Liberal Party, and it appeared that the days of their duels were over. In November 1875, Disraeli had taken his first major step in foreign policy, which indicated his ambition to play a more forceful part on the international stage, and to take over from Palmerston the role of forcefully defending perceived British interests throughout the world. His success in doing this led to the Tories acquiring the reputation of being 'the patriotic party', which greatly increased their electoral appeal, particularly among working-class voters. The ruler of Egypt, the Khedive Ismail, facing bankruptcy, offered to sell his minority 40 per cent stake in the Suez Canal to French financial interests, which would have left the canal totally in French hands. Disraeli moved sharply in, made an improved offer, and bought the shares for the British government, with the aid of a large loan from the Rothschilds. The impression was created that Britain now controlled the canal, which proved a highly popular move. At about this time, several revolts against Turkish rule broke out in Bulgaria and Bosnia-Herzegovina, and, when the Ottomans moved to crush them, Russia threatened war against the Turks. Stories of brutal Turkish massacres of Bulgarians caused great indignation, and forced Gladstone out of his retirement, to lead a stirring campaign to drive the Turks 'bag and baggage' out of Europe. Beaconsfield, as he now was, dismissed the massacre stories as 'exaggerated' and was much more concerned with preventing Russian encroachments into the Balkans than in reprimanding the Turks, for whom he retained his youthful sympathy. He proposed a con-ference of the great powers of Europe (Austria, Britain, France, Germany, Italy and Russia), to try to persuade the Russians to hold their hand and the Turks to introduce long-overdue reforms in their subject territories.

To this, he sent Lord Salisbury, rather than Derby, the Foreign Secretary, from whom he was becoming increasingly estranged. The Conference, held in Constantinople, was a failure (see Chapter 19), but it had the totally unex-pected effect of turning Salisbury into an international statesman of great renown. Russia now declared war on Turkey, and – after overcoming stubborn and prolonged resistance before the Bulgarian town of Plevna – its forces swept to the gates of Constantinople, where they imposed the humiliating Treaty of San Stefano on the Turks, stripping the country of large parts of its territory. Beaconsfield then ordered the mobilization of troops to put pressure on Russia, leading to the resignation of the peace-loving Derby, and his replacement by Salisbury, who – as recounted in Chapter 19 – now took a leading role in forc-ing the Russians to back down. They agreed to attend a Congress in Berlin, presided over by the German Chancellor, Bismarck, but where Beaconsfield created a tremendous impression, with his charm and panache, though most of the serious negotiation was conducted by Salisbury. Dizzy got on brilliantly with Bismarck, who made the famous comment 'Der alte Jude; das ist der Mann'. The result of the Congress was that Russia was forced to disgorge most of its gains, while the Turks handed over the island of Cyprus to Britain, as an east Mediterranean base. Beaconsfield and Salisbury returned in triumph to London, claiming to have brought back 'Peace with Honour'. Victoria wished to honour her favourite Prime Minister by making him a Duke. He declined, but accepted the Garter, on condition that it was also bestowed on Salisbury.

Dizzy remained Prime Minister for nearly another two years, basking in the glory of Berlin, but not attempting many fresh political initiatives. His health was not good – he suffered from gout, asthma and, perhaps, Bright's disease, a kidney disorder. Then – in March 1880 – misled by two Tory victories in by-elections, he called a general election, a year before it was due. It was a disaster: the Liberals won 414 seats, and the Tories only 238. Beaconsfield had hoped that his foreign policy successes would bring him victory, but more relevant to the voters was the bleak position of the economy, after six successive bad har-vests and an industrial recession. His previously popular imperialist policies also cost him some support, following humiliating British defeats in Zululand and Afghanistan.

A rejuvenated Gladstone replaced him as Prime Minister, and Disraeli settled down to finish a further novel – *Endymion* – on which he had been working over many years. Lightly based on his own early political career, it was well received, and netted him another £10,000. Five months later – on 19 April 1881 – he died at Hughenden, after a severe attack of bronchitis, aged 76. A greatly concerned Queen Victoria had proposed to visit him during his last days, but Disraeli, whose mordant humour had not yet deserted him, replied 'No it is better not. She would only ask me to take a message to Albert'.

Altogether, Disraeli led his party in Parliament, first in the Commons, later in the Lords, for rather over 20 years, for less than seven of which he was Prime Minister. He was a supremely accomplished parliamentarian, but hardly a great Prime Minister. He was to lead a moderately reformist government, which had one major success in foreign affairs, the Congress of Berlin, for which he must share the credit with his Foreign Secretary, Lord Salisbury. Disraeli's greatest contribution was the legacy which he left to the Conservative Party. It had been effectively smashed by him in the 1840s, but he slowly rebuilt it, and left behind him a party which was to be an extremely successful competitor for many years to come, under the newly enlarged electorate, which he had created by his 1867 Reform Bill. Disraeli was not, in practice, a notable social reformer, but – more because of his writings, *Sybil* in particular, than the legislation for which he was responsible – he acquired a durable reputation of being one. This has continued to inspire Conservative leaders, with some notable exceptions, including Margaret Thatcher, until the present day. His concept of bridging the gap between the 'two nations' has been a potent rallying cry, even though subsequent Tory governments have seldom shown great assiduity in pursuing it.

Works consulted

Robert Blake, 1969, *Disraeli*, London, Methuen.
Sarah Bradford, 1982, *Disraeli*, London, Weidenfeld & Nicolson.
Benjamin Disraeli, 1954, *Sybil or The Two Nations*, Harmondsworth, Penguin Books.
Christopher Hibbert, 1981, (ed.), *Greville's* England, London, Folio Society.
Christopher Hibbert, 2005, *Disraeli: A Personal History*, London, Harper Perennial.
André Maurois, 1978, *Vie de Disraeli*, Paris, Gallimard.
W.F. Monypenny and G.E. Buckle, 1910–1920, *The Life of Benjamin Disraeli, Earl of Beaconsfield*, 6 vols, London, John Murray.
Parry Jonathan, 2004, Article in *Oxford Dictionary of National Biography*.
D.C. Somervell, 1926, *Disraeli and Gladstone*, New York, Garden City Publishing.
John Vincent, 1990, *Disraeli*, Oxford University Press.
Stanley Weintraub, 1993, *Disraeli*, London, Hamish Hamilton.

18

William Ewart Gladstone – From 'Stern Unbending Tory' to 'the People's William'

The Right Honourable
WILLIAM EWART GLADSTONE M P

For nearly three decades – from 1852 to 1881 – two men – Benjamin Disraeli and William Gladstone – were to dominate British politics. To say that they did not get on would be a monumental under-statement. They came to hate each other with a visceral fury. Nor was this attenuated by any respect for each other's personal qualities. For Gladstone, Disraeli was nothing more than a 'charlatan', while Dizzy regarded Gladstone as a 'humbug'.

Of the two, Gladstone came from a much more conventional background. His parents were Scottish Presbyterians, transplanted to Liverpool, where they joined the Church of England, favouring its more Evangelical wing. William Ewart Gladstone was born on 29 December 1809, the fifth child and youngest son of John Gladstone and his second wife, Anne Mackenzie Robinson. A self-made man, John Gladstone (originally Gladstones, he dropped the final 's' before his arrival in England), made a fortune as a trader with America and the West Indies, dealing in sugar, cotton and slaves. In Liverpool, he became a pillar of the local Tories and was instrumental in persuading George Canning to stand for the constituency in 1812. John Gladstone himself was also elected to the Commons, serving 'from 1818 to 1827 for a series of corrupt boroughs' (Matthew, 1986, p. 4). He was, according to Matthew, a classic Samuel Smiles character, 'mixing duty, probity and religion with materialism, initiative and a strong drive for worldly success' (Ibid.). Matthew goes on to describe the home atmosphere in which the young William grew up. It was:

> moderately Evangelical, with the Evangelicals' strong emphasis on the reading of the Bible and on personal duty, family obligation, sin and atonement. Religion brought joy to the Gladstone women, but it weighed heavily on the men, and especially upon William... William's mother believed that he had been 'truly converted to God' when he was about ten. (Ibid. p. 6)

William was heavily influenced by his mother, and his elder sister, Anne, both of whom were very – but cheerfully – pious, and were regarded by him as saints. Anne was to die, still unmarried, at the age of 26. She and her mother possessed

> the Evangelical religious assurance, repose and sense of grace which Gladstone never throughout his life gained. For him, awareness of sin... was always uppermost, never its atoning opposite. His mother and sister represented to him, therefore, a quality of holiness which both inspired him and intensified his sense of inadequacy. (Ibid, p. 7)

Following the example of the elder Sir Robert Peel, who, having 'made his pile', determined that his children should enjoy the privileges and opportunities open to the aristocracy, John Gladstone sent three of his four sons to Eton, the two daughters being educated at home by governesses, while the remaining brother – at his own insistence – went to the Royal Naval College at Portsmouth. Neither of William's brothers distinguished themselves at the school, but, in Roy Jenkins's words, 'William took to Eton like a duck to water' (Jenkins, 1995, p. 12). A tall, good-looking and ferociously hard-working young man, who felt no sense of inferiority to his aristocratic schoolmates, he was a notable success, both academically and socially. He was soon co-opted to the school elite, becoming a member of the Eton Society (later known as 'Pop'), where, from the outset, he acquired a formidable reputation as a debater. Yet, comments Jenkins,

> For an outstanding orator, which he was already on the way to becoming, he was singularly lacking in neatness of phrase...His force depended essentially on his flashing eyes and the physical authority of his presence. Thus the printed records of his speeches do not compare with those of Chatham [the Elder Pitt], or Burke or Canning or Abraham Lincoln, or even with the contrived epigrams of Disraeli, whose flippancy was so antipathetic to Gladstone. (Jenkins, p. 13)

He made a number of close friends, one of whom – Lord Lincoln, the heir to the dukedom of Newcastle – was later to be instrumental in launching his political career. He also had a highly charged 'on-off' relationship with Arthur Hallam, the brilliant and dangerously attractive son of a constitutional historian, who was two years younger than Gladstone but was generally held to outshine him. Hallam was to die tragically at the age of 22, and was the subject of Tennyson's famous poem *In Memoriam*. Jenkins commented that 'there is no evidence of any homosexual behaviour', but 'what was most remarkable, however, was that, as Professor Robert Martin's life of Tennyson points out, 'sixty years after his [Hallam's] death the Prime Minister and the Poet Laureate were still jealous of each other's place in his affections' (Jenkins, p. 18).

In his fourth year at Eton – on 16 July 1825 – he wrote the first entry in the diary which he was to continue until he was 85. His purpose, he later wrote, was to 'tell, amidst the recounting of numberless mercies...a melancholy tale of my own inward life' (Matthew, 1986, p. 7). In fact, it is largely a catalogue of the books which Gladstone read – over 20,000 in all – the events he attended, and the people he encountered – some 22,000 – in his long life, interspersed with agonizing introspections as to whether he was truly acting out God's purpose in his life. The entire diary, brilliantly edited by M.R.D. Foot and, in particular, H.C.G. (Colin) Matthew, was published in 14 volumes, between 1968 and 1994, under the title *The Gladstone Diaries with Cabinet Minutes and Prime-Ministerial Correspondence*. Thanks to this Herculean effort, more is known of the private and public life of Gladstone than of any other nineteenth-century politician.

Gladstone did not find the teaching at Eton very inspiring, and later wrote that the one thing the school taught him was the importance of strict accuracy in everything he attempted. Otherwise, according to Matthew, it made him: 'proficient in Greek and Latin, competent in French, barely adequate in mathematics, and largely ignorant of the sciences. Yet his self-education in English literature, history and theology was already considerable, and the school had achieved his father's objective of grafting him onto the metropolitan political elite' (Matthew, 2004).

In October 1828, Gladstone, aged nearly 19, went up to Christ Church, Oxford, then – and for much of the nineteenth century – the most intellectually distinguished of Oxford colleges. Here he excelled himself, taking double firsts in *Literae Humaniores* and Mathematics, in the autumn of 1831, 22 years after Robert Peel had performed the same feat (see Chapter 12). Yet studying was perhaps merely incidental to Gladstone's life at Oxford; it was a major formative influence both in his religious and political development. In religion, he drifted away somewhat from his Evangelical roots, and associated himself more with High Church figures such as Edward Pusey, John Keble, F.D. Maurice and John Henry Newman, several of whom – to Gladstone's dismay – later joined the Roman Church, as did another future cardinal with whom he became acquainted, Henry Manning, who was at that time rather Low Church. Some, at least, of Gladstone's fellow students found him an intolerable prig, and late one evening his rooms at Christ Church were invaded by a group of college 'hearties', who proceeded to beat him up. Gladstone recorded the occasion in his diary, in these words:

> Here I have great reason to be thankful to that God whose mercies fail not... 1) Because this incident must tend to the mortification of my pride, by God's grace... It is no disgrace to be beaten for Christ was buffeted and smitten... 2) Because here I have to some small extent an opportunity of exercising the duty of forgiveness. (Jenkins, 1950, p. 21)

At about this time, Gladstone thought seriously about offering himself for ordination as a priest, and wrote to his father asking permission to do so. The elder Gladstone had much grander ambitions for his son, and wrote back strongly discouraging him, and Gladstone – possibly secretly relieved – readily complied and seems never to have had any regrets. Gladstone, who had already shone at Eton, was by a wide margin the best debater of his time at Oxford. He honed his skills in an essay club which he founded along with a group of Old Etonian friends. Intended as a counterpart of the Cambridge Apostles (of which Arthur Hallam was a member), it was known as the Weg (after Gladstone's initials). Unlike the Apostles, it did not survive the departure from the University of its founders. Yet Gladstone's finest performances were reserved for the Oxford

Union, founded only five years earlier. Elected its President, his most notable speech, on 17 May 1831, was a vehement attack on the Reform Bill, then making its troubled way through Parliament. He spoke for 45 minutes, and carried the resolution against the Bill by 94 votes to 38. Also speaking on the same side in the debate, though with far less impact, was his Old Etonian friend, the Earl of Lincoln. He was deeply impressed by Gladstone's performance.

Gladstone left the university at the end of 1831, and two months later set off for the 'Grand Tour', ending up in Rome in July 1832. In the meantime, the Reform Bill was passed, and preparations were made for the general election of the reformed House. One of the strongest opponents of the Bill was the Duke of Newcastle, who was the proprietor of a series of rotten or pocket boroughs. Several of these had been eliminated by the Bill, but he still had a predominant influence in the Nottinghamshire constituency of Newark. At the urging of his son, Lord Lincoln, the Duke wrote to John Gladstone asking whether William would be interested being one of the two Tory candidates. John Gladstone thought the offer was a bit premature, but wrote to his son in Rome, who accepted it with enthusiasm. The following December, he was duly elected, heading the poll, with 887 votes, against 798 for his fellow Tory, and 726 for the sole Whig candidate. He was just short of his twenty-third birthday. He made his maiden speech on 3 June 1833, and his choice of topic was unfortunate. He was opposing the government's Bill to abolish slavery in the British Empire, which he did not object to in principle, but questioned the provisions for compensating the slave-owners, who included his father, who owned plantations in Jamaica. In his subsequent speeches, Gladstone made a considerable impression on the House, and was soon seen as a 'coming man', the historian Macaulay referring to him in an article as 'the rising hope of those stern and unbending Tories' (Matthew, 1986, p. 29). When Peel formed his minority Tory government in December 1834, Gladstone, aged just 25, was included as a Junior Lord of the Treasury. Within a month he was promoted to Colonial Under-Secretary, in which post he served for less than three months before the resignation of the government in April 1835.

In opposition, Gladstone's main concern was the protection of the role of the Anglican Church against what he saw as Whig attempts to undermine its privileges, particularly in Ireland, where Lord John Russell unsuccessfully sought to divert part of its tithe income to secular purposes (see Chapter 13). At this time, Gladstone held semi-theocratic views, believing that the state had a duty, through the established Church, to impose a Christian morality on its subjects. He argued the case for this in two books, *The State in its Relations with the Church* (1838) and *Church principles Considered in their Results* (1841). He became closely involved with the Tractarian movement (also known as the Oxford Movement) of High Church Anglicans, attended Church daily and, in 1838, drew up proposals for what he called a 'Third Order', a lay brotherhood of persons in public life. This was never formally established, but Gladstone with a number of like-minded friends later set up a small private all-male group, which they called 'the Engagement'. They met regularly together for prayer sessions and discussions on the religious life, committing themselves to devote a proportion of their incomes, and a great deal of their spare time, to charitable activities.

During the late 1830s, Gladstone made proposals of marriage to three aristocratic ladies. He proved himself an awkward and unpersuasive suitor, and was given short shrift by Caroline Farquhar, a society beauty who later married a son of Earl Grey, and by Lady Frances Douglas, daughter of the Earl of Morton. He had more success with Catherine Glynne, the sister of Sir Stephen Glynne, who had been with him both at Eton and Christ Church, and who was the owner of the Hawarden castle and estate in North Wales. They were married on 25 July 1839, at Hawarden parish Church, when Gladstone was 29 and Catherine, 27. She shared his strong Christian beliefs, but their characters were very dissimilar, she being much more informal, vague and untidy, in contrast to her husband's methodical and meticulous ways. Gladstone proved himself an uxorious husband, and the marriage was largely successful, though they tended to drift apart in later years. In the first 12 years of their marriage, four sons and four daughters (one of whom died in infancy) were born.

Sir Robert Peel was deeply impressed by Gladstone, whom he saw as a young man very much in his own image, and when he again became Prime Minister, this time of majority Tory government, in 1841, he appointed Gladstone Vice-President of the Board of Trade. The President was the Earl of Ripon, a former Prime Minister under the name of Viscount Goderich. A veteran politician who had rather run out of steam, the effective head of the department was Gladstone. Two years later Ripon retired, and Gladstone took his place, joining the Cabinet at the age of 33. Strongly influenced by Peel he became a fervent advocate of free trade, and carried a major piece of legislation – the Railways Act – through the Commons. His reputation as a hard-working, decisive and formidably well informed minister soared, and he was tipped by John Stuart Mill to become Peel's successor as Tory leader. Publicly successful, he went through a deep religious and sexual crisis during these years. It began painfully to dawn upon him that his theocratic ideas were impracticable, and his attitude to the Conservative Party insensibly changed. Formerly, he had seen the party as the chosen instrument of God's will for the nation, but increasing familiarity with his fellow Tory MPs slowly disillusioned him.

Now he viewed the party more in terms of being marginally preferable to the Whigs and much more so to the Radicals, rather than a thing apart. He also suffered from acute sexual frustration. According to Matthew, he was almost certainly a virgin at the time of his marriage, but was highly sexed, and found it difficult to abstain from sexual relations with Catherine during her repeated long periods of pregnancy when, according to Victorian custom, intercourse was strongly disadvised. He sought relief in furtive reading of pornography, but was driven more and more to his 'night-time work' of attempting to rescue 'fallen women'. This he had begun in 1840, as his chosen charitable work within the Engagement group, but – despite the meagre success of his efforts – he estimated that only one of the first 80 or 90 women he took up with was redeemed, he now stepped up his activities, which continued, including during his premierships, until his old age. He made little effort to conceal what he was doing, often taking the women he had encountered back to his house for a meal with Catherine, who approved her husband's activities, though it is doubtful if she knew their full extent. For Gladstone was physically attracted by many of them, and often succumbed to temptation, and then flagellated himself in atonement, signifying the occasions with a symbol resembling a whip in his diary. It is doubtful if he ever went 'the whole way' and indeed 17 months before his death he wrote a solemn declaration to his son, the Rev. Stephen Gladstone, now the Rector of Hawarden, assuring him that he had never 'been guilty of the act which is known as that of infidelity to the marriage bed' (Matthew, 1986, p. 93). Nevertheless, his diaries make it clear that he felt a very strong sense of having sinned on a number of occasions. Many of Gladstone's friends and colleagues became aware of his midnight prowls, and were concerned that they might cause a scandal, but not a mention appeared in the press until well after his death. This side of Gladstone's life was virtually ignored in the famous three-volume biography written by his friend and colleague John Morley, and it was only in 1927, during the course of a libel action between his son Herbert and a scurrilous author called Captain Peter Wright, that it became known to the general public. The jury in this trial, giving judgement in favour of Herbert Gladstone, added a note to the effect that the evidence had 'completely vindicated the high moral character of the late Mr W.E. Gladstone' (Jenkins, p. 106). It was not until the publication of Gladstone's diaries in the final third of the twentieth century that the full extent of Gladstone's nocturnal activities and his own sense of shame became known to scholars.Gladstone's cabinet career was interrupted in February 1845, when he resigned in protest against the decision to make a small grant to Maynooth College, in Dublin, a seminary for the training of Catholic priests. He felt that, as a stalwart defender of the Church of England, he could not be associated with this action. It amazed many of his colleagues that this apparently highly ambitious minister should risk his career over such a trifle, but it was not the first sign he had given of an over-sensitive conscience. Peel, however, was determined to bring Gladstone back to his team, and when he reconstructed his cabinet, after the defection of Lord Stanley over the projected repeal of the Corn Laws, the following December (see Chapter 12), he persuaded Gladstone to accept the post of Colonial Secretary. This obliged him to resign his seat, and fight a by-election, but the Duke of Newcastle – a strong supporter of the Corn Laws – refused to back him as a candidate for Newark. This put Gladstone in the anomalous and historically unique position of serving in the Cabinet without being a member of either House. As Colonial Secretary, Gladstone showed himself to be a strong advocate of home rule for the inhabitants of British colonies, particularly in Canada and New Zealand.

Gladstone was again in opposition after July 1846, when the Peel government was defeated on the morrow of the repeal of the Corn Laws. He had unhesitatingly backed Peel in the party split, and appeared not to find the division in the party especially painful, probably because he had already lost his faith in its divine mission. He remained out of Parliament until the 1847 general election, when he was returned as one of the two Members for Oxford University, which he represented for the next 18 years. He now had to concern himself very much with family problems. One arose from the collapse of the business activities of his brother-in-law, Stephen Glynne, who was facing bankruptcy, putting his continued ownership of the Hawarden estate at risk. Gladstone, who on his marriage had taken up residence there with Catherine, now moved sharply to take over control of Glynne's affairs, and over a period of years managed to re-establish them, with financial help from John Gladstone. In the process, he gradually – if gently – squeezed Stephen out of his position as the head of the household of Hawarden. Gladstone also discouraged Stephen's younger brother, the Rev. Henry Glynne, from embarking on a marriage, which might have produced an heir, in the apparent hope that the eventual ownership of the estate would fall to his own eldest son, Willy.

Gladstone was also deeply concerned over the delicate health of his infant daughter Mary and took her to Naples for four months between October 1850 and February 1851. In Naples he attended the trial of a leading liberal opponent of the Bourbon régime and visited a notorious prison, where political prisoners were kept in appalling conditions. On his return to London, he published two indignant *Letters to Lord Aberdeen*, a former Foreign Secretary who, since the death of Peel in July 1850, was the recognized leader of the Peelites, condemning the Kingdom of the Two Sicilies as 'the negation of God erected into a system of government'. Gladstone's published letters deeply embarrassed Aberdeen, who had no wish to be involved in the controversy, but they gave Gladstone an overnight international reputation. He was seen by conservatives throughout Europe as a dangerous supporter of revolutionaries, but was heroised by liberals. It was the first of many passionate pronouncements by Gladstone on foreign affairs, which sat ill with his domestic reputation as a cautious politician, who still considered himself a Conservative.

In December 1851, John Gladstone, who had been made a baronet in Peel's resignation honours in 1846 – more a tribute to the son than the father – died at his Scottish home, four days short of his eighty-seventh birthday. William was at the bedside of his formidable father, and recorded in his diary that 'I thrice kissed my Father's cheek & forehead before & after his death: the only kisses I can remember' (Matthew, 2004). His mother had died 16 years earlier, at the age of 64. Henceforth Gladstone regarded himself as the head of the family, though he was the fourth of four brothers. He was particularly concerned about the fate of his younger, unmarried sister, Helen, who became addicted to alcohol and drugs, and – perhaps worse in Gladstone's eyes – converted to Catholicism. They were estranged for many years, but were reconciled before her death in 1881.

When Lord John Russell's Whig government was defeated in a parliamentary vote in February 1852, Gladstone was invited to join the minority Tory government led by Lord Derby. He was tempted, but declined – for three reasons – the unwillingness of Derby at this stage to renounce protectionism, the failure to include all the leading Peelites in the invitation and – perhaps crucially – Gladstone's determination not to serve in a subordinate role to Disraeli, the Tory leader in the Commons. While Dizzy would have been prepared to efface himself if Palmerston – also targeted by Derby – had been willing to join the government, there was no question of his making way for Gladstone. Had Gladstone accepted Derby's invitation, he might well have emerged as his eventual successor and a future Tory Prime Minister. His refusal opened the way – though it was far from clear at the time – to a quite different destiny.

A decisive step in this new direction was Gladstone's speech – a great parliamentary triumph – condemning the budget which Disraeli, as Derby's Chancellor of the Exchequer, presented in December 1852 (see Chapter 17). Showing complete mastery of the subject, and extraordinary forensic power, Gladstone effectively destroyed the whole intellectual basis on which the budget had been constructed and removed any remaining possibility that it would be accepted by a majority of MPs. The dramatic effect of his intervention was enhanced by a fierce thunderstorm which raged outside, with frequent flashes of lightning visible through the windows of the Chamber. The government was defeated in the ensuing vote, and immediately resigned, being replaced by a coalition of Peelites and Whigs, led by Lord Aberdeen. It was no surprise after this performance that Gladstone was appointed Chancellor of the Exchequer in the new government, and on 28 December 1852, he began the first of his four chancellorships.

It is an open question whether Gladstone was the greatest man ever to be Britain's Prime Minister. Roy Jenkins thought he was, when he concluded his biography, but later changed his mind and awarded the palm to Churchill. Yet his primacy as Chancellor of the Exchequer has never been challenged. He effectively created the post, as it has existed in modern times, and none of his successors has rivalled the impact which he made. His first period in this office opened with an unedifying quarrel with his predecessor, Disraeli. The

Chancellor's official robes, first worn by the Younger Pitt, had been passed on to each of his successors, who bought them from their own predecessors, but Disraeli insisted on keeping them (they are still on display in his home at Hughenden Manor, now owned by the National Trust), and a disgruntled Gladstone was forced to have a new set made at his own expense. This dispute, and a parallel one about paying for furniture at the Chancellor's official Downing Street residence, only served to confirm the extremely low opinion each of them had already formed about the other.

Gladstone presented his first budget on 18 April 1853. His speech, which lasted for four and three-quarter hours was every bit as much a triumph as his destruction of Disraeli's budget four months earlier, and it set the new Aberdeen government off to an encouraging start. It was as if he was carrying on where Peel left off – the centre piece of the budget was another large step towards free trade, removing tariffs altogether from 123 items, and reducing them on another 133. This was to be financed by broadening the base of income tax, which he described as 'an engine of gigantic power for great national purposes' and extending it for a further seven years, an unheard proposition for what was regarded only as a temporary tax, renewable – if at all – only on a yearly basis. Nevertheless, he proposed a steady diminution of its rate, and that it should be finally phased out by 1860 – a proposal rendered impracticable by the outbreak of the Crimean War two years later. Gladstone's performance in 1853 can be seen as the first modern budget. He instituted the practice of presenting it with a detailed annual account of the nation's finances, and made this presentation one of the central occasions of the parliamentary year. His chancellorship marked the effective ending of the Prime Minister's functions as First Lord of the Treasury, and clearly established that the Chancellor should normally be seen as the second man in the government, even though the office continued – in formal terms – to be junior to those of the Secretaries of State. Altogether, Gladstone introduced eleven budgets during his two chancellorships in the 1850s and 1860s, and, in the words of a later Chancellor (Roy Jenkins) gave them 'such a sweep and force that their presentation became a fixture of the national life comparable with Derby Day or the State Opening of Parliament' (Jenkins, 1998, p. 6). Apart from 1853, his most notable budgets were in1860 and 1861. In the first of these, he proposed the abolition of paper duties (which had made newspapers prohibitively expensive) only to have his proposal thrown out by the Lords. The following year he tried again, but this time presented it, together with all his other proposals, in a consolidated Finance Bill (the first time this had been done), and challenged the Lords to reject it – an action which they never again contemplated until – with fateful results – they threw out Lloyd George's 'People's Budget', in 1909. One of Gladstone's persistent aims as Chancellor was 'retrenchment'. He had a horror of what he regarded as unnecessary public expenditure, and once famously said that 'No Chancellor of the Exchequer is worth his salt who is not ready to save what are meant by candle-ends and cheese-parings in the cause of his country' (Speech at Edinburgh, 29 November 1879).

Apart from his budgets, Gladstone's main activity during the Aberdeen government was in overseeing parliamentary bills designed to reform the two ancient universities. As an MP for Oxford University, he took a close interest in their contents and managed to ensure that they were moderate in their scope, preserving the collegiate structure of the universities. Perhaps more significantly, he commissioned the Northcote-Trevelyan Report on recruitment to the Civil Service, which led to meritocracy replacing patronage as the basis for future appointments. Gladstone initially supported the Crimean War, despite his strong disapproval of the Turkish regime, and took energetic steps to raise revenue to pay for it, in an attempt to prevent the national debt from rising steeply. His close friend Lord Lincoln, who was now the 5th Duke of Newcastle, was Secretary for War and was more directly involved in the military preparations. When Aberdeen was forced to resign over the conduct of the war, Newcastle left with him. Gladstone and most of the other Peelites joined Palmerston's new government, but resigned after a few weeks, partly because they saw little point in continuing the war after the initial pretext – the Russian occupation of the two Romanian principalities – had come to an end.

Gladstone spent the next four years in opposition, and risked political isolation. He immersed himself in classical studies, publishing the first of several works on Homer in 1857, and for the remainder of his life produced a steady stream of articles and books, as well as translations, of classical authors, notably Horace, Homer and Dante. He pursued his course with enormous energy: his diary records that he read the *Iliad* 36 times during the course of his life.

When Lord Derby again became Prime Minister of a minority Tory government in 1858, he approached Gladstone once again to join his administration, but once more he declined. He did accept, however, an offer to go to the Ionian Islands, a former Venetian territory, which had been a British protectorate since 1815, as Lord Commissioner Extraordinary, a decision regarded as eccentric by his political supporters. Gladstone's mission which lasted four months was not a success, and bordered on being a fiasco. He was intended to investigate the state of opinion within the islands and to advise on their future. He undertook this with his customary diligence, but he did not endear himself to the overwhelmingly Greek population by addressing them either in Italian or in ancient Greek, which was quite incomprehensible to them. The predominant feeling was in favour of *Enosis* (union with Greece), with which Gladstone was not unsympathetic, but he thought it premature, and recommended instead accelerated progress towards Home Rule. His own mission ended prematurely, when difficulties arose over his membership of the House of Commons, which was deemed incompatible with his role as Lord

Commissioner, and Governor-designate. He hastened back to London to reclaim his Oxford University seat in an uncontested by-election. He travelled back through North Italy, stopping to have dinner with Count Cavour, the Piedmontese Prime Minister, on the eve of Napoleon III's war with Austria, which was intended to deliver the whole of North Italy into Piedmontese (Sardinian) hands. This journey served to reignite Gladstone's enthusiasm for Italian unity, which had first been sparked by his earlier visit to Naples in 1850–1.

Within three months of his return, the Derby–Disraeli government was defeated in a parliamentary vote, in which Gladstone perversely voted on the Tory side, while the other Peelites sided with the Whigs. In the ensuing general election, the Tories (while making up some ground) came a clear second to the newly created Liberal Party. This had been hurriedly established at a meeting at Willis's Rooms, on 6 June 1859, and brought together the Whigs, Radicals and Peelites (see Chapters 13 and 16). Gladstone did not attend this meeting, but despite this, he was immediately invited to join the government which Lord Palmerston formed following the election. Gladstone thoroughly disapproved of Palmerston, who was second only to Disraeli as his *bête noir*, but during the election campaign Palmerston had come out strongly in favour of Italian unity, which now came high on Gladstone's list of priorities. This and Palmerston's hostility to parliamentary reform, about which Gladstone was still at this stage highly sceptical, was enough to bring them together. Gladstone peremptorily demanded the chancellorship, saying he would accept no other post, and Palmerston acceded, glad to have a firm hand at the Treasury to underpin his adventurous foreign and imperial policies. Gladstone never got on well with 'Pam', but served out the whole seven years of his premiership, which only ended with his death in 1866, without once threatening to resign – quite a feat for him.

Joining Palmerston's government put an end to Gladstone's political isolation, and set him firmly on the road to the Liberal leadership and eventual premiership. He was not the second person in the government – that was Russell, the Foreign Secretary, who claimed seniority as a former Prime Minister, but he was already elderly. Moreover, Gladstone's potential rivals among the ex-Peelites nearly all died off during this period – Aberdeen in 1860, Sidney Herbert and Sir James Graham in 1861 and Newcastle (Lincoln) in 1864. In addition, the most able of the younger Whigs, George Cornewall Lewis, the Home Secretary, was to die, aged 57, in 1862. The reaper was ruthlessly clearing the way for Gladstone's advance. Not that Gladstone was particularly backward in pushing himself forward. He was the acknowledged author of one of the most significant achievements of Palmerston's second government, the Anglo-French Trade Treaty, negotiated in Paris by Richard Cobden in 1860. Four years later, he made himself the hero of the Radicals by reversing his previously negative attitude to extending the franchise to working-class voters. In a Commons speech, responding to a Private Member's Bill, he said: 'I venture to say that every man who is not presumably incapacitated by some consideration of personal unfitness or of political danger is morally entitled to come within the pale of the constitution' (Hansard, 11 May 1864).

This was taken to be an endorsement of universal manhood suffrage, which was perhaps rather further than Gladstone really intended to go, at this stage. He also set about building up for himself a mass following outside Parliament, speaking at packed public meetings throughout the country. He was the first politician to take advantage of the opportunities presented by the railway age. It was noted that he was particularly effective speaking to meetings of working men, and he was dubbed 'the People's William' by the *Daily Telegraph*, then a Liberal newspaper, which, like several others, had been able to reduce its price to one penny, following Gladstone's abolition of the paper duties, and whose circulation had then expanded rapidly, overtaking that of *The Times*. Other papers had benefited in the same way, and their proprietors were grateful to Gladstone, and rewarded him with an exceptionally favourable press. They reported his speeches word for word, which meant that their impact far exceeded their original audience. Other politicians, notably Disraeli, belatedly attempted to emulate Gladstone, but none of them enjoyed anything like his success.

In the 1865 general election, Gladstone lost his seat at Oxford University, having upset many of its graduates over his support for university reform, as well as on details of Christian theology and by joining the Liberals. He took the precaution of also standing for the South Lancashire constituency, a three-member seat, where he sneaked in in third place behind two Tories. The overall result was a Liberal triumph, but before Parliament could meet, Palmerston died, and was replaced as Prime Minister by Earl Russell. Gladstone continued as Chancellor, and also became Leader of the Commons. Russell, now 73, had only one ambition for his second government, which was to carry a new Reform Bill, having been restrained from introducing one earlier by Palmerston's stubborn opposition. The main provision of the measure, which it was Gladstone's task to carry through the Commons, was to reduce the property qualification in borough constituencies from £10 to £7 a year. The Bill, as it stood, had few supporters in the Commons. The Radicals thought that the threshold should be reduced to £6, or lower, the Tories were solidly opposed to the Bill, and so were the right-wing Liberals (or 'Adullamites'), who refused to accept any extension of the franchise. In the Commons proceedings, Disraeli completely out-manoeuvred Gladstone, and succeeded in defeating the Bill, leading to the government's resignation, in June 1866. Lord Derby then became Prime Minister for the third time, again leading a minority, and Gladstone suffered the mortification of seeing his arch-rival, Disraeli, carry through a measure which went significantly further than his own Bill, providing household suffrage in borough constituencies (see Chapters 14 and 17). Nevertheless, Gladstone was to be the first beneficiary of the 1867 Reform Bill, as the Liberals won the subsequent general election, in November 1868, with a majority of 112, and Disraeli, who had succeeded Derby in the premiership 10 months earlier, promptly resigned. Gladstone had lost his Lancashire seat in the election but was returned for Greenwich instead. Given that Russell had earlier announced that he would not seek office again, he was the only conceivable choice as Prime Minister.

A telegram was duly delivered to Hawarden, announcing the imminent arrival of Queen Victoria's private secretary, General Charles Grey, with a commission inviting him to form a government. It was an intriguing detail that Grey was the husband of Caroline Farquhar, who had turned Gladstone down 30 years earlier, but this did not appear to have caused either man much embarrassment. Gladstone was busy felling a tree on the estate – a frequent occurrence in which he took both pride and pleasure – when the news arrived. He paused to read the telegram, famously declared 'My mission is to pacify Ireland', and carried on with his axemanship. Gladstone had recently become obsessed with Ireland, currently the scene of a rash of terrorist incidents by the Fenians, and concluded that two steps were urgently necessary to remove the justified grievances of the Catholic majority. One was a major programme of land reform, at the expense of the largely absentee landlords of the Protestant ascendancy. The other was the disestablishment and disendowment of the Anglican Church in Ireland, a measure which he had strongly resisted when Lord John Russell had made some tentative steps in this direction in the 1830s. He now resolved to make them the two priority items in his government's programme.

Gladstone was a few weeks short of his fifty-ninth birthday when he became Prime Minister for the first time on 3 December 1868. The government he formed was rather over-weighted by Whig grandees, though it included the leading Radical, John Bright, as President of the Board of Trade, and younger, more reformist ministers such as Edward Cardwell (War Office) and W.E. Forster (Education). His somewhat surprising choice as Chancellor of the Exchequer was Robert Lowe, leader of the 'Adullamites', who had scuppered Russell's Reform Bill in 1866. Gladstone was to be disappointed by Lowe's performance, and switched him to the Home Office in 1873, taking on the chancellorship himself. The Foreign Office was entrusted to the experienced hands of Lord Clarendon, who had twice served before as Foreign Secretary. He was to die in 1870, and was replaced by Lord Granville, the Leader of the House of Lords, and perhaps Gladstone's closest colleague. One leading Whig who was disgruntled to be fobbed off with a relatively junior office was the Marquess of Hartington (later the 8th Duke of Devonshire). He became Postmaster-General, having served as Secretary for War in Earl Russell's Cabinet in 1866. After two years, he was switched by Gladstone to become Chief Secretary for Ireland – again a post which he did not relish.

Gladstone started his premiership with great *brio*, determined to mark each session with a major Bill, which he would himself carry through all its stages in the Commons, and which would act as a shop-window for his administration. For the first session he chose the Irish Church Bill, a highly complicated and controversial measure, whose purpose was to disestablish and disendow the Church in Ireland, though it made no provision, as some had argued, for endowing the Catholic and Presbyterian Churches, to which the great majority of Irish adhered. He got it through the Commons, with majorities of over 100 at all its stages, but had to compromise on its financial terms to carry it through the Lords, where the Tory majority threatened to veto the Bill. Gladstone freely admitted during the parliamentary debates that he had changed his views on disestablishment, but clothed his explanation in such lofty terms that he left little doubt in the minds of his listeners that he believed his present position was divinely inspired. This led the Radical politician Henry Labouchere to make his famous remark, often wrongly attributed to Disraeli, that he didn't object to Gladstone always having the ace of trumps up his sleeve, but merely to his belief that the Almighty put it there.

The Liberals saw the passage of the Bill as a great triumph, and Gladstone sought to consolidate his success with a repeat performance in the 1870 session, with the Irish Land Bill. His original aim had been to extend traditional tenants' rights in Ulster to the whole 32 counties of Ireland, but fierce resistance by Whig landowners in his cabinet forced him to backtrack. The Bill as it was presented, and passed, merely gave statutory force to these rights in Ulster, but for the remainder of Ireland, while it provided for compensation to tenants who made improvements to the farms which they rented, it did not greatly improve their position vis-à-vis their landlords. The Bill was passed and though it had some beneficial effect in Ireland, it did little to remove the causes of rural discontent. Meanwhile, other ministers were primarily responsible for carrying measures which contributed to Gladstone's 1868–74 government being seen as a great reforming administration. Chief among these were W.E. Forster's Elementary Education Act of 1870, Cardwell's Army reforms, abolishing the purchase of commissions, and the Ballot Act of 1872, finally establishing the secret ballot in elections, thereby protecting tenants and employees from intimidation by their landlords or bosses. This measure was twice rejected by the Lords – in 1870 and 1871 – but at the third time of asking they reluctantly gave way. Another measure, about which Gladstone was initially sceptical, but which he ended up by introducing himself in the Commons was the University Tests Bill, which removed most of the remaining restrictions on non-Anglicans holding posts in the universities of Oxford and Cambridge.

In foreign policy, Gladstone gave a strong impetus to the cause of international Arbitration by agreeing to refer the festering dispute with the United States over the *Alabama* affair (see Chapter 16) to an international tribunal in Geneva. This set the amount of compensation to be paid at £3.25m, about one-third of the US claim. This was an unpopular move with the voters, but it put Anglo-American relations back on a good footing, and probably relieved Gladstone's conscience for the strongly pro-Confederate speech he had made at the outset of the Civil War, and which he later regretted. When war broke out between France and Prussia in 1870, he saw merit on both sides, and was resolutely resolved to stay neutral, though he signed a treaty with both powers to recognise Belgian neutrality, and prepared to send an expeditionary force if 30,000 men if either side reneged. It was this treaty which was cited in 1914 to justify Britain's declaration of war on Germany. When the 1870 war ended, Gladstone was appalled by Germany's annexation of Alsace-Lorraine, without a plebiscite being held, but was over-ruled by his Cabinet when he proposed to organize a joint protest with other neutral countries. Gladstone was even more upset by the declaration of papal infallibility at the Vatican Council in 1870, which he largely blamed on his former Oxford friend, Cardinal Manning, who had become a leader of the extreme 'ultramontane' faction in the Roman Catholic Church. Gladstone attempted to mobilize diplomatic opposition by other European governments to the declaration, but had little success.

Gladstone overshadowed all his ministerial colleagues, but was by no means the unchallenged master of his own house. Roy Jenkins aptly described him as pre-eminent, but not predominant, and over several issues he was over-ruled by his Cabinet. He also experienced difficulties in his dealings with Queen Victoria, whom he tried to chivvy into playing a more active and public role, believing that her decade-long period of grieving for Albert was harmful both to the country and the monarchy. He also tried, with little success, to get her to allow the Prince of Wales to play an active part in public affairs, for example as Viceroy of Ireland. Although he invariably treated her in a respectful way, she soon tired of hearing the earnest arguments which he put to her, and complained that he addressed her like a public meeting. She pined for her beloved Disraeli. After the early bout of legislation, by 1872, the government was beginning to run out of steam, and was internally divided on many issues. The opposition Conservatives took heart and Disraeli in a famous speech in Manchester, in April 1872, excoriated the government, saying:

As I sat opposite the Treasury bench the ministers reminded me of one of those marine landscapes not very uncommon on the coasts of South America. You behold a range of exhausted volcanoes. Not a flame flickers from a single pallid crest. But the situation is still dangerous. There are occasional earthquakes , and ever and anon the dark rumbling of the sea. (Blake, p. 523)

Even Gladstone's titanic energy seemed to be wilting, and for a time he was seriously distracted by what Jenkins describes as 'an infatuation' and Matthew as 'a platonic extra-marital affair'. This was with Laura Thistlethwayte, a former courtesan, who had made an advantageous marriage to a wealthy, but otherwise uninteresting gentleman. Gladstone quickly got into the habit of writing long letters to her, and seeking out her company, showing no regard for discretion. The relationship was at its most intense in 1869, but it dragged on spasmodically for several more years. It has been compared to Asquith's infatuation with Lady Venetia Stanley, to whom he wrote several letters a day at the height of his wartime premiership (see Leonard, pp. 63, 68), but Gladstone managed to keep his feelings under tighter control. One consequence of his relationship with her is that his night-time activities with street prostitutes tailed off considerably during this period.

If Gladstone's first government began with a bang, it sadly ended with a whimper. He was largely responsible for creating his own troubles. Against the wishes of most of his Cabinet, he insisted on bringing in a third Irish measure, the Irish Universities Bill, whose main aim was to open them up to Catholic students. He handled the issue maladroitly, succeeding in antagonising not only the powerful lobby of Trinity College, Dublin, but also many secular educationalists and, fatally, the Roman Catholic hierarchy. When the Bill came up for its second Reading, on 13 March 1873, a large number of Liberals, mostly but not exclusively Irish Members, voted against, or abstained, and the government was defeated by three votes. Gladstone immediately resigned, and with perhaps indecent haste, Queen Victoria invited Disraeli to take his place. Yet the wary Tory leader declined. He had no wish to emulate Lord Derby's experience, on three occasions, of leading a minority government, and was by now confident enough to believe that if he held off until the next general election he would gain an elected majority. It was the last occasion in British history when an opposition leader refused to accept office.

The government limped on for nearly another year, but repeated Conservative successes in by-elections gave it little confidence that it would survive the general election. This was not due until 1875, but Gladstone decided on a bold stroke and sought dissolution early in 1874. He made the abolition of income tax the central feature of the Liberal election platform. He managed to persuade himself that it was justified on economic grounds, but, in reality, it was no more than a blatant electoral bribe, which sat ill with the high moral tone which he habitually adopted. Nor was it successful: Disraeli instantly followed suit, but when he assumed office found it utterly impractical, and the tax has remained the main source of government revenue ever since. During the election campaign, Gladstone was extraordinarily passive, speaking at only three meetings, all of them in, or near, his Greenwich constituency, which he had represented since 1868. The election result was a majority of 50 for the Tories, while Gladstone suffered the indignity of coming in second place at Greenwich, behind the leading Tory candidate who was a brewer. This election marked the beginning of a long tradition, still continuing, of massive financial support from the brewing industry for the Conservative Party, and Gladstone wrote to his brother that 'we have been borne down in a torrent of gin and beer' (Mathew, 2004). This was a direct consequence of the government's unsuccessful attempt to bring in a Licensing Bill in 1871.

Gladstone, now 64, assumed that his political career was virtually over, and had no desire to lead the Liberal Party in opposition. At the earliest opportunity, he handed over the leadership in the Commons to the Marquess of Hartington MP, while Earl Granville continued to lead in the Lords. Gladstone determined to devote what he saw as the few remaining years of his life to writing on classical and ecclesiastical topics, though he retained his seat in Parliament. Whether it would have proved possible for such a driven and restless character to remain for long out of the political limelight is highly doubtful. The revolts against Turkish rule in 1876 in Bulgaria and Bosnia-Herzegovina, and subsequent Turkish atrocities, settled the issue for him. Outraged at the indifference of Disraeli's government to the growing slaughter of Orthodox Christians by the Ottoman Turks, he published his most famous pamphlet, *The Bulgarian Horrors and the Question of the East*, and launched a massive campaign of public meetings throughout the country, at which he demanded that the Turks be expelled 'bag and baggage' from their European territories. Letting it be known that he would not be fighting his Greenwich seat again, he arranged – partly through the good offices of the young Scottish Liberal peer, the Earl of Rosebery – to contest the Midlothian constituency, then regarded as a safe Tory seat. The Liberal leadership, and many leading right-wing Liberals, were deeply embarrassed by the fury of Gladstone's campaign, but rank-and-file Liberals, mostly non-Conformists suddenly warmed to this High Church Anglican who articulated so well their own feelings, responded to him with great enthusiasm, and he was hailed as a hero wherever he went. He expanded his target to include the whole range of Disraeli's foreign and imperial polices, which he denounced as 'Beaconsfieldism', following Dizzy's elevation to the peerage. By this, he meant unprincipled adventurism. In the 1880 general election he was easily elected for Midlothian, ousting the Earl of Dalkeith, the son and heir of the Duke of Buccleuch, his former colleague in Sir Robert Peel's cabinet.

Nationally, the Liberals were returned to power, with a majority of nearly 200, including their large band of Irish supporters. It is doubtful whether Gladstone's campaign played more than a marginal part in the overall Tory defeat, which was largely due to economic issues (see Chapter 17), but he was very widely given the credit. Queen Victoria desperately sought to avoid appointing him as Prime Minister, preferring either Hartington or Granville, but Gladstone firmly persuaded both of them to advise her that he was the only possible choice, in the country's interest.

The Gladstone who returned to office in 1880 was a different character from the one who had been defeated in 1874. In the words of the Gladstonian scholar Eugenio Biagini, his 'semi retirement', in 1875, had 'marked a watershed in his career from the executive politician of the Peelite tradition to the charismatic leader of a new and more democratic age' (Biagini, p. 201). Gladstone's later career was, in fact, the prototype on which Max Weber based his famous theory of charisma in politics. Previously, essentially a cautious politician, Gladstone now increasingly threw caution to the winds, depended more and more on his own whims rather than on the counsel of colleagues, and became much more 'left wing', as he grew older, though still insisting that he was not an egalitarian. His reputation with the poor, and the working class soared, but he was increasingly seen by 'men of property' as a dangerous demagogue.

He again chose to be his own Chancellor of the Exchequer, though relinquishing the post to Hugh Childers, in 1882. Granville was again Foreign Secretary, and Sir William Harcourt became Home Secretary. The Radical leader, Joseph Chamberlain, became President of the Board of Trade, while Hartington was appointed Secretary for India, moving on to the War Office after two years. In 1882, also, the 15th Earl of Derby, a former Foreign Secretary, who had crossed the floor from the Tory benches, joined the government as Colonial Secretary. Unlike his first administration, Gladstone's second government was not hailed as a great reforming ministry, though it did pass the 1884 Reform Bill, which effectively completed the work of the 1867 Act, by introducing male household suffrage to county as well as borough constituencies. Lord Salisbury, formerly a stubborn opponent of reform, who had succeeded Disraeli as the Tory leader, threatened to defeat the Bill in the Lords, but after negotiation with Gladstone agreed to let it through, provided it was accompanied by a redistribution of seats, which saw the replacement of almost all the two-member seats by single-member constituencies. As he foresaw, but the Liberals did not, this proved greatly to the advantage of the Tories (see Chapter 19).

At the outset of the government, the now 70-year-old Gladstone, who initially saw his premiership as only a stopgap arrangement for a year or two at most, concentrated on foreign affairs, determined to put an end to Beaconsfield's adventurism and to curb the excesses of his imperialism. Gladstone's mentor in foreign affairs had been Lord Aberdeen, whose pacific approach to potential conflicts, based on a strong preference for diplomatic negotiation rather than sword-rattling, had greatly influenced him. He had, accordingly, set out six principles of correct international behaviour in a speech in Midlothian, on 27 November 1879 (Mathew, 2004). In practice, he found these principles more difficult to apply than he had imagined, and his determination to prevent further imperialist expansion proved elusive. Nowhere more so than in relations with Egypt, where British influence continued to grow following Disraeli's purchase of the Suez canal shares, so that it was fast becoming a British protectorate, though it remained technically part of the Ottoman empire. Gladstone initially encouraged nationalist sentiment in Egypt, but reluctantly agreed to the bombardment of Alexandria by a British fleet in June 1882, after riots had broken out, and then to a full-scale invasion, after it had been demanded by all his cabinet ministers except John Bright, who resigned in protest. The country was completely in British hands by September 1882, and the nationalist leader, Arabi Pasha, was deported and imprisoned in the Seychelles. Unfortunately, the British commitment did not end there. Sudan, an Egyptian dependency, was the scene of a rebellion by a fanatical Moslem leader, known as the Mahdi, and General Charles Gordon was despatched with a small force to rescue isolated Egyptian garrisons in the country, and evacuate them. Gordon, a war hero from the Crimean and Chinese Wars, exceeded his instructions, and established himself in Khartoum, where he hoped to keep the Mahdi's army at bay. Instead, he was besieged there, and his situation became progressively more hopeless. For long, Gladstone resisted pressure to send a relief force, but when he finally agreed it was too late, and the force arrived in Khartoum two days after it had been over-run, and Gordon and all his troops killed. Gladstone's reputation was badly damaged; he survived a Commons censure motion by only 14 votes. The Tories gleefully reversed the acronym GOM (Grand old Man), by which he was becoming widely known, to MOG (Murderer of Gordon).

When Gladstone returned to power in 1880 he had not expected that Ireland would again be the dominant issue facing his government, but so it proved to be. His 1870 Irish Land Act had failed to dampen discontent, and rural violence had greatly increased. Meanwhile, Charles Stewart Parnell, the Protestant leader of the predominantly Catholic Nationalist movement had built up a formable electoral machine, which had made a virtual clean sweep of the Irish constituencies outside Ulster, with an insistent demand for Home Rule. Gladstone's response was two-fold; he introduced another Land Bill, which went a great deal further to meeting Irish demands than his earlier measure, and accompanied this with a Coercion Bill, giving the Viceroy powers to detain people indefinitely, without bringing them to trial. Parnell and several of his associates were arrested, and held in Kilmainham jail for several months. Then in May 1882, Lord Frederick Cavendish, the Irish Chief Secretary, who was married to Catherine Gladstone's niece, was murdered by Fenians in Phoenix Park, Dublin, together with his Permanent Under Secretary, T.H. Burke. Gladstone was severely shaken by this event, but probably concluded about this time that Home Rule was the only viable long-term solution, though he did not reveal this to any of his colleagues. In the meantime, an even stronger coercion bill was passed. This upset Parnell and his party, previously allied to the Liberals, and in June 1885 they voted with the Tories to defeat the budget.

Gladstone immediately resigned, and Lord Salisbury formed a minority Tory government. A relieved Victoria then offered Gladstone an earldom, which he unhesitatingly rejected. In November 1885, Salisbury called a general election, in which he failed to win a majority, but remained in office with the support of the Parnellites. At around this time, Gladstone approached Arthur Balfour, Salisbury's nephew, to see whether a bipartisan agreement on some measure of Home Rule might be reached (see Chapter 19). Salisbury flatly refused, and Gladstone's youngest son, Herbert, then leaked to the press that his father was converted to Home Rule.

This was good enough for the Parnellites, and they promptly abandoned their temporary alliance with the Tories, defeating the government in the Queen's Speech debate on 27 January 1886. Salisbury resigned, and Victoria, anxious to avoid a third Gladstone government at all costs, put out feelings to George Goschen, a former Liberal cabinet minister, who now often voted with the Tories, to see if he would head a coalition government. Goschen refused, and after three days, she bowed to the inevitable, and sent her secretary to call on Gladstone with 'the Queen's Commission', which, as he recorded in his diary 'I at once accepted'. He had difficulty in forming the government: several prominent Whigs, led by Lord Hartington, whom Gladstone had treated most insensitively in the past, and including both Derby and Goschen, refused to serve, because of their strong opposition to Home Rule. Two leading Radicals, Joseph Chamberlain and Sir George Trevelyan, accepted office, but resigned soon after for the same reason. Victoria continued to make difficulties, turning down Gladstone's first two choices for the Foreign Office, Lord Granville and the Earl of Kimberley, and insisting instead on the young Earl of Rosebery. Undeterred, Gladstone pressed ahead, and introduced his Home Rule Bill, in April 1886. After 16 days of debate, it was defeated by 30 votes on the Second Reading, on 8 June 1886, with only two-thirds of Liberal MPs voting with the government. Gladstone immediately asked for, and was granted a dissolution, and went down to heavy defeat in the subsequent general election, which produced the following result:

Conservatives	316
Liberals	190
Liberal Unionists	79
Irish Nationalists	85

The Liberal Unionists, who included a large element of the former Whigs as well as Joe Chamberlain's formidable Birmingham-based group of Radicals, threw in their lot with the Conservatives, with whom they eventually merged to form the Conservative and Unionist Party. Gladstone's third government had lasted a mere 169 days, and Lord Salisbury became Prime Minister for the second time, with a large majority. Many of the Liberals who stayed loyal never-theless blamed Gladstone for the recklessness with which he had split his party. They agreed with him in principle on Home Rule, but did not believe that its importance outweighed all other considerations. They felt that he should not have sprung the issue on the party, without spending a great deal more time in gentle persuasion. This, however, was not the way of the older Gladstone, who, in Lord Randolph Churchill's words, had become 'an old man in a hurry'.

The now 76-year-old Gladstone had no thought of retiring, but sat out the six years of Salisbury's term, continuing to make Home Rule his over-riding prior-ity, and forming a close alliance with the Irish Nationalists, sometimes using Parnell's mistress, Kathy O'Shea, as a go-between. When Kathy's husband, Captain W.H. O'Shea MP, cited Parnell as a co-respondent in his divorce case, Gladstone sanctimoniously threw up his hands in horror, though he was well aware of what had been going on. He urged Parnell to retire temporarily from public life, and withheld his support when Parnell's Catholic supporters turned on him. Parnell, a broken man, died within the year, aged 46. The GOM's abandonment of Parnell, and the consequent fatal split in the Irish Nationalist party was highly damaging to the Home Rule cause. A string of by-election successes had led to high hopes of a massive Liberal victory at the forthcoming general election, with a majority large enough to secure not only the passage of a Bill through the Commons but also to deter the Lords from applying a veto. In the event, some 355 supporters of Home Rule were returned in the 1892 election, and 315 opponents – a clear majority, but a bitter disappointment after the earlier high hopes. Salisbury resigned, and in August 1892, aged 82, Gladstone embarked on his fourth government. His cabinet included three subsequent Liberal Prime Ministers – Rosebery, Henry Campbell–Bannerman and H.H. Asquith, but his closest associate was John Morley, the Irish Chief Secretary, who was later to write his biography in three extensive volumes. His last premiership lasted for one year, and 199 days, and was totally domi-nated by the issue of Home Rule. Gladstone received little support from his Cabinet colleagues, only two of whom – Morley and Lord Spencer, a former Irish Viceroy – were wholeheartedly behind his efforts. The two most senior figures – Harcourt, the Chancellor of the Exchequer, and Rosebery, the Foreign Secretary – were determinedly obstructive, while most of the rest of the cabinet were sullenly resentful that what they regarded as a quixotic enterprise should take precedence over all other government business. Gladstone himself was far from optimistic about the outcome, and, now half blind as well as half deaf, had serious misgivings about his own his own capacity, confiding to his diary: 'Frankly from the condition (*now*) of my senses, I am no longer fit for public life; yet bidden to walk in it. "Lead thou me on" ' (Jenkins, p. 585).

Yet, he rose sublimely to the occasion, Jenkins commenting that: 'Even among his bitterest opponents, there was a sense of witnessing a magnificent last performance by a unique creature, the like of whom would never be seen again' (Ibid., p. 603).

Virtually single-handedly, Gladstone assumed the entire burden of carrying the Bill through the Commons, speaking frequently and impressively at all stages – nine days of debate at Second Reading, 53 days for the Committee stage, nine for the Report stage, and three for Third Reading, altogether the greater part of 82 sittings of the House. In the end, the Bill was passed by a majority of 34. The House of Lords was not impressed, and certainly not over-awed. It spent only four days on the Bill, and then rejected it by 419 votes to 41, one of the most one-sided votes in its entire history. They did not stop at that, going on to defeat or truncate several other Liberal Bills over the following months. Gladstone was indignant that the Tory leader, Lord Salisbury, should take such liberties with the programme of a recently elected government, and proposed to his colleagues that an immediate election should be fought on a 'Peers ver-sus People' prospectus, and that – in the event of victory – the Bill should be re-introduced. The Cabinet, sensing – probably correctly – that this was a rec-ipe for electoral disaster, unanimously turned him down. Gladstone resigned his premiership shortly afterwards, having been overwhelmingly defeated in a cabinet vote on Naval rearmament, which he strongly resisted. The Queen, who treated Gladstone in the churlish way to which she had become accus-tomed, did not ask his advice on the succession. If she had, he would have proposed Lord Spencer; the choice of Liberal MPs would probably have been William Harcourt. Showing cross misjudgement, she chose instead the Earl of Rosebery, who turned out to be one of Britain's least successful premiers (see Chapter 19). Gladstone left office on 2 March 1894, in his 85th year. In total, he had been Prime Minister for 12 years and 126 days, then the fourth longest in British history, though he was subsequently overtaken by Salisbury. Gladstone lived on for another four years, dying of cancer on 19 May 1898, aged 88.

Gladstone was one of the most remarkable men ever to serve in 10 Downing Street. The sheer length of his political career was in itself daunting. Over 62 years as an MP (narrowly second only to Churchill among Prime Ministers), 27 years as a minister, he spanned the period between George Canning, whom he knew as a young man, and Asquith, who served in his last Cabinet. He transformed the office of Chancellor of the Exchequer, was the first politician to campaign actively throughout the whole country and was the virtual crea-tor of the modern Liberal Party. He then badly split it, by driving out most of the former Whigs, while compensating by building up a great bond of trust among working-class voters. The effect of this was probably to delay the crea-tion of a viable Labour or Socialist party until after his death, while this devel-opment occurred notably earlier in most other Western European countries. Regarded as 'mad' by Queen Victoria, many of his Liberal colleagues thought that he had lost all sense of proportion over Ireland, and that the strength and persistence of his commitment to Home Rule was a grave error. Nevertheless, if his efforts had been crowned with success, more than a century of turmoil, including two long periods of terrorist, and counter-terrorist, violence would have been avoided, and Ireland would conceivably have remained within a devolved United Kingdom. Gladstone was, more than any other British leader, strongly and publicly motivated by his Christian beliefs which were undoubtedly sincere, though he was not above cutting corners and indulging in sharp practice, from time to time. Disraeli should not be taken at his word when he complained that 'he did not have a single redeeming defect'. It would also not be true to picture Gladstone as consistently solemn and humourless. He had a lively sense of fun, and his speeches, though over-long, were enlivened by flashes of wit, which were not, however, the equal of those of his more mercurial rival. Perhaps, above all, Gladstone should be seen as an archetypal figure of the Victorian age, though he was never appreciated by its figurehead, whose interests he had tried so devotedly and so unrewardingly to serve.

Works consulted

Eugenio Biagini, 1998, 'William Ewart Gladstone', in Robert Eccleshall and Graham Walker (eds.), *Biographical Dictionary of British Prime Ministers*, London, Routledge.

Robert Blake, 1966, *Disraeli*, London, Eyre & Spottiswoode.

Peter Clarke, 1992, *A Question of Leadership: From Gladstone to Thatcher*, London, Penguin Books.

Roy Jenkins, 1998, *The Chancellors*, London, Macmillan.

Roy Jenkins, 1995, *Gladstone,* London, Macmillan.

Dick Leonard, 2004, *A Century of Premiers: Salisbury to Blair*, London, Palgrave-Macmillan.

H.C.G. Matthew, 1986, *Gladstone 1809–1874*, Oxford, Clarendon Press.

H.C.G. Matthew, 1995, *Gladstone 1875–1898*, Oxford, Clarendon Press.

H.C.G. Matthew, 2004, Article in *Oxford Dictionary of National Biography.*

19

Robert Cecil, 3rd Marquess of Salisbury – Skilful Opponent of Reform

The third Marquess of Salisbury* was one of the longest-serving of British Prime Ministers. His three terms of office stretched to 13 years and 252 days, a total exceeded only by three of his predecessors (Walpole, the Younger Pitt and Liverpool), and by none of his successors. He also had a distinguished record as Foreign Secretary – a post he continued to hold during the greater part of his time as Prime Minister – and he was, together with Gladstone, the dominant political personality during the final three decades of the nineteenth century. Yet he quickly became an almost forgotten and disregarded figure. It is only recently – 100 years after his death – that the full extent of his (largely negative) achievements has come to be widely recognised. At the beginning of the twenty-first century, he is at last being given the recognition that he was denied during the 20th. This is partly, but not entirely, due to the publication, in 1999, of the mammoth biography by Andrew Roberts, *Salisbury: Victorian Titan*, written with full access to the voluminous Salisbury papers, preserved at his stately home at Hatfield House.

Superficially, Salisbury strongly resembled the long series of aristocrats who led the majority of British governments throughout the eighteenth and nineteenth centuries. Educated at Eton and Oxford, elected to a 'family borough' while still in his early twenties, inheriting a peerage and large estates in his forties, his c.v. matched those of such predecessors as the Earl of Derby, Viscount Melbourne and Earl Grey. Yet, temperamentally, he was far from falling into this mould. Born on 3 February 1830, the third son of the second Marquess of Salisbury – a direct descendant of Lord Burghley and Robert Cecil, the chief ministers of Elizabeth I and James I – he was a sickly and unsociable child who had no appetite for the favoured pastimes of his class. He detested games, and throughout his life abstained alike from hunting, shooting and fishing. Instead, he spent long hours in the well-stocked library of Hatfield House, his ancestral home, and developed marked intellectual tastes from an early age. This did him no good at Eton, where he was so badly and incessantly bullied that his father agreed to take him away at the age of 15 and entrust him to a private tutor.

At 17, Lord Robert Cecil, as he was then known, went up to Christ Church (Oxford), where he felt more at home than at Eton, and showed a keen interest in politics, becoming successively secretary and treasurer of the Union, where he made his mark as a stern and orthodox Tory. But his health broke down after two years and he had to leave prematurely, being awarded an honorary Fourth Class degree in Mathematics. In view of the sad fate of his elder brothers, one of whom had died in infancy, while the other (Lord Cranborne) was a permanent

---

*Salisbury's premiership straddled two centuries. This chapter is an adapted and extended version of that which appeared in my earlier volume, *A Century of Premiers: Salisbury to Blair* (Palgrave-Macmillan, 2004).

invalid, his father agreed in July 1855 to send him on a long voyage to recover from what his doctor described as 'the complete breakdown of his nervous system.'

This voyage, which lasted 22 months and included lengthy stays in South Africa, Australia and New Zealand, was the making of Cecil. Not only did it permanently strengthen his health, but, according to a biographer, A.L. Kennedy, it

> broadened his mental outlook, afforded him close contact with types of humanity he would not otherwise have met, and gave him one or two of the permanent characteristics of his statesmanship, not the least of which was a profound belief in the Empire, by no means common among his contemporaries. (Kennedy, pp. 14–15)

Yet the man who returned from the voyage had little confidence that he would make anything of his life. Writing to his father, he discussed dismissively the prospects of a career in politics, the Church or the bar:

> 'My chances of getting into the House of Commons are practically nil ... [Holy] Orders is the profession I should place next to it [politics] in usefulness: but from my uncertain health and my inaptitude for gaining personal influence I am as little fitted to it as any man I ever met', he wrote, adding that 'I am as likely to attain eminence in it [the bar] as I am to get into Parliament'. (Kennedy, p. 16)

Only three months elapsed, however, from his return from New Zealand, in May 1853, before he was elected MP for Stamford. Effectively a pocket borough, it was in the gift of his cousin, the Marquess of Exeter. Cecil was unopposed in the by-election which followed the death of the previous Member, and he never had to fight a contest during the 15 years that he represented the seat. His father, who was himself later a Tory Cabinet minister in the second Derby government, used his influence to secure him the candidacy, and must have hoped that Cecil would now conform more closely to the accepted pattern of life for a country gentleman of high birth. He was due for two grievous disappointments. In April 1855 the colonelcy of the Middlesex militia fell vacant. As Lord-Lieutenant of the county, the appointment was in the Marquess's hands, and he resolved to confer it on his son, writing to offer it to him in the most enthusiastic terms. Cecil's blankly refused, saying 'I detest all soldiering beyond measure' and that his usefulness for the militia command was 'ludicrously glaring'. (Kennedy, pp. 27–8)

Worse was to follow. Cecil might not have been generally considered a particularly eligible bachelor. 'A tall, stooping, myopic intellectual recluse, he was also an untidy unprepossessing man' (Taylor, p. 4), but it was taken for granted that he would eventually make an appropriate match with the daughter of another aristocratic house. When Cecil announced in 1856 that he was to marry Georgina Alderson, the dowerless daughter of a judge, his father promptly forbade the marriage. Cecil was obdurate, and his father eventually relented, though setting his allowance at so meagre a level that he was forced to seek a supplementary source of income – journalism.

This proved a blessing in disguise. For the type of journalism to which Salisbury devoted himself was at the highest intellectual level – long articles (33 in all), each of 20,000 words or so, for the *Quarterly Review*, supplemented by over 600 shorter pieces for the weekly *Saturday Review*, edited by his brother-in-law, Alexander Beresford-Hope. Such articles required a great deal of research, and Cecil expended much energy in informing himself and thinking through his position on all the major issues of the day. Although the majority of the articles dealt with domestic politics, the most trenchant are undoubtedly on foreign policy, including two brilliant historical studies of the Younger Pitt and Castlereagh, whom Cecil clearly regarded as appropriate role models (several of these articles are reprinted in Paul Smith (ed.), see below).

Perhaps the most significant of all his articles, which appeared in April 1864, was a critique of the policies carried out by the then Foreign Secretary, Earl Russell, and the Prime Minister, Lord Palmerston. He was especially scathing about their nonchalance in encouraging Denmark to stand up to Prussian and Austrian demands over Schleswig-Holstein, but then leaving the Danes in the lurch when it was clear that the two Germanic powers were bent on war. 'Peace without honour is not only a disgrace, it is a chimera', he wrote, in words which almost precisely prefigured the Munich agreement of 74 years later.

In a survey covering the eight years between 1856 and 1864, Cecil discerned a pattern of British bullying of weak countries (six examples), while using only menacing language against more powerful countries (first Russia, then Prussia, then the United States), followed by a hasty retreat when it became clear that they were in earnest. The conclusion he drew was that provocative words should only be used when there was a firm intention to back them up with action. Theodore Roosevelt's later dictum – 'Speak softly but carry a big stick' – surely encapsulated the lesson which Salisbury drew from his study of Russell and Palmerston, and it was one he faithfully applied on most occasions during his subsequent conduct of foreign policy.

If his financial dependency had the beneficial effect of preparing him intellectually much more thoroughly for ministerial office, its cause – his 'inappropriate marriage' – had no less happy an effect. Lord Blake describes it as:

> one of the wisest decisions in his life ... [Georgina Alderson] was of the same High Church persuasion as he was. Religion played a vital part in both

their lives. She also had a similar sense of humour. But unlike Cecil she was sociable, gregarious and extrovert. She was highly intelligent and ready to talk about all the topics of the day; she suffered from none of the nervousness, the introspection, the shyness which afflicted him from his youth, but which evaporated to a great extent as their married life went by. She was his prop and invaluable support for forty-two years till she died in 1899. (Blake and Cecil, p. 3)

Although Cecil's articles were contributed anonymously, the identity of the author rapidly became known among political circles. He soon gained renown as a sceptical, shrewd and informed commentator whose views, though firmly based on Conservative principles, were not bound by narrow party political considerations. It was his writing, rather than his rather fitful and idiosyncratic parliamentary activity which gradually built up Cecil's political reputation during the 1850s and early 1860s. He was, however, overlooked by Lord Derby when he formed his short-lived Conservative administration of 1859–60, in which Cecil's father served as Lord President of the Council.

Still feeling under keen financial pressure, with a rapidly growing family to support, Cecil resolved to give up politics and seek an office of profit under the Crown. The most promising vacancy was for a Clerk to the Privy Council, now in the gift of his father. The second Marquess was willing to appoint him, but was over-ruled by the Cabinet who balked at this act of nepotism. So Cecil redoubled his journalistic efforts, but his situation was transformed in June 1865, with the death of his elder brother, Lord Cranborne. From being a mere younger son, he became the heir to the marquessate and to one of the largest estates and fortunes in the country. His father substantially increased his allowance, and his days of relative penury were over.

Cranborne, as he now became, had strongly criticized Benjamin Disraeli, whom he regarded as a mountebank, in several of his articles, but the Conservative leader in the Commons did not hold it against him. When Lord Derby again became Prime Minister in 1866, Disraeli readily agreed to the appointment of Cranborne as Secretary of State for India, and went out of his way to be friendly to him.

Cranborne's first cabinet post lasted for less than nine months. In March 1867 he resigned, with two other colleagues, in protest against the terms of the second Reform Bill, which extended the vote to all heads of households in urban constituencies. Cranborne made it clear that his objection was as much to what he regarded as Disraeli's unprincipled manipulation as to the actual terms of the bill, which was duly voted into law. Cranborne's resignation was no sudden fit of pique. No great believer in democracy, he appeared to feel that the settlement reached under the 1832 Reform Bill had produced an almost perfect balance between the different classes of society. The untrammelled power of the aristocracy had been trimmed, and representatives of the middle classes had been admitted into the decision-making process. Cranborne had no objection to working class representatives also being involved, but he did not wish them to be admitted in such numbers as to swamp the interests of the propertied classes. His quasi-Marxist analysis led him to conclude that giving power to the workers would inevitably lead to the despoliation of the other classes. His favoured solution – which was incorporated in the original draft which Disraeli presented to the Cabinet – was that the extension of the franchise should be balanced by plural voting rights for the propertied and better educated.

On his own account, Cranborne was notably disinterested, but not so on behalf of his class or of his party. He regarded the ownership of property as an essential basis for political leadership, and his opposition to the 1867 Reform Bill owed much to a study which he undertook of its likely political consequences. These, he concluded, would be injurious to the Conservatives, particularly in the smaller boroughs (Clarke, pp. 48–9).

Cranborne's resignation did little, if any, harm to his reputation. Rather, it confirmed him, at least in Conservative circles, as a man prepared to put principle before his own political career. Nor did Disraeli take offence, inviting him to rejoin the Cabinet when he succeeded Derby as Prime Minister in January 1868. Yet Cranborne was adamant, writing at this time:

> If I had a firm confidence in his principles or his honesty, or even if he were identified by birth or property with the Conservative classes in the country – I might...work to maintain him in power. But he is an adventurer and I have good cause to know he is without principles or honesty'.
> (Taylor, p. 28)

At this stage, he once again thought of abandoning politics, writing to a Liberal friend (John Coleridge): 'my opinions belong to the past, and it is better that the new principles in politics should be worked by those who sympathise with them heartily' (Kennedy, p. 64).

In April 1868 his father died, and he inherited his seat in the House of Lords as well as the family estates. The new Marquess's character and beliefs had long been fully formed. At their root was a strong Christian faith. Salisbury was no less committed a Christian than Gladstone – indeed had been strongly influenced by the teachings of the same Bishop Butler, whose works Gladstone was to edit and annotate. Yet, whereas Gladstone's Christian faith tormented him, Salisbury's brought him calm and reassurance. It also made him a profound pessimist, with few illusions about the perfectibility of man. Yet Salisbury was also a utilitarian, influenced by Jeremy Bentham with his doctrine of the greatest happiness of the greatest number. He was a very English character, who took it for granted that English ways were best, though he was sharply critical of signs of racial superiority exhibited by British colonists and administrators in South Africa or India. No social snob, he was more aware of the responsibilities than the privileges of the landed class, and considered public service an inescapable duty. Painfully shy in private, he never flinched from playing a public role. The natural authority which he exhibited may have owed much to his social position in an age of deference, but it was also due in part to his strength of character and the unaffected candour of his speech. His conservatism did not take the form of a blind resistance to change, indeed he regarded change as inevitable and beneficial. What he was against was sudden, revolutionary upheaval; change he believed should be something organic, as in nature. Nor did he believe in dying in the last ditch even against changes which he considered objectionable; they should instead be accepted as an accomplished fact, and energies should thereafter be directed to making them work out with the least undesirable consequences. This was certainly the spirit in which he accepted the 1867 Reform Bill once it had been passed, and it greatly influenced his attitude, as we shall see, to the subsequent Bill of 1884.

His new position led to a considerable broadening of his interests: he took his duties as a landowner and farmer extremely seriously, and showed a benevolent and highly practical interest in the welfare of his many tenants. As a keen amateur scientist, he set up his own laboratory at Hatfield House, which became one of the first private houses in England to be connected with electricity, or to have a telephone. He became an accomplished photographer, and even contributed a learned article on the subject to the *Quarterly Review*. In 1869 he became Chancellor of Oxford University, while a year earlier he became chairman (and effective general manager) of the Great Eastern Railway – a post which he successfully held for four years, and which gave him invaluable experience of business and commerce.

And there was the House of Lords, a chamber not especially revered by Salisbury, who once described it as 'the dullest assembly in the world'. Yet he played a considerable part in its proceedings during the six years of Gladstone's first government, which lasted until 1874. His position was somewhat anomalous. Easily the most effective debater in the House, he played no formal role in the Conservative opposition. Though he usually sided with them in debate, he continued to show the same independent streak that he had in the Commons. On one notable occasion, he rounded on Tory peers who had sought to modify the trust deeds of a charitable bequest intended to provide doles for old people. They had argued that it was bad for the poor to receive money without working for it. 'Lord Salisbury, furious and sarcastic', a biographer wrote 'mocked the hypocrisy of a House, which, living for the most part on inherited wealth, was denying the solace of an unearned pittance for the poor' (Kennedy, p. 76).

Salisbury continued to regard Disraeli with contempt, and it was ironic that he owed the resurrection of his political career entirely to his sustained patronage and support. Without this, he would only be remembered now – if at all – as an eccentric grandee and intellectual maverick.

When Disraeli unexpectedly won the 1874 election, and embarked on his second ministry, one of his first concerns was to recruit Salisbury to his Cabinet. Salisbury showed extreme reluctance, writing to his wife that the prospect of having to serve again 'with this man' was 'like a nightmare'. The wily Disraeli used Salisbury's step-mother, now married to the 15th Earl of Derby (son of the former Prime Minister and himself Foreign Secretary in the new government), as a go-between. Her urging and that of Salisbury's few intimate friends proved sufficient to overcome his doubts, though he still spent three days making up his mind. He returned to his previous post in the India Office, and from then onwards his distrust of Disraeli gradually diminished and something approaching friendship developed between the two men.

The decisive moment in Salisbury's political career came two years later, in 1876. Uprisings in Herzogovina and Bulgaria against Turkish rule, which had been suppressed with the utmost barbarity, had stirred consciences throughout Europe, especially that of Gladstone, who embarked on his missionary campaign to turn the Turks 'bag and baggage' out of Europe. Disraeli, fearful that if no action was taken, Russia – which had already vastly extended its territories by the virtual annexation of Turkmenistan, Khiva and Bokhara – would undertake this task for its own aggrandisement, proposed a conference of the great powers of Europe (Austria, Britain, France, Germany, Italy and Russia) to persuade the Turks to reform their administration. The Russian government was unexpectedly willing to go along with this proposal, and itself convened a conclave at its embassy in Constantinople to which the other powers were invited.

The obvious British representative was the Foreign Secretary, Lord Derby. But he was increasingly at odds with Disraeli, who chose Salisbury to go in his place. The consequence was to turn Salisbury from a little-known British politician into a statesman of international renown. He set off for Constantinople in November 1876, stopping off on the way at the main European capitals to discuss the situation. In Berlin he met Bismarck, the German Chancellor, and the Emperor, William I, and in Paris, Vienna and Rome had long discussions with the leading political figures. No British politician since the Congress of Vienna 60 years earlier had had such extensive contact with his foreign counterparts. Salisbury's private views at this stage were not very different from Gladstone's; he was pre-disposed to a pro-Russian viewpoint, unlike Disraeli (now Lord Beaconsfield) and a majority of his Tory colleagues. At Constantinople he made common cause with the amiable but artful Russian representative, General Ignatiev, though he subsequently realised that he had been manipulated by him. The conference itself went remarkably smoothly, and an agreed list of demands was presented to the Sultan, Abdul Hamid II. These he promptly rejected, and the plenipotentiaries returned home feeling that the venture had been a failure. So, in substance, it had, but for Lord Salisbury it had been a triumphant success, putting him on the map internationally, and he returned home, to his amazement, to a hero's welcome.

The subsequent war between Russia and Turkey, which broke out in April 1887, led to Salisbury becoming more and more critical of Russia, as the threat increased of its occupation of Constantinople and the conversion of the whole of Turkey's European possessions into virtual Russian satellites. He repeatedly demanded a British show of force – such as sending a fleet to the Dardanelles – to warn the Russians off, but the majority of his cabinet colleagues were reluctant, and only finally agreed in February 1878 when the Russian troops were at the gates of Constantinople. The following month the Turks were induced to sign a peace treaty with Russia at San Stefano.

This treaty carved a large Bulgarian state out of Turkey's European territories, extending from the Danube to the shores of the Aegean, from the Black Sea to the Albanian border. Nominally under Turkish suzerainty, the terms of the treaty made it clear that it would, in fact, be a Russian satellite. The British government's reaction was that the Treaty breached the terms of the Treaty of Paris, which ended the Crimean War, and that it should not be ratified unless its terms were approved by all the signatories of the earlier treaty. When Russia sent an evasive reply, the Cabinet decided to transport troops from India to the Mediterranean to be in a position to intervene, if necessary, on behalf of the Turks. This decision provoked the resignation of Derby, to the relief of Beaconsfield, and Salisbury was the inevitable successor. He did not wait until his formal appointment, on 2 April 1878, before taking the most decisive step in his career. On the night of 29 March, returning to Hatfield from a dinner party, he retired to his study, and without any help or consultation with Foreign Office staff, composed a circular, which a subsequent Prime Minister, Lord Rosebery, described as one of the 'historic State papers of the English language'. Approved by the Cabinet the next day, it went out to the capitals of the other five European powers – St. Petersburg, Vienna, Berlin, Paris and Rome.

The circular made clear that each and every one of the provisions of the San Stefano Treaty must be re-examined at a congress of the European powers, and left little doubt in the minds of its readers that British military intervention would follow if Russia did not agree to this. Salisbury followed up the circular with secret negotiations with the Turks for the transfer to Britain of Cyprus, to provide a suitable base for such intervention either immediately or in the future. The circular had the effect of stiffening the other powers, notably Austria-Hungary, and Russia climbed down and agreed to the summoning of the Congress of Berlin. Here Bismarck was able to pose as an 'Honest Broker', and Beaconsfield basked in the limelight of what proved to be the twilight of his premiership. Yet it was clear to all the participants, as Beaconsfield generously conceded, that Salisbury was the real architect of the Congress and its settlement (which greatly reduced the size of the new Bulgaria, restored conquered territories to Turkey and confirmed the British take-over of Cyprus), and that without his decisive initiative the Russian war gains would have remained intact. In the words of A.L. Kennedy, 'The discomfiture of Russia at San Stefano was probably the most single-handed achievement in the whole long history of British diplomacy' (Kennedy, p. 137).

In retrospect, it appears less of an unmitigated triumph. Salisbury himself later came to question the wisdom of cutting Bulgaria down to size, the collapse of the Ottoman Empire was deferred rather than averted, and Britain was saddled with a new colony that proved less of a strategic asset than it appeared and which stored up troubles for the future. Less transitory were the benefits (primarily to his own party) of his two great contentions in domestic politics with Gladstone during the following decade.

After Beaconsfield's death, in 1881, Salisbury led the Tories in the Lords, but shared the party leadership with Sir Stafford Northcote, who was the leader in the Commons. The determining event which resulted in his supplanting Northcote as the most likely choice for a Tory Prime Minister was the 1884 Reform Bill, which extended the principle of household suffrage to the Tory heartland – the county constituencies. Salisbury was not above threatening to veto the bill in the House of Lords, and rather than provoking a Lords vs. Commons showdown, Gladstone invited the Tory leaders to a meeting with the objective of negotiating a bi-partisan compromise. At this meeting, Salisbury played the dominant role, entirely putting the passive Northcote in the shade. In exchange for letting the Reform Bill through, he insisted, there must be a general redistribution of seats, in order to maintain the influence of the rural and suburban areas against those of the larger towns, which formed the core of Liberal support. This objective he achieved, and in particular he secured the virtual ending of the long-established system of two-member constituencies. Henceforward, the great majority of seats would return only a single member, which turned out to be a significant disadvantage to the Liberal party. This party embraced a wide range of interests, ranging from right-wing Whigs to left-wing radicals. A great many local Liberal associations had followed the practice of offering a 'balanced ticket' by nominating both a Whig and a Radical candidate, and this option would no longer be open to them.

Ever since Disraeli had split the Conservative Party in 1846, and the subsequent link-up of the Peelites with the Liberals, the Tories had been very much the minority party, winning only one election (that of 1874) in a 40-year period. It was Salisbury's long-term objective to reverse this situation by luring the Whigs away from the Liberals, to form a 'moderate' alliance with the

Tories, embracing the centre and right of the political spectrum, confining a Radical-dominated Liberal Party to the left. Salisbury's handling of the 1884 Reform Bill was directed towards this end, but it was the Irish Home Rule crisis of 1885–6 which provided the catalyst.

The crucial moment came towards the end of Salisbury's first, minority, premiership, which lasted from June 1885 to January 1886. Gladstone, who was already convinced of the necessity of Home Rule, approached Salisbury, through his nephew, Arthur Balfour, with a proposal that the Irish question should be settled on a non-partisan basis. In practice, this could only take the form of some kind of all-Ireland assembly, with guarantees for the Protestant minority, and reserve powers for the Westminster Parliament. Salisbury rejected the approach out of hand. He was already on record as a convinced opponent of Home Rule, but it must also have occurred to him that such a settlement would divide his own party. The alternative – of leaving Gladstone himself to legislate for Home Rule – would be far. more likely to lead to the very split in the Liberal Party which he had long sought.

This is precisely what happened the following year when Gladstone introduced his first Home Rule Bill and was abandoned – not only by the Whigs under Lord Hartington, but by Joseph Chamberlain's Radicals as well. Salisbury's tactful handling of the Liberal Unionists led to their permanent detachment from the Liberal Party and their eventual absorption into the Conservative and Unionist Party.

Salisbury's own recipe for Ireland was to combine firm government ('coercion') with measures designed to remove the economic causes of discontent. In 1887 he appointed his nephew as Chief Secretary for Ireland with a mandate to carry out this policy, which he accomplished with limited success, earning the sobriquet 'Bloody Balfour' in the process.

Salisbury's three terms as Prime Minister (1885–6, 1886–92, 1895–1902) were hardly notable periods for domestic reform, though a number of useful bills were passed. The two most significant were probably the Education Act of 1891, which provided for free primary schooling, and the Local Government Act 1888, which established elected county councils. Other Local Government Acts provided for elected authorities in Ireland, Scotland and London boroughs, while there were a number of other legislative measures concerning Irish land tenure, safety in coalmines, working-class housing and, in particular, improving the lot of agricultural labourers.

In large part, however, Salisbury was more interested in providing calm and efficient administration rather than in innovation. He proved himself a skilful cabinet-maker, promoting effective colleagues such as Hicks-Beach, W.H. Smith and C.T. Ritchie to senior posts and then, on the whole, leaving them to get on with their jobs with a minimum of interference. His major personnel problem was in handling the popular, energetic but disloyal Lord Randolph Churchill, whose burgeoning ambitions clearly represented a threat to Salisbury's own leadership. He comprehensively outmanoeuvred Churchill, whose impetuous resignation as Chancellor of the Exchequer, in December 1886, effectively ended his political career. Thereafter Salisbury's domination over his cabinets was virtually complete until his final years in office when his authority was visibly failing.

For 11 of the nearly 14 years of his premiership, Salisbury combined the office with the Foreign Secretaryship, something no subsequent Prime Minister has attempted, apart from Ramsay MacDonald in 1924. It was the principal focus of his interest, and it has even been suggested that Salisbury's only, or at least main interest in being Prime Minister was that it meant he could run his own foreign policy without having a senior colleague looking over his shoulder and restricting his freedom of action. Salisbury put the furtherance of the interests of the British Empire at the head of his priorities, but his preferred method of settling disputes was by international negotiation, actively seeking to revive the Concert of Europe.

He was firmly against embroiling Britain in permanent alliances, believing that national security depended, above all, on the strength of the British navy. He was the originator of the 'Two Power Naval Standard', that is, that the British fleet should be equal in strength to that of the combined forces of the next two biggest navies. He maintained particularly good relations with Germany, especially until the fall of Bismarck in 1890, but he rebuffed approaches to turn them into a formal treaty of alliance, either on a bilateral basis, or with the Triple Alliance of Germany, Italy and Austria-Hungary. The last attempt to formalize a treaty with Germany, strongly pressed by Joseph Chamberlain, was killed stone dead by a magisterial memorandum composed by Salisbury in May 1901.

With France his relationship was more difficult because of a multitude of conflicting interests in various parts of Africa, culminating in the Fashoda incident in 1898, which brought the two countries to the brink of war. Salisbury took an exceptionally firm line, insisting that the French should back down, which they did, but then negotiated a *modus vivendi*, leaving Britain a free hand in the Nile Valley, in exchange for French expansion in West Africa.

Eight years earlier he had agreed a comparable *quid pro quo* with Germany, ceding Heligoland (in spite of the reluctance of Queen Victoria) in exchange for British hegemony in Zanzibar, Uganda and Kenya. Salisbury, who remained cool towards the aspirations of Joseph Chamberlain and Cecil Rhodes to establish an unbroken British north–south link between Cairo and the Cape, nevertheless was vigilant to prevent any other colonial power, whether France, Germany, Belgium or Portugal, establishing an east–west trans-continental link. He was able to avert this possibility by a series of diplomatic negotiations, and though the 'scramble for Africa', which substantially coincided with Salisbury's periods in office, resulted in many crimes and horrors, these did not include any wars between the European colonial powers. This was largely Salisbury's achievement.

He has been pictured as a reluctant imperialist, adverse to British annexations, much preferring indirect to direct rule and hesitating for years before approving the reconquest of the Sudan, culminating in the Battle of Omdurman in September 1898. Yet the fact remains that under his premiership, as A. L. Kennedy points out, the British Empire expanded 'by six million square miles, containing populations of about a hundred million – a record – which no other Prime Minister in British history since the elder Pitt could approach' (Kennedy, pp. 341–2).

Salisbury's handling of the Fashoda incident was almost the last occasion on which he was able to demonstrate his leadership abilities. From then onwards it was downhill almost all the way. His physical and mental powers were in decline – he failed to recognise cabinet colleagues and on one occasion had a lengthy conversation with the African explorer Sir Harry Johnson under the misapprehension that he was the Commander-in-Chief of the British army, Lord Roberts. There was a major reshuffle of the government in 1900, when Salisbury relinquished the Foreign Office to Lord Lansdowne, but packed his ministry with so many relatives that it was caricatured as the Hotel Cecil.

More serious still had been the general lassitude which had afflicted him during the long-drawn-out illness and death of his wife, in 1899. During this period Britain had drifted into the Boer War, much against Salisbury's instincts, but he had lacked the ability or the will to control the actions of his bellicose Colonial Secretary, Joseph Chamberlain or of Lord Milner, the British commissioner in the Cape Colony. Had he still been at the height of his powers, it is scarcely conceivable that the war would have broken out nor that it would have been prosecuted with such little sense of purpose.

Yet, even when Queen Victoria died in 1901, Salisbury did not take the obvious opportunity of standing down, but laboured on for nearly two more years. His clinging to office was not the least paradox of his career, for he had been genuinely unwilling to take office, seeking to excuse himself on each of the first two occasions when the Queen had summoned him to take charge. By this time however, his fine intellect was blunted, his natural scepticism was suspended, and he allowed himself to succumb, as do many long-serving leaders, to the illusion that he was indispensable. Or, as his younger son, Lord Robert Cecil, put it more charitably in an article contributed anonymously to the *Modern Review*, shortly after his death:

> Probably the greatest trial of his patriotism and courage was reserved for the end of his career. Only those in his most intimate circle know how distasteful office had become to him in his later years. He hated war, and his

hatred of it grew as he grew older. He was borne down with domestic grief and physical weakness; and yet he felt himself unable to lay down his burden lest the enemies of his country should take courage from the ministerial and electoral difficulties that might, and indeed did, follow his resignation. He remained at his post. (Kennedy, p. 328)

By hanging on into the twentieth century, Salisbury severely damaged his reputation. Had he died or resigned in 1898 or 1899, he might well have been assessed as one of the most successful leaders ever to have held the top office. Yet, three developments, in particular, owe more to him than any other single person. First, the dominance during most of the twentieth century of the Conservative Party, of which he – rather than the more celebrated Disraeli – was the main architect. Second, the persistence of the Irish problem until our own day, which may well be traced back to his refusal to agree a bi-partisan policy with Gladstone over Home Rule. Third – but more contentiously – his veto of an Anglo-German alliance, as late as 1901, has been blamed, notably by Julian Amery in his biography of Joseph Chamberlain, as leading to the First World War and, by implication, to all the horrors which came after (Amery, p. 158).

Salisbury could be regarded as the ultimate High Tory, and it is perhaps appropriate that what will almost certainly come to be regarded as his definitive biography has been written by a High Tory historian, Andrew Roberts. Roberts wrote that:

> Early in life Salisbury recognised that the institutions he cherished were coming under grave threat. The Established Church, the British Empire, the House of Lords, High Tory and High Church Oxford, Crown prerogatives, the rights of property, the landed aristocracy, the Act of Union – all that he regarded as the very foundations of English governing society…His was consciously a lifelong rearguard action. (Roberts, p. 851)

His stubborn efforts to hold back what others regarded as the march of progress are lauded by Roberts. Another renowned High Tory, however, believed that he rather overdid his resistance to change. Lord Curzon, one of his more distinguished successors as Tory leader in the Lords, was to describe him, in a rather bemused tone, as 'that strange, powerful, inscrutable and brilliant obstructive deadweight at the top' (Midwinter, p. 130).

Works consulted

Julian Amery, 1969, *The Life of Joseph Chamberlain*, Vol. IV, London, Macmillan.
Lord Blake and Hugh Cecil (eds.), *Salisbury: The Man and his Policies*, 1987, London, Macmillan.

Peter Clarke, 1992, *A Question of Leadership: From Gladstone to Thatcher*, Harmondsworth, Penguin.

A.L. Kennedy, 1953, *Salisbury, 1830–1905, Portrait of a Statesman*, London, John Murray.

Andrew Roberts, 1999, *Salisbury: Victorian Titan*, London, Weidenfeld & Nicolson.

Paul Smith, 1972, (ed.), *Lord Salisbury on Politics*, Cambridge, Cambridge University Press.

Paul Smith, 2004, Article in *Oxford Dictionary of National Biography*.

Robert Taylor, 1953, *Lord Salisbury*, London, Allen Lane.

Eric Midwinter, 2006, *Salisbury*, London, Haus Publishing.

20

Archibald Philip Primrose, 5th Earl of Rosebery – Seeking 'the Palm without the Dust'

Archibald Primrose, the fifth Earl of Rosebery is reputed to have said as a young man that he had three ambitions in life – to win the Derby, to marry a great heiress and to be Prime Minister (McKinstry, p. 43). He obtained all three objectives, indeed winning the Derby three times, but much of his life can be accounted a long-drawn-out failure, and his achievements during his short premiership were virtually nil, despite his undoubted gifts.

The blame for this has been attributed by one writer (Iremonger, pp. 147–156) almost entirely to his severe deprivation of parental love during his childhood. He was born on 7 May 1847, the eldest son and third child of Lord Dalmeny, also named Archibald Primrose, and the heir to the Rosebery earldom, and his wife, Lady Wilhelmina Stanhope, a beautiful and highly cultivated, but intensely selfish woman. The young Archie was doted on by his father, who unfortunately died when he was only three, but was almost totally neglected by his mother, who instead lavished whatever love she was capable of giving on his younger brother, Everard.

Archie himself became Lord Dalmeny on the death of his father, and was to inherit the earldom from his grandfather when he was just short of 21. Three years after his father's death, Lady Wilhelmina married for a second time, to Lord Henry Vane, later the Duke of Cleveland, an amiable but ineffectual grandee, who nevertheless failed to establish a close relationship with any of his four stepchildren. Archie proceeded to Eton when he was 13, where he impressed both the masters and his fellow pupils not only by his intellectual precocity and social assurance, but also by his apparent indolence. He was taken up by William Johnson, a highly erudite teacher and poet (the author of the words of the Eton Boating Song), who was scarcely able to conceal his homo-erotic interest in the boy. He wrote a series of letters to the Duchess of Cleveland, as she now was, recording the progress of her son, who, he said, had 'in himself wonderful delicacy of mind, penetration, sympathy, flexibility, capacity for friendship – all, but the tenacious resolution of one that is to be great' (Rhodes James, 1963, p. 30). Writing to a fellow Eton schoolmaster, Johnson made an even shrewder remark, which presciently foreshadowed the young Lord Dalmeny's later career: 'He is one of those who like the palm without the dust' (McKinstry, p. 20). Dalmeny was by no means the only schoolboy who attracted Johnson, who, ten years later, was forced to leave Eton under a cloud, changing his name to Cory.

From Eton, Dalmeny proceeded, in 1866, to Christ Church, Oxford. Here he mixed with a boisterous crowd of Etonians, including Lord Randolph Churchill, who became for a time a close friend, joined the Bullingdon club, renowned for its drunkenness and general loutishness and infuriated his tutors by his unwillingness to conform. According to the recollections of a fellow student: 'His patrician hauteur was unmistakable. Not an offensive hauteur but that calm pride by which a man seems to ascend in a balloon out of earshot every time he is addressed by one not socially his equal' (McKinstry, p. 18).

For many he appeared a conundrum. Highly intelligent and considered physically attractive, though baby-faced and not very tall, he was extraordinarily sensitive, and unable to abide criticism. He appeared to neglect his studies, but read widely, often appeared boorish, but could light up a room by a sudden smile, and – when he could be bothered – was a scintillating conversationalist. Moody, capricious, for long periods he would prefer his own company to anyone else's, but would then ingratiate himself with his fellows by conspicuous displays of bonhomie. Aged 20, he inherited the earldom on the death of his grandfather, and with it two grand residences in Scotland, and an income of at least £30,000 a year, which he proceeded to spend at a great rate, gambling and losing vast sums on horse racing. He bought his own racehorse, named Ladas, which he confidently predicted would win the Derby. Despite all his distractions, he achieved First Class results in his preliminary examinations, and his tutors expected him to obtain a First in his final degree. It was not, however, to be. The University authorities discovered a regulation forbidding the ownership of racehorses by undergraduates, and gave Rosebery an ultimatum to get rid of the horse or be sent down. To their amazement, he haughtily refused to comply, and left the University without taking a degree. He was later to regret this, particularly when the Derby was run, and Ladas came in last.

Rosebery took his seat in the House of Lords within a week of his twenty-first birthday, in May 1868. Coming from a Whig family, he naturally sat on the Liberal benches, though he had been approached a year earlier by Darlington Tories who wanted him as their parliamentary candidate. He had no great respect for the House, where the Liberals were in a permanent minority, describing it as 'a gilded dungeon', and there is little doubt that his subsequent political career suffered from his never having been an MP. Winston Churchill, who started life as a great admirer of Rosebery, was later to lament: 'I feel that if I had his brain I would move mountains. Oh that he had been in the House of Commons! There is the tragedy. Never to have come into contact with realities, never to have felt the pulse of things – that is what is wrong with Rosebery' (McKinstry, pp. 36–7).

In the following years, Rosebery was moderately active in the Lords, but preferred speaking to public meetings, where his wonderfully melodious speaking voice made him a great attraction, and he was soon seen as a 'coming man' in the Liberal Party, where – at this stage – his views veered very much towards the Radical wing of the party. Though strictly paternalist, he showed great sympathy with working-class people, exposing the exploitation of children in the Glasgow brickfields, becoming President of the Edinburgh United Industrial School and calling in 1871 for 'a union of classes without which power is a phantom and freedom a farce' (Davis). Gladstone was much taken with him, and wanted to recruit him for office, but felt strongly that he – like other promising young recruits – should serve an apprenticeship in more menial roles before moving to a senior post. There thus began a long series of incidents when Rosebery was offered appointments and turned them down, ostensibly because he felt himself poorly qualified, but in reality because he thought they were beneath his dignity. Gladstone and other senior Liberals found this intensely irritating, but rank-and-file Liberals were thoroughly seduced by his glamour, and he rapidly became, after Gladstone, the most sought-after public speaker in the party, particularly in Scotland.

What gave Rosebery's political career a crucial upward push was his immediate support of Gladstone, when he emerged from his 'retirement', in 1876, to campaign against Turkish atrocities in the Balkans (see Chapter 18). Gladstone effectively swept back into the Liberal leadership, unceremoniously thrusting aside Lords Hartington and Granville, who had been elected respectively as leaders in the Commons and the Lords. Yet having declared that he would not fight again in his Greenwich constituency, he needed another seat to contest, and Rosebery exerted himself to obtain a nomination for him in Midlothian, a county constituency surrounding Edinburgh, where his residence at Dalmeny, overlooking the Firth of Forth, was situated. When Gladstone launched his famous Midlothian campaign in advance of the 1880 general election, he based himself at Dalmeny, and Rosebery footed the bill for the campaign. This, he estimated, amounted to £50,000; a figure which one of his biographers reckons was exaggerated (Rhodes James, 1975, p. 149). Rosebery was not content to act just as Gladstone's quartermaster. He himself played a very active part in the campaign, speaking to numerous meetings, where he invariably electrified the audience. He was one of the best 'stump' speakers of his day.

Rosebery was very attractive to women, and was regarded as a supremely eligible bachelor – many were the aristocratic ladies who saw him as the ideal mate for their daughters. So there was general consternation – which was felt at least equally in the Jewish community – when his engagement was announced to Hannah de Rothschild, the heiress of the fabulously wealthy Baron Meyer de Rothschild. No great beauty, being plump and rather gauche, she had a very pleasant disposition and much commonsense (which her new husband notably lacked). He had originally met her ten years earlier, when she had been introduced to him by Disraeli. They married in March 1878, when he was nearly 31, and she 27. Neither she nor Rosebery (a Presbyterian) changed their religion. The marriage brought to Rosebery the enormous Rothschild residence of Mentmore, in Buckinghamshire, stuffed with art treasures, to add to his two Scottish homes, his London residence in Berkeley Square, and the Durdans, a country house near Epsom, which he had bought in 1872. It was obvious that Hannah totally adored Rosebery, but he tended to treat her in a rather offhand manner. They had two daughters, followed by two sons, in less than five years, but in 1890, after 12 years of marriage, Hannah was to die of typhoid, at the age of 39. It was only then that he fully appreciated her, and he entered a deep depression, which lasted for over a year, during which he withdrew himself from almost all human society, and from which he perhaps never fully recovered.

Forming his second government, following the 1880 election, Gladstone offered Rosebery the Under-Secretaryship at the India Office. Disappointed not to be included in the Cabinet, he declined, saying he did not want to appear to be receiving a pay-off for his role in the Midlothian campaign. He did, however, accept the post of Under-Secretary at the Home Office, with a brief to handle Scottish affairs, in August 1881, only to resign less than two years later. His reasons for resigning, according to John Davis:

> combined the principled and the petty: his belief that London habitually neglected Scottish business and his fear that this neglect would spawn a Scottish home-rule movement; his overreaction to criticism of the Home Office in the Commons; his difficult relationship with the Home Secretary, Sir William Harcourt; and the fact that he was bored with his work. (Davis)

Perhaps his incompatibility with Harcourt, which was later to blight his premiership, was the determining factor. Gladstone did not give up on him, offering him the post of Minister for Scotland, created under the Local Government Board Act of 1883. Rosebery demurred, partly it seems because it was not in the Cabinet, and departed in a huff for a tour of the United States and Australia. While on this tour, he made a famous speech at Adelaide calling for the British Empire to be converted into a 'commonwealth of nations', the first time that this phrase had been used. On his return he took the first of several initiatives to reform the House of Lords, proposing the appointment of a Select Committee to look into its efficiency. His motion was defeated. In November 1884, Gladstone finally offered him a cabinet post: that of Commissioner of Works, perhaps the least glamorous office in the government. Rosebery again declined, but three months later changed his mind, when the post was combined with the title of Lord Privy Seal. He was to serve out the remaining four months of Gladstone's second government, until it resigned in June 1885, after the Irish Nationalists ganged up with the Tories to defeat it on the budget.

During the short interim of the first Salisbury government (June 1885– January 1886), Gladstone's conversion to Home Rule in Ireland had a devastating effect on the unity of the Liberal Party. Lord Hartington MP, and other senior Whigs, refused to serve in the third Gladstone government, while the Radical Joseph Chamberlain agreed to do so, but resigned shortly afterwards. Furthermore, another leading Radical, Sir Charles Dilke, much fancied as a potential Foreign Secretary, was involved in a sensational divorce case at this time, and the ensuing scandal effectively destroyed his political career. This left something of a vacuum at the top end of the party, and this greatly facilitated

Rosebery's rise. Lord Granville, who had been Foreign Secretary in Gladstone's first two administrations, was becoming increasingly decrepit, and Queen Victoria refused to accept him for a third term. She then opposed Gladstone's choice of the Earl of Kimberley, and strongly pressed for Rosebery, who had charmed her almost as much as her late lamented Disraeli. Gladstone thought Rosebery, then 38, too young for the post, but nevertheless offered it to him. Rosebery made his customary noises about being unfit for the office proposed, writing to Gladstone:

> I have absolutely no experience of the Foreign Office, which I have never entered except to attend a dinner. My French is I fear rusty. I have never had to face anything like what you would call hard work. I have no knowledge of diplomatic practice or forms and little of diplomatic men. And I am sensible of many deficiencies of temper and manner. Moreover the Foreign Office is usually considered, and I think justly so, to be the chief of all offices. I should gladly have climbed into it in ten or twenty years, had I been fit for it then. But I know very well that I am not fit for it now. (McKinstry, p. 147)

Nevertheless, he accepted the offer, and was clearly as pleased as punch at the prospect. It was noteworthy that, this time, it took only a few hours for him to overcome his qualms rather than months or years, as on previous occasions. In the event, Rosebery's first tenure of the Foreign Office proved to be a notable success, and perhaps the apogee of his political career. He was in office for just over five months, Gladstone's third government going down to a heavy electoral defeat, following the rejection of its Home Rule Bill, and the defection of most of the Whigs and the Chamberlainite Radicals from the Liberal Party. But during this short time, he proved himself to be firm and decisive, and revealed an unexpected talent for administration. Not all his fellow Liberals were delighted, however, that he aimed at pursuing a bipartisan policy, and was determined to achieve a maximum of continuity with his Tory predecessor, Lord Salisbury. 'The second rate foreign policy which is continuous', he later said, 'is better than the first rate foreign policy which is not' (Davis). The only potential crisis with which he had to deal concerned Bulgaria, which in 1885 annexed the neighbouring Turkish province of Eastern Roumelia, after defeating a Serbian army at the Battle of Slivnitsa. This could easily have sparked a wider Balkan War, in which Russia would have been directly involved, but Rosebery's cool handling of the issue, enabled it to be settled with a minimum of international discord. Gladstone was delighted, and wrote warmly congratulating him. When he left office, Queen Victoria said to him: 'You have a great political future ahead of you' (McKinstry, p. 159), while Gladstone in a speech at this time said: 'I say to the Liberal Party that they see the man of the future'.

Rosebery was far from being an enthusiastic supporter of Home Rule, and remained in the party largely out of loyalty to Gladstone, whom he greatly admired. He was, however, greatly distressed by the exit of the great majority of his fellow Whigs, which – in particular – left the Liberals in an even smaller minority in the House of Lords than before. This only confirmed Rosebery in his view that the composition of the House of Lords was in urgent need of reform, and over the years he launched a series of initiatives with this in view, including the appointment of life peers. None of his proposals came near to being adopted. On one occasion, he even contemplated contesting a seat in a by-election to put to the test the established view that a peerage was incompatible with membership of the Commons (a step actually taken by Tony Benn some 70 years later), and consulted a former Liberal Lord Chancellor, who advised him against taking this step. Instead, he stood for election to the newly established London County Council, in 1889, and being successful was immediately elected as the first chairman of the Council. The Liberals were in a majority in the Council, and Rosebery quickly acquired a reputation as a municipal reformer, collaborating closely with Fabians, such as Sidney Webb, in promoting a wide range of progressive policies, particularly in housing and education.

Rosebery was now widely seen as Gladstone's probable successor as Liberal leader, but the sudden death of his wife, Hannah, in November 1890, completely disoriented him. He dropped all his political activities, and spent long periods alone in his castle at Barnbougle, mourning inconsolably. The insomnia, which had periodically afflicted him since his youth, became chronic. He determined never to be a minister again, and expressed deep disdain for party politics, but again fought the London County Council (LCC) election in 1892, and resumed the chairmanship of the Council. He was gloomy about Liberal prospects for the general election in the same year, but out of loyalty to Gladstone agreed to speak at a number of meetings, some of his reported speeches indeed upsetting Queen Victoria by their Radical tone. As usual, Gladstone, now an elderly and rather decrepit figure, made Dalmeny his base for the campaign, but found his host moody and uncommunicative. The election result was a deep disappointment to Gladstone, who had looked forward to winning a clear majority, but found himself some 40 seats adrift of the Tories, and able to govern only with the aid of the 81 Irish Nationalists, themselves deeply split by the disgrace and death of their former leader, Charles Stewart Parnell (see Chapter 18).

The Liberal leader gathered his leading supporters around him in London, urgently discussing how they might form a government in anticipation that Lord Salisbury would soon resign, which he did a month after the election. All this time Rosebery dawdled in Scotland (Achilles in his tent!), letting it be known that in no circumstances would he consider entering the government. Meanwhile virtually all his former colleagues, including his arch-rival

Sir William Harcourt, convinced themselves that his presence was a *sine qua non*, and that almost any price should be paid to secure his agreement. It was only after John Morley had been dispatched to Dalmeny, where he begged almost on his knees for Rosebery to come to see Gladstone in London, that he agreed to do so, still determined to tell the GOM that he would not serve. At the meeting Gladstone failed to obtain an acceptance from Rosebery, who did, however, agree that he should tell the Queen that he wished Rosebery to be appointed. Gladstone left for his appointment with the Queen, who was at Osborne, her Isle of Wight residence, and Rosebery departed for a two-day visit to Paris where he communed alone. Informed by telegram that the Queen had agreed to his appointment, he sent back a cryptic reply 'So be it, Mentmore [the name of his Buckinghamshire home]'.

Rosebery resumed the Foreign Secretaryship with mixed feelings, but on one thing he was determined; that he should run his own policy, and permit only a minimum of consultation with his cabinet colleagues. The policy he intended to pursue was, however, not likely to commend him to the majority in his party. Determined, as before, to keep in step with his predecessor Salisbury, he was far more of an imperialist than most of the other leading Liberals, Gladstone in particular. Two major incidents occurred, in both of which Rosebery was at odds with majority Liberal opinion. The first concerned Uganda, where the British East Africa Company was effectively in control of the territory. It was threatened with bankruptcy, and Rosebery, backed by his Under-Secretary, Sir Edward Grey, and the Tory opposition, proposed to take it over and declare a British protectorate. This was too much for Gladstone, and Rosebery reluctantly agreed a compromise under which the company was kept afloat by an interim subsidy. He, however, prepared plans for annexation, which went ahead in 1894, after Gladstone's retirement.

The second flowed from the British occupation of Egypt, which had continued for ten years, following the decision, which Gladstone had taken with great reluctance in 1882, to impose a virtual protectorate on the country, which was still technically part of the Ottoman Empire. The effective ruler was the British proconsul, Sir Evelyn Baring (later Lord Cromer), an over-bearing figure who, for 24 years from 1883–1907, thought nothing of issuing detailed instructions to the Khedive on how to man and manage his administration. Gladstone, still keen to secure the withdrawal of British troops, responded encouragingly to an informal approach by the French ambassador suggesting that the two governments should jointly consider the problem of the future control of Egypt. Rosebery hit the roof, saying that it was a grave diplomatic solecism for the ambassador to by-pass the Foreign Secretary in seeking a meeting with the Prime Minister. Gladstone meekly apologized, and the ambassador was withdrawn soon afterwards. Nothing more was heard of Anglo-French co-operation, and when Cromer requested a further reinforcement of British troops, Rosebery arranged for a battalion of the Black Watch en route for India to be diverted to Port Said. In his second term as Foreign Secretary, he appeared to be a commanding figure, and his international reputation soared. He also received a glowing press in Britain, and his popularity reached fresh heights. Yet his relations with Gladstone seriously deteriorated, and were not improved by his failure to give strong support to the Prime Minister in his struggle to carry the Irish Home Rule Bill, which was the central objective of his last government. Nor were many of his Cabinet colleagues enthralled by his imperious ways. The Queen, however, was a different matter, and – in August 1893, he recorded in his diary a 'long and curious talk' he had had with her at Osborne, in which she said that: 'It was ridiculous for a man of 83 to be Prime Minister. "You ought to be there, Lord Rosebery, I wished you to be there and I hope you will be there. You are the only one of the Ministry with whom I can talk freely"' (McKinstry, pp. 258–9).

When Gladstone resigned six months later, in March 1894, there were at least two senior Liberals in the House of Commons who had good claims on the premiership, notably Sir William Harcourt, the Leader of the House and Chancellor of the Exchequer, but also, John Morley, the Irish Secretary, and Gladstone's closest colleague. Yet, without any consultation, Victoria sent unhesitatingly for Lord Rosebery. It is doubtful if she was doing him a favour, and certainly not the Liberal Party or the country as a whole. Rosebery himself had his usual qualms about taking office, though he immediately accepted when the Queen invited him to form a government. He had, however, set out in a private memorandum the reasons why he thought it a mistake. One of these was the great difficulty that a Liberal Prime Minister would have in leading a government from the Lords, where there were now only about 20 Liberal peers in a House of 560, following the mass defection of Whigs over Home Rule. In many ways, Rosebery would have preferred to remain as Foreign Secretary, and serve under Harcourt, despite their sharp differences, but was aware that Harcourt was deeply unpopular within the Cabinet, despite his large following among Liberal MPs as a whole. Harcourt's supporters, led by his son Lewis, universally known as 'Loulou', had waged an energetic campaign to secure the premiership for him, but had been blocked by Morley, formerly an ally, who came out strongly in support of Rosebery, partly it seems because he had hopes of succeeding him as Foreign Secretary. Harcourt was furious when Rosebery was named as Prime Minister, and he was tempted to refuse to join the government in the hope that Rosebery would be unable to proceed without him. But he held back, perhaps because Victoria might, in these circumstances, have sent for Lord Salisbury, rather than himself. Instead, he insisted on onerous terms, including the retention of both his posts, freedom to express his views publicly on any subject and the right to be fully consulted on all foreign policy issues, as well as on patronage. Rosebery, sensing that this would effectively mean a joint premiership, agreed with the greatest reluctance. Unlike Harcourt, Morley was in no position to drive a hard bargain. Rosebery declined to make him Foreign Secretary, insisting on choosing a fellow peer, the inoffensive Earl of Kimberley, who shared Rosebery's imperialist instincts, whereas Morley was a prominent advocate of the 'Little Englander' views, predominant among rank-and-file Liberals. Morley was not even able to secure the India Office as a consolation prize, and was forced to continue as Irish Secretary.

The government took office on 5 March 1894, when Rosebery was nearly 47. It got off to the worst of starts, with its three leading members deeply disgruntled and hardly on speaking terms with each other. Within less than a week, the new Prime Minister committed an appalling blunder, which upset the great bulk of his own supporters. Replying casually to a point made by Lord Salisbury, the Leader of the Opposition, he agreed that Home Rule would not be practicable until a majority of English, as distinct from British, MPs were in favour. He also tactlessly referred to England as the 'the predominant partner' in the Union, which deeply offended Scottish, Welsh and Irish MPs, the great majority of whom were Liberals or Nationalists. The deeply divided government was unable to present a coherent programme of intended legislation, offering instead a series of minor, if often contentious proposals, of which the most notable was a Bill to disestablish the Anglican Church in Wales. Its first important piece of business was the budget, which needed to raise considerably more revenue to pay for the expensive programme of naval rearmament, of which Rosebery had been a strong advocate, and which was the proximate cause of Gladstone's resignation (see Chapter 18). Harcourt proposed to raise the bulk of the extra £5 million he needed to balance the budget by the introduction of graduated death duties, which appalled Rosebery who, apart from any personal considerations, feared that this would drive away from the Liberal Party the few wealthy landed supporters that it retained. He sent a detailed memorandum to Harcourt setting out his objections, which the Chancellor of the Exchequer contemptuously rejected. Not wishing to be depicted 'as a rich man who disliked being taxed', as his son-in-law and first biographer, Lord Crewe, put it (Walker, p. 227). Rosebery refrained from challenging Harcourt within the Cabinet and was then mortified when the Chancellor achieved a great parliamentary triumph in carrying his proposals through. The government then suffered a considerable international humiliation, when it negotiated an Anglo-Belgian treaty, leasing to King Leopold II substantial tracts of land in the Upper Nile basin in order to forestall French infiltration into the area. The treaty infuriated anti-imperialist feeling in the Liberal Party, and then had to be abandoned when the Belgian King, fearing French retaliation, refused to ratify it. Meanwhile, the government seemed to be drifting aimlessly along with no co-ordination between its leading members, and the conspicuous absence of any leadership from Rosebery. The one striking event, which – temporarily at least reignited Rosebery's flagging popularity – was when his horse, Ladas II, won the Derby in June 1894. (He repeated this achievement the following year with another horse, Sir Visto).

Even this, however, did not go down at all well with the influential Nonconformist elements in the Liberal Party, while Rosebery was rebuked by Queen Victoria for the frivolous tone of several of his speeches. He at last attempted to give his government some direction by calling for a bill to restrict the veto powers of the House of Lords, which he intended to make the centrepiece of the Liberal Party's next election manifesto. But there was little enthusiasm for this; the Lords had not made themselves unpopularr by blocking Home Rule, which was not supported by the majority of English voters. He was heavily criticized in debates in the House of Commons, and very little attempt was made by Liberal ministers, notably Harcourt as Leader of the House, to defend him. Rosebery petulantly summoned a meeting of the Cabinet in February 1895, at which he announced that he would resign because of their lack of support. He withdrew the threat two days later after receiving protestations of support from his leading colleagues, though they continued to grumble about him behind his back. In April 1895, he had a serious attack of influenza followed by an almost complete nervous breakdown, which effectively put him out of action for several months. Given his hyper-sensitive temperament, the breakdown could well have been caused by the strain of leading a fractious government in unfavourable conditions, but it seems probable that it was also brought on by Rosebery's fear of being exposed in a homosexual scandal – the Oscar Wilde affair, which was reaching its climax in April and May 1895. There is no direct evidence that Rosebery was homosexual, but it was widely assumed in 'society' that he was, on the basis of certain effeminate traits, his apparent lack of interest in seeking a second marriage, and his habit of surrounding himself with attractive young men as his secretaries and assistants. One of these had been Viscount Drumlanrig, the 25-year-old heir to the mad 5th Marquess of Queensbery, whom he appointed as his Private Secretary, when he was Foreign Secretary in 1892. Queensberry, already disgusted by the relationship of his younger son, Lord Alfred Douglas ('Bosie'), with Wilde, convinced himself that Rosebery, whom he referred to as a 'snob queer', had seduced his heir. He followed Rosebery to Bad Homburg, where he was on holiday, intending to horsewhip him, but was apprehended by local police and deported. Two years later, in 1894, Drumlanrig had become engaged to be married, and then went off to join an aristocratic shooting party. He became separated from the group, who heard a single shot fired, and found him dying in a neighbouring field. The inquest verdict was that he had accidentally shot himself, but the general belief was that it was suicide, and it was suspected that he was being blackmailed about his alleged relationship with Rosebery.

The government's law officers were terrified that Rosebery's name would be mentioned in Wilde's libel action against Queensberry, or in the subsequent first trial of Wilde for gross indecency. The jury failed to agree, and the harsh and unexpected decision of the law officers to subject him to a second trial has been attributed to their fear that if they did not press the charges it would be seen as a cover-up to protect Rosebery. In the event, Wilde was convicted and given two years with hard labour, an effective death sentence, while Rosebery emerged unscathed.

He resumed his government duties, but the inter-ministerial squabbling continued unabated, and the feeling spread that the government was doomed. In June 1895, the government was unexpectedly defeated in a parliamentary ambush during a debate on the alleged shortage of cordite for the army. The War Secretary, Sir Henry Campbell-Bannerman insisted on resigning, and though the vote could easily have been reversed on a confidence motion, the Cabinet unanimously decided instead on collective resignation. As Asquith, the Home Secretary, rhetorically asked: 'Is there any member of Rosebery's Cabinet, in either House, who wishes to see it assembled again for any purpose under heaven?' (McKinstry, p. 378).

As for Rosebery himself, he felt the profoundest relief, saying a few years later: 'There are two supreme pleasures in life. One is ideal, the other real. The ideal is when a man receives the seals of office from his Sovereign. The real pleasure comes when he hands them back'.

His premiership had lasted a mere year and 109 days. The Queen immediately sent for Lord Salisbury, who requested, and was granted, a dissolution. In the subsequent general election, the Liberals went down to a resounding defeat, the Tories emerging with an overall majority of 152, the largest since the 1832 Reform Act. Among the Liberal losses were those of Harcourt and Morley, to Rosebery's ill-concealed satisfaction. He had taken no part in the campaign, instead going for an extended cruise in his yacht. He welcomed the extent of the Liberal defeat, saying it had been 'purged as with fire', and now had the opportunity of regrouping itself on what Rosebery regarded as a more realistic basis. He carried on as party leader for another 15 months, but resigned in October 1896, when Gladstone emerged from his retirement to make a fiery speech in Liverpool attacking Armenian massacres by the Turks. Rosebery felt this was undermining his own position, and with few regrets handed over the leadership to Harcourt. He was still under 50, and was to live another 33 years, until 1929. Yet his political career was virtually over, though it did not appear so at the time. He retained a strong following, particularly among younger Liberals, and those who supported his imperialist approach. Among these were three of the abler younger ministers in his government, Asquith, Sir Edward Grey and R.B. Haldane. This trio formed the core of the Liberal Imperialist faction, who strongly supported the Tory government's conduct of the Boer

War, and who looked forward to Rosebery's return, perhaps at the head of a coalition government committed to imperialism abroad and social reform at home. Every now and then, Rosebery would make a well-publicized speech full of bright ideas, which would dominate the headlines for a few days or weeks, but he never had the patience or consistency to follow them up with an organized campaign. In his book *Great Contemporaries*, Winston Churchill charted the waning enthusiasm of his followers: 'At first they said, "He will come." Then for years "If only he could come;" And finally, long after he had renounced politics for ever, "If only he would come back"'.

The end of the Boer War, in 1902, and the recovery of Liberal unity under Campbell-Bannerman, effectively ended the possibility of Rosebery's return to the leadership even if he had desired it. It was perhaps in recognition of this that he declared in a long-anticipated speech at this time that 'I must plough my furrow alone'. Nevertheless, he appeared to be disappointed, when Campbell-Bannerman formed his government in December 1905, not to be given the opportunity of declining a Cabinet post. One was offered to him by Lloyd George in his coalition government in 1916, but by then all remnants of his political ambition had long been extinguished. The following year he had a debilitating stroke, and though he survived for another 12 years, it was as a sad, lonely and pitiful invalid.

For one who had aroused such strong hopes among so many people, his career was a bitter disappointment. No subsequent writer has been able to make out a case that he had any solid achievements to his credit, and most of them have been highly critical of his self-indulgence and dilettantism. The cruellest verdict was that of Philip Guedalla, who, in his book, *The Gallery*, published in 1924, wrote that Rosebery's: 'long career has been a painfully prolonged adolescence. Sometimes he would play quietly with his toys for years together. But at intervals, swept by those dark impulses which devastate a nursery, he dashed them on the floor and went off to mutter in a corner'.

This was perhaps a bit hard, but in truth Rosebery should never have tried his hand at politics. He had altogether the wrong temperament: he was much better suited to be an artist rather than a politician. He had wide cultural interests and was a gifted writer, publishing perceptive biographical studies of Chatham, Pitt, Napoleon and Lord Randolph Churchill. These were all decisive and ruthless men, everything in fact that Rosebery might have wished to be, but all too evidently was not.

Works consulted

John Davis, 2004, Article in *Oxford Dictionary of National Biography*.
Lucille Iremonger, 1970, *The Fiery Chariot*, London, Secker & Warburg.
Leo McKinstry, 2005, *Rosebery: Statesman in Turmoil*, London, John Murray.

Matthew Parris, 1995, *Great Parliamentary Scandals*, London, Robson Books.

Robert Rhodes James, 1963, *Rosebery*, London, Weidenfeld & Nicolson.

Robert Rhodes James, 1975, 'The Earl of Rosebery', in Herbert Van Thal, (ed.), *The Prime Ministers, Vol. II*, London, Allen & Unwin.

Graham Walker, 1998, 'Archibald Philip Primrose, Fifth Earl of Rosebery', in Robert Eccleshall & Graham Walker, (eds.), *Biographical Dictionary of British Prime Ministers*, London, Routledge.

Appendix – Prime Ministers of the Nineteenth Century

Name	Party	Age at first appointment	Dates of Ministries	Total time as Premier
1. William Pitt, born 28 May 1759, died 23 Jan. 1806, unmarried.	Tory	24 years, 205 days	19 Dec. 1783–14 March 1801, 10 May 1804–23 Jan. 1806	18 years, 343 days
2. Henry Addington, 1st Viscount Sidmouth, born 30 May 1757, died 15 Feb. 1844, married (1) Ursula Hammond, 17 Sep. 1781 (2) Mary Anne Townsend, 1823, 4 sons, 4 daughters	Tory	43 years, 291 days	17 March 1801–10 May 1804	3 years, 54 days
3. William Grenville, 1st Baron Grenville, born 24 Oct. 1759, died 12 Jan. 1834, married Anne Pitt, 18 Jun. 1792, no children	Whig	46 years, 110 days	11 Feb. 1806–25 March 1807	1 year, 42 days
4. William Cavendish-Bentinck, 3rd Duke of Portland, born 14 April 1738, died 30 Oct; 1809, married Lady Dorothy Cavendish, 8 Nov. 1766, 4 sons, 2 daughters	Whig, then Tory	44 years, 353 days	2 April 1783–18 Dec. 1783, 31 March 1807–4 Oct. 1809	3 years, 82 days
5. Spencer Perceval, born 1 Nov. 1762, died 11 May 1812, married Jane Spencer-Wilson, 10 Aug. 1790, 6 sons, 6 daughters	Tory	46 years, 338 days	4 Oct. 1809–11 May 1812	2 years, 221 days

Continued

Appendix: Continued

Name	Party	Age at first appointment	Dates of Ministries	Total time as Premier
6. Robert Banks Jenkinson, 2nd Earl of Liverpool, born 7 Jun. 1770, died 4 Dec. 1828, married (1) Lady Louisa Hervey, 25 Mar; 1795, (2) Mary Chester, 24 Sep; 1822, no children	Tory	42 years, 1 day	8 Jun. 1812–9 April 1827	14 years, 305 days
7. George Canning, born 11 April 1770, died 8 Aug. 1827, married Joan Scott, 8 Jul. 1800, 3 sons, 1 daughter	Tory	57 years, 1 day	12 April 1827–8 August 1827	119 days
8. Frederick John Robinson, 1st Viscount Goderich, 1st Earl of Ripon, born 30 Oct. 1782, died 28 Jan. 1859, married Lady Sarah Hobart, 1 Sep. 1814, 2 sons, 1 daughter	Tory	44 Years, 305 days	31 Aug. 1827–8 Jan. 1828	130 days
9. Arthur Wesley (Wellesley), 1st Duke of Wellington, boirn 1 May 1769, died 14 Sep; 1852, married Lady Kitty Pakenham, 10 April 1806, 2 sons	Tory	58 years, 266 days	22 Jan. 1828–16 Nov. 1830, 17 Nov. 1834–9 Dec. 1834	2 years, 320 days
10. Charles Grey, 2nd Earl Grey, born 13 March 1764, died 17 Jul. 1845, married Mary Ponsonby, 18 Nov. 1794, 10 sons, 7 daughters (one illegitimate)	Whig	66 years, 254 days	22 Nov. 1830–9 Jul. 1834	3 years, 229 days
11. William Lamb, 2nd Viscount Melbourne, born 15 Mar 1779, died 24 Nov. 1848, married Lady Caroline Ponsonby, 3 Jun. 1805, 1 son	Whig	55 years, 123 days	16 July 1834–14 Nov. 1834, 18 April 1835–30 Aug. 1841	6 years, 255 days

Continued

Appendix: Continued

Name	Party	Age at first appointment	Dates of Ministries	Total time as Premier
12. Sir Robert Peel, born 5 Feb. 1788, died 2 July 1850, married Julia Floyd, 8 Jun. 1820, 5 sons, 2 daughters	Conservative	46 years, 308 days	10 Dec. 1834–8 April 1835, 30 Aug. 1841–29 June 1846	5 years, 57 days
13. Lord John Russell, 1st Earl Russell, born 18 Aug. 1792, died 28 May 1878, married (1) Lady Adelaide Ribblesdale, 11 April 1835, (2) Lady Frances Elliot, 20 July 1841, 3 sons, 3 daughters	Whig, Liberal	53 years, 316 days	30 Jun. 1846–21 Feb. 1852, 29 Oct. 1865–26 Jun. 1866	6 years, 111 days
14. Edward George Stanley, 14th Earl of Derby, born 29 Mar. 1799, died 23 Oct. 1869, married Emma Bootle-Wilbraham, 31 May 1825, 2 sons, 1 daughter	Conservative	52 years, 331 days	23 Feb. 1852–17 Dec. 1852, 20 Feb. 1858–11 June 1859, 28 Jun. 1866–25 Feb. 1868	3 years, 280 days
15. George Gordon, 4th Earl of Aberdeen, born 28 Jan. 1784, died 14 Dec. 1860, married (1) Catherine Hamilton, 28 July 1805, (2) Harriet Hamilton, née Douglas, 4 sons, 4 daughters	Peelite	68 years, 326 days	19 Dec. 1852–30 Jan. 1855	2 years, 42 days

Continued

Appendix: Continued

Name	Party	Age at first appointment	Dates of Ministries	Total time as Premier
16. Henry John Temple, Viscount Palmerston, born 20 Oct. 1784, died 18 Oct. 1865, married Emily, Lady Cowper, 16 Dec. 1839, no legitimate children	Liberal	71 years, 109 days	6 Feb. 1855–19 Feb. 1858, 12 Jun. 1859–18 Oct. 1865	9 years, 141 days
17. Benjamin Disraeli, Viscount Beaconsfield, born 21 Dec. 1804, died 19 April 1881, married Mary Anne Wyndham Lewis, 28 Aug. 1839, no legitimate children	Conservative	63 years, 68 days	27 Feb. 1868–1 Dec. 1868, 20 Feb. 1874–21 April 1880	6 years, 339 days
18. William Ewart Gladstone, born 29 Dec. 1809, died 19 May 1898, married Catherine Glynne, 25 Jul. 1839, 4 sons, 4 daughters	Liberal	58 years, 340 days	3 Dec. 1868–17 Feb. 1874, 23 April 1880–9 Jun. 1885, 1 Feb. 1886–20 July 1886, 15 Aug. 1892–2 March 1894	12 years, 126 days
19. Robert Arthur Cecil, 3rd Marquess of Salisbury, born 3 Feb. 1830, died 22 Aug. 1903, married Georgina Alderson, 11 Jul. 1857, 5 sons, 3 daughters	Conservative	55 years, 140 days	23 Jun. 1885–28 Jan. 1886, 25 July 1886–11 Aug. 1892, 25 Jun. 1895–11 July 1902	13 years, 252 days
20. Archibald Primrose, 5th Earl of Rosebery, born 7 May 1847, died 21 May 1929, married Hannah de Rothschild, 20 Mar. 1878, 2 sons, 2 daughters	Liberal	46 years, 302 days	5 Mar. 1894–22 Jun. 1895	1 year, 109 days

Index

Note: Page numbers in **bold** refer to chapter titles